IDI AM...

Mark Leopold is Lecturer in Social Anthropology at the University of Sussex.

Further praise for *Idi Amin*:

'A wonderfully written, original account of the enigmatic Idi Amin.' Simukai Chigudu, author of *The Political Life of an Epidemic*

'Amin was a much more complex person than most think. And his relationships with Britain were also more complex than it is often safe to admit. Leopold's book restores complexity and detail to the man in a way that instructs us never to look superficially at tragedy.' Stephen Chan, author of *Grasping Africa*

'This biography of the Ugandan dictator Idi Amin sifts through the many myths and fictitious claims that have long shaped public understanding of his early life and his later rule as president of Uganda from 1971 to 1979. In so doing, it reaches a more nuanced assessment of the man than previously available.' Nicolas van de Walle, *Foreign Affairs*

'Instead of the caricature of a merely evil buffoon, the Idi Amin who emerges from this fascinating book is all too chillingly human.' Andrew Harding, BBC Africa Correspondent

MARK LEOPOLD

IDI AMIN

THE STORY OF AFRICA'S ICON OF EVIL

YALE UNIVERSITY PRESS
NEW HAVEN AND LONDON

For information about this and other Yale University Press publications, please contact:
U.S. Office: sales.press@yale.edu   yalebooks.com
Europe Office: sales@yaleup.co.uk   yalebooks.co.uk

Set in Minion Pro by IDSUK (DataConnection) Ltd
Printed in Great Britain by Clays Ltd, Elcograf S.p.A

Library of Congress Control Number: 2020942589

ISBN 978-0-300-15439-9 (hbk)
ISBN 978-0-300-26088-5 (pbk)

A catalogue record for this book is available from the British Library.

10 9 8 7 6 5 4 3 2 1

CONTENTS

List of Plates		*vi*
Preface		*viii*
Map		*xiv*
	Introduction: Idi Amin Dada, Man and Myth	1
1	'Wrung from the Withers of the Western Nile': Background, Birth and Youth, 1928(?)–46	24
2	'He Comes from a Fighting Race': Life in the King's African Rifles, 1946(?)–59	55
3	A Resistible Rise? 1959–65	91
4	Amin and Obote, 1965–69	125
5	'Martial Music': The Build-up, the Coup and the Aftermath, 1969–71	163
6	A Honeymoon and Four Divorces: The First Two Years of Uganda's Second Republic, 1971–73	202
7	The Centre Cannot Hold: President Amin, 1973–76	239
8	Decline and Fall: Idi Amin and Uganda, 1977–79, and After	276
Afterword		*310*
Notes		*315*
References		*337*
Index		*345*

PLATES

1. General Amin as commander of the Ugandan army and air force, *c*. 1969–70. Central Press/Getty Images.
2. Major-General Amin gives his first press conference as president of Uganda, 27 January 1971. AP/REX/Shutterstock.
3. Amin driving past cheering crowds to attend a ceremony for the newly liberated politicians, January 1971. AP/REX/Shutterstock.
4. Amin meets Golda Meir, Israel, 1971. David Rubinger/CORBIS/Corbis via Getty Images.
5. President Amin with King Faisal of Saudi Arabia, 11 November 1972. © Keystone Press Agency/Keystone USA via ZUMAPRESS.com.
6. Amin releases English writer Denis Hills to British Foreigh Secretary James Callaghan, 12 April 1975. Keystone/Stringer/Getty Images.
7. President Amin arrives at JFK International Airport, New York, 1 October 1975. AP/REX/Shutterstock.
8. Amin attends Kenyan President Jomo Kenyatta's funeral, Nairobi, 31 August 1978. Sayyid Azim/ AP/REX/Shutterstock.
9. Amin in a tracksuit, 1970s. AP/REX/Shutterstock.
10. Amin takes part in an exhibition bout, December 1973. Anonymous/ AP/REX/Shutterstock.
11. Amin warming up before a basketball game with Ugandan soldiers, near Kampala, 7 March 1977. Richard Tompkins/AP/Shutterstock.
12. Amin happily accompanying the Uganda Air Force Band on his accordion, 10 April 1972. Bentley Archive/Popperfoto/Getty Images.
13. Al-Hajji Field Marshal Dr Idi Amin Dada, VC, DSO, MC. AP/REX/ Shutterstock.

14. Amin at a press conference, 1973. © Keystone Press Agency/Keystone USA via ZUMAPRESS.com.
15. Amin as chancellor of Makerere University at a degree ceremony, October 1976. AP/REX/Shutterstock.
16. Amin riding a bicycle ambulance during festivities, Kitgum, late 1970s. AP/REX/Shutterstock.
17. British and other white residents of Uganda pledge loyalty to Amin, September 1975. Bettmann/Getty Images.
18. Amin at Entebbe airport, 27 February 1977. Trinity Mirror/Mirrorpix/Alamy Stock Photo.
19. Amin and his first official wife, Maryam. © Africa Media Online/Mary Evans.
20. Amin in exile in Saudi Arabia. © Africa Media Online/Mary Evans.
21. Front covers of official government publications. Author's photos.

PREFACE

Idi Amin was no ordinary man, and this is not a conventional biography. Its origins lie in the ethnographic research I conducted in Amin's home area of Uganda, known as West Nile, in the 1990s. I went to investigate how the local people – most of whom had become refugees following Amin's overthrow – were rebuilding their society after returning from exile. However, by the time I got there, other conflicts had broken out, and the focus of my research became the prevalence of violence in the region's history, and how each generation, in turn, had been viewed by outsiders as tainted by this history – as somehow intrinsically violent. West Nile had been fought over by Africans, Arabs and Europeans since the nineteenth century, and it now lies at the intersection of three troubled countries: Uganda, the Democratic Republic of Congo, and South Sudan. Idi Amin was West Nile's most famous son, but the district's association with violence long pre-dated his birth. When I was living in the district capital, Arua, in 1995–97, I found that his presence haunted the place, and his deeds hung over its population as a permanent cloud. He came to haunt me, too.

I have written elsewhere about the wider history; here my aim is to focus on the individual, and ask the biographer's usual questions: who was this man, what did he do, and why? That is where the problems arise, because Amin – both during his life and since – has been turned into a figure of myth, an evil monster rather than a human being. He has become an almost supernatural icon of intrinsic evil: a sadist, torturer, murderer, racist, fascist, cannibal . . . the list of accusations goes on, and so do the numerous books, articles, films and online material about the former Ugandan president. In Uganda itself, his rule is invoked whenever people want to criticise the government.

Academics are used to studying things no one else knows or cares about, but with Idi Amin it seemed that everyone, from my students to my hairdresser, knew about him, his evil deeds, and his mad and bad character. This interest in my subject was heartening, but it was also part of the problem in writing about the man. Notoriety is the enemy of historical analysis. How can one write the biography of such a mythologised figure, accounts of whose life are saturated with unreliable anecdotes and outright fabrication? Some historians, of course, are specialists in doing just this, especially in the case of the distant past, where there is very little hard evidence. As the classicist Catharine Edwards wrote, reviewing a biography of the notorious Roman emperor Caligula, 'Mad emperors are an embarrassment to serious historians . . . [W]e are not in a position to distinguish "embellishment" from any core of historical truth in the fantastic anecdotes told about emperors. . . . It is impossible to isolate a "kernel of truth" in this kind of story.'[1]

I was aware of these problems when I started the book. My intention at that time was to try to bring together what we actually know about the man, and contrast this with the multiple myths that have grown up around him. Each chapter, I thought, would try to disentangle these things as the book progressed through his life, leaving the reader with a fairly clear picture of what in the story of Idi Amin is true, and what is fantasy. In the course of writing, however, I came to realise that this was an impossible task. The nature of both the primary and secondary historical evidence is too contested, contradictory and infected with myth to allow a simple, disinterested search for the truth to work. I began by interviewing people in Uganda and the UK but I found that, although they all knew for sure the truth about Amin, they tended either to contradict each other, or to repeat the same stories that were in the popular books. When questioned, their accounts were almost always based on what they had heard from others, rather than actually seen.

By far the biggest primary source on Amin's life is to be found in the UK National Archives. However, the messages and memos of British diplomats are as full of myths and misconceptions, tied up in racial assumptions, and keen to focus on amusing anecdotes, as many of the published works. Some of the popular contemporary accounts of Amin's life were written by his political enemies, others by journalists with an eye for a good story rather than the truth. Some contain wholly invented tales, which found their way into contemporary human rights reports, and later into serious academic histories of Uganda. Like the people I interviewed, contemporary written accounts contradict each other even on basic issues of fact (such as dates and places), and many even contradict themselves. The situation is further complicated by Amin's own penchant for propagating legends about his life. I found it increasingly impossible to pick apart the reality from the myth, and it became more and more clear to me that much of what had been accepted as the truth was in fact a farrago of myth and supposition.

It seemed that, because of the myths, the subject ought to be the representations of Idi Amin, rather than the facts. The easy way out would have been to abandon any hope of writing history, and instead to look at what has been published about the dictator, without worrying too much about the truth of it. That would have been a radically relativistic approach, which perhaps fitted the dubious nature of much of the material, but did not fit at all with my experiences of meeting and working with real Ugandan people who had been affected by Amin himself, by the consequences of his rule, or by the ways his life has been represented. The people of West Nile, in particular, suffered a good deal due to their association with the former president, and I felt they deserved an attempt to assess the historical evidence. My approach, though, had to shift from a relatively straightforward historical biography, to one that developed the account of Amin's life alongside a careful assessment of where the information came from, and its reliability. The story became one that brought together, rather than picking apart, the truth and the fiction, and that sought to bring out the important elements of the myth, however speculative or even supernatural they appeared.

An amazing series of fantastic stories and surprising twists and turns emerged, as did a critique of the accepted historical truth about Amin, and the sources it is based on. Widely held assumptions, about questions such as who was behind Amin's coup, his responsibility for expelling Uganda's Asians, and how many people he killed, were shown to be false or, more often, unknowable. Instead of two carefully distinguished piles of true and false statements, I uncovered a complex web of myth making, deliberate or accidental obfuscation, and plain lying. In working through all this, the book develops a kind of ethnography of historical knowledge, an investigation, through a very particular and unusual case study, of how what we 'know' about the past is produced.

This required an unusual approach to writing the book. One anonymous reader of an early draft commented that 'Frankly, no historian would even consider doing it this way.' I am no historian; I am an anthropologist, and I have chosen to deal with the complexities of the evidence by being open about the dubious nature of much of it, and by using a *polyphonic* approach. Each chapter outlines and assesses contesting views of what happened, bringing together archival material, popular journalistic accounts, contemporary memoirs, and serious historical work by Ugandans as well as Westerners. In this way, I aim to show the multiple contexts and agendas through which postcolonial politics has been described and through which postcolonial history can be written. In consequence, the book has a far higher proportion of direct quotation than most historical writing, allowing the reader to see the flaws and contradictions in the sources and to judge them by their own words. My voice, and my conclusions about the sources, are always there, but they sit alongside other accounts and interpretations of the truth. Perhaps this approach could be called a *demonography*, a book that aims to show how a monstrous icon of evil is created – by human beings.

I began the project with the typical anthropologist's idea that the key to understanding Amin's life would be found in his social and cultural background and its long-term historical development. As the research and writing went on, I became increasingly aware that the role of my own country was at the heart of the story. From the controversies that surround his birth, to his eventual overthrow and retirement, Amin's story was shaped as well as interpreted by British people and British history, to a much greater degree than I had thought. Amin's ancestors had historical links to the East and West coasts of Africa, the Middle East and the wider Arab world, and to Belgian as well as British colonialism. His own life and career, though, were most intimately linked with Britain, in both its late imperial and immediately post-imperial phases. The British Empire, in particular its military institutions, formed Idi Amin from childhood, and made him the man he became (whether, at any given time, he was fighting for the Brits, or railing against them). As I will argue, his complex and fluctuating relationship with the British state was probably the most important and enduring relationship in Amin's life. However, he was always first a Ugandan, and his roots lay in the country's polyglot variety of ethnic groups, religions and cultures, its complex history, and its network of relations with the wider world. In particular, Amin was a West Niler and his life exemplifies the history of his homeland as a whole; its violence, marginality and complexity.

All this indicates why an anthropologist may be the best person to write about Amin. A study of his life has to go well beyond its factual details, even where these are known, and to look past the historian's distinction between fact and fiction to examine the myths accreted around him. Although myths are, of course, always strictly false, or have only the most tenuous link to actually occurring events, they survive and are reiterated because they embody a deeper, metaphorical truth about the cultures they spring from or are absorbed into. In addition, representations create their own realities. In his lifetime, which stories people believed about Amin determined how they behaved towards him. In a more diffuse sense, the image of Amin has deeply influenced (or perhaps reinforced) Western attitudes to Africa, its political leaders and Africans in general. This book therefore focuses on the myths as well as the reality of Amin's life, and considers how and why Amin became seen as an icon of evil, while at the same time describing the known realities of his life and times. It is an amazing story, of how an illiterate peasant, from one of the most remote and undeveloped parts of Central Africa, not only managed to advance himself in the service of the state and then capture state power for himself, but to become the most notorious dictator in the continent, possibly the world.

This has been a long and difficult project, which has taken me, on and off, more than ten years to complete. In that time I have accrued a massive amount of information, and only a small portion of the primary archive and interview material can be discussed in the book. Many Ugandans, in particular, will regret the omission of their favourite Amin story, or some explanation of a key event, for which I can only apologise. I could not have written this without considerable help from many people, and I can only mention a few here. First of all, I thank those I have interviewed and spoken with, in Uganda and the UK: even when I have not used your words, they have informed my judgements. In particular I owe an immense amount to the people of Arua, who have battled for dignity and respect in a Uganda which associates them completely with Idi Amin; I particularly thank John Alokore, Jason Avutia, Nahor Oyaa Awua, Nathan Droti, Kitami Ali Garawan, Samson Geria, Doka Ali Kujo and Simon Vigga. Above all, I am grateful to the late Lulua Odu, pioneer of West Nile history writing. I would never have begun to study Idi Amin, or West Nile, without the inspiration of two great mentors, Barbara Harrell-Bond and Wendy James. When things got tough, I have depended on the practical support of my colleagues at the University of Sussex, especially successive heads of the Anthropology Department: Filippo Osella, Geert de Neve and Jon Mitchell. Essential psychic support was provided by my psychoanalytic psychotherapist, Heather Chamberlain. I am especially grateful for the advice and encouragement of those who read and commented on the book as it evolved, especially James Fairhead and Luise White, who kept me going by getting what I was trying to do and believing in it, even when I didn't quite do so myself. Most of all, though, I have depended throughout, in all these ways, on the intellectual and personal help, advice and support of JoAnn McGregor, to whom this book is dedicated.

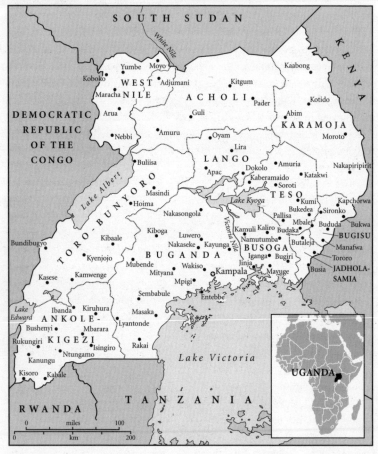

Uganda

INTRODUCTION
IDI AMIN DADA, MAN AND MYTH

Idi Amin Dada[1] was the president of Uganda between 1971 and 1979. Since then, he has become a man of mystery and of myth. More than forty years after his overthrow and eighteen years after his death, he remains a key point of reference in Ugandan culture and politics. Elsewhere in the world, his name has become synonymous with brutal and psychotic African dictatorship. In the Western popular imagination, he is a mainstay of books and TV series with titles like *The Fifty Most Evil Men and Women in History*, *The World's Most Evil People*, *The World's Most Evil Dictators*, or simply *Monsters*.[2] He has a place in the cultural commentator Peter York's guidebook to the interior decor of *Dictators' Homes*, and also in Clark and Scott's *Dictators' Dinners*, described on its jacket as 'the world's most gruesome cookbook'.[3] In many of these works, he is the only African subject. Popular, journalistic accounts of the more notorious aspects of his rule – such as the 1972 expulsion of the 'Ugandan Asians', or Israel's 1976 raid on Uganda's Entebbe airport – continue to be published, while Kevin Macdonald's 2007 movie, based on Giles Foden's novel *The Last King of Scotland*, impressed a new generation with its fictionalised horrors of his regime.[4]

Amin's name comes up in the media whenever contemporary African dictators are discussed, though many of them are nothing like him. In the West, he exemplifies both a personal notion of evil, characterised by cannibalism and sadistic pleasures, and a political notion of evil, seen as unconstrained dictatorship. These go together with strong suggestions of a 'reversion' to some primitive African past, and a concept of masculinity drenched in violence and (hetero)sexuality. Amin embodies the stereotype of Africans associated with Joseph Conrad's novella *Heart of Darkness*, but

1

revisited in the late twentieth century. This is not an accidental connection; Conrad's story was actually inspired by events that took place near Amin's home area in north-west Uganda, and which were to have a direct connection with his rule. Idi Amin can, in fact, only be understood in the context of the history of the place he came from, and the times he lived through. In this, at least, he is like the rest of us.

Appropriately for such a figure of myth, even Amin's place and date of birth, as well as his parentage, are matters of dispute. Most accounts suggest that he was born between 1925 and 1928 near the small town of Koboko in West Nile district, close to Uganda's borders with Congo and Sudan, of a Muslim father from the Kakwa tribe and a mother from the neighbouring Lugbara people. A widespread rumour in Uganda is that his real father was the Kabaka, or King, of Buganda, the largest and most powerful of the pre-colonial southern Ugandan kingdoms, after which the country was named. He himself often claimed to have been born in or near the Ugandan capital, Kampala,[5] and this is what his family believe.[6] Hostile commentators, on the other hand, frequently suggest he may not have been born in Uganda at all.[7]

In some of the cruder accounts of Amin's life, the Kakwa are depicted as a particularly ferocious ethnic group. Amin's former commanding officer (CO) in the British Army calls them a 'warrior tribe' and tells us that they and other West Nile tribes engaged in 'sacrifices of animals and humans'.[8] Henry Kyemba, a southern Ugandan who worked for Amin as a senior civil servant and cabinet minister, and wrote one of the most influential accounts of his rule, suggested that cannibalism is common among the Kakwa.[9] Already, in his younger years, growing up in and around the army regiment known as the King's African Rifles, Amin was the subject of rumours and anecdotes, contradictory accounts of his actions and motivations, together with widely varying (though usually strong) impressions among those who encountered him. The stories grew in the telling, especially after his 1971 seizure of power.

Most Ugandans and historians of Uganda agree that his rule, covering eight years in the 1970s, was a crucial period in the collapse of the Ugandan economy and society, though the process worsened after his departure. The main reasons for this were the economic destruction caused in part by his expulsion of the Asian population of the country, who had run most of its formal economy, the internal disorder and violence created as a result of undisciplined military rule, and Amin's habit of making powerful external enemies, in East Africa and more widely. However, most informed analysts also agree that Amin's predecessor and successor as president, Apolo Milton Obote, was probably responsible for more deaths than Amin, over a shorter time period.[10] Unlike Obote during his second period in power, Amin did not specifically target mass violence towards civilians from particular tribes, and Obote's earlier expulsions of Kenyan and Rwandan workers are not remembered alongside Amin's targeting of the Asians, although the Kenyans and Rwandans were greater in number.[11] Why, then, is Amin repeatedly singled out, by Ugandans and other Africans as well as Western commentators, for special condemnation? That is one of the central questions this book seeks to address. In contrast to the critics, Amin and his supporters have consistently represented him in political terms as, above all, a Black African nationalist; his son quotes him in exile as saying, 'The people will appreciate what I was trying to do for the Indigenous African. ... God will be my Judge.'[12] For many contemporary Ugandan intellectuals, on the contrary, he was clearly a colonial stooge; as the Marxist academic and lawyer, Dan Wadada Nabudere (who was released from Obote's prisons by Amin, and put in charge of Uganda's railways) put it, Amin 'governed for imperialism'.[13]

Popular books about Amin often have titles like *Uganda Holocaust* or *Idi Amin Dada, Hitler in Africa*,[14] but genocide is not the word for Amin's rule; it was far more chaotic and unorganised than that. He certainly killed, or caused to be killed, anyone who got in his way, while allowing his troops considerable licence to act on personal grudges and further their private economic aims. Amin specifically targeted soldiers from the Acholi and Langi tribes, and later other groups, within the army, because he suspected their loyalty was to Obote. However, there is no clear evidence he ever ordered mass pogroms against Acholi or Langi civilians in their home areas. Obote, on the other hand *did*, in his second period as president, attempt to exterminate large, ethnically defined groups of civilians, both in West Nile itself and among the Baganda of the Luwero Triangle in the south of the country.[15] The description of Amin as a 'village tyrant' by the British lecturer Denis Hills, who was jailed and nearly executed for writing it, is not the whole truth;[16] Amin was more powerful, and therefore able to be considerably worse, than that. But it is closer to the truth than depicting him as an

3

evil Hitler-like monster. Meanwhile, Milton Obote has never been seen internationally as an icon of African evil, although most historians of Uganda believe he killed more people, in less time, than Amin did.

Why is this? It is easy to see Amin as a man who conveniently fits colonial racial stereotypes of 'the (male) African'; violent, uneducated, primitive, a fantasy figure exemplifying the Western portrayal of the continent as a 'heart of darkness'. He certainly does this, but it is also true that Amin's image as an icon of evil is more than a racist Western cliché; it is shared by many Ugandans, and African writers have played a big part in painting this picture. One reason for the contrast between representations of Amin and of Obote, is that the latter was a modern, educated, Westernised figure, with scant respect for African tradition. He could talk the languages of global diplomacy and world socialism. Amin, an uneducated soldier with an accent (in any of his several languages) painful to the southern Ugandan ear, seemed not only to be a primitive reversion but also to glory in the role. Once he assumed power, the British media almost immediately made him notorious for his grandiose anti-colonial statements – often deliberately rather than accidentally funny – which were quickly parodied, notably by the British humourist Alan Coren in a long-running column in *Punch* magazine, supposedly written by Amin, using a grotesque pidgin English.[17]

However, almost equally caricatured depictions of Amin as a primitive reversion come from African writers, some of whom, such as the eminent political scientist Ali Mazrui, even celebrated this image as authentically African. In the Ugandan media today, Amin remains a touchstone of illegitimate and violent authority, and a perpetual embarrassment to the country. He is the almost inevitable point of comparison for any criticism of government action, and as such is, in a sense, still part of Ugandan society and political discourse many decades after his fall from power. The image of tribal atavism runs through virtually all the literature on Amin, both 'Western' and African. Throughout his rule and since, both his supporters and detractors have emphasised his ethnicity, seeing the source and inspiration of his regime as based on his heredity. In many of the popular and sensational texts, a racist anthropology relates Amin's atrocities to the supposed traditional ways of the Kakwa tribe; in some of the more academic work his origins link his actions, through deep historical roots, to aspects of Nile Valley history and the wider North-East African past.

HISTORICAL BACKGROUND

In the late nineteenth and early twentieth centuries, before being incorporated into Britain's Uganda Protectorate, the area that became West Nile had been a part of the Belgian Congo and then of the Anglo-Egyptian Condominium of Sudan. In European conceptions of African geography, this made the area part of 'West Africa' and then 'North Africa', before settling down as part of East Africa. In Uganda and more widely across the region, Amin is often seen as exemplifying the image of West Nile, whose people have had stereotypes of violence and marginality attached to them long before he was born, probably since the first half of the nineteenth century. It was at this time that slave raids into the area created the first contacts between local people (later divided by colonial anthropologists and administrators into the Lugbara, Kakwa, Madi and Alur tribes) and others from very different cultures, who possessed radically more powerful technology, especially guns. The raids were organised by North African slave traders and carried out by groups of soldiers, themselves mostly slaves, though sometimes powerful and wealthy ones. The slave-soldiers would seize children and adults to refresh their ranks, for onward sale in the slave markets of North Africa and the Middle East, or to be exchanged for valuable items, especially elephant tusks. A widespread tripartite trade in guns, slaves and ivory developed, with a simple and remarkably consistent exchange rate of 1 healthy slave = 1 working gun = 1 complete tusk. Western powers, particularly Britain, sought to stamp out the practice of slavery and so gain control over the highly lucrative ivory trade.[18] By the 1870s, the Anglo-Egyptian regime ruling what was to become Sudan, sent armed forces into the south of the country, which had previously been almost entirely ungoverned. Many of the troops were themselves former slave-soldiers. One of these groups was commanded by a German doctor and Muslim convert known as Emin Pasha. In the late 1880s, an Islamic insurrection, which historians of colonialism call the Mahdist rebellion, caused Emin and his troops to be driven southwards up the Nile, towards an area later known as the Lado Enclave, the southern part of which was later to be named West Nile – Amin's homeland.

In 1889, Emin was 'rescued' by the explorer and journalist Henry Stanley, in a major international media event which became the inspiration for Joseph Conrad's *Heart of Darkness*, a book later described by Chinua Achebe as expressing the 'dominant image of Africa in the Western imagination'.[19] Most of Emin's soldiers remained behind in the Enclave, where many were picked up a few years later by Captain Frederick Lugard of the Imperial British East Africa Company – in effect, a private colonial army. Lugard saw these people as potentially 'the best material for soldiery in Africa',[20] and he used them to carve out the colonial territories that were to become modern-day Uganda and Kenya. In this role, the former slave-soldiers became known as 'Nubi' or 'Nubians' (a word that is applied to a number of completely unrelated groups in different parts of Africa, connoting both 'black' and 'slave'). Many of them were later integrated into the official British Army formation known as the King's African Rifles (KAR), where they fought for colonial rule in East Africa and elsewhere. From the days of the slave armies they had been Muslims and, in fact if not in theory, the identity became an elective, strategic one, which West Nilers and others could choose to adopt when they moved to towns and joined the army or took up other coercive trades of the state, such as police and prison officers. To become Nubi, they simply had to convert to Islam, and learn to speak some KiNubi, a form of vernacular Arabic, or the related KiSwahili, the language of command in the KAR.[21]

The contested history of West Nile meant that its people in general were considered by the British to be 'a warrior folk', less intelligent and civilised than southern Ugandans, therefore unsuited for most productive economic activities and discouraged from entering them. This was one of the main reasons why so many of them joined the army, police or prison service, thereby becoming Nubis. Idi Amin's father, as a Muslim in the colonial forces, was regarded as one of these, and his boy was brought up within and around the subculture of the British colonial military, policing and prisons system. Many commentators have seen his Nubi background as determining, at least in part, his violent inclinations and behaviour,[22] just as others have explained it in terms of his Kakwa origins.[23]

Idi Amin, like his father before him, was born a Nubi as well as a Kakwa. He was raised in and around the bases of the 4th Battalion of the King's African Rifles, and in Uganda's biggest city, Kampala. He often claimed to have fought as a child soldier with the KAR in Burma during the Second World War, but records show he was not officially enlisted until 1946. Amin became very popular with his British officers, making a powerful impression as an extremely athletic, strong and obedient soldier. He rose through the ranks as quickly as an African soldier could do. He fought against the Mau Mau uprising in Kenya, winning promotion to the KAR rank of 'Effendi', equivalent to a warrant officer in the regular British Army. This was the highest military rank a black African could then aspire to; the Queen's Commission held by officers was reserved for whites.

Amin's former commanding officer in the KAR, Iain Grahame, told me he was one of the two best soldiers he ever commanded, and other officers agreed with his assessment. Over the course of the 1950s, in the run-up to African independence, the KAR slowly realised that African soldiers would now have to be promoted. Despite his reputation for violence, the British continued to promote Amin until, when the country gained independence in 1962, he was one of only two Ugandan commissioned officers in the military. He quickly made himself irreplaceable to the new nation's first president, the very *un*military, left-wing nationalist intellectual Dr Apolo Milton Obote, and in 1965 he became the head of the Ugandan Army. Obote quickly fell out of favour with both the powerful Baganda leaders and the British. In the Cold War context of the 1960s, he was regarded as suspiciously socialistic and, with at least tacit support, advice and approval from Israeli and (to a lesser degree) British diplomats, in January 1971 Amin took over in a military coup, to widespread acclaim in both Uganda and the West.

This honeymoon period, however, quickly ended. By 1973 Amin had fallen out with the Israelis and British, and had thrown Uganda's Asian population out of the country (as we shall see, Obote had intended to expel them himself, but did not get round to it before he fell). The country's infrastructure crumbled and, as Asian properties and businesses were distributed to soldiers, Nubians and West Nilers, the army itself began to fall apart. As one former military officer, a West Niler, told me in 1997, 'by 1977–79 there was no army. . . . The military, that way of life got lost completely. They were now living lifestyles, extravaganza lifestyles, and civil ones, not military at all.'[24] Meanwhile, exile groups were conspiring in neighbouring states and, after an ill-advised incursion into Tanzanian territory in 1978, Uganda was invaded and Amin deposed by Tanzanian troops, together with some Ugandan refugees. Most of the West Nilers fled over the nearby borders into Sudan or Zaire and, after a series of very short-lived regimes, Milton Obote returned to power in 1980, in a rigged election. This initiated the period known in Uganda as 'Obote II', during which, according to most historians, more people were killed than under Amin. In 1986, following a bloody civil war, Obote was himself overthrown by the Tanzanian-backed Yoweri Museveni, who combined the political intellectualism of Obote with a military experience comparable to Amin's, albeit gained in guerrilla insurgency rather than conventional armed forces. Unlike both Obote and Amin, however, Museveni has always been careful to keep in favour with world powers, which has enabled him to rule Uganda longer than all its other post-independence leaders put together. After being ousted, Amin himself fled into exile, briefly in Libya and then, in 1981, to a peaceful retirement in Saudi Arabia, where he died in 2003.

REPRESENTATIONS OF AMIN

The many popular books on Amin, and their continued production and consumption into the twenty-first century, are symptomatic, not of a widespread Western interest in Ugandan history and postcolonial politics, but of European and North American attitudes towards African people. As Chinua Achebe wrote:

> it is the desire – one might indeed say the need – in Western psychology to set Africa up as a foil to Europe, as a place of negations at once remote and vaguely familiar, in comparison with which Europe's own state of spiritual grace will be manifest. ... Herein lies the meaning of *Heart of Darkness* and the fascination it holds over the Western mind: 'What thrilled you was just the thought of their [Africans'] humanity – like yours ... ugly.'[25]

Achebe is alluding here to the Freudian concept of 'projection', a psychological process in which some undesirable aspect of the self is buried, being imagined as part of another person instead. In this respect, *Heart of Darkness*'s fiction can be replaced here with the thrilling real life of Idi Amin Dada. In the popular accounts of his rule, Amin seems to represent the complete opposite of Western society's self-image. He is perceived and portrayed as animalistic, violent and hyper-sexual, quintessentially uncivilised/un-'developed', stupid, ignorant and a 'buffoon', somehow ridiculous as well as scary. The stories of cannibalism and body parts stored in fridges epitomise this image. He is, in fact, presented as wholly 'Other' in relation to Western men and women; '*they*' have these evil political and personal vices, '*we*' have none of them. A moment of projection, indeed, and one repeatedly evoked when Amin is mentioned. But to say this is to emphasise, not dismiss, the continuing importance and relevance of Amin's life, his personality and the many myths that have accreted to his reputation. It also goes some way towards explaining the strange fascination he seemed to generate, perhaps especially among the British people who met him.

The very first book on Idi Amin, published in 1973, was the work of a Hungarian aristocrat and journalist married to an Anglo-Irish earl. Judith, Countess of Listowel, met Amin in 1969, when he was commander of the Ugandan Army, and she was working on a BBC documentary about Obote's Uganda. Amin's son, many years later, described her as 'Dad's official biographer'.[26] According to Lady Listowel's obituary in the *Daily Telegraph* (she died in 2003, aged 100):

> Her biography of Idi Amin . . . led to serious trouble. She completed it in six weeks for a fee of £300, and the new Ugandan leader was so delighted that he invited her out for a party. But her plane came down in the bush between Uganda and Sudan, forcing the passengers to manage with two bottles of water and a 5lb cheese until they were rescued after two days. . . . [A] couple of weeks after her return to England, Milton Obote, whom Amin had ousted, sued over some remarks about gold smuggling. Although her Irish publisher went bankrupt, and she had no insurance cover, Lady Listowel fought the case. She had to apologise and faced damages of more than £80,000, which were eventually reduced to a fraction after the case had come before Lord Denning.[27]

It was something of a rushed job, but Listowel's book is notable for having been written before Amin's rule had really got under way, and thus before the emergence of his powerful image as a psychotic monster. Consequently, she portrays him as a more complex, sophisticated and attractive character than later writers.

As Amin became increasingly notorious, during and especially after his rule, accounts of his life and career proliferated. Former military comrades (such as Grahame) and political allies (Kyemba), journalists (Martin, 'Donald', 'Kamau and Cameron'), civil servants (Kato), Western diplomats (Smith, and Melady and Melady), teachers and lecturers (Benson, Hills), nurses (Hale), telecoms engineers (Measures and Walker), broadcasting executives (Lawoko), a long-standing expatriate technical advisor to the Ugandan government ('Gwyn') and even a British senior member of the Ugandan judiciary (Allen) – all these have produced book-length memoirs and accounts of his time in power, each with its own story of encountering the monster.[28] These writers are from Uganda, Zimbabwe, Britain, the USA, Canada, Australia and New Zealand. Interestingly, several of them – 'Gwyn', 'Kamau and Cameron', 'Donald' – use pseudonyms. Such books were in demand, as the Western reading public lapped up the exotic doings of a psychopath who represented the epitome of primitive savagery. In the contemporary world, this material has been added to by websites and self-published, print-on-demand books. There is a lot of repetition in these works, but also a degree of variety: while I emphasise the consistency of the picture they paint of Amin, each also tells its own tale. But they are all, inevitably, also by unreliable narrators. As Peter Nayenga perceptively put it, in a review of three of these books (by 'Gwyn', Kyemba, and Melady and Melady), 'Respectable as these authors are, however, the question which still remains unanswered is: what portion of their writings is a myth and what can be taken as a reality?'[29] It is worth noting that this was written while Amin was (just) still in power.[30]

All these books, and the persistence of the legend, means that in a sense there are many lives of Idi Amin. Like any mythical being – a chimera, a unicorn, a fairy, or indeed a demon – there is a more or less universally agreed core of characteristics defining the imaginary beast, but this is always embroidered with wildly differing and highly implausible stories and inter-pretations. In this book, I attempt to unpick the embroidery, while at the same time appreciating the very real historical impact of its depiction. I look at both the well-known and the more obscure aspects of Amin's life, giving due weight to both the facts in the historical record, and the stories that accreted around Amin from his early days in the British Army to the present day, while discussing the theoretical implications of his persona, and his status in the Western imagination.

My own view is, to put it simply, that Amin's image as an icon of evil came about because he fits, almost parodically, the long-standing stereotype of

African masculinity as intrinsically violent, irrational, autocratic and dangerous: the perfect foil, as Achebe wrote, to white 'Western' man's rational, liberal self-image.[31] When, in November 2016, the US satirical TV programme *The Daily Show* wanted to attack America's new president-elect, Donald Trump, they replayed spoken phrases of self-aggrandising braggadocio from his speeches, alongside recordings of Amin saying very similar things.[32] It was both funny and politically pointed precisely because it dared compare the 'Leader of the Free World' with the archetypal African monster, pairing a perceived white supremacist with a quintessentially black man, and a democratically elected president with the ultimate African dictator. A key aspect of this book, then, is a close examination of the making of a Western Other.

AN ICON OF EVIL

To show how someone becomes an icon of evil, we need to understand the concept. The nature of evil has been analysed at length by philosophers and theologians, though anthropologists tend to shy away from it. David Parkin's 1985 edited collection *The Anthropology of Evil* is an exception. In the introduction, Parkin refers to evil as 'an odd-job word', suggesting that 'it is precisely because the term has been so loose analytically that it has been able to reveal so much empirically'.[33] A key aspect of this 'looseness' is an ambiguity at the heart of the concept. In one sense of the word, a weak one, the meaning of 'evil' is broadly similar to that of 'bad', or 'very bad', along a moral continuum in which human acts may be graded from 'very good' to 'very bad'. In a much stronger sense, however, 'evil' goes way past 'very bad' as a condemnation. It signifies an excess well beyond normal human badness, denoting behaviour that cannot be described as simply 'bad', but is literally inhuman, even demonic. This is what philosophers since Kant have called 'radical evil', and it is discussed in the Parkin collection by Martin Southwold, who points out that, in this sense of the word, to paraphrase 'evil' as 'extreme badness' is in effect to condone it: '[i]f one were to describe and discuss what the Nazis did at Auschwitz and elsewhere in pursuit of their Final Solution, and conclude with the judgement that such conduct was "bad", or "wrong" or "immoral", one would outrage one's readers'.[34]

The origins of the word are obviously associated with a religious context. Donald Taylor tells us that the Hebrew word *ra*, translated in the King James version of the Bible as 'evil', originally referred to the weak sense of the concept, rather than the radical one,[35] but the English word signifies something beyond this. Its root (and that of the Dutch *euvel* and the German *übel*), goes back to a Teutonic term, *ubiloz*, the primary sense of which, according to the *Oxford English Dictionary*, 'would be either "exceeding due measure" or "overstepping proper limits"'.[36] Parkin emphasises that 'In a number of languages ... some terms translatable as bad or evil also have a sense of physically rotten, misshapen, and ugly.... [T]he evil powers of madness are semantically linked to ugliness and dirt.... [M]any other terms in other societies, rendered by us as evil or bad, denote blackness [*sic*], obscurity and unfulfillment.'[37] Wherever it is used, there is always a potential slippage between the weak and strong senses of the word, and this is what gives it much of its power.

These are not just technical linguistic definitions; such words have moral weight and historical consequences. What moves normal human badness towards radical evil is the sense of an otherness. Those who are called evil have gone so far beyond normal wickedness that they have become other than human; they are demons or monsters. As David Pocock argues: '[T]he word "evil" has, for the majority, a totalising force that, we can properly say, makes "evil people" monsters in the sense that they are denied all admirable human attributes such as love or loyalty.'[38] He explicitly connects this with racism and colonialism, writing of:

> a view commonly held in nineteenth-century western society that human beings, while remaining human, can be graded on a scale of moral excellence such that some achieve a condition of refined humanity in relation to which the less advanced are ... as it were, members of an inferior genus. ... [In racist societies] the inferiority is located in the physical appearance of beings who are simultaneously recognised as human and denied full humanity.[39]

Pocock concludes with the remark that: 'I am very struck by the fact that in primitive societies evil is attributed ultimately to monsters that cannot exist (demons, evil spirits, witches, etc.), whereas in our society it is attributed to monsters that do.'[40] All of which, of course, brings us back to Idi Amin.

The anthropologist Jean La Fontaine wrote, in a study of satanic ritual child abuse allegations in late twentieth-century England, that:

In most of the societies anthropologists have traditionally studied, inhuman evil is personified in the form of the witch. Whatever the local term that is translated 'witch' by anthropologists, it refers to those who commit acts perceived as transgressing the fundamental moral axioms on which human nature, and hence social life, is based. The sins attributed to witches may vary somewhat in their detail and emphasis according to the culture in question, but they commonly concern sex, food and killing. . . .

In modern England evil inheres in similar acts: in the sexual abuse, ill-treatment and murder of children, in cannibalism and human sacrifice.[41]

Representations of Amin in the West have almost invariably depicted him as an epitome of evil. As far as I know, no one has accused him of paedophilia, but certainly sexual violence is part of the picture, as is killing, and accusations of cannibalism add food to the sex and violence. In many of the popular books on him, Amin is pictured as an inhuman monster, evil through and through. Again and again, this is associated with his ethnic origins – as an African in some of the cruder work, and as a Kakwa and/or a Nubi in more sophisticated accounts. Judith Listowel clearly did not see Amin as evil, but as a rather appealing figure. However, the next book on Amin to be published in the West was considerably more critical, and influential, than Listowel's: this was *General Amin*[42] by the British journalist and Obote admirer, David Martin. Both Listowel's and Martin's books were published before the more sensational stories about Amin emerged, and neither of them mentions sexual sadism or cannibalism. What both books emphasise, though, is the supposed link between Amin's violence and his tribal background. The Kakwa and the Nubi are depicted as particularly 'primitive' groups, in comparison with the 'civilised' Baganda and, of course, Europeans. Martin writes of the Nubi that: 'among their fellow countrymen they enjoyed an unenviable reputation of having one of the world's highest homicide rates. The Nubians were renowned for their sadistic brutality, lack of formal education, for poisoning enemies and for their refusal to integrate, even in the urban centres.'[43] Both he and Listowel repeatedly link the idea of 'primitiveness' with that of 'violence', an association also, as we shall see, to be found in many of the British diplomatic assessments of Amin. In fact, Amin was carefully trained to be violent, in the British armed forces.

The two most influential works on Idi Amin were written in the later years of his rule, by people who knew him well and focus on their own memories of the man. These were the books of Henry Kyemba and Iain Grahame, published in 1977 and 1980 respectively, which introduced many of the stories, themes and tropes that were repeated again and again in subsequent work on Amin, including the stories of cannibalism. Henry Kyemba is a Muganda aristocrat who, he wrote, 'was born with the tradition of government behind me'.[44] He was Obote's private secretary and went on to do the same job for Amin, later becoming the latter's health minister, before defecting in 1977. Kyemba seems to have been the first to claim that Amin was an enthusiastic cannibal, arguing that this (along with his violence in general), was characteristic of his primitive ethnic background as a Kakwa and a Nubi:

> To understand Amin's reign of terror it is necessary to realize that he is not an ordinary political tyrant. He does more than murder those whom he considers his enemies: he also subjects them to barbarisms even after they are dead. These barbarisms are well attested. It is common knowledge in the Ugandan medical profession that many of the bodies dumped in hospital mortuaries are terribly mutilated, with livers, noses, lips, genitals or eyes missing. Amin's killers do this on his specific instructions; the mutilations follow a well-defined pattern. . . .
>
> There is of course no evidence for what he does in private, but it is universally believed in Uganda that he engages in blood rituals. Hardly any Ugandan doubts that Amin has, quite literally, a taste for blood.
>
> Amin's bizarre behaviour has much to do with the peculiarities of his own aberrant personality. It also derives partly from his tribal background. Like many other warrior societies, the Kakwa, Amin's tribe, are known to have practised blood rituals on slain enemies. These involve cutting a piece of flesh from the body to subdue the dead man's spirit or tasting the victim's blood. . . .
>
> I have reason to believe that Amin's practices do not stop at tasting blood: on several occasions he has boasted to me and others that he has eaten human flesh. . . . [H]e went on to say that eating human flesh is not uncommon in his home area. He justified the practice in coolly practical terms: 'in warfare, if you do not have food, and your fellow soldier is wounded, you may as well kill him and eat him to survive'.[45]

In his book *Amin and Uganda: A Personal Memoir*, published three years after Kyemba's work, Amin's former CO, Iain Grahame, stops just short of directly accusing him of eating human flesh. He does, however, believe that ritual cannibalism was used by the 'Mau Mau' fighters he and Amin fought in the 1950s, and writes that 'in Amin's area of West Nile, it [cannibalism] was within living memory a by no means rare occurrence'.[46] Before the arrival of the Muslim slave traders, he misinformed his readers: 'West Nile ... people had all been pagans, worshipping animal totems, ancestral spirits and other heathen idols. Priests and witch doctors had divine powers to order armed raids against their enemies, or to make sacrifices of animals and humans.'[47] He also claimed, of the Kakwa's near neighbours over the Congo border, that 'among the latter, cannibalism was still practised'.[48]

In the same year that Grahame's book came out, the former United Nations (UN) diplomat George Ivan Smith published his *Ghosts of Kampala*. In this, he told his readers that:

> The southern Ugandans are particularly contemptuous of the southern Sudanese and the Nubis ... as wild and uncivilized. It is from them that we have reports of Amin and his Nubis tasting the blood of their victims and eating their livers and the explanation that such a custom is either a Nubi or Kakwa rite. There is strong evidence that Amin and some of his henchmen did engage in this sort of thing, but as an instrument of terror, not as a tribal custom.[49]

Smith provides none of the 'strong evidence' for 'this sort of thing', but the first sentence might well refer to Henry Kyemba, whose book remains one of the few works on the country's postcolonial history that is both readily available and affordable in Ugandan bookshops. Kyemba acted as an advisor for the movie *The Last King of Scotland* and, along with Iain Grahame, remains to date an important source for TV documentaries and other accounts of Amin's life and times.[50]

Given Kyemba's repeated statements that Amin's cannibalism was well known in Uganda, however, it seems strange that none of the Ugandan historians who have written about the Amin period seem to take the accusations seriously. Omara-Otunnu, Mutibwa, Kasozi, Kanyeihamba and Makubuya all write extensively about Amin's rule, but none of them mentions cannibalism.[51]

Otunnu does refer to the story, but only to dismiss it, writing that Amin's disrespect for British authorities was represented by 'many political commentators [he cites, Kiwanuka, 'Gwyn', Kyemba and the Meladys] as a clear indication that Amin was suffering from schizophrenia'. He goes on:

> According to them, what they presented as a series of confused orders, 'senseless killings', 'sadism' and 'involvement in "blood rituals"' by Amin confirmed their medical 'diagnosis'. The commentators ... also attempted to explain some actions by the 'patient' in terms of Amin's Kakwa warrior tradition, superstitions and witchcraft. For example, they claimed that, in accordance with the Kakwa warrior tradition, Amin ate the flesh of his victims to prevent them from haunting him. What the commentators, who do not understand Kakwa traditions and were not qualified medical experts in the field, failed to understand was the legitimation functions of the drama ... [which] made Amin extremely popular in the country because he had humiliated white men. To ordinary Ugandans this was a payoff moment.[52]

Amin's British associate, Bob Astles, broadly agrees with this assessment. In his memoir he writes, I think rightly, that:

> Over the years, Amin's antics have made good copy to sell newspapers.... He was human enough to know that by 'putting his foot in it', he was giving them a good story but they rarely acknowledged that he had helped their careers. Much has been written about him both in praise and execration. We should forget stories about keeping heads in refrigerators and eating human flesh. They are accusations without evidence, which is not surprising, as they never happened. Africans do not believe such stories, which make the Western press look ridiculous to them.[53]

Although throughout history some individuals have eaten human flesh, for reasons ranging from extreme hunger to mental illness, most anthropologists who have written on the subject have concluded that the existence, anywhere, of socially sanctioned anthropophagy, is a myth.[54] Rumours of cannibalism are not unusual in parts of North-East Africa, always among other tribes, of course, not one's own. E.E. Evans-Pritchard investigated widespread cannibalism stories about the Azande people of South Sudan,[55] finding the accounts to be highly unreliable in every case. Even some southern Ugandan groups have acquired a reputation for cannibalism.[56] However, in my own research since the late 1990s, I have found no evidence at all that the Kakwa or Nubi practise, or have ever practised, cannibalism. More significantly, no one I have spoken to from the neighbouring tribes (the Lugbara, Madi and Alur people) ever suggested this to me, though one or two did believe that Amin himself was a cannibal.

The early books on Amin were written during or shortly after his time in power, but since then the cannibalism story has become accepted fact in much of the popular writing about him, which represents him as a twentieth-century icon of evil. It is, unfortunately, impossible to discuss these works without quoting some of the fevered fantasies of their authors, which are usually either unsourced, or hyped-up versions of anecdotes taken from earlier works such as those of Kyemba and Grahame. These are at the heart of the demonographical aspect of the Amin story, and it is worth quoting them here to show the persistence of the myth of Amin as an evil monster. Here is a fairly representative example, from Diane Law's book, *The World's Most Evil Dictators*:

> At home, Amin kept a harem of wives and an estimated twenty-five to thirty-five children. He had in his home a collection of 'trophies' from those he had killed. When one of his wives, Kay, died in a bungled abortion attempt he insisted that her legs and arms be removed and re-attached with the legs at the shoulders and the arms at the pelvis as a warning to the other wives.[57] He kept the head of Jesse Gitta, the former husband of his wife Sarah, in his freezer (referred to as his 'botanical room'). Among many others was the head of Ruth Kobusinje, a one-time girlfriend whom he had suspected of infidelity. One nurse testified to decapitating six bodies and sending their shaved and preserved bodies to Amin's home. He also confessed proudly to Henry Kyemba, the Ugandan Health Minister, during a dinner party that he had eaten the flesh of his human victims on many occasions.[58]

Miranda Twiss, author of *The Most Evil Men and Women in History: The Book of the Channel 5 TV Series*, goes even further, attributing to Amin's thugs the unusual tactic of forced auto-anthropophagy:

17

Cruising through the streets of Kampala in their imported cars, wearing their uniform of gaudy shirts and bell-bottom trousers ... [Amin's agents] openly arrested ordinary townspeople. And at their headquarters, only a few hundred yards from Amin's home, they ruthlessly butchered their victims. One of Amin's ministers later compiled a list of the tortures that they inflicted. They are as follows:

Slow killing was common practice. A man would be shot in the arms, chest and legs and left to bleed to death.

There was a technique for cutting a victim's flesh and force-feeding it to him raw until he bled to death.

A man's flesh would be cut, roasted and he would be forced to eat it until he died.

Certain prisoners were kept in very deep and dark holes. These holes are filled with ice-cold water in which the prisoners were kept and tortured to death.

Sticking bayonets through prisoners' anuses or genitals.

Women were raped or had their reproductive organs set on fire whilst still alive.[59]

Neil Blandford and Bruce Jones put Amin at the head of their list of *The World's Most Evil Men*, a book which brings together many of the most lurid tales about him, but strangely omits cannibalism. We are told that, 'One hot August night in 1972, dinner guests at Amin's palace, State House in Entebbe, were shocked and revolted when he left the table and returned from the kitchen with the frost-encrusted head of Brigadier Hussein from the freezer.'[60] Like many of the other accounts, the book also tells the story of the post mortem mutilation of Amin's wife: 'Kay Amin's mutilated torso lay on the operating table. Her head and all her limbs had been amputated. Her head had been reversed and sewn back on face down on her torso. Her legs had been neatly sutured on to her shoulders and her arms attached firmly to her bloodstained pelvis.'[61]

The popular historian Simon Montefiore is less sure of the cannibalism accusations than Kyemba, Law or Twiss; he calls them 'rumours', but he sees them as important enough to take up a paragraph of his brief account of Amin's life, complete with the characteristic pseudo-anthropological language of African 'blood rituals' and 'tribal rites', and the depiction of these as the opposite of the 'western norm'. According to Montefiore's book, *Monsters: History's Most Evil Men and Women*:

> Rumours began to emerge that Amin practised blood rituals over the bodies of his victims, even indulging in cannibalism. Many of the bodies, dumped in the Nile, or on the streets or found hooded and tied to trees, were sliced open with organs missing, clearly the victims of tribal rites. Amin himself often asked to be left alone with bodies in the morgues, which he visited frequently, and it was clear that he tampered with the cadavers. 'I have eaten human flesh', he boasted, 'it is saltier than leopard flesh.' The terror extended to his own wives: the beautiful Kay died during an abortion, but Amin had her body dismembered and then sewn together. Lesser women suspected of disloyalty were simply murdered.[62]

There is no need to continue to pile up these examples. To summarise, Amin is repeatedly described in the popular literature in terms that characterise Western culture's notion of evil. His life is seen as a series of episodes which twine together aspects of sexuality and forms of violence, while also combining the personal and the political senses of the word 'evil'. This is perhaps most clearly encapsulated in the cannibalism stories, which bring together so many of the tropes associated with the concept of evil, but it permeates virtually all these books, even those which avoid tales of anthropophagy. These associations of sex and violence are almost always related to aspects of Amin's ethnicity, whether as a Kakwa, a Nubi, or simply an African. The popular books on Amin consistently represent him in terms of masculinity, violence and sexuality, linked to an atavistic racial primitivism and a frontier historical tradition, both of which are exemplified by his West Nile origins.[63] Of course, this also reflects a more general association in Western culture between African men and hyper-sexuality, plus a propensity to violence. It can all be neatly summed up in the multiple meanings of the word 'primitive'.

In fact, the themes of masculinity, sex and violence were developed in contemporary academic debates on Amin's rule as well as the popular literature. Two of the most interesting accounts were expressed in the course of a debate between the British social anthropologist Aidan Southall, who had done extensive ethnographic fieldwork in West Nile, and the Kenyan academic Ali Mazrui (mentioned earlier).[64] Both Mazrui and Southall considered that Amin's Nubi ancestry, with its long history of militarisation and slavery, was the key to understanding his rule, though Mazrui took a more ambivalent – and changing – attitude to Amin than Southall. Both knew Amin personally, and both had taught at Makerere; Southall in the 1960s and Mazrui during Amin's early years in power, when the president was a very active chancellor of the university. By 1975, when their debate on the nature of Amin's rule began, both were working in the United States.

Mazrui's writings about Amin are complex and sometimes contradictory, like their subject. He developed a pan-African figure of 'the warrior' who exemplifies self-reliant, and therefore anti-colonial, adulthood, arguing that '[T]he struggle against dependency as exemplified by Field Marshal Amin at his best, is, in an important sense, a reactivation of the ancestral assertiveness of warrior culture.'[65] Amin also exemplifies an extreme heterosexual masculinity:

> What should not be overlooked is the sexual dimension of the warrior culture. ... Virtues like courage, endurance, even ruthlessness, were regarded as hard, masculine virtues. The statement 'he is a real man' could mean either he is sexually virile, or he is tough and valiant. ... Given the link between manliness and warfare there could also be an easy link between violence and sexuality.[66]

Political, military and sexual aspects are merged in this masculine paradigm:

> When we relate charisma to the warrior tradition in Africa, there is one quality which demands particular attention. We call this quality political masculinity. ...
>
> The political masculinity of the General [Amin] does not lie merely in his size, though he is impressively tall and broad. Nor does it lie merely in his insistence that he fears no-one but God. Yet these factors are part of the story, combined with the additional factor that an affirmation of fearlessness and an athletic build have indeed been part of the total picture of martial values within African political cultures.[67]

Mazrui's articles about Amin usually included a token reminder that the warrior tradition was a cruel one, but the overall tendency of his work in the 1970s was to celebrate both that tradition and Idi Amin as its exemplar.

Aidan Southall broadly accepts Mazrui's picture of Amin as the incarnation of an African warrior tradition but, unlike the Kenyan, he wholly deprecates this. He situates Amin within Ugandan, and especially West Nile, history, rather than in relation to continent-wide political structures, and he sees the general's rise as the outcome of a long developmental process, as opposed to Mazrui's evocation of a recrudescence from the pre-colonial past. Evoking the martial history of the Nubi and the geo-political marginality of the Kakwa, Southall presented Amin as 'an exceptional person ... [who] is the product of a series of events and a concatenation of forces which seem ineluctable'.[68] 'Central to my interpretation', he writes, 'is the fact that General Amin is a Nubi, and that the history of the Nubi is important for the understanding of contemporary events. The present regime is more and more predominantly a Nubi regime, and its core strength is a Nubi strength.'[69] Like Mazrui, Southall emphasised the long history of West Nile marginality, linking this with Amin's violence: 'Remote from the centre and from the benefits of education and income opportunities, [the West Nilers] ... seem fertile ground for fairly bitter resentment and potential hostility to other Ugandans, which may have found its outlet through the army.'[70]

However, Southall parts company explicitly and forcefully with Mazrui's celebration of the warrior tradition, which he saw as fundamentally based on a colonial racial stereotype. He concludes:

> I will be bold and state my conviction that the warrior tradition is neither relevant nor useful for contemporary Africa. It inevitably summons up the colonial image of the noble savage ... every inch a man and visibly male, honest and clean, lion-spearing, the virtuous though primitive contrast to the lying thieving, spoilt 'mission boy' [an implicit reference to Obote]....
>
> In so far as the warrior tradition continues to find expression in the verbal bellicosity and excessive military spending of some African leaders, it is a suicidal mockery, effectively destroying any hope of sound economic development....
>
> Moreover, the African people whose poverty and economic backwardness are exploited to perpetuate the sentimental warrior image ... are

those who have been left high and dry in inaccessible and inhospitable areas ... so that, faute de mieux, their primal existence has continued colourful and unchanged.[71]

There are deep and insidious dangers, as well as intellectual fallacies, in fostering the warrior image as a positive symbol in contemporary Africa and, as an example of it, flattering Field Marshal Hajii Idi Amin Dada.[72]

Many of the early accounts by people who had known Amin depicted him as not just one murderous dictator among many in the world, but a demonic monster, an icon of evil, and a recrudescence from the ancient African past. More recently, historians in both Uganda and the West have taken an increasingly nuanced and analytical approach to the Amin period, and the man himself.[73] While this has had an impact on academic historians of Africa, however, it has not changed the popular image of Amin, in or outside the continent. Recent Ugandan writing on Amin tends to be more knowledgeable and nuanced than the older material, while lacking the racial presuppositions of most of the British commentators, and regarding him as one nasty dictator among others, rather than a non-human monster. A good example of this is in a thoughtful 2019 newspaper article by the journalist Daniel Kalinaki:

Today is 40 years to the day Idi Amin was driven out of power by Tanzanian soldiers and Ugandan exiled fighters. Yet his eight years in power cast such a dark shadow over the country that it is not uncommon, in foreign lands, for one's Ugandan identity to immediately trigger inquiries or sympathetic grunts about Amin. It does not seem to matter that he died a decade and a half ago, or that eight out of every ten Ugandans alive today were not even born when he was ousted; Amin is a stubborn stain in our socio-political fabric.

Surprisingly for someone who had so much impact on the country, there is very little original scholarship or literature on Idi Amin. A lot of what exists, certainly in the popular media, is written, created or curated by foreigners, often with embellishments. So apart from the myths (the human head in the refrigerator, a taste for human flesh, et cetera), other important questions, such as the exact number of people killed under this hand and regime, remain answered inconclusively. Even basics, such as whether compensation was paid to departing Asians for their properties remains unsettled.[74]

The most intriguing recent Ugandan book on Amin, which I have used throughout, with caveats, is his son Jaffar's somewhat repetitive and rambling work, *Idi Amin: Hero or Villain?*[75] Together with its associated website,[76] this is a unique account from within Amin's own family, and was apparently written with the approval of its senior members. However, the book needs to be used cautiously by historians. Jaffar's use of supernatural forces to explain many of the events in Amin's life indicates that it is following an agenda other than that of rationalist historical scholarship. This does not mean that it is unusable, but the book's reliability has to be appraised and explained; it cannot be accepted uncritically as a source. I have tended to take up the book's first-hand accounts of Amin's personal and family life (often we have no others), but to question many of Jaffar's statements about his father's public career. He often gets dates wrong, and his focus on the role of portents, dreams and curses makes much of the material in the book difficult to use – which has not stopped historians from doing so.

So what is the truth about Idi Amin Dada? Why did he, rather than other political leaders of his day, become such a lasting icon of evil? How was he able to rise to power in the military, and then in politics? What did the Ugandan background he came from, and the British military upbringing and training in which he grew up, contribute to the man he became? Why did he exercise such a strange fascination on so many of the British and other Western people he met? How does his record compare with those of other dictators? With other African nationalist leaders of his era? With other presidents of Uganda? How can (or should) an account of Amin's life try to distinguish myth from reality, and what was his own contribution to the establishment of his iconic image? None of these questions is simple or straightforward, but I attempt to answer all of them in the course of this book, showing how the truth and the myth are embroiled together at each stage of Amin's life, by bringing together Ugandan and Western voices in a polyphonic account of events. In my view, his rule, and his myth, are both inexplicable except in the context of his upbringing and training in the British Army, and the latter's role in the wider world of the British Empire. These are the main focus of the next three chapters.

1

'WRUNG FROM THE WITHERS OF THE WESTERN NILE'
BACKGROUND, BIRTH AND YOUTH, 1928(?)–46

Idi Amin's adult life, in the British and Ugandan armies and in government, was seen and commented on by a range of outside observers, but there were no such witnesses to his early years. All we have are widely varying accounts, created after he had already become a largely mythical figure. As a result, this chapter, even more than the rest of the book, must focus to a large extent on representation rather than primary documentation, and I will be quoting extensively from the wildly contradictory (popular and academic) secondary literature. Some of this is quite strange, often rather overwrought, and occasionally downright offensive. I will also be using the work of Amin's son, Jaffar, on his father's early life and their family history.[1] This, despite its oddities, has to be seen as a key source, probably the most significant one on Amin's childhood and background. I will use all this material, together with the few relevant archival sources, to look at the varying accounts of Amin's birth, parentage, ethno-historical background and childhood.

THE BIRTH OF A LEGEND

While a conventional biography would probably begin with its subject's date and place of birth, Amin, as I have suggested, is unsuited to conventional biography, and even his birthplace and birth year are matters of dispute (which has been important to those wanting to portray him as not really Ugandan). For many British and Baganda commentators, the world is – or ought to be – divided into discrete, ethnically homogeneous nations, each having a language and culture that differentiates it from its neighbours.

From this point of view, the trans-border cosmopolitanism of the West Nile tribes, especially the Kakwa, and still more the Nubi, is not just unusual, or a product of colonial border creation, but a departure from the natural order of things, almost an abomination. In fact, such cross-border ethnicities are very common in postcolonial Africa, with similar consequences. As the Nigerian historian Ade Adefuye put it:

> [T]he British attempt to partition the Kakwa between Uganda and the Sudan did not affect the peoples' feelings of brotherhood towards one another. The Kakwa of the Sudan and Uganda showed clearly the artificial nature of the colonial boundaries inherited by the independent African countries.... [T]he Kakwa still regarded themselves as one and worked together.... [I]n spite of their location in Uganda and Sudan, the Kakwa retained their ethnic identity in utter disregard for the boundary imposed by the colonial authorities.[2]

Amin himself seems to have given varying accounts of where and when he was born, and told his first biographer, Judith Listowel, that he did not know the date:

> General Idi Amin Dada knows that he was born in a small village near Koboko in the West Nile Province of Uganda, bordering on the Sudan and the Congo. But he does not know when.... Idi Amin says that he is forty-six years old, which would mean that he was born in 1926, but the family's observant neighbours, who like many Africans have remarkably retentive memories, think that he may have been born in 1925.
>
> There is no doubt about Amin's ancestry; he is a Kakwa, although his mother came from a related Nilotic tribe called the Lugbara ...[3]

Listowel goes on to point out that several of the first generation of African nationalist leaders were equally unsure of their birth details; colonialism in early twentieth-century Africa had not developed the state to the point where the mass of people had their births registered by it.

Many writers of popular works on Amin, however, are more certain on these questions than he was himself. Their accounts are also often vividly coloured by what, to the contemporary eye, looks very like racist fantasy.

One relatively sober, though not unbiased, book, by the British journalist David Martin, provided some (unsourced) details of Amin's background:

> Amin was born in Koboko county, the smallest in Uganda's West Nile District, which is the rough boundary of the 50,000-strong Kakwa tribe. His father was a Kakwa, who had spent much of his life in the southern Sudan and his mother was from the neighbouring and ethnically related Lugbara tribe. His parents separated at his birth with his father continuing to scratch a subsistence living on his small holding [*sic*] near Arua.
>
> Both his parents' West Nile tribes are frequently described as Sudanic-Nubian, and like his parents Amin became a Muslim . . .[4]

The Nubi or Nubian population of the country, as we have seen, is often regarded by southern Ugandans as inherently 'Sudanese' rather than truly Ugandan. Despite Amin's Kakwa and Lugbara parentage, which is broadly accepted by most commentators, many believe he must have been born outside Uganda. This view was often picked up and repeated by Western commentators. 'David Gwyn', the pseudonym of a British former technical advisor in Uganda, wrote that, 'Amin's roots are not in Uganda. He has gathered round himself other rootless horrors [presumably a reference to his Nubi supporters].'[5] 'Gwyn' goes on to say that:

> Amin is now about 48 years old [i.e. he was born in 1928]. He is a Nubian Kakwa, of the Sudanic tribal group. He was born in Buganda (and has once claimed Buganda parentage), although Buganda is not his tribal area. He is a Muslim in a predominantly Christian country. He is, in sum, about as atypical of the people of Uganda, a tribally structured country, as he can possibly be.[6]

George Ivan Smith, a UN diplomat much involved with Uganda during Amin's rule, outlines the liminal nature of the area Amin came from. He writes that 'the Kakwa tribe ... congregates in the north west corner of Uganda where the southern Sudan and Zaire [today the Democratic Republic of Congo] blur their borders together. ... In that area borders are clearly defined only on a map. ... [T]here is no way of proving whether he was born in a hut in Zaire, in Uganda or in the southern Sudan.'[7] Later, however, like most of the other writers on Amin, he settles on the Ugandan district of Koboko as the site of the birth:

> To the Lugbara mother and the Kakwa father a son was born, Idi Amin. The precise date of birth is not known. It was some time between 1925 and 1928 in the Koboko district, so close to both the Sudanese border and that of Zaire as to make it very doubtful whether one could call him a Ugandan.
>
> What does matter is that his father was a Kakwa. They spoke a Sudanic language and were Nilotic tribes and whereas about six thousand of them lived in Uganda, a much larger number lived in the Sudan and Zaire. Amin came from a corner of three countries and from two tribes – his mother's Lugbara also Sudanic, also spreading across the borders of three countries.[8]

Another diplomat, US Ambassador Thomas Melady, speculated that 'Amin started out as a young boy with a tenuous family relationship. He probably did not know who his real father was, and if he did, it is not likely that he saw him very often. ... He is believed to have been born in 1925, but no birth records exist.'[9] Mary Hale, an American nurse working in Uganda in the 1970s, declares, with unjustified confidence, 'Idi Amin Dada was born on January 1 1924 at Arua, in Uganda's remote West Nile District belonging to the small dominantly Muslim Kakwa tribe. ... Amin was half Kakwa and half Nubian with Sudanese blood.'[10] Semakula Kiwanuka, a Muganda from the south of the country,[11] wrote that 'Koboko in Kakwa land may stick as his birth place not because he himself was sure that he had been born there but because the idea had been drummed into his head.'[12] Another southern Ugandan, Wycliffe Kato, wrote that 'According to one particular story, Amin himself was a Nubian but had to claim to be Kakwa so that he could pose as a Ugandan.'[13] The anthropologist Barbara Harrell-Bond's account of the West Nile refugee movement which followed Amin's overthrow (see Chapter 8) describes Amin as 'a Kakwa speaker (said to have been born in Zaire)'.[14] The largely pro-Amin southern Ugandan businessman Christopher Sembuya will have none of such stories. 'In an apparently futile bid to cleanse the country of a perceived evil', he wrote in 2009:

> some Ugandan politicians have continued to hunt for evidence showing that Idi Amin was not a fellow Ugandan. Attempts have been made to

make him a Sudanese or Congolese, especially since he hails from the border district of Koboko. His distinctly Arab-Swahili names and the absence of a name that sounds African has made it easy to sell this popular lie especially to an unsuspecting public.

There are many uncertainties over the dates and places of Amin's birth. Most biographical sources hold that he was born in either Koboko or Kampala around 1927.[15]

Aidan Southall, a British social anthropologist who had done extensive fieldwork in West Nile, and knew Amin, wrote that:

Anyone in the Uganda army with such a name is inevitably assumed to be a Nubi. Among the more closely informed, Amin is indisputably regarded as a Kakwa. He treats the Kakwa country in the far northwest corner of Uganda as his home, though some argue that he is Sudanese and others that he is Congolese, for the Kakwa have the melancholy distinction of being chopped into three by colonial boundaries.

I suggest that Kakwa is a strategic identity for Amin since it carries at least the possibility of being a native Ugandan, whereas the Nubi are still looked upon as of Sudanese extraction.[16]

Perhaps the most detailed and highly imaginative account of Amin's background and childhood was supposedly written by two pseudonymous Kenyan journalists, calling themselves 'Joseph Kamau' and 'Andrew Cameron', in a book published while he was still in power. In fact, the real author was a white Rhodesian journalist named Angus Shaw, who had reported from Amin's Uganda. Much of his book is fictional, but it is well worth quoting, both for its luxuriantly overwritten literary style and its lurid assemblage of the fantastic African stereotypes which have always clustered around Amin's popular image:

January 1 1928. It was the twilight hour, the brief span between the end of another African day and an African night. Inside, the hut was already dark, fetid with the smell of a woman's labour. She lay on the wicker bed moaning and sweating. The village midwife grunted as she wiped the woman's brow. It was going to be a difficult birth. The baby was bigger than normal. Aiyee, moaned the woman, as another pain convulsed her. . . .

A great agony racked her body. The midwife struggled, stumbling in the dark as night came down swiftly.

The labour continued far into the night while the midwife cursed and comforted, and the father snored away his fatigue in another hut. In the morning, the long hours of pain were ended. The new baby was at least 12 pounds in weight, if not more, and the women who crowded into the hut were overcome with awe.

Outside the men of the village laid down their tools and, dressed only in genital cloths, tall of carriage, proud and erect, settled down to celebrate the birth.... Inside the mother nursed her son and dozed, exhausted. She was sick of the pain and the struggle for existence ...[17]

Someone who, unlike Shaw, knew Amin well, was his former commanding officer (CO) in the King's African Rifles (KAR), Iain Grahame, who wrote rather more circumspectly:

A maze of conflicting accounts shrouds the origins of Idi Amin. It has been suggested by some that his mother practised witchcraft; by others that she was a tropical version of Eskimo Nell, parading her wares from one soldier's bed to another in the Nubian encampment at Bombo, a few miles to the West of Kampala, where the young Idi Amin's father was a policeman. While the latter may or may not be correct, Idi himself told me on a number of occasions that she was indeed a witch-doctor. More significant, however, is that she was a Christian from the Lugbara tribe, while his father was a Moslem and a Kakwa. Like many West Nilotes, Idi Amin therefore had complex ethnic and religious affiliations for, as a Kunubi-speaking Moslem whose ancestors had come from the Sudan, he was also allowed to consider himself a Nubian.[18]

Academic accounts, and official British government records,[19] have tended to put the birth date as 1925. The Canadian historian Jan Jelmert Jorgensen, in his *Uganda: A Modern History*, writes (citing the Ugandan academic Omari Kokole) that:

Idi Amin Dada was born around 1925. His mother was of mixed Kakwa-Lugbara descent. His Kakwa father had been christened into the Catholic faith as Andrea Dada, but was converted to Islam by Ali Kenya Midia, who was the Kakwa chief in Koboko, West Nile, between 1910 and 1920. On conversion to Islam, Idi Amin's father took the name Amin Dada. In the 1920s Amin Dada rose to the rank of sergeant in the Uganda Police and served at Katwe. His superiors nicknamed him Simon. Idi Amin Dada was himself nicknamed Andrea by soldiers familiar with his family's background . . .[20]

More recently, some scholars[21] have come to accept, perhaps for want of any contrary evidence, much of the account given by Amin's children. Family stories may, of course, be just as inaccurate as any others (more so, a Freudian might say), and several elements of this particular one are clearly mythical, but, lacking other reliable sources, it seems a reasonable starting place for an account of his birth. According to the version by Amin's son, Jaffar, Idi Amin Dada was born on the Muslim feast day of Eid Ul Adha in 1928.[22] 'Idi' is an East African form of the Arabic 'Eid', which denotes the two most important annual Islamic religious festivals, Eid Ul Fitr (at the end of Ramadan) and Eid Ul Adha. In Western terms, this means that Amin's birth occurred on Wednesday 30 May 1928 (at 4 p.m., according to Jaffar Amin). His birthplace was in central Kampala, Uganda's capital, inside the Shimoni Police Barracks on Nakasero Hill, where his father was a police officer. Today this is an upmarket area of the city and it has long been associated with the Buganda royal family. Idi Amin's father, Amin Dada Nyabira Tomuresu, had originally been christened as a Roman Catholic and given the name Andrea. Like many Ugandans who joined the British colonial military forces, however, he converted to Islam when he became a boy soldier, eighteen years before Idi was born, and he then took the names Amin Dada, the former being a version of a widespread Arabic name signifying 'Faithful'.[23]

The meaning of 'Dada' is, like so much else about Amin, disputed. In his army days, it was widely believed that the name came from the KiSwahili word for 'sister', and was a kind of nickname, affectionate or otherwise. According to Amin's first biographer, Judith Listowel, the name came from an incident in which Amin was discovered by a British officer with two women in his barrack quarters. Asked to explain, he is said to have replied, pointing, 'This one is my wife.' 'And who is the other one?', the officer enquired. 'She is my elder sister, my Dada,' was the quick reply. Listowel tells us that: 'The story went round the barracks, and it is since then that the General is called Idi Amin Dada. Amin likes to tell this story to friends and even to distinguished visitors, and laughs at his own quick-wittedness.'[24] Amin's former commanding officer, Iain Grahame, tells a similar story. The former UN diplomat, George Ivan Smith, tells a different tale:

> There are three or four versions of why he became known as Idi Amin Dada. One of them is his alleged cowardice ... [when he ran away after an attempted assassination of Milton Obote in the late 1960s]. He acted like a woman and escaped. Although 'Dada' is used to mean sister, and 'sissy', Amin's father had the given name of Dada. ... It was in 1968 that Idi added the Dada to his name, but it did not become generally recognised and used until after the cowardly escape Amin made after the attempted assassination of Obote – it was used in the context of a 'sissy' who fled from duty.[25]

However, by most accounts, Amin's use of the name pre-dates this, and Amin's son, Jaffar, gives a more straightforward explanation: that Dada is the name of a Lugbara clan, widely but not universally used as a personal name by its members, which included Idi Amin. This seems far more likely than that Amin himself happily adopted a name with derogatory implications.

According to Jaffar, his father's family background was troubled:

> Grandpa's father, Nyabira Tomuresu rejected his wife Atata, forcing her to abandon the family home and return to her childhood homes. ... As Grandpa's mother Atata left her husband's homestead, following the rejection, she was so angry that she dumped the cradle protecting the young Grandpa in a tree trunk. Her actions prompted Grandpa's thirteen year old brother to stand guard over the toddler the same way Moshe's [Moses'] sister did when the Israelites were being oppressed in Egypt and Moshe's mother placed him in an Ark and hid him in the reeds by the bank of the Nile River. ... [U]ntil their maternal uncles the Godiya-Gombe (Kelipi) [a Kakwa clan to which Amin's grandmother belonged] came to their rescue.[26]

Jaffar was told by his father that:

> [B]efore Dad was born, my Grandpa was a practising Roman Catholic with the first name Andrea up to and including the first decade of the 20th century. ... In 1910 however, Grandpa converted to Islam and changed his first name from Andrea to Amin.... At the time of Grandpa's conversion ... he had been conscripted as a bugler in Sultan Ali Kenyi's army.[27] He served as a bugler in the Sultan's army from 1910, the year he converted to Islam, until 1913 when he joined the Colonial Police Force and served as a policeman at Nsambia Police Barracks in Kampala, Uganda from 1913 to 1914.
>
> In 1914, Grandpa and others were forcibly conscripted into the King's African Rifles – a multi-battalion British Colonial Regiment raised from the various British 'possessions' in East Africa from 1902 until 'Independence' in the 1960s.
>
> After being forcibly conscripted into the King's African Rifles, Grandpa served as a soldier between 1915 and 1921 and fought in the First World War ... alongside colonial soldiers in Tanganyika which became part of present-day Tanzania.[28] Upon being honourably discharged from the King's African Rifles in 1921, Grandpa and other veterans were allotted plots [of land] in a village in Arua, Uganda, christened Tanganyika Village, after the veterans' successful Tour of Duty in Tanganyika.
>
> The same year, 1921, Grandpa rejoined the Colonial Police Force at Nsambia Police Barracks in Kampala but he maintained the plot he had been allotted at Tanganyika Village, in honour of his contribution to the First World War as a loyal soldier of the colonial powers.
>
> When Dad was born in 1928, Grandpa had been transferred to the Shimoni-Nakasero Police Barracks where Dad was born.[29]

Idi Amin was the third child of Amin senior and Aisha Aate:

> Grandpa's first son, Dad's older brother Ramadhan Dudu Moro Amin was born to Grandpa and Grandma Aisha Aate in 1919. Then a daughter was born in 1925 but she passed away as a toddler and then Dad was born in 1928 at Shimoni Police Barracks in Kampala where Grandpa was stationed as a Police Officer. By the time Grandpa retired from the Police

Force in 1931 and accepted the job at the District Commissioner's office in Arua Township, he and Grandma had shifted to Kololo Police Barracks in Kampala.[30]

A FAMILY ROMANCE

Idi Amin's mother, Aisha (or Asha) Chumaru Aate (or Atate), was, as Jorgensen suggested, from a tribally mixed family, part Kakwa like her husband, but also partly Lugbara, the largest ethnic group in the West Nile region. Almost all accounts say that she was a traditional healer and a midwife. Jaffar was told by his aunts that his father's birth was accompanied by a violent hailstorm, considered a propitious omen among Kakwa people, and Aisha is said to have delivered her own son as the hailstones fell. According to Jaffar, his grandmother told his own mother that 'as she performed a self-delivery and gave birth to Dad with no one else in attendance, her newborn son landed on a pile of hailstones. This set off a resounding scream that reverberated around the Shimoni Hill Police Barracks.'[31] Aisha was the second wife of Amin's father, and Amin himself was her second son. According to the family story, as a traditional healer, Aisha had been consulted by the Queen of the Baganda people, Irene Druscilla Namaganda, and had cured her of infertility. This connection with the Baganda royal family led to a widespread belief that the child's real father was the Kabaka (king) of the Baganda, at the time a British puppet ruler named Daudi Chwa. As Jaffar Amin puts it: 'Grandpa had continued to listen to vicious rumours spread by gossiping Ganda (Baganda) and Nubi (Nubians) alleging that King Daudi Chwa of the Great Kingdom of Buganda fathered the baby Grandma was carrying and not him.'[32] Sigmund Freud wrote about a widespread fantasy he called the 'family romance', in which a person believes they were born from nobler, more important people than their actual parents. This is at the root of the 'foundling myths' seen in fairy tales and mythological stories from many cultures around the world. In these legends, a baby is abandoned by its powerful and eminent parents (often to save it from enemies, or for supernatural reasons), and taken in by ordinary folk, to claim its rightful inheritance in later life.[33] Amin's family romance, however, was not his own account of his true paternity (though, like many of the stories about him, he was very happy to use it when the situation warranted), but a common rumour that is still widely believed in Uganda, especially in West Nile and Kampala; it was mentioned to me by several people in the 1990s that Amin's real father had been the Kabaka.

According to Jaffar Amin, many rumours about the baby's 'true' paternity were spread by his father's childless senior wife, Miriam Poya, who was jealous of Aisha for having borne two sons. The child was named 'Awon'go', meaning 'noise' or 'din' in the Kakwa language, alluding to the noisy gossip about his royal paternity, as well as to the new born's screaming on the hailstones. Jaffar comments:

> [I]n accordance with Kakwa naming tradition she meant for Dad's name Awon'go to have a deeper meaning than a screaming infant. True to his name Awon'go, Dad continued to cry excessively as a baby but he and Grandma shared a very close relationship and they had a very strong bond. ... Dad ... also grew up to be and live what was implied in his Kakwa name. He lived the meaning of the name ... to the fullest extent in relation to the 'noise' arising from being 'talked about' during and after his rule in Uganda. The 'noise' and 'din' arising from backbiting and false rumours followed Dad throughout his life ...[34]

The family story goes that, because of the rumours about the Kabaka, Amin senior was persuaded by tribal elders that the baby should undergo a 'paternity test', which involved being left alone in a forest on the slopes of Mount Liru in Koboko county, the home of the Kakwa people. After leaving the infant in the wild for four days, the elders returned to find Awon'go still alive. Aisha, in Jaffar's account, often told her son that during his ordeal in the wild, 'Nakan, the legendary seven-headed serpent ("sacred" snake) had saved [him].' 'Grandma', Jaffar writes, 'insisted that Nakan had come to Dad and wrapped itself around Dad for warmth, as it would do around its own eggs. "Nakan placed its head on the crown of baby Awon'go's head for the duration of the ordeal", Grandma always emphasized.'[35] This account was corroborated to Jaffar by his cousin, Major Dudu Alias Adume:

> He said that the Temezi (Elders) from their Adibu Likamero clan actually encountered Nakan, the legendary seven-headed Serpent ('sacred' snake)

still wrapped around the infant Dad when they came to check on the results of the 'paternity test'. On seeing the sacred snake, the elders felt all was lost only for the 'great' python to unwind its great length and gracefully slither away into the jungle.... According to Dudu Alias Adume the Elders were so astonished at this mystical event that they all nodded to each other, uttering 'Behold the Mata (Chief)' as they approached the baby, who kept marking time with his feet in mid air like someone riding an inverted tricycle.[36]

Idi Amin's uncle Siri'ba told Jaffar that Aisha was furious at the elders' suspicions about the baby's parentage:

Like an Avenging Angel, your Abuba (Grandma) ... strode with fury in front of her husband and the ... Kakwa Elders.... At the next assembly, she placed an ancient King's African Rifles (KAR) rifle on the ground and pronounced a solemn curse on her husband.... She proclaimed 'If this child is not yours ... let him languish in poverty and misery. But if he is of your blood, then let him prosper and succeed in this world to the highest position of the land and may you, his father, not see any of his wealth and prosperity.

According to Dad's uncle Siri'ba, Grandma then stepped over the KAR rifle to invoke this powerful curse. The assembly was awestruck by Grandma's curse since just the fact that the infant survived the jungle was good enough for justice to the mother and child.

This occasion made it impossible for my grandparents to live together again as husband and wife.... [T]heir marriage had disintegrated beyond repair.[37]

According to Jaffar Amin, the couple lived together in Shimoni Police Barracks for a few years after Awon'go's birth but when the boy was 4, they separated and divorced. The father returned to the West Nile District, settling in his Tanganyika Village home in Arua town. Most accounts suggest that Amin went with his mother.[38] In Jaffar Amin's version, however, the boy initially went with his father, as is Muslim custom, while his mother stayed in Buganda with relatives and continued her association with the royal family.

'STEEPED IN WITCHCRAFT': AISHA AATE AND THE WATERS OF YAKAN

Many of the popular books on Amin suggest that Aisha was not just a healer and midwife, but also a prostitute and a witch. According to 'Kamau and Cameron''s overwrought account, when she left the boy's father,

> [S]he packed her scanty belongings and hoisting the boy on her back in a sling began the long walk to the main dirt road to wait for the occasional bus. ... There would be business, she was sure, for her ripe, overflowing body and for the ancient alchemies she had learnt from her mother's lips even when she was at the breast. Soon the customers were seeking her out for love charms and potions, for malignant curses on a hated enemy and some for more physical comforts.[39]

Smith writes that 'Amin's mother ran away from his father while Idi was still a baby. ... As a witch and "available", she then moved to the outskirts of the barracks of the King's African Rifles at a place called Buikwe.'[40] Martin takes a similar view, telling his readers that, 'Amin's mother, with her newly born son, after separating from her husband moved to one of the Nubian colonies in Uganda at Lugazi ... [She] was what used to be called a camp follower. ... [and] had practised witchcraft since moving to the area – and possibly before.'[41]

'Witchcraft' was, of course, used by European writers as a general disparaging term for a variety of traditional African religious, medical and agricultural practices. For the Kakwa and Lugbara people of West Nile, as for others in Africa, religious beliefs may have been at the heart of their resistance to the imposition of colonial rule. Ten years before Amin's birth a social movement, which became known to the British as the 'Yakan' (or 'Allah Water', or 'Lion's Water') uprising, had emerged among the Lugbara and Kakwa people of West Nile, and this was regarded by the local colonial authorities as a potentially dangerous organised insurrection against imperial control.[42] By 1928, Amin's mother seems to have been very much part of this religious movement, and it is frequently mentioned by the popular writers, though in somewhat contradictory ways. Judith Listowel mentions 'a Kakwa ... cult called "the water of Yakan" ... which Amin may have learned to make when he attended meetings in his early youth [and which] is mixed with a drug called kamiojo ... a powerful drug which causes excitement and elation; taken in large quantities, it leads to frenzy'.[43]

Repeating Listowel's adjectives, 'Kamau and Cameron' say the potion was drunk by the Kakwa men to celebrate Amin's birth: 'Elation followed swiftly as they drank the water of Yakan, a raw native liquor for elders only, mixed with a drug extracted from a local plant. Soon elation became frenzy'.[44] George Ivan Smith believed that Yakan water was 'the LSD of Central Africa in the latter part of the last century'[45] and worked as an aphrodisiac as well as an intoxicant and a war potion: 'Amin's mother was a Lugbara. She was known to be steeped in witchcraft, consulted by soldiers for that, and for other services. She would have known how to prepare the "lion's water" of the Lugbara which made men strong for war or love.'[46] He describes Amin himself as a 'boy wrung from the withers of the tribes around the Western Nile, drawn in from the twilight of the witchcraft and the superstition surrounding them, a boy of "the waters of Yakan"'.[47] In Smith's account, the Yakan water even had an unexplained effect on Amin's later taste in torture techniques:

> The water symbol touched his life at many points. Its tribal mystical influences in its younger days were later followed by more terrible associations and manifestations, such as the 'water treatment' meted out under his rule when the victim's head was held under water until he drowned.[48]

For many of the popular writers on Amin, the Yakan movement and its 'Allah Water' were a key to Amin's life and background. George Ivan Smith told his readers that:

> One herb of the field in the Kakwa country is called kamiojo, a plant of the daffodil species. It is the source of a drug which puts the magic into the waters of Yakan, Allah Water. The drug produces illusions and visions. It causes excitement, elation, a sense of frenzy, when taken to excess. ...
> In the last century tribesmen of the Sudan, Congo, Kenya and Uganda drew from the water the false courage to attack armed garrisons. The cult spread. ...
> Once I saw tribesmen in the Congo lying stiffly on the earth. Their fellows said they could not be dead. They had been protected by 'The

Water'. Nor were they sleeping. They had their ears to the ground. They were listening to the talk of the enemy. At night they would return with their secrets.

The manifestations of this water cult at different times and places have in common the belief that man can be protected by the power of the magic water: not only against bullets from guns, but from thunderbolts seemingly sent by Divinities.[49]

The word 'frenzy' is used to describe the effects of Yakan waters, first by Listowel, then 'Kamau and Cameron', and now by Smith. It is also used by 'Trevor Donald', in a strange book purporting to be a collection of writings by Amin himself 'in his own words', including supposed diary entries (it is hard to think of anyone less likely to keep a diary than Idi Amin). The book is an almost parodically overheated example of the journalistic literature on Amin. It shows very clearly how the 'Water of Yakan' comes to symbolise the violent, irrational 'primitive savagery', which is attributed to Amin, and also to the Kakwa and the Nubi in general. 'Donald' writes, with apparently intimate knowledge:

It was while he was still with the [Kakwa] tribe that Idi became a drug-taker. He was introduced to it when he joined the tribal cult called the Water of Yakan. . . . He learnt then how to mix the secret ingredients of a potent mixture that, when drunk, caused excitement and elation. Taken in large quantities, it leads to frenzy. This mixture is – perhaps appropriately – called Lion's Medicine . . .

Idi constantly has the mixture at his hand. He sips from it and takes it in deep draughts according to his moods. . . . . Aides say he eventually loses all sense of control and normality, that he becomes like a man whose body and mind are possessed by the Devil.

He has, for instance, under the influence of the drug, ordered his aircraft on full alert to fly him to London for an immediate audience with the Queen. . . . He once stripped himself naked in the middle of a dance with his troops and their wives and girlfriends and turned on the wildest African tribal dance that Kampala has yet seen. . . .

The drug provides a great deal of the bravado that Idi musters to make speeches. . . . It is said that Idi drinks deeply from his flask of

Lion's Medicine before going onto a rostrum. He usually has a hollow head, a mind devoid of any idea about what he will speak. As he begins, thoughts flood into his brain and pour from his mouth, and he turns them into policies. Later, rather than lose face, he orders his Government and his Ministers to carry out the proposals he has espoused under the influence of the drug.

Idi is the first to explain that the Lion's Medicine is responsible for his ability to see so clearly into the future. For instance he says he knows exactly when, where and how he will die.[50]

The Amin family account of the meaning of Yakan is, of course, rather different. Jaffar Amin writes that '[t]he "Yakanye Order" was a secret African society that reportedly used sacred water and other mystical powers to instigate and win insurrections and wars. . . . Grandma was a part of this secret society and served as its priestess.'[51] He suggests that this was what originally led Daudi Chwa, the Kabaka of Buganda, to become interested in Aisha:

During his rule, the Ganda Priesthood would often wonder how the Nubi . . . and Lugbara managed to gain power militarily through the 'Yakanye Order' and how their King could acquire those powers. Moreover the King would have gained the information about the 'Yakanye Order' that Grandma belonged to from his subjects as the information continued to flourish at King George Garrison Jinja which Grandma frequented and 'all roads seemed to lead to Grandma Aisha Aate's shrine'. In Buganda while Grandma was the High Priestess of the 'Yakanye Order' amongst the King's African Rifles Nubians, word of her prowess got through to the embattled and politically impotent Kabaka.[52]

THE BIRTH OF COLONIAL POWER: A TALE OF TWO ANNEXATIONS

Amin's connection with the Yakan movement demonstrates how close in time his birth was to the very beginning of British rule over Uganda. His parents would have spent most of their lives in a pre-colonial West Nile, which was only annexed to the Uganda Protectorate in 1914. Although, prior to that, the district was technically part of the (Anglo-Egyptian-ruled) Sudan Condominium, in practice colonial rule from Cairo never fully extended that far south. Due to the First World War, effective British rule over West Nile, as part of Uganda, only began in 1918, less than a decade before Idi Amin's birth, and the Yakan movement played an important part in the establishment of imperial government in the district. Yakan has gone down in African history as an anti-colonial resistance movement alongside many others at the time, but its real origins and purposes are unknown. It first appeared in written documents as associated with a group of rebels against British authority in 1919, shortly after colonial administration began in the district.[53]

British rule over southern Uganda had begun considerably earlier. The missionaries arrived first, with a Church Missionary Society (Anglican) mission to Buganda in 1877. They reported conflict within the Baganda royal court and widespread use of slavery, which were useful pretexts for British intervention. In 1887, the British government granted a royal charter to the Imperial British East Africa Company (IBEAC), in order, as Jorgensen puts it, 'to open East Africa to legitimate commerce to replace the allegedly widespread slave trade'.[54] Not entirely coincidentally, the vice president and treasurer of the Church Missionary Society was also a director of the IBEAC.[55] As a private colonial endeavour, the IBEAC collapsed, and the government formally took over its role in 1894. Shortly afterwards, British military forces consisting mainly of Nubi soldiers enabled Buganda to defeat and annex part of the neighbouring kingdom of Bunyoro. The missionaries had done their job well, and rivalries between Catholic and Protestant groups split the courts of the southern Ugandan kingdoms, much to the advantage of the British 'divide and rule' strategy. Uganda was declared a British 'Protectorate' in 1900. Using indentured Indian labour, the government built a railway from the British port at Mombasa on the Kenyan coast, to Buganda. Begun in 1891, this was completed in 1902, at a (then massive) cost to the British government of £5.3 million. It dramatically cut the price and time involved in moving goods (agricultural commodities and, especially, ivory) from Uganda to the coast. Uganda was henceforth integrated into the growing world capitalist economy. It was also the building of the railway that first brought substantial numbers of South Asian people into the country.[56]

A key aspect of Ugandan colonial history, which has had powerful repercussions down to today's Uganda, is the 'special relationship' between the British and the Baganda. When the first British explorers arrived in the region in the mid-nineteenth century, they were astonished to find not only a political system they could recognise as a monarchy but also a society where, unlike all the surrounding people, the aristocratic elite actually wore clothes, made from tree bark which was soaked and hammered into thin cloth. This was a powerful marker, indicating to the Victorian mind that these people must be, uniquely, more 'civilised' and 'advanced' than other Africans. The attitude, and its racist ethnic basis, is perfectly summed up by Winston Churchill's account, in his 1908 book *My African Journey*:

> The Kingdom of [B]uganda is a fairy tale. You climb up a railway line instead of a beanstalk, and at the end there is a wonderful new world. The scenery is different, the vegetation is different, the climate is different and most of all the people are different from anything elsewhere to be seen in the whole range of Africa.
>
> In the place of naked, painted savages, clashing their spears and gibbering in chorus to their tribal chiefs, a complete and elaborate polity is presented. Under a dynastic King ... an amiable, clothed, polite and intelligent race dwell together in an organised monarchy.[57]

If the aristocracy of Buganda represented, to the colonial mind, something like the most 'advanced' condition Africans could possibly attain without Western assistance,[58] the people of West Nile, especially the Kakwa, were seen as pretty much the opposite. Amin's first biographer, Judith Listowel, herself an aristocrat, contrasted the two societies:

> The Kakwa have a great respect for personalities, but not for rank or position. They never had chiefs or recognised clan leaders. . . . Amin was brought up to believe that all Kakwa tribesmen are equal. . . . A chiefless African society can have disadvantages. Among the Baganda . . . a chief's headquarters was in every sense the centre of tribal life. . . . Parents sent their children to the chief's enclosure to be his men- and maid-servants as only in that way could they obtain advancement. . . . Amin could have had no such training because the Kakwa had no chiefs. Some of his recent measures [in the early months of his presidency] illustrate all too well that he had to leap into the complicated politics of the modern world without any intermediate feudal preparation.[59]

41

Southern Ugandans, perhaps unsurprisingly, tended to agree with this estimation of Kakwa primitiveness. Wycliffe Kato, who was Uganda's Director of Civil Aviation under Amin, before he was arrested in 1977, wrote that 'Amin's tribesmen, the Kakwas [were] a very small tribe.... Unfortunately for him, the Kakwas were not only one of the most insignificant [tribes] numerically, but were also hopelessly backward.'[60] Many of the British concurred. In an official letter to the head of the Foreign Office East Africa desk (EAD)[61] in 1977, A.C. Stuart, at the time based at the British Embassy in Jakarta, but formerly stationed in Uganda, wrote:

I am, as it happens, one of those who used to know Amin reasonably well. ... I think it would be a mistake to forget that he is a real primitive, with virtually no education or cultural background. As such he still seems to act, just, within the limits of what one would expect of a primitive bushman who, for the first time in recent history, has been suddenly thrust into the control of a reasonably modern State, whose complexities he does not at all understand, and into the possession of virtually unlimited power.

The Kakwa are among the most primitive tribes in Uganda. Their key position in the army is an historical accident. ... They are infinitely behind the southern Bantu tribes, particularly the Baganda, and behave accordingly. Amin obviously has, to an exaggerated degree, the primitive's shrewdness, humour, cruelty, cunning and childishness. And he has always been like this ...[62]

In 1914, six years after Churchill's trip up the beanstalk to visit the Buganda fairyland, the West Nile district was added to the Uganda Protectorate. The only part of the country situated west of the river Nile, the area had previously been part of the Belgian Congo, then of the Sudan Condominium,[63] but neither of these had established any real control on the ground, or even made much contact with the local people. The British sent a young colonial officer named Alfred Evelyn Weatherhead to take over the region as district commissioner (DC). It was believed, because of the history of the Nubi, that the West Nilers were particularly suited to fighting and warfare, and Weatherhead's main job during the First World War was to recruit soldiers. This met with very limited success at first, and by 1916 only 14 had been signed up, but the figure had risen to 300 men by the end of the war.[64] These men were collected and handed over by local elders, identified by the British as 'chiefs' and well rewarded for their efforts, but as long as this was the only obvious result of colonial rule it did not at first seem to provoke much local opposition.

Then, in 1917, the government tried to introduce taxation into the district. This represented the first widespread use of money in West Nile, forcing many young men to go south, to work for wages in the Lugazi sugar plantations in Buganda or to join the colonial military forces (using this term in the widest sense, including for example the police and prison guards). The only alternative to paying tax was forced labour for no wages at all (it is difficult to see how this differs significantly from slavery, but to the British authorities it certainly did). Limited at first, in 1918 the tax was extended to the whole district. The imposition of taxation and forced labour was still remembered and resented in the 1960s and 1970s,[65] and was even mentioned by elderly people I spoke to during my doctoral fieldwork in 1996–98. At around the same time as this introduction of taxation, military service and forced labour, the district was also hit by simultaneous outbreaks of smallpox, meningitis and blackwater fever between 1914 and 1918,[66] and by a serious local outbreak of the global flu pandemic of 1918. In March 1918 Weatherhead tried to set up an 'isolation camp' for smallpox victims, and by May of that year a famine had broken out[67] and sacks of grain had to be shipped from southern Uganda.[68] The same year saw British administration strengthened by a military detachment (of the KAR) large enough to be headed by three British officers, and by the addition of two new assistants for Weatherhead, Assistant District Commissioner J.H. Driberg and R.E. McConnell, both keen amateur anthropologists who later published the first academic articles on the local people.[69]

'A PARTICULARLY INTOXICATING DRINK': THE YAKAN MOVEMENT AND WEST NILE RESISTANCE TO COLONIAL RULE

This was the background against which the Yakan movement, to which Aisha Aate belonged, and which was known to the Europeans at the time as 'Yakani' or the 'Allah Water Cult', emerged into colonial knowledge, as a form of organised resistance to British rule. It seems to have existed as a healing movement since at least the 1890s, and local people, who associated the epidemics of 1914–18 with the arrival of the Europeans, responded by calling on Yakan as they had done before in response to widespread disease and infection.[70] The British, however, believed that, whenever the movement arose, 'On every occasion the medical aspect is shortly superseded by the revolutionary idea', as ADC 'Jack' Driberg later put it.[71] The idea that Yakan was, among other things, an anti-imperialist movement, is supported by Amin's son Jaffar, who said that, 'genuine independence . . . is what the secret "Yakanye Society" that Grandma belonged to wanted for African tribes and communities'.[72] Whatever the West Nilers thought was the purpose of the Yakan movement, the British apparently believed it was a coordinated conspiracy which represented a serious challenge to colonial rule. Weatherhead and Driberg saw the 'cult' as being behind widespread refusal of forced labour, and sent in troops with a machine gun to quell the rebellion. Fifteen local 'chiefs' (colonial appointees in the first place) were deported, to be followed the next year by another eight.[73] They were replaced by some of the Nubi British soldiers who had put down the 'rebellion', and others loyal to Weatherhead's administration. However, the case for deportation was disputed, and some of Driberg's and Weatherhead's superiors cast doubt on their evidence. Alan Hogg, the Attorney General of the Protectorate, asked for further evidence, and then concluded that:

> I have carefully read these supplementary affidavits and I regret that I cannot advise His Excellency to grant Deportation Orders. I do not think that they show that any of the persons named have caused disaffection or have actually intrigued against the Government. As far as I can gather from the affidavits, 'Allah Water' appears to be a particularly intoxicating drink but does not appear to be anti-governmental.[74]

In the event, Hogg was overruled and the deportations went ahead.

I have argued elsewhere[75] that Hogg was probably correct to conclude that no real uprising had occurred on this occasion. However, it is also clear that the Yakan movement was about a lot more than just the consumption of a potent local brew. Yakan certainly had associations with the healing of sickness, and its rites were probably also used in coping with the imposition of colonial rule. It is hardly surprising that sickness and conquest were considered by local people to be similar things and, in fact, in epidemiological terms it probably *was* the invading outsiders who brought the new diseases into the region in the early 1890s and 1910s. Contemporary accounts (from the trial) mention Yakan rituals which incorporated European symbols of power such as cashboxes, rectangular buildings (as opposed to the round local dwellings), flag-pole-like 'Yakan poles' and a 'parade ground' on which a version of military drill may have been enacted, using imitation wooden or grass 'rifles'.[76] This resonates strongly with Jaffar Amin's description of his grandmother stepping over the KAR rifle to curse her enemies after the child's paternity was disputed, ten years after the 'rebellion' in West Nile. Jaffar also writes that Nakan, the 'seven-headed serpent ("sacred" snake)', which wrapped itself around the infant Amin during his abandonment in the forest, was considered 'the source of the sacred water used by the powerful "Yakanye Order" that Grandma served as priestess for'.[77] Jaffar tells us that in later life, 'Dad ... regularly told us stories about his birth to the Adibu Likamero Kakwa clan and Grandma's account to him relating to Nakan (Yakan) the Legendary seven-headed serpent ... that saved him as an infant.'[78] According to Jaffar: 'The focus of the Yakanye order was to expel foreigners and it started [presumably around the 1880s] with a bitter experience against the Arab slavers ...'[79] Jaffar Amin's account of Yakan adds considerably to the material we have on the movement, and seems broadly to confirm King's interpretation of it, as both a medical and an anti-colonial force.[80]

In the decade between the events of the 'Yakan uprising' and Idi Amin's birth, the chasm between the West Nilers and the southern Ugandans, particularly the Baganda, widened. The former, along with other northern tribes, were regarded as excellent material for soldiers, and many of them, like Amin's father, converted to Islam in the KAR, thus becoming 'Nubis'. The southerners, meanwhile, were encouraged to produce cash crops, were educated by British missionaries and allowed to keep their kings and aristocrats (while real power, of course, was in the hands of the British). The northern soldiers helped keep the southerners in order. It is not clear to what extent the Baganda adopted the British idea that the northerners were more primitive and violent than they were, and how far the British simply accepted what the 'uniquely civilised' Baganda told them about their northern neighbours.

'A WARRIOR TRIBE': THE KAKWA AND THE NUBI

This, then, was the world into which Idi Amin was born, and the background he came from. He was not only considered inferior as an African in a land dominated by European colonial power, but doubly inferior, as a member of the 'primitive' Kakwa tribe in a country dominated (insofar as Africans had any power in the system) by the Baganda and other southern groups. It has been important to look at the history of his ancestral home area and his family's ethnic background, not least because of the role it plays in explanations for his later political motivations and his approach to government. During Amin's rule, both British and southern Ugandan writers (as well as other Westerners and other Africans) tended to explain him in terms of his tribal origins, as Kakwa, Lugbara or Nubi. These West Nile groups are almost universally portrayed as not only particularly 'primitive' but also intrinsically 'violent',[81] lacking – as Judith Listowel had noted – the aristocratic graces of the Baganda. Frequently, as we have seen, this characterisation includes the allegation that human sacrifice or cannibalism is characteristic of West Nile society. Amin's CO, Iain Grahame, calls the Kakwa 'a warrior tribe'[82] and says that they, and other West Nile tribes, regularly carried out 'sacrifices of animals and humans'.[83] Henry Kyemba, a Muganda, wrote that, 'Like many other warrior societies, the Kakwa, Amin's tribe, are known to have practiced blood rituals on slain enemies. . . . Such rituals still exist.'[84]

Even a renowned African nationalist intellectual such as the Kenyan writer Ali Mazrui, emphasised the primitive nature of the Kakwa in his largely positive analysis of Amin's rule, using it to explain the expulsion of Uganda's Asian population from the country:

Amin has brought other cultural imports into the political process in Uganda derived from his peasant origins. His entire style of diplomacy is striking for its lack of middle-class 'refinements'. . . .

Some of these tendencies are personal to Amin rather than to his social origins. But the very fact that he lets his personal tendencies have such free play while occupying the top office of his nation might have been influenced by the relative spontaneity of rural upbringing among the Kakwa . . . humanitarian arguments quite often are arguments steeped in middle-class assumptions and are therefore more likely to impress an African intellectual than an African peasant with memories of having been insulted over the years by Asian shopkeepers or Asian employers. The style of Amin's expulsion of the Asians was in this sense an aspect of his peasant origins.[85]

Mazrui uses the adjective 'primordial' to describe Amin's approach to politics, and explains this in terms of his origin (appealing to the work of unspecified anthropologists):

General Amin is in some respects deeply primordial in his attitudes and presuppositions. His demands on the Asians echoed some of the anthropological findings about traditional political societies in Africa. Amin has been primordial in his demand for cultural identification and biological intermingling; he has also been primordial in his tendency to regard complete aliens as basically potential enemies; and thirdly he has been primordial in his distrust of private choice in matters of public concern.[86]

Other African historians have taken a similar position on the importance of Amin's Kakwa background, with its 'primordial' superstitions, for his later policies and practices. Adefuye wrote that:

There is abundant evidence that Amin, even as late as 1972, exhibited characteristics similar to those of the typical Kakwa with their strong belief in the supernatural. Amin often claimed to be acting on the instructions of his witch doctors and from messages he received in dreams. . . . Although some of Amin's demonstrations of belief in witchcraft were interpreted as evidence of his eccentricity, what is often not realised is the fact of his complete commitment to Kakwa culture, including the efficacy of customary rituals and sacrifices. His village, Koboko, was close to the grove of Nguleso, the Kakwa supreme god, and he saw the protection of fellow-Kakwa, whether in Uganda or the Sudan as his primary responsibility. In addition, he felt it was his right to call on them for aid when he needed it.[87]

Western writers, on the other hand, have often focused on the Nubi, rather than the Kakwa, aspect of Amin's background to explain his apparent taste for violence and murder. David Martin says of the 'Nubians' that 'among their fellow countrymen they enjoyed an unenviable reputation of having one of the world's highest homicide rates. The Nubians were renowned for their sadistic brutality, lack of formal education, for poisoning enemies and for their refusal to integrate, even in the urban centres'.[88] Grahame, who commanded many Nubi soldiers in the KAR, wrote that 'the Nubians became the most feared and influential ethnic group in Uganda, mercilessly suppressing uprisings and tribal disputes at the behest of their British masters. It was the success of these early operations [such as the shutting down of the Yakan movement in West Nile] that gave them a contempt for all pagan and Christian tribes in the country'.[89] Smith refers to the Baganda stories of cannibalism, but seems unsure whether they refer to the Kakwa or the Nubi:

The southern Ugandans are particularly contemptuous of the southern Sudanese and Nubis (not of other northern tribes) as wild and uncivilised. It is from them that we have reports of Amin and his Nubis tasting the blood of their victims and eating their livers and the explanation that such a custom is either a Nubi or Kakwa rite.[90]

The pseudonymous 'David Gwyn' described Amin as 'a Nubian Kakwa, of the Sudanic tribal group'.[91] Many southern Ugandan writers are similarly unsure about whether to place Amin as a Kakwa or a Nubi or both, and portray the Nubi as being a Sudanese people, not really Ugandan at all. Kato writes about Amin's time in power that:

Amin's tribesmen [were] the Kakwas, a very small tribe in the north western corner of Uganda. ... Accordingly he enlisted Nubians from southern Sudan across the international borders. ... According to one particular story, Amin was himself a Nubian but had to claim to be a Kakwa so that he could pose as a Ugandan.[92]

I have outlined the history and development of the Nubi in the introduction. It is perhaps unsurprising, with their links to slavery and militarism, that many Ugandans would want to deny them a Ugandan identity. However, as we have seen, Nubi identity was adopted by many West Nilers, including Amin's family, and, in effect, the denial of the Nubis' 'Ugandanness' amounts to a refusal to accept that the West Nile itself is properly part of the country.

THE BOYHOOD OF IDI AMIN

Like the magical circumstances of his birth and infancy, Amin's childhood has produced a rich vein of imaginative speculation by the various commentators on his life. A widely recycled account by the pseudonymous 'Joseph Kamau and Andrew Cameron' told readers that:

> When his mother was busy he would play outside. School was not for him or his agemates. They wrestled in fun and played ancient games, but sometimes the witch's boy could be rough. If any displeased him, he would resort to painful methods of showing his anger. It was an indolent childhood, an education of gossip and tribal legends and of superstition and fear. He learnt many dark arts from his mother and in play he had discovered the secret of power. At 12, he was well established as the leader of the village children – a domineering, resourceful, brute-strong youth with a pronounced streak of sadism. In the sundown hours of play he would overcome any opposition by simply grasping his opponent's genitals and crushing them in his great bear paw of hand [sic].[93]

Thirty-five years later, the real author of the book, the Rhodesian journalist Angus Shaw, wrote in his memoirs:

> It was to be an instant book to snatch sales while the news was still fresh in people's minds. With the time constraints of such an instant book, I had used creative licence to flesh out Amin's childhood. He probably did use his bear-like fists to bruise the testicles of the children in his village. George Ivan Smith, an Australian academic, later wrote a paper on the psychosis of mass murderers and used Amin's testes bashing as an early sign of his. This was to be perpetuated as fact in the archives of the British Library and the US Library of Congress.[94]

Judith Listowel, who seems to have been rather less keen than Shaw to invent stories and also, unlike most of the other writers on Amin, had met and interviewed him at some length, wrote that:

> His father was a peasant and Amin likes to reminisce about the hardships of his childhood; 'I came from a poor family: when I was young, I had to herd goats, carry water, cook and even dig in the evenings to earn money for my parents'. . . . Amin's father worked the land in the immensely fertile brown earth of the West Nile. . . .
>
> The childhood home of Amin was a typical Kakwa house, made of wattle and clay, neatly smeared with cement. If the white ants destroyed the wattle, the clay held firm. His father's granary was formed of wicker-work perched on upright stone or hard wood pedestals. Their diet was monotonous – as that of many Africans is – and Amin only had one meal a day. The Kakwa, like many Nilotic people, did not cover their bodies until the arrival of the Europeans . . . and as late as the 1950s many of them still went about wearing only a genital cover.[95]

Later, she writes that:

> Amin was educated at the local mission school intermittently because, according to himself, he had to help his father on the land. Many Africans in the early 1930s were not very aware of the blessings of education and the Kakwa were not among the most progressive tribes. But at school Amin at least learned Swahili. . . .
>
> He grew into a strong lad, six-foot four-inches tall, who was to outshine his contemporaries by his physical prowess and his leadership qualities.[96]

Most accounts of Amin's childhood agree that his parents split up shortly after his birth. Martin says that:

> The full extent of his mother's influence on his life is unclear, but his upbringing was certainly far from traditional. His mother was what used to be described as a camp follower, and she finally moved to Buikwe, about twelve miles from Jinja. African soldiers serving at Jinja remember that she had been living with a man about her age until 1954 when she

moved into the Jinja barracks to live with Corporal Yafesi Yasin, a clerk in 'D' Company of the 4th King's African Rifles.

The corporal was in his early twenties and about half her age, and his friends had laughed at him for living with such an old woman. Amin's mother had practised witchcraft since moving to the area – and possibly before, and this was her only means of livelihood until she moved into the camp. One of the soldiers serving there recalls a woman nicknamed 'Pepsi Cola' who they all believed was mad. She was brought to Amin's mother, and in a darkened room with flashing lights and ringing small bells she sought to drive the evil spirits from the woman.

It seems the treatment failed, for 'Pepsi Cola' continued to be regarded as being as mad as ever. But the cynicism as to the magic powers of Amin's mother were soon to be shaken. Corporal Yasin tired of the woman and ordered her to leave the camp, and she went back to Buikwe. A few days later, the corporal reported one morning that he was feeling sick. The orderly sergeant sent him to the doctor, but before he could be examined, he died. Whether a post mortem was carried out was not known, but the belief in Jinja was that he had been poisoned or bewitched.[97]

The UN diplomat George Ivan Smith (who adopts both the genital crushing story from 'Kamau and Cameron', and the 'Pepsi Cola' story from Martin) speculates that:

[The] sense of being a Nubi, a stranger within the gates, would have been strengthened by the kind of life that the boy Idi would have led in the dusty surrounds of the barracks of the King's African Rifles. Most of the children he played with would like himself have been Nubian/Kakwa, or Nubians related to some other minor tribe. They were part of the life on the edge of the barracks as marine slugs and starfish are part of the life on the edge of the sea. . . .

Between 1930 and the middle forties, Amin's mother with her visions, use of bells, lights and potions, toted the child about in the fogs of their lives.[98]

Idi Amin's family have a less exotic tale to tell about his boyhood than the mystical fantasies in the popular books on him. In Jaffar Amin's version of

51

his father's life, unlike most of the secondary accounts, when his parents split up Idi Amin initially went with his father, back to West Nile:

> My grandparents' marriage could not withstand the continuing and persistent false allegations that King Daudi Chwa or others fathered Dad and not Grandpa. It could not withstand the Lan'ga na Da (stepping over the King's African Rifles rifle [*sic*]) ritual that Grandma performed at the assembly following the 'paternity test' Dad was subject to, to invoke the powerful curse she pronounced on Grandpa. Moreover, Grandpa's first wife Mariam Poya continued the relentless gossip about other men being Dad's father. So my grandparents separated and subsequently divorced....
>
> In 1932, Grandpa retired from the Colonial Police Force and returned to live in Tanganyika Village in Arua.... Following his retirement and move back to Arua, Grandpa served in the District Commissioner's Office in Arua until the 1940s.
>
> Between 1932 and 1936 during the time Dad was aged 4 to 8 years ... he attended Arua Muslim School under the care of his stepmother Mama Poya where he now resided. By this time, his own mother my Grandma had completely given up the ghost of her marriage to Grandpa and headed for Semuto in Buganda to live among her relatives who had retired from the King's African Rifles. Mariam Poya had no recourse but to look after the child of her rival because Muslim culture insists the children remain with the father after a divorce. So, Dad's older brother Ramadhan Dudu Moro was living in his father's house as well.[99]

According to his son, between the ages of 4 and 8, the young Idi Amin lived with his father's family and attended Arua Muslim School. Several of his classmates there, Jaffar says, became close associates after Amin's coup. One boy, named Kiiza, came from the southern tribe, the Bunyoro (long-time rivals of the Baganda), though his mother was from the West Nile group known as the Alur. Kiiza's sister Nyakayima became Idi's first girlfriend. According to Jaffar, he wanted to marry her but his father refused permission, as he believed the Alur were inclined to be witches. 'In Nubian culture', Jaffar writes, 'the father usually makes the first choice of wife for the son, the second, third and fourth choices are his own after that. So Dad gave up his marriage to Nyakayima.'[100] Kiiza became an electrician, and told Jaffar

Amin about a later encounter he had with his father: 'the up and coming Idi Amin came to my workshop with his gramophone so that I could repair it. ... However, when the repair was done Idi came in, picked up the machine and as he attempted to walk out, I asked for my money only to get an Nkonzi/ Ngolo (knuckle rap) on my head.'[101]

Amin's mother, meanwhile, continued to live in Buganda, enjoying the patronage of the Kabaka, and Jaffar believes the young Idi visited her at the royal court in Mengo. However, she moved away from the court when she married a retired soldier whom Jaffar calls 'Mze Ibrahim'. According to Jaffar, when the 8-year-old Idi finished at Arua Muslim School, his mother sent a delegation of Nubi Muslim scholars ('Ulama') to Arua, to persuade his father to allow the boy to go south, to be educated at a religious school known as 'Sheikh Mahmood's Madrasa for Garaya'. So, from 1937 to 1940, between the ages of 9 and 12, Amin lived in Buganda, first at the school and later with his mother. He became renowned for his skills in memorising and reciting the Koran, and worked intermittently, like many of his mother's family, as an indentured labourer in the sugar plantations owned by the Asian Mehta family. Jaffar says: 'I strongly believe that Dad began despising Uganda's Elitist system during the time he lived and worked at the Metha [*sic*] Sugar Plantations.'[102] In his account, the supposed Sudanese origin of the Nubians led to them being refused educational opportunities in Uganda beyond the fourth year of primary schooling. He writes: 'According to Dad, he participated in riots organized by the Nubi (Nubians) to protest the injustice of being denied education. This had happened when he was twelve years old. During these riots, Dad was injured and arrested but released.... This is also the specific time thoughts of joining the King's African Rifles loomed large in Dad's mind.'[103]

This was the obvious route for an ambitious boy from Amin's background. The only alternatives open to a young West Niler – subsistence farming (which frequently entailed starvation), or indentured semi-slavery and hard physical labour cutting sugar cane for the Mehtas – would have been much less appealing. Amin probably joined the British Army, not so much because of any sadistic leanings he might have had, but as the only available route out of extreme hardship and deprivation. Whatever his initial motivations, his army life was perhaps the key experience that made him into the person he became. It was also the period in which he first began to appear on a wider stage and come to public attention and appraisal. The next chapter will look at Amin's military career, and at how it has been represented by the various writers on his life.

In this chapter, I have looked primarily at the published representations of Amin's background, birth and childhood. Both the popular and the more academic books considered here have served to produce and reproduce the many contradictory stories – both realistic and supernatural – that have accreted around the few established facts of Amin's birth and childhood. The impossibility of distinguishing fact from fantasy is complicated in this case both by the politics and ideologies of Ugandan ethnicity, and by Idi Amin's own habit (or tactic) of encouraging, and telling, wild and untrue stories about himself. It is a reasonable, pragmatic decision for an historian to work on the basis that Jaffar Amin's account is the most detailed and convincing we have for Amin's early life. However, such an historian then has to face up to the implications of the more mystical elements in Jaffar's story for its truth status. As an anthropologist, however, I am more interested in the social meanings attributed to both the Yakan movement and the other supernatural elements of this story, rather than simply their historical origins and factual veracity.

2

'HE COMES FROM A FIGHTING RACE'
LIFE IN THE KING'S AFRICAN RIFLES, 1946(?)-59

The young Idi Amin's career in the British colonial army regiment called the King's African Rifles (KAR) had a major influence on later events. It could be said, with only a small exaggeration, that the KAR made him the man he became. His military life certainly established many aspects of the mythical figure he turned into; his reputation for immense strength, his use of violence, apparent lack of intelligence, and buffoonish sense of humour all date from this period. It was here that he learned to succeed in the eyes of his British masters, and he also learned to kill. For this period of Amin's life, there are some witnesses among the officers he served with, who either published accounts of him or gave information to the British authorities later in his career, some of which has found its way into the archives. It should be noted, though, that these stories were mostly written many years after the events they describe and, crucially, after Amin's takeover of power in Uganda. They were written, that is, not as purely disinterested contemporaneous observation of a remarkable soldier, but as later contributions to the ongoing creation of the legendary monster known as Idi Amin. His caricatured representation, in other words, was already established before any of the military memoirs appeared. It should also be noted that one major lack in the historical account is that of other Ugandan voices, those of the African soldiers he served with, rather than the white officers he served under. Their accounts of Amin's military career might have offered an illuminating contrast to the ones we have now. As it is, the stories about this period in Amin's life offer little more hard evidence than those of his childhood. What I have tried to do here is to allow the colonial officers' voices to speak for themselves – giving them enough rope, as it were – while attempting to distinguish clearly between my voice and theirs, and at the same time trying not to patronise a past world.

THE KING'S AFRICAN RIFLES

The KAR has already been mentioned several times. Here it is important to outline something of the regiment's history and character at the time the young Idi Amin joined up, and to look briefly at the role it played in imperial East Africa in the first half of the twentieth century. The KAR was formed in 1902 from three previously existing regiments: the Central African Regiment, the Uganda Rifles and the East Africa Rifles, which themselves had their origins in the Imperial British East Africa Company. As the regiment's official history puts it, 'The establishment of armed forces within the African Protectorates was an essential step in the early development of these territories.'[1] The former KAR officer turned military historian, Lieutenant Colonel H. Moyse-Bartlett, depicts the founding of these forces as a benevolent exercise undertaken in order to fight against both slavery and what we would now call 'radical Islamism', especially in Sudan and Somaliland. Both these aims involved defining the same enemy – 'the Arabs'[2] – who apparently threatened the peace-loving people of East and Central Africa, so that the latter had to be defended by British (or rather British-trained and led) troops.[3] As I have suggested, the Nubi played a key role in this. In the case of the Uganda Rifles, Moyse-Bartlett tells us that: 'In Uganda, certain Sudanese troops, formerly of the Khedive's army, became the nucleus of the Uganda Rifles.'[4] These, as we saw in the introduction, were among the Anglo-Egyptian forces which fought the radical Muslim leader known as 'the Mahdi' in Sudan. They included the remnants of Emin Pasha's troops – Frederick Lugard's 'best material for soldiery in Africa' – and represented the core of what became the ethnic, or ethno-military, group called the Nubi.

The establishment of the KAR as an inclusive East African unit came about shortly after the turn of the century because, Moyse-Bartlett tells us:

> The main object was to make the Protectorates militarily independent as a whole, while at the same time ensuring the internal security of each. Neither East Africa nor Uganda was yet sufficiently strong to cope with

serious trouble single-handed. The old policy of strengthening local defence by calling on our troops from India had proved very expensive and was increasingly unpopular with the [British colonial] government of India. After the Ashanti Campaign [in West Africa] the capabilities of African soldiers were much more widely recognised. On the other hand, the Sudanese mutiny had shown the need for caution. It was felt that some Indian garrisons must be retained for a time, but that African troops might solve the important question of an emergency reserve, the need for which had been repeatedly demonstrated during the past few years. Such a reserve must be stationed centrally and if possible consist of askaris [low-ranking African soldiers] with no local affinities in the areas where they might be called upon to operate.[5]

Accordingly, in 1902 the Uganda Rifles became the 4th Battalion of the KAR. In the First World War the regiment fought to annex the German colonies of East Africa (primarily the mainland part of present-day Tanzania) for the British Empire. Many of its troops, as we have seen, were more or less forcibly recruited into military service. They probably included Amin Dada senior, as Jaffar Amin records, and this is why, after the war, the colonial authorities gave him a plot of land in Arua town's 'Tanganyika Village'. '4KAR', as it was known, also included many other men and boys from the West Nile region. The KAR perpetuated the traditions inherited from the 'Khedive's Army', of soldiers becoming Muslim and learning a form of vernacular Arabic on joining the army; the KAR's language of command was KiSwahili, and many soldiers spoke the related KiNubi, both based to a large extent on an Arabic vocabulary. In the case of people like the young Idi, however, there was little need for such an acclimatisation to the military life – the family was deeply embedded in the British forces, and many of them already spoke KiNubi and followed the Muslim faith. Jaffar Amin explicitly links his family's military history to the birth of the Nubi:

[M]y family's history with the King's African Rifles dates back to the 19th century political upheavals in Africa that were linked to the colonisation of sub-Saharan Africa. During the time in 1914 when Grandpa [i.e. Idi Amin's father, Amin Dada Nyabira Tomuresu] was forcibly conscripted into the King's African Rifles in order to fight the First World War (WWI) alongside colonial soldiers, many other members of my family were also forcibly conscripted to fight in the same war.[6]

He goes on to recall some of the cultural impacts of this military livelihood on an African society:

Dad's family hails from Koboko, home of the Kakwa tribe in Uganda. However the family settled in Tanganyika Village of Arua after the First World War, following Grandpa's forcible conscription. ... This made it easier for family members to become amalgamated to the Nubi (Nubians). Even though the bulk of my immediate family lived in Arua and Arua became the family's primary abode, Grandpa and other family members encouraged regular trips back to Kakwaland to continue to maintain the family's Kakwa roots. However, despite these efforts, many family members continued the process of amalgamation with the Nubi (Nubians) with colloquial Arabic becoming the widely spoken language by members of my family along with the Kakwa language and other languages.[7]

Later, Jaffar discusses the relationship between the Amin family, including Idi himself, and the KAR:

By the time Dad was born in 1928, our family had been heavily 'invested' in the King's African Rifles (KAR). ... So, it was only natural that he would aspire for a career in the Armed Forces. Over the years, the King's African Rifles had employed more members of my immediate and extended family and become a career path Dad would also aspire to as a child. As Dad searched for better opportunities, he would periodically spend time at the Al-Qadriyah Darasah Bombo [a military base in Buganda] and work as a Kasanvu [indentured labourer] at the Metha [sic] sugar plantations, like several members of our immediate family.[8]

By 1940, the 4th Battalion of the KAR had become a major source of employment, not just for the Kakwa and the Nubi, but for other West Nile groups, such as the Lugbara and Madi people, and also for the larger tribes from the central northern region, particularly the Acholi. This powerful ethnic

group was both much more numerous, and more coherent and long established, than the West Nilers, with their complex, fluid ethnicities.[9] Because of
this, the Acholi were – and are – often seen by Baganda people and other
southerners as representative of the North as a whole.[10] By the time of the
Second World War, there were more Acholi in the army than Kakwa and Nubi
soldiers.

The characteristic attitude of the British KAR leadership towards the
African soldiers they commanded is well summarised by their official historian, Moyse-Bartlett. Concluding his two-volume history of the regiment
between 1890 and 1945, he writes:

> No single factor is of greater importance with colonial troops than the
> choice of suitable European leadership. In war and peace this has been
> repeatedly proved. To be led by officers who know and understand him
> and who speak his language is a vital necessity for the African. But the
> personnel of all military units constantly changes, and of colonial battal-
> ions more frequently than most. So much the greater, then, must be the
> value placed in such regiments as the KAR upon the influence of a sound
> military tradition, fostered in the present by an understanding and
> appreciation of the past.[11]

Moyse-Bartlett's references to Lord Lugard's agreement with Emin Pasha
make it clear that this military heritage includes that of the slave armies
from which the Nubi arose.[12] In the last paragraph of the book, he continues:

> There are in Eastern Africa today many tribes whose young men possess
> the proved capacity to become good soldiers. That they cannot be
> expected to attain a European standard needs no saying, but in bush and
> jungle warfare, when conditions are particularly rough and supplies are
> limited and few, their hardy physique, simple needs and cheerful outlook
> are of outstanding value. The history of the past 50 years has furnished
> repeated proof of the loyalty and courage that can be founded upon these
> basic qualities.[13]

A more recent history of the KAR, by another ex-officer, Malcolm Page,[14]
brings the story up to the disbanding of the regiment in 1963, though the

post-Second World War era is covered only by scattered reminiscences of former officers, taken from their regimental magazine *Rhino Link*, edited by Page. The book contains no mention of Idi Amin, probably the KAR's most famous old soldier.

RECRUITMENT AND ENLISTMENT

The question of exactly when Idi Amin joined the British Army, like the date of his birth, has been the subject of some disagreement and dispute. Even the British government later had problems ascertaining when he joined up, and whether he had fought in the Second World War. Shortly after the coup in 1971, a biography prepared by the Foreign Office's Information Research Department stated that: 'His military career began when he joined the former British regiment, the King's African Rifles, as a private, and he saw active service in Burma during the Second World War, in Kenya during the Mau Mau crisis, and in Somalia and Ethiopia.'[15] Later that year, a British Foreign Office report on 'Leading Personalities in Uganda' stated that Amin had: 'Joined KAR about 1945 as a private soldier and saw service in the Burma campaign. Served in Kenya during the Mau Mau emergency when he did well and rose to rank of Warrant Officer.'[16] At around the same time, Lt Col. B.H. Bradbrooke, a 'defence advisor' in the British Embassy in Kampala, in a lengthy report on Amin's coup, wrote that: 'He joined the KAR about 1943, served in Burma in World War II, and later in Kenya during the Mau Mau trouble.'[17] By 1975, however, the Foreign Office had amended the date of his enlistment to what had by then become the accepted year. A lengthy Foreign Office document titled 'Leading Personalities in Uganda 1975' stated, under the section on Amin, that he 'Joined KAR about 1946 as a private soldier. Served in Kenya during the Mau Mau troubles when he did well and rose to Warrant Officer.'[18] This became the official line, and was echoed in the briefing for a 1975 visit to Uganda by the Foreign Secretary, James Callaghan (see Chapter 7). He was informed that Amin 'Joined King's African Rifles 1946, rising to Warrant Officer during the Mau Mau troubles in Kenya.'[19]

This was to remain the officially agreed date in the British government files. However, it is by no means impossible that, while Idi Amin *officially* signed up in 1946 (hence the British account, based on written records), he was informally taken on, as what we would now call a 'child soldier', some time earlier. Jaffar Amin's account has him 'enlisting' as a 12-year-old:

> At 12 years old, Dad landed a gig in the Kitchen Mess of the King's African Rifles aboard the Navy Ship named SS *Yoma* during the Second World War. According to him and others, he started his career in the King's African Rifles in 1939 when he landed the gig at the King's African Rifles Kitchen Mess as a Kitchen help. He would eventually join the Fighting Unit. . . .
>
> Dad's gig in the King's African Rifles Kitchen Mess took him aboard the Navy Ship SS *Yoma*, which plied the following sea route and back between the World War II years . . .
>
> Mombasa Port
> Cape Town
> Madagascar . . .
> Mombasa Port
> Mogadishu
> Djibouti
> Aden
> Port Sudan
> Suez Canal.[20]

According to Wikipedia (which is usually reliable on Second World War military history), the *Yoma* had, before the war, been a commercial vessel plying the route between the UK and its colony of Burma. After 1939, it continued to sail this route commercially, travelling in naval-escorted convoys from Liverpool to Rangoon, until January 1941, when it was requisitioned and turned into a troop ship. On 18 February, *Yoma* sailed from Glasgow to Freetown (Sierra Leone), on to Cape Town, and then round the Cape of Good Hope into the Indian Ocean. There, the ship spent the next two years 'moving troops mostly between Mombasa, Aden, Bombay, Colombo and Bandar Abbas'. Her last Indian Ocean voyage was in April 1943, after which *Yoma* was transferred to the Mediterranean and sailed from Gibraltar to Alexandria via Tunisia and Libya. While on the second trip over this route, carrying 1,128 British soldiers and 665 Free French Naval Forces, *Yoma* was sunk by a German U-boat submarine on 17 June 1943.

What are we to make of this? There is some overlap between Jaffar's account and the historical record on the SS *Yoma*; the route outlined in the former is not dissimilar to *Yoma*'s 1941–43 itinerary, though it is not exactly the same and, if his son's information is correct, Idi Amin seems to have sailed only as far as Egypt. However, this was clearly not a route the ship plied for the whole duration of the war, as Jaffar suggests, as it was transferred to the Mediterranean and then sunk. If Amin *was* a kitchen boy on the boat for a time, it would provide a partial justification for his frequent claims in later life to have fought in the Burma Campaign during the Second World War. Jaffar Amin's account is partly based on memories of the tales his father used to tell about his military life, but also on an interview he had with a man named Ronny Bai, who said he had joined up at the same time as Idi Amin. Jaffar claims he subjected Bai to 'Stasi-style' interrogation to ascertain the truth of his story,[21] and appears to have gone to some lengths to confirm it by fact-checking. According to Jaffar,

> In the stories Dad had told about the Second World War, he had claimed that during the war, he was on board a ship that was downed by a U-Boat and an American Destroyer rescued them. Records show that the Navy Ship SS *Yoma* was sunk on June 17 1943, between the Port of Alexandria and the Libyan Coast. So Dad's story definitely has some truth in it.
>
> Moreover, according to Dad, the rescue team had wanted to send them all the way to the United States of America! In jest, Dad used to say 'All of my seeds, all of you, would have ended up being Niggers'. . . . Dad liked to crack jokes and laugh even though some of his jokes could be very annoying and in terrible taste. . . . Dad regularly talked about the African Slave Trade and the deplorable conditions Africans were subjected to as they were being transported to the Americas to work as slaves.[22]

The date of the sinking of the *Yoma* is right but, according to Wikipedia, the ship's crew were rescued, not by an American destroyer, but by two Australian corvettes, two British minesweepers and a merchant ship. These vessels rescued 1,477 sailors and troops, while 484 people died, including the *Yoma*'s captain. This rather destroys Amin's 'joke' about his children becoming African Americans, and casts further doubt on Jaffar's account.

But, if the story was fabricated, why are so many of the details right, or nearly so? One possibility, as I have suggested, is that Amin *did* work on the ship for a time as a young boy; another might be that he knew someone who had been on it, and had appropriated the story for himself. As with so many tales about Amin, it is impossible to know for sure.

Whatever the truth in his war stories, Amin certainly does seem to have *officially* enlisted in the KAR very shortly after the end of the Second World War, in 1946. The popular books on Amin all describe his recruitment and early military career in a similar way. They also tend to stress how keen the British officers were to recruit him, and how popular Amin was with them. Characteristically, 'Kamau and Cameron' (Angus Shaw) summarise it vividly and imaginatively:

> In the young Idi Amin, the British officers of the 4th Battalion, King's African Rifles, found all the qualities for which they were looking. Intelligence was not one. The main criteria for the selection of African troops were height, physique and the ability to shut one eye – the prerequisite of being able to shoot a rifle.
>
> Enlisted as a private in 1946, it took Idi Amin seven years of dogged soldiering to make lance-corporal. His boots were always immaculately polished, their toecaps shining like mirrors. His starched khaki uniform crackled, its creases were like razors. Amin showed respect and admiration for his superiors, he became assiduously loyal and pro-British and developed a fierce regimental pride. He was a boon on the sports field, but most of all he obeyed commands unquestioningly.
>
> To the British officers, Amin was ideal KAR material. 'Not much grey matter', as one of the officers put it, 'But a splendid chap to have about'. . . .
>
> Recalled a British Sergeant Major in the KAR, 'He was rather quiet, not the rowdy type at all and the only thing that perhaps distinguished his from the other *askari* [KAR troops] was his zest for military knowledge. Everyone really liked him, especially the Europeans – they thought the world of him.'[23]

Most of the writers on Amin emphasise this appeal he had for his military superiors. Another pseudonymous writer, 'David Gwyn', also cites the

1946 date for Amin's enlistment, rejecting the claim that he had been involved in the Second World War. He writes that:

> Amin's original recruitment, and his survival in the army until 1964, can be attributed to the attitude of some British army officers posted for duty to the 4th Battalion of the KAR in Uganda. Amin was the type of soldier whom these British officers preferred. Large and physically impressive, he had little education. The theory was that those with least education made the best troops because they would obey orders more readily. Without the intellectual capacity to question, they would supposedly accept discipline automatically.... It would be wrong to assume that all British army officers in Uganda took this view, but there were enough....
>
> A few of the British looked on Amin's manifest sadism as praise-worthy and ideal material for the army.[24]

It is difficult to tell here whether 'Gwyn' holds Amin's intellect, or that of his British army officers, in greater contempt. It is difficult to imagine that the latter were quite as stupid as he suggests; why would anyone think that unintelligent or uneducated people are more controllable than intelligent, educated ones? The KAR certainly chose recruits on the basis of tribal, ethnic, stereotypes, and they were recruited on physical rather than mental attributes. But this is not the same as picking individuals *because* they were unintelligent. It is hard to accept the insistence, shared by so many of the writers as well as retired KAR officers I spoke to, on Amin's own lack of intelligence. His career certainly exhibits some luck, and considerable ruthlessness, but it is hard to see how it could all have happened to someone quite so lacking in intelligence as the Idi Amin depicted in these books. While he certainly had little formal education, it is difficult to see how a child from such a deprived and marginalised background could have risen so far, if he really had little or no intelligence. This raises the interesting question of how and why Amin was able to hide his intelligence from most of his officers, or perhaps how and why they missed it.

One thing that is clear from all accounts is that the British military selected on the basis of perceived tribal (ultimately, that is, racial) physical characteristics. In Uganda, this meant mainly recruiting from the Acholi and Langi people of the central north, and the various West Nile tribes from the north-west. Idi Amin exemplified what the KAR were looking for in their recruits; he *was* the martial paradigm. Major R.D. West, who was attached to 4KAR between 1958 and 1960, described how the selection process worked from a British point of view, in answer to a questionnaire sent to former KAR officers in 1979:

> Basically, one arrived in Uganda, was given a job and got on with it. The only special training was the learning of Swahili.
>
> The Uganda [Protectorate] government laid down the tribal structure of the Battalion – in simple terms, we concentrated on the Northern Tribes and left out the so-called 'non-warriors' of the South. Idi Amin, of recent notoriety, was a Sergeant then a Warrant Officer in my Company. At that time he was excellent at his job.
>
> I think this field tribal structure as laid down by the Administration was wrong and that subsequent events in Uganda might have been avoided if the clever but 'non-warlike' tribes had been represented well before Independence. I speak mainly from hindsight, but I feel there was always a hangover in Colonial administrations of the Indian Mutiny of the Bengal Army which caused a universal distrust of the educated or intelligent native – the Mission Boy.[25]

These were the two main ethnic stereotypes that persisted throughout the British African empire; the Warrior Tribes, represented in Uganda by the northerners (particularly the Acholi and the West Nilers), and the Mission Boys, represented by the southerners (particularly the Baganda). Major West's analysis shows clearly why the appearance of stupidity might well be a useful mask for a clever soldier from the north to assume, though it would, of course, be imputed regardless. The tribal quotas were taken seriously, and the northern districts were where the recruiting drives took place.

Another respondent to the KAR questionnaire, Lt Col. H.K.P Chavasse, (seconded to 4KAR from 1960 to 1962), gave a fairly detailed picture of this:

> Recruiting was carried out in an annual safari to the tribal areas. . . . The Acholi tribe was the most numerous in 4KAR and we could easily have filled the battalion with them. However, they were limited to 40% of the strength in order to keep some tribal balance. The Lango, Teso and

the West Nile tribes formed the majority of the remainder. The Acholi and the West Nile tribes were considered the best soldiers on average....

Idi Amin, who came from one of the West Nile Tribes, was an outstanding individual. I knew him first as an Effendi, when he was a first rate platoon commander, although he showed a touch of ruthlessness at times, especially if detached on his own. He was one of the first two to receive the Queen's Commission, and subsequently commanded the Recce Platoon, which gave him more independence and responsibility than any other senior African. He accepted this without difficulty, but needed supervision on inter-tribal operations, otherwise he would exceed his instructions and treat suspects with an unnecessary degree of ruthlessness, and, although never proved, outright cruelty. At that time we considered that he would be a Company Commander in due course, but that would be his ceiling![26]

The two former colonial officers, it should be noted, were writing here about the period in which they served in 4KAR, more than a decade after Amin's recruitment and only a year or two before Uganda's independence. They were also looking back on this period from the perspective of hindsight, having seen Amin's time in office. However, their analysis of the consequences of the KAR recruitment processes was shared by other British officials at the time. After the new president turned against British interests, the acting British high commissioner in Uganda, Harry Brind, wrote in his valedictory despatch, dated 16 July 1973:

What went wrong? I think we must find the root cause in the tribal structure of Uganda. Not surprisingly for a country in the middle of Africa, there are great contrasts in its peoples, Bantu in the south, Nilotic in the North. No single tribe accounts for more than a fifth of Uganda's population. The differences between north and south have been compounded by the fact that the majority of the army, and to a lesser extent the police, were recruited from two or three Northern minority tribes ...[27]

In September 1973, the head of the Foreign Office East Africa desk, Martin Ewans, blamed the situation in Amin's Uganda on: 'our habit of bequeathing to successive independent governments, in Uganda as elsewhere, an army and police that in the colonial period had been largely recruited from minority tribes'.[28]

The Australian diplomat George Ivan Smith spoke to many who had known Amin, and gives a slightly more nuanced analysis of Amin's appeal to the KAR than most writers, arguing that it rested in part on their perception that he was stupid and potentially malleable, rather than his actual possession of these qualities:

> He was a 'natural' for the recruiting eyes of an army seeking 'black chaps' to use in its patrolling, fighting section. Politics, nil. Nubian neutral [sic]. Height (very important for presentation purposes) unusually good – 6 ft 4 ins. Good for a ceremonial, even better for scaring hell out of those to be policed. Undoubtedly charismatic presence. If the chap could be told what to do and when to come back he was the good stuff that the bottom part of such an army was made on [sic].
>
> He had the brawn that gives a solid foundation to the platoon. Strong, obedient, quick to learn the army jargon – 'Yes, Sir', 'No, Sir', 'Say again, Sir'....
>
> It was his size and nature that made him I think what the British army would call one from the 'warrior tribes'. Big, black, willing to obey orders.[29]

The Kenyan political scientist Ali Mazrui also suggested that specific biological characteristics were sought by the KAR recruiters:

> Just as the British had made assumptions about extra martial prowess among the Ghurkas and Punjabis, so they made assumptions about such prowess among the Nilotic and Sudanic peoples of northern Uganda.... Nilotes and Sudanic tribes produced a disproportionate number of men who were tall and slim. This particular kind of physique was interpreted in the colonial period as additional evidence of military suitability. The 'tall and lean' were regarded as 'good drill material'.... [T]he recruitment officers of the imperial power in Uganda came to look at Nilotic and Sudanic communities as being physically better 'drill material' than most of the people of the Bantu kingdoms [such as the Baganda]....

It was against this background that Amin became a significant military figure. He was a good physical specimen, drawn from a region with more than its share of Uganda's tall people, and less than its share of the country's rich people. A combination of economic and physical factors had set the stage for a remarkable career.[30]

Some of the specifics of Mazrui's account are questionable, but it is clear that the British military did tend to select on the basis of perceived tribal (ultimately, racial) physical characteristics.

The most widely quoted account of Amin's army days is provided by his former commanding officer, Iain Grahame. The first chapter of his 1980 book on Amin contains a fictionalised reconstruction of a 1948 KAR recruitment drive in Northern Uganda, five years before Grahame himself joined the regiment. In this account, the British officers were testing potential soldiers for their fitness and appearance:

> In Koboko . . . only two of the . . . candidates could write their own names, but this in itself did not debar them from military service. . . . [W]hat the officers were looking for was a strong physique, stamina, speed of reaction and an upright bearing. . . . Any military task that required a modicum of intelligence was carried out by European officers or NCOs [non-commissioned officers].[31]

Over the course of the chapter, the imagined convoy winds its way around the north of Uganda, providing a narrative framework for Grahame to outline some relevant history and geography of the region. At the end, the soldiers and their new recruits return to Kampala:

> When the convoy finally reached the tarmac streets of Kampala itself, the safari commander headed for the Imperial Hotel. There he and the medical officer went inside to slake their thirst, leaving the senior African warrant officer to prepare the soldiers for the final few miles' drive to the barracks.
>
> Just as the two officers were emerging and preparing to re-enter their jeep, they suddenly found themselves accosted by the hotel bell-boy. Standing smartly to attention, he said to them in simple Swahili:

'Sir, I want to join the KAR.'

The officers looked up at this huge figure with a fine, impressive physique, the tribal scars on his cheeks identical to others that they had seen at Koboko.[32]

'All right', replied the safari commander, feeling exceptionally benevolent after a couple of ice cold lagers. 'Jump in the truck.'

The name of the new recruit was Idi son of Amin.[33]

Jaffar Amin's account of his father's 1946 recruitment is not very different from Grahame's reconstruction. According to Jaffar, when Idi Amin returned from his stint on the SS *Yoma*, having failed to get into a fighting unit of the KAR due to his youth, he went to live in Kampala with relatives. The teenager got a job at the Grand Imperial Hotel 'as a Bellboy of sorts', as Jaffar puts it, '[i]t would be at this hotel that Dad would meet a Scottish Officer, assert his interest in joining the … King's African Rifles and be formally recruited into the Fighting Unit of the Colonial Army. … This is the scene of the account by Dad's biographer Judith Listowel.'[34] In fact, however, Listowel's account, presumably based on what Amin told her, did not include the bellboy story. In her version, Amin was recruited in West Nile: 'The Regiment had had heavy losses in Burma, where 1,924 African private soldiers were killed. On its return to East Africa, the 4th Battalion was stationed at Langata Camp, outside Nairobi. From there, a recruiting safari was sent to northern Uganda where it signed up a group of Kakwa, including Amin.'[35] Jaffar has perhaps confused Listowel's account with Grahame's. Elsewhere, however, even his son seems unsure about how Amin was enlisted, and relies on Grahame's fictionalised story:

There are two versions to Dad's conscription into the King's African Rifles. One version that Dad regularly told in typical Kakwa Adiyo (oral historical narrative account of history and events from the past) narration style was that he was busy selling mandazi (doughnuts) on the streets when he was grabbed and forcibly conscripted by a Scottish man, at the probable age of twelve.

The second version that Dad's biographer pens down is that Dad was a Bellboy of sorts at the Imperial Hotel when he requested a British Officer to join the King's African Rifles.

Regarding the correct version, the Scottish man who grabs him off the street is more in line with the Kitchen Mess gig aboard the ... SS *Yoma*. ... The 'bellboy' version is more in line with his recruitment into the Fighting Unit of the Army in 1946....

For the 'Bellboy version' people in the know recount that Dad smartly stood to attention and said in simple Swahili 'Sir, I want to join the KAR'. According to them, the Safari Commander looked up at this huge figure with fine, impressive physique, the tribal scars identical to others they had seen at Ko'buko (Ko'boko) during a 'recruiting safari' sent out to recruit members of the Kakwa tribe into Colonial Uganda's Army at Nyarilo (Ko'buko's Headquarters) and said 'All right. Jump in the truck' – a 3-ton truck.[36]

A SOLDIER'S LIFE

Whenever and wherever Amin really did join up, he quickly appeared to justify his recruiters' assumptions about his natural abilities as a warrior. He seems to have had early success in the KAR, coming to the notice of the British officers, especially through his devotion to, and skill in, sports and games of many kinds. These were of massive importance to the British officers, and their accounts of the young soldier often emphasise his sporting ability, especially in boxing. According to Listowel, in his first posting, in Kenya:

Amin's main concern was to carry out his military duties, and he soon attracted the attention of officers by his sense of responsibility and intelligence. He also participated in all games and soon stood out as an athlete and a boxer. He became so proficient as a boxer that in 1953 he entered the Ugandan light-heavyweight championship and won it, retaining the title for nine years.[37]

'David Gwyn', unlike most of the other writers (and also the former KAR officers I spoke to in 2007–8, including Iain Grahame), is somewhat dismissive of Amin's sporting prowess, writing that: 'He had an above-average ability at sports. He became a successful boxer, though not distinguished for his style, and also took up rugby.'[38] George Ivan Smith mentions Amin's rugby skills, but also the barriers to his progression in the sport:

> The colour bar still operated. We know that Amin was a keen and quite good rugby forward. There was a pathetic desire on the part of the African soldiers ... to model themselves on the British pattern. . . . Amin was for ever trying to please, and he was the only African member in what they called the Nile Rugby Club. Sometimes, when they went across to play in Kenya, while the rest of the team were attending the reception after the game, Amin would have to sit outside the Club House in the bus that was going to take them back.[39]

Iain Grahame does not stint his praise of Amin's athletic abilities:

> Another quality that endeared him to all ranks within the battalion was his exceptional ability at every sport to which he turned his hand. His physique was that of a Grecian sculpture, and no matter to what form of athleticism he turned his hand, he excelled and he conquered. During the latter part of 1954 ... Idi won the 100 yards and 200 yards sprints against no mean opposition. He was anchor man in the winning tug of war team, and he quickly put on the canvas all opposition in the heavyweight boxing championships. He later went on to win the national title at this event, and it was to be nine years[40] before he finally hung up his gloves, still undefeated.[41]

Jaffar Amin's account of his father's sporting life is closely based on Grahame's, and it is interesting that he provides so few stories directly from his father in this part of his book. On page 99, he repeats Grahame's sentence comparing Amin's body with 'a Grecian sculpture' verbatim, but not in quotes. He does, however, add that in the 1950s his father ran a hundred yards in less than 10 seconds (which would have been a world record at the time). He also provides slightly more detail than Grahame of Idi Amin's boxing career: 'Dad ... quickly put on the canvas conquering all opposition in the heavy weight championships [sic]. He later went on to win the National Title at this event and it would be nine years before he hung up his gloves still undefeated.... [H]e had one cardinal rule, much in the mould of Sonny Liston and Mike Tyson. He loved to knockout (KO) opponents ...'[42]

Another European, who encountered him a couple of years later, gives a different account of Amin's boxing successes. This was Peter Jermyn Allen, at the time a senior police officer, later a judge in Amin's Uganda. In his published diary, the entry for 4 November 1956 describes his first encounter with the young soldier:

> In its doorway stood a tall, well-built young man wearing a white shirt and Khaki drill trousers. He looked like a fairly typical Nubian from the Sudan. ... The constable introduced him as his relative, Sergeant Idi of 4KAR and the present heavyweight boxing champion, over from Jinja army barracks for training for the Uganda Amateur Boxing Association Championships [held the previous day]....
>
> Four of our men [police boxers] reached the finals but three of them lost their fights. The last fight of the evening was the heavyweight finals between Les Peach of the Police and the newly promoted Sergeant Major Idi, who, when still a corporal two years earlier, had defeated Peach to become champion. They slugged it out for the full three rounds, each knocking the other down for partial counts. Peach then delivered a punch that put Idi through the ropes for the full count – our only win of the evening.[43]

This obviously does not support the usual story that Amin held the national heavyweight boxing championship, undefeated, for nine years or so. Allen also says that Peach, a white British former KAR soldier,[44] beat Amin again, on points, in the following year.[45] I have been unable to trace any reliable records of the Uganda heavyweight amateur boxing title and, as with so many other aspects of Idi Amin's life, the myths seem to obscure the truth. Perhaps all that can be said with confidence is that he was, at least, a very successful amateur boxer at national level for some years. Boxing, of course, is a contact sport that demonstrates controlled violence and aggression, as well as depending on tactical and defensive abilities. It had been associated in the European mind with a stereotype of black masculinity for a long time before Amin's successes, but it is difficult for today's reader to understand why men of different 'races' were allowed to thump each other for public entertainment, but not, for example, to eat or drink together in the same military canteens.

Amin's army career, even before his boxing achievements, was one of fairly rapid success. According to Listowel (as well as Smith and Grahame), he was promoted to corporal in 1948, after only two years as a private, and 'distinguished himself in expeditions against tribal marauders in northern Uganda'.[46] She says that although 'questions were not infrequently asked about the harsh methods he used', he would explain his actions to his superiors respectfully, 'in amusing Swahili', to their satisfaction. In the autumn of 1952, his company was sent to Kenya to counter the growing Mau Mau insurrection among the Kikuyu people, against British rule. This was probably the first time Amin took part in serious military action, and it happened to be during what is now widely acknowledged as one of the dirtiest 'little wars' in Britain's colonial history.[47] His commanding officer was Major A.E.D. Mitchell, who remembered Amin as 'very quiet, well mannered, respectful and loyal . . . a good shot, in fact a remarkable marksman on the range, always alert and noticed the slightest movement. He had extraordinary eyesight.'[48] In 1954, the battalion moved back to Uganda briefly, for the Queen's opening of Owen Falls Dam and other royal ceremonies, including presenting new colours (ceremonial flags) to 4KAR. 'Corporal Idi', Listowel tells us, 'was everywhere to the fore in the preparations for the royal visit.'[49] Then it was back to Kenya, where Amin's behaviour was, Major Mitchell told Listowel, exemplary. He served in many different parts of the battalion, including the mortar platoon, the transport company and the signals section. Mitchell apparently tried to have Amin promoted to sergeant, but at first he had problems with the English-language exams. However, after taking lessons and cramming English textbooks each morning before duty, Amin duly passed and was promoted in 1955.

Some of the most persistent stories about Amin's time in the KAR involve extreme sexual violence of various sorts, and the linkage between sexuality and violence is central to the legend of Idi Amin.[50] 'David Gwyn', who seems to have spent several years in Uganda and to have known many of the white population there, says that some British officers approved of Amin's 'manifest sadism'. He writes that one of these told him an anecdote about the future president's approach to disarming a group of Karamojong cattle herders (a semi-nomadic people living in the north-east of Uganda near the Kenyan border). Amin's task was to make the Karamojong men hand over their spears and shields. In 'Gwyn''s account:

> Amin's method, praised by British officers in the mess, was to bring the Karamojong tribesmen before a safari table, place the man's penis on the table, hold up a panga (a particularly lethal Uganda machete), and threaten to sever the penis unless the spears and shields were produced. The method was described as effective.[51]

It seems quite likely, however, that this anecdote came, not directly from a KAR officer, but from the earlier book by David Martin. His version of the story runs:

> In Uganda, the north-eastern Karamojong tribe, who traditionally go about naked, were notable cattle rustlers who periodically had to be disarmed. Naturally they were reluctant to surrender their spears and shields, and another British officer who served with Amin at the time, has boasted that Amin was remarkably successful in persuading them. He claimed that Amin made them stand with their penes on a table and then threatened to cut the organs off with a machete unless they told him where their spears and shields were hidden.[52]

George Ivan Smith tells more or less the same story, with a few variations:

> Records state that Amin's company shot many . . . and left them unburied to be eaten by hyenas. Although his basic orders were to disarm the rustlers, he apparently used his usual methods to get the Karamojong to surrender their weapons by forcing them to lay their penises on a table. The phrase he is reported as using was 'they would be de-gooded' unless they admitted that they had been involved and told him where their spears were hidden. On one occasion, he had cut off the genitals of eight Karamojong before getting the confessions he wanted. He got away with it. Were his British officers unaware that he was using these methods, or were they content that his brutality was producing results?[53]

If he really got the story from 'records', Smith would surely know at least some of the answer to the last question. As with 'Gwyn', it seems quite likely that Smith, too, has appropriated and embroidered on the tale in Martin's earlier book. On the surface, his account is phrased as a critique of the KAR but, put together with the other versions of the story, the repetition of gruesome accounts of sexualised torture reveals some of the complex and twisted forms of colonial desire that lie within the Amin myth. These anecdotes of his army years, offensive and distasteful in so many ways, are central to the development of the legend.

'Kamau and Cameron' present, as the reader will expect by now, one of the most lurid and violent versions of Amin's KAR years. The book returns frequently to the theme of testicle twisting which, as we saw in the previous chapter, the author admits inventing. On patrol in Kenya, having found 'a group of cattle rustlers' Amin is said to have:

> indulged himself, bringing roars of laughter from his men, as he twisted the scrotums of his captives before bayoneting them and leaving them to bleed to death.
>
> The uniform of the KAR was a protective shield which gave him strength. He could hear again the screams of the victims as he prolonged the pleasure of his torture. Too bad, he regretted, that one of the privates had reported his behaviour to the RSM [regimental sergeant major]. Amin had marked the man for vengeance, after his facile explanation and respectful manner had cleared him with the officers who questioned him. White men responded to respect. It did not do to let them see your thoughts.[54]

Amin's sporting prowess is again stressed. We are told that he enjoyed 'the inherent brutality of the boxing ring, the close bodily contact in the rough and tumble of the Rugby field' where, inevitably:

> Sometimes in the scrum he would resort to his old boyhood trick of squeezing one of the opponent's genitals. He never resented, or showed resentment if the opponents replied in kind. Sheer strength, an unquestionable charisma, made certain Amin had been marked for other things by his superiors.[55]

The book goes on to recount a long, obscene and gruesome story, which seems to be pure (or, rather, impure) fantasy. It begins with Amin waking up with a hangover in a Mogadishu brothel, and hearing the sound of the Muslim call to prayer. He kneels and prays, then shakes awake and beats up the woman he has been sleeping with, ordering her to pray while he admires himself in a mirror. He returns to camp 'before 6.15', Shaw tells us with implausible precision[56] and later that day moves with his platoon towards the Somalia-Kenya border. Here Amin contrives to shoot in the back the Kakwa private who had informed on his torture and murder of prisoners. In a subsequent enquiry into the death of the *askari*, according to Shaw, Amin was commended for his 'initiative and courageous devotion to duty'.[57] We are told that, 'For Amin, the experience was salutary. He had learnt that he could kill and that, with guile, he could do so with impunity.'[58] Perhaps the writer forgot that, in the same book, Amin had already learned this lesson several pages earlier in a different country, by killing the Kenyan cattle rustlers.

Martin claims that 'Africans who served with him in the King's African Rifles recount that [Amin] was frequently in trouble.'[59] Apparently, on one occasion he was caught in bed with a colleague's wife and chased down the street. Martin recounts the widespread story that Amin acquired syphilis in the KAR, quoting a later *Daily Telegraph* interview with an unnamed British officer who told the paper: 'In 1955 there was only one blot on his copybook. His records show that he had venereal disease which made him ineligible for a good conduct stripe.'[60] Despite these rumours, the young Kakwa private was quickly promoted to corporal. According to Smith:

In 1948 Idi became a corporal. His height, his presence, his desire to please and to win badges of merit, marked him for promotion. A medical report halted him for a short time. In 1950 venereal disease was recorded and hindered his progress. Did he take counsel from his mother, the witch, who was still alive? Did they have recourse to potions and medicines or the beheaded flying chicken, ready to drop on some point of the compass to lead the eye to where the trouble lay? Idi was only baulked.

As I went through his papers, and through the outlines of his presidential life, I saw Amin as a ventriloquist's doll on the knees of the British army. He was the figure, head to one side, seeking to understand and then repeat his master's voice. . . .

There is a touch of pathos about this aspect of Amin. Former British officers of the KAR who had recruited, promoted and commanded him, spoke to me about him with language that had the whiff of beer, smoke and grape shot of Kipling's Barrack-room Ballads. Idi was 'a good chap'. He was 'a bit thick' – 'a little short of the grey matter, you know'. His strength, his obedience, his pathetic desire to please within patterned grids of behaviour in the flat world of the army made him among the best of a poor lot. . . . Idi was a man of the barracks as well as of the Waters of Yakan.[61]

OFFICERS AND MEN

Iain Grahame first encountered Idi Amin in 1953. He had been given command of number 13 platoon of 'E' Company, and Amin was in another platoon of the same company. Grahame even remembers Amin's service number – N44428 – which is also cited by Jaffar Amin.[62] Although he seldom met *askaris* from other platoons, nevertheless, Grahame wrote: '[i]n any regiment . . . certain individuals soon acquire a degree of fame or notoriety, and it was not long before the deeds of Corporal Idi Amin were coming to my ears'.[63] In fact, Grahame said very little about the later famous corporal in the first book on his KAR days, *Jambo Effendi*, published before Amin's coup. In this, he gives Amin the name 'Saidi' and introduces him during an account of a 1962 operation to disarm ('de-spear') a group of pastoralists in north-east Uganda (Karamoja District). He describes Amin as one of three 'extremely capable'[64] platoon commanders under his command on the operation, 'Saidi, a six-foot four giant from West Nile who had been the heavyweight boxing champion of Uganda for ten years, had been one of the first two Africans from 4 K.A.R. to be given the Queen's Commission in July 1961.'[65]

By 1980, however, in his second book, *Amin and Uganda: A Personal Memoir*, written while Amin was still in power but published shortly after his downfall, the tall boxer has become central to Grahame's memories of his KAR days. In this book, Grahame's account of the period combines events he witnessed and others he heard about, providing both first-person evidence and regimental gossip, truth and fiction, which are indistinguish-ably described, with the vivid detail of a popular novel. This presents consid-erable problems for the researcher, because Grahame is usually treated as a primary source and has been interviewed as such by many, probably most, of the writers on Amin (including me), as well as filmmakers, since the appearance of his 1980 book. As we shall see, he was also consulted by the Foreign Office from time to time during Amin's rule.[66] Grahame undoubt-edly produced, in this second work, the most influential and detailed account of Amin's army life.

The year 1953 was one of rising violence in the British war against the Kenyan insurrection known as Mau Mau. This was the name of an anti-colonial secret society, which became associated by the British with any and all agitation against colonial rule among the Kikuyu people. Unlike Uganda, Kenya had a substantial and privileged white settler minority which (quite correctly) saw its very comfortable existence as being under threat from Mau Mau, and indeed any other expression of African nationalism. The human cost of this conflict is laid out in stark terms in David Anderson's history of the insurrection: between 1952 and 1960 Mau Mau fighters killed 32 white settlers, just under 200 colonial police and soldiers, and more than 1,800 African civilians. The British security forces killed somewhere between 12,000 and 20,000 rebels in combat, imprisoned more than 150,000 Kikuyu people in detention camps, and hanged 1,090 of them for Mau Mau-related crimes; 'many more', Anderson tells us 'than in all the other British colonial emergencies of the post-war period – in Palestine, Malaya, Cyprus and Aden'.[67] Amin's, and Grahame's, KAR Company was heavily involved in this brutal conflict, and many of Amin's 'deeds' that Grahame had heard about happened as part of it. One unfortunate result of the uncovering of the truth about Mau Mau by historians such as Anderson and Elkins was an increased reluctance on the part of ex-KAR officers to speak about their roles in the insurgency, as I found in my interviews with some of them in 2008–10.

The significance of Mau Mau in African history, however, may lie not only in its effects on those involved in the uprising, but also on the soldiers who put it down. Grahame writes, with his habitual sneer at African resist-ance to colonial rule, that 'the Mau Mau phenomenon was not only one of the first manifestations of what so often goes under the guise of "nationalism" in Africa, but also provided the first form of active service experienced by Idi Amin and many of his contemporaries.'[68] He goes on to provide both first- and second-hand examples of these experiences. According to Grahame, on one occasion, towards the end of 1953, Corporal Amin was leading a patrol with three other *askaris* when they came across a group of Mau Mau fighters and ambushed them. Grahame writes that, '[s]ix terrorists were killed and a seventh wounded and captured. ... Five rifles and some important documents were recaptured.'[69] While Grahame says he was not present at this operation, he *was* involved in another the following year, during which his and Amin's patrol killed three men and a woman and, according to Grahame, discovered evidence of 'bestial rites', 'satanic oaths', child sacrifice and cannibalism among the Mau Mau fighters.[70] Both this patrol, which Grahame says he took part in, and the previous one which he only heard about, are described in the same, detailed, pacy manner. I have been unable to find any record of these events in the British archives, but that is not surprising; historians of Mau Mau such as Anderson have commented on the large amount of 'missing' material in the British archives for this period, only some of which has been recovered. However, the Mau Mau events had demonstrated Amin's value to the British military. Grahame blames the atrocities committed by the British forces on the *askaris*, rather than those who gave the orders, writing that 'the Mau Mau campaign, in which no quarter was given nor expected, served to accentuate the innate cruelty and ruthlessness of many of Uganda's northern warriors, none more so than the Nubians'.[71] Characteristically, the extreme violence of the British response to Mau Mau is attributed to the African cruelty of the soldiers, rather than the imperial harshness of their orders.

Just as Angus Shaw's Amin stories often involve testicle twisting, Grahame's repeated trope is to end his anecdotes with the brawny soldier hoisting someone onto his shoulders. One occasion he writes about was a Christmas party, for which a 'local Indian conjuror-cum-contortionist had been hired'.[72] At the climax of his act, the conjuror lay down with a 'huge concrete block' on his chest and invited the members of the audience to come forward and pulverise it with a sledgehammer:

All eyes focused on Sergeant Idi, the acknowledged Atlas of the battalion. Chuckling to himself and cheered on by the spectators, he strode to the fore, rolling up his sleeves and flexing his muscles. A sudden silence descended and everyone's attention focused on the puny, pale brown frame of the Asian. With a mighty heave, Idi hoisted the weapon high above his shoulders, paused momentarily, and brought it down with a resounding thump on the block of concrete. The concrete disintegrated in a shower of chip and grey dust, and we all rushed forward to see what had become of the frail little man. For a moment he lay quite still, eyes cast upwards to where his deity presumably resided, then gradually the eyes rolled round and he began to recover. Idi thereupon dropped the sledgehammer, threw the Asian up onto his shoulders and marched off to the African Sergeants' Mess,[73] where a series of stiff drinks soon restored our intrepid entertainer.

Idi, son of Amin appeared to have a bright future in the King's African Rifles.[74]

Grahame relates this anecdote as a scene at which he had been present, but the same story appears, with slight variations, in Listowel's book published seven years before his. In this, the events take place on the annual regimental sports day, rather than a Christmas party. She describes Amin's encounter with the Asian conjuror as 'borne out by many eyewitnesses',[75] so it is possible that Grahame was one of these, and he may have told her the story in the first place, rather than having appropriated it from her account. Jaffar Amin, who, as we saw in relation to the tales of his father's sporting prowess, says surprisingly little about his father's army days, tells the same story, citing Grahame's version as the source. Is Grahame the origin of the tale of the Asian conjuror, or Listowel? Why does Jaffar not focus more on his father's own stories of KAR life, rather than quoting Grahame's book at such length? Perhaps Idi Amin did not talk much to his sons about his army days. If so, why might this be? In any case, the different, echoing versions of this anecdote exemplify the 'wilderness of mirrors'[76] presented by the literature on Amin, and the near impossibility in this context of distinguishing truth from fiction.

A later anecdote of Grahame's is set during an annual training exercise, which involved the whole company in a 90-mile route march carrying full battle equipment, which had to be completed in 72 hours. The story demonstrates the ambivalent attitude of his British officers to Idi Amin the young soldier, revealing a genuine admiration, always combined with a degree of contempt:

> Throughout that long and painful night, one man was an example and inspiration to us all. As we finally passed the finishing post, Idi Amin was marching beside me at the head of the column, head held high and still singing 'Tufunge safari' ('let us complete the march') for all he was worth. Across one shoulder were two bren guns and over the other was a crippled *askari*. It reminded me of a translation of another KAR marching song:
>
> > It's the Sudi my boy, it's the Sudi,
> > With his grim-set ugly face
> > But he looks like a man and he fights like a man
> > For he comes of a fighting race.[77]
>
> Idi was certainly an outstanding soldier, within the context of that period, and yet his very qualities of leadership and loyalty, brute force and bravery served merely to accentuate the very fragile thread on which the future of Uganda then stood.[78]

Another former KAR officer, John Cleave, gave a similar assessment of Amin's marching abilities. He remembered that:

> Sergeant Major Idi Amin ... did not make much impression on me at the time. He was properly supportive of his platoon commander and carried out orders effectively. He had a raucous sense of humour that was popular with the troops. And for all his bulk, he was very fit. On my second assignment ... it was decided to send out a series of patrols of platoon strength. ... One thing that stands out in my memory of that spell is that although I was in good shape and counted myself a fast and experienced walker, keeping ahead of Idi on the march was no mean feat.[79]

Jaffar Amin has an earlier anecdote, writing that, in 1949–50, the young corporal's unit was sent on a tour of duty to Somalia. On that trip, Amin told his children, he had been mauled by a crocodile but had a lucky escape, getting away with a wound on his ankle, which he would show the family when he recounted the tale, using the formal Kakwa historical story-telling genre known as *Adiyo*, mentioned earlier. Jaffar also says he spoke to another Kakwa soldier who was present at the incident, a retired lieutenant named Musa 'Dimba, who gave a broadly similar version of the tale. 'Dimba also confirmed to Jaffar that Idi Amin had fathered two children in Somalia, a son and a daughter, by different mothers, a story which Amin himself had previously told his son, who had not fully believed it until it was confirmed by 'Dimba. While stationed in the country, according to Jaffar, his father also knew Siad Barre, later president of Somalia, who became an ally of Amin's during the latter's presidency but who, at the time, was 'a policeman in the Italian Somali Police and a good friend to Dad'.[80]

Jaffar goes on to describe another encounter with a future African leader, which he says occurred in Kenya a few years later, during the Mau Mau campaign. This time, his father is said to have saved the life of Jomo Kenyatta, the Kenyan nationalist leader (and also an anthropologist). According to Jaffar Amin, 'Colonial Intelligence' had told the KAR that Kenyatta – being hunted by the British for instigating Mau Mau – was hidden aboard a truck. At a roadblock, Corporal Amin found the future leader of Kenya hiding under some sacks, but told his superiors that there was no one there, covering the fugitive up again. According to Jaffar: 'Later in the 1970s when war almost erupted between Uganda and Kenya after Dad became President of Uganda, Kenyatta quickly cooled and diffused the standoff when Dad revealed that he, Idi Amin, was the Indigenous Sergeant who saved Kenyatta's life during the Mau Mau days.'[81] Jaffar also says that Idi Amin fathered two more children at this time, with Kikuyu mothers. Apparently, he mentioned this on a state visit to Kenya in the 1970s, when he asked after the where-abouts of his children, Njoroge and Njuguna (their genders are not given by Jaffar). Jaffar's account of Amin's early army days thus involve fathering children, and meeting future East African leaders, in both Kenya and Somalia. I have been unable to find any mention of these events elsewhere, which does not necessarily mean they are untrue.

A very different account of Idi Amin's time in the KAR, and of his sexuality, is given in a biography of Robert Fraser, a British art dealer, doyen of 'swinging London' in the 1960s, and flamboyantly promiscuous gay man about town. In his youth in the 1950s Fraser had been a KAR officer, and former colleagues confirmed to his biographer, Harriet Vyner, that he had overlapped with Amin at some point during his army years. The singer Marianne Faithfull, a close friend of Fraser, told Vyner,

> Idi Amin was a sergeant, Robert was a 2nd Lieutenant. Robert had a fling with Amin and spoke about it years later. I didn't actually ask him if Amin was good in bed, but it was obviously an interesting relationship. Probably just a one-night stand. If he'd said he'd had an affair, that would be quite different. He saw Amin for what he would have been at the time – a nice, big, strong – well, I don't know about nice, but a big strong lad in the army, under him, ready for a bit. Robert would blush, look pleased with himself, whenever Amin was on TV.[82]

Fraser certainly served in the KAR in Uganda at the relevant time, but he was also a well-known fantasist and the fact that he told the story to Faithfull (and probably others) does not mean it was true. No other source alludes to Amin being in any way 'bi-curious'. More broadly, Fraser's story makes one wonder how common consensual gay sex, or perhaps sexual assaults on African soldiers, was in the KAR. At the very least, it confirms that British military officers had a lot of tales to tell about Idi Amin Dada, and provides an interesting variation on the usual association of Amin with heterosexual hyper-masculinity.[83]

Summing up his own experience of commanding Amin, Iain Grahame wrote:

> Not only did I admire his devotion to duty, his innate gift of leadership and his endless enthusiasm for whatever military task that we had to perform, but I found him a genuinely likeable person. These feelings, I know, were shared by every other European in the battalion. Like them, I regarded it as an immense tragedy that a man with such outstanding natural qualities should be debarred, through his own very limited educational standards, from ever rising much further in the army. . . . As a platoon commander, however, I found him first class. It was always his unit that had the best esprit, discipline and standards of field training. With the simple methods by which we operated, where the written word

was kept to the minimum and where a natural eye for the ground was more important than the calculation of a grid reference on a map, his low intellect was only a minor handicap.[84]

Grahame was indeed by no means alone in his high estimation of Amin's qualities as a soldier. When even the officers of the KAR began belatedly to realise that the British Empire was not going to continue for ever, the muscular NCO was picked out for advancement. If the regiment *had* to be handed over to African control, Idi Amin was the sort of man who would see to it that at least some of the British military traditions of the regiment would be perpetuated into the postcolonial era. In the late 1950s, Amin went on a series of training courses, and was promoted to warrant officer platoon commander (WOPC) in 1958. According to Grahame, this was 'after I and others had spent every spare minute at our disposal in giving him extra tuition in the three Rs. Although he tried his best, we found it an uphill struggle.' The following year, he was promoted again, to 'Effendi'. This rank was considered the equivalent to the former colonial Indian Army's highest rank for 'native' soldiers, known as a 'Viceroy's Commission' (rather than 'the Queen's Commission', which conferred the substantive rank of officer and was recognised throughout the British military, not just within its colonial outposts). By the end of the 1950s, only two Ugandan soldiers had achieved even this relatively junior position, Idi Amin and a southern Ugandan from the Iteso tribe, named Shaban Opolot (spelt Opoloto in some British accounts). Smith cites a comment by Iain Grahame, from the *Sunday Times* newspaper in the 1970s:

When Independence had first been mentioned, we looked along the ranks of our soldiers and thought [for the first time, it seems] 'who the hell are going to be the officers?'. On recruiting Askaris, we always went for the chaps who were tough and strong and ran quicker than anyone else. It was a terrible mistake. Faced with the prospect of finding African officers, we had a choice between the loyal long-service chaps who were absolutely reliable, but incredibly limited by their lack of intelligence – Idi was a typical example – or newly recruited chaps with slightly more intelligence but absolutely no experience.[85]

A handwritten note preserved in the British archives, dated 18 February 1964, addressed to 'Mrs Chitty' and signed 'JSC' states that: 'Idi Amin is a splendid type and a good rugger player; Opoloto is what my Canadian friends would call a shiffler-shouk [*sic*] – but both are virtually bone from the neck up, and need things explained in words of one letter.'[86]

To sum up, one of the key themes of this chapter is that, by the end of the 1950s, Idi Amin had spent his entire adult life being told what to do by people who firmly believed that he was – genetically, intrinsically and inevitably – stupid. This attitude, based on racial stereotypes such as the myth of the warrior tribes, was pretty much universal among his senior officers. One of them described Amin in 1964, when he was second in command of the Ugandan army, as: 'a splendid man by any standards ... held in great respect and affection by his British colleagues. He is tough and fearless, and in the judgement of everybody a year ago, completely reliable. Against this he is not very bright and will probably find difficulty with the administrative side of command.'[87] In these circumstances, he had perfected, consciously or unconsciously, the persona that so endeared him to his British superiors, that of the bluff, honest, not very intelligent but wholly trustworthy soldier; loyal, brave and strong, with a good sense of humour. If, as I suspect, Amin was by no means stupid, he may well have felt some contempt towards those who thought he was. Whatever his intellectual powers, this image the British had of him was to prove very useful indeed later in Amin's career. Perhaps the ambivalent attitude of his British superiors towards the ambitious young soldier later played a part in Amin's own ambivalence towards the British. Jaffar Amin tells an implausible anecdote, which may sum up, not so much something that actually occurred, as an event that he and perhaps his father both *wanted* to have happened:

It was 1959. Dad had been promoted to the Honorary Rank of Affende [*sic*] – the highest rank awarded to Black African members of the King's African Rifles at the time. On this day, Dad dared to march into the 'Whites Only' Officers' Mess at 1st Battalion, Jinja, after getting tired of moving with a rank that did not hold water. He moved up to the 'Whites Only' Officers' Mess instead of going to the Sergeants' Mess and ordered a drink. When the White bartender told Dad off and 'barked' for him to go to the Sergeants' Mess, Dad grabbed the Bartender by the collar and pulled him straight over the counter. He then let rip with a resounding right to the Englishman's chin, to the hushed silence of the whole room, full of shocked White Officers.[88]

It would be spurious to claim that the KAR, or even the British Empire, was wholly to blame for what Amin later became. Many Africans went through the racist mill of the colonial army without becoming either murderous dictators or extreme parodies of the KAR's own racial stereotypes. But his experiences in the regiment, and the attitudes of his superior officers as recorded here, must have had a deep effect on him, transforming his life and attitudes in ways that his family marvelled at. Beyond this, it is difficult to assess the reliability of memories which emerged only in the light of later events, and tend to project the events of the post-independence era back into the colonial past.

THE CONTAMINATION OF THE PAST BY THE FUTURE

Indeed, a key problem in assessing the published and unpublished material on this period in Amin's life is the contamination of the past – or our knowledge of it – by the future. Most of the material cited here was written quite a while after the events described, and also after Amin had taken power and his iconic evil image was fully formed. People remember things which fit with this, and forget those that do not. We have seen how Grahame's first volume of memoirs, written before Amin's rise to power, barely mentions the big soldier, while his second, written after the 1971 coup (and while Grahame himself was on the way to becoming the British government's go-to expert on Amin) places him right at the centre of Grahame's army experiences. A more overt example of this contamination comes in the memoirs of another former KAR officer, which demonstrate very clearly the way that events which are yet to happen (in this case, the stories of Amin's murderous presidency) lead to the reinterpretation of our memories of earlier ones. J.J. Hespeler-Boultbee, a Canadian officer in the Tanganyika Battalion of the KAR (who developed strongly anti-British views after leaving the regiment), encountered Amin during the Mau Mau operations in Kenya, when different KAR battalions were mixed together and he wound up commanding a platoon of Ugandans. In his 2012 book *Mrs Queen's Chump*, past and future are clearly mixed together:

> Quite by chance, the largest man in the battalion was assigned to me, along with his section of nine men. It was in this manner that I came to be acquainted with Corporal Idi Amin.
>
> It would have been impossible at the time to have assessed what the man was later to become. The thousands he would kill were yet as unimagined as they were destined to become nameless. The thought of feeding to the crocodiles large numbers of those who displeased him, once he became President, would have been an unutterable barbarism even for that coarse moment of colonial mayhem. ... Or so thought those of us who had yet to learn the finer details of Rule Britannia. The acts of violence Idi Amin was shortly to commit were beyond our wildest imaginings.
>
> Death by crocodile? Ye Gods!
>
> For my own part, I was primarily conscious of the man's extraordinary size. Well above six feet and several inches, and proportionately wide, he would fill any doorway absolutely. ... More than that, though, I quickly became aware of his efficiency as a soldier. One would think ... that someone of such generous dimensions would have a voice to match, but ... [h]e was inclined to be soft-spoken, as a matter of fact....
>
> Amin's size alone was sufficient to dominate the soldiers of the platoon, I reckoned. ... On parade he would move among them swiftly, loftily, a word here, a muffled bark there, as he stepped forward to straighten a belt or correct a cap angle. But suddenly our parades took on an improved polish and efficiency. The men stood taller and straighter, somehow, and moved about with greater precision ... they worked better than I had ever seen them work before.[89]

Later, the two men were both in a regimental boxing tournament, and Hespeler-Boultbee gives a colourful description of Amin's sporting appearance:

> Once encamped in Nairobi I was able to take a good look at this jolly giant of a man who always smiled more than he glowered. ... In the ring his oversized feet would be stuffed into a pair of high-sided gym shoes,

no socks, and he would leave the top few lace-holes unthreaded. . . . His boxing trunks were black, our team colour, and he wore no shirt so that one could see at a glance the full size of his belly, torso and arms. Above the waistline his body resembled three black refrigerators laid sideways and stacked one on top of the other. He had no neck that you could discern, but a massive head shoved pugnaciously forward on his shoulders. His arms were the girth of sewage pipes and his fists were packed into gloves that resembled potato sacks. Between the mountainous gluteal muscles that filled his trunks and the shuffling of his sloppy gym shoes, his powerful legs moved back and forth like engine pistons as he stalked about the ring, sure-footed as a leopard. . . .[90]

The Canadian officer seems to have been fascinated by the huge soldier:

We were in awe of the corporal's size. Watching him on the inner side of the ropes was like looking into the cage of a pacing feline. . . . His personal appearance, his bulk, actually repulsed me, a bit like feeling nausea at being given a heaped serving on one's dinner plate. . . . But I was drawn, fascinated, by his boxing. To this day I have yet to see another such enormous person move himself with equal speed. He was far and away the fastest man I have ever seen flashing his way around the inside of a boxing ring. . . . He was like Saint Elmo's fire crackling along the ropes. He carried his enormous bulk from corner to corner with a dancer's skill and balance. The force of his blows would crash through his opponent's guard, sufficient to stop and stun some wild beasts. Direct hits about the head were devastating.[91]

After one workout in the gym, the two soldiers went with others to one of the few bars where blacks and whites could socialise, where they had soft drinks and a conversation which seems to have been recalled in considerable detail by the writer, more than half a century later (while his impersonation of Amin's speaking voice reads very like Alan Coren's parodies in *Punch* magazine):

'What do you think of your chances on Thursday night?', I asked our heavyweight. His laughter rumbled up out of his belly and he showed all of his teeth. 'I don't know who I be fightin' Thursday, but I put him away sure. They other tribes, they just Mau Mau, so I put him away, you see.' 'Come on corporal', I teased him 'you think all other tribes are just Mau Mau?' 'All of them! All but Kakwa, like me!' He laughed and slapped the sides of his ample stomach, then fluttered his hands womanishly under his face. The gesture registered with me because of the extraordinary size of his mitts and the expressiveness of his movement. . . . 'I'm not Kakwa, but I'm not Mau Mau either', I told him, curious as to his reaction. 'No, you're of the English tribe. The English, they the worst Mau Mau of all!' He was still laughing. He liked this play. 'Ah-ha, you are wrong there, Amin', I exclaimed. 'I am not English at all. Like you I am a foreigner fighting an Englishman's war.' His smile faded as he looked at me, 'Why?' He was not amused at me stopping him mid-joke, as it were. For an instant, I thought I could see thunder behind his eyes, a moment of confusion in his demand to know why I should be fighting someone else's war. Then he pushed it away like a toy he did not really want to play with anyway, and his back-slapping joviality returned. 'So we both be foreign Mau Mau fighting the Mau Mau!', he roared jovially, 'You good man, Sah! Very generous. Mrs Queen get good mileage outta you! You be Mrs Queen's Prawn [*sic*].'[92]

Hespeler-Boultbee concludes his memories of Amin:

I met Corporal Idi Amin only a few times after that evening in Nairobi. Many months later, after I had left Kenya, I heard that he was one of the first of the *askaris* of the East African battalions to be selected for officer training at Sandhurst. The news did not surprise me. I had a feeling about him, and remembered him for years afterwards. He had been a good and willing soldier, pleasant-natured and a lively person to be around. Fun, even. But then I started to read about him in the newspapers, how he had become the leader of his country's military forces, and then staged a coup d'état and not long afterwards anointed himself President of Uganda.[93]

Amin's time in the KAR both built the basis of his later career, and formed him as a man. The British Army taught him how to dissemble, how to manipulate people, and how to kill. Unfortunately, very little reliable, contemporary material on his time in the British Army has survived. In particular, as I suggested at the beginning of this chapter, we lack any accounts from other African soldiers, which would have deepened and strengthened the very partial picture provided by the colonial sources. For the young officer's later military career, and its evolution into a more political role, we do have a little more information from African sources, as well as much more British archival material.

3

A RESISTIBLE RISE? 1959-65

The first half of the 1960s was an eventful and pivotal time for Idi Amin. He began the decade as a colonial soldier, and Ugandan independence, which arrived on 9 October 1962, at first changed little in the military life. As the new East African nations gained their independence one by one, their KAR battalions took on new, national names. The Ugandan 4th Battalion, as a new independent national army, reverted to its early colonial designation 'the Uganda Rifles', but it continued to be run by white British officers more or less as before, though there was, of course, an increased push towards 'Africanisation' of the senior ranks. Even the most blinkered and reactionary military officers began to recognise the inevitability, if not always the desirability, of the need to develop African national armies, and quite a few, like Iain Grahame, retired rather than take part in this decolonisation. But the Mau Mau uprising had contributed to a major shift in British opinion and policies towards Africa. Many members of the British ruling class had family and friends among the Kenyan settlers, and their views on the need for a new, post-imperial policy towards Africa were heavily influenced by the Kenyan conflict of the early 1950s. As Lord Carver, former head of the British Army, said in 1980, Mau Mau 'had a profound effect in persuading Conservative political figures in Britain to bow to the wind of change in Africa':[1] the allusion is to Prime Minister Harold Macmillan's famous 1960 speech heralding (or accepting) the end of empire.

For Idi Amin, however, independence brought little immediate change to his position and role. The army was not the only branch of the state to remain, for a while, more or less as it had been under colonial rule. Many other aspects of Ugandan life also continued to be run by white officials after independence, including the police, the legal system and most of the economic infrastructure (roads, rail, posts and telecommunications). Formal economic activity, from commercial agriculture to retail sales, where it was not British-controlled, was almost entirely in the hands of 'Indians' (that is, people of South Asian descent). This initial lack of change on the ground was not unusual in the decolonisation process; it takes time to shift a behemoth. As the Kenyan scholar Simon Gikandi wrote: 'decolonised situations are marked by the trace of the imperial pasts they try to disavow'.[2] This chapter will consider the years both immediately before and after the 'moment' of *Uhuru* (freedom/Independence), without a chapter break as the conventional signal of a shift from colonialism to independence.

Gradually, over the first half of the 1960s, Amin rose from being a very junior officer under British rule to become the powerful head of independent Uganda's armed forces. His role became increasingly political rather than military, as he was more and more embroiled in the lively and often acrimonious politics of post-independence Uganda. His career became increasingly a matter of public record, and we are less reliant on partisan witnesses looking back over decades, or journalistic speculation. Amin, in other words, now enters 'history', in the sense that he enters the archive. The 'public record' is not, of course, an objective, neutral arbiter whose word can be taken for truth. The British and Ugandan civil servants whose prose sits in the archives at Kew Gardens and Entebbe produced, as I have already suggested, a deep seam of opinion, guesswork and bias, as well as registering things that actually happened. As we saw in the previous chapter, historians looking for missing Mau Mau files found that an unknown but large number of official documents had 'disappeared' before the files were handed over to the UK Public Record Office (now the National Archives). Some intelligence-related documents from the period, and some that might embarrass living people, are still withheld from public access (although it is now possible to challenge this legally),[3] and sometimes files are found to have been hidden away in obscure and unlikely places. Despite all these gaps and suppressed evidence, however, the official record does provide a different dimension from the accounts we have been looking at so far. Its big advantage over other sources of material on Amin is not that the archives provide unbiased, objective evidence, but that they are less tainted with hindsight: they are *contemporary* documents: reports, letters and memos.

From now on, I will be using such material, together with the published work of historians (including Ugandan historians), to a much greater extent than I have been able to do so far in this book. I should say that my account of Ugandan political history, in this and the next three chapters, is necessarily partial and incomplete. Post-independence Ugandan politics was very complex; Ugandans were sometimes divided on ethnic lines (particularly 'northerners' vs 'southerners'), sometimes along religious ones (Catholics vs Protestants), and sometimes on class alignments (traditional tribal aristocrats vs a growing bourgeoisie). Usually it was a combination of all these factors. Much of the complexity cannot be fully untangled here; this is not a history of Uganda but a biography of Idi Amin, and the reader will have to be content with the broader political/historical context as a vague shape in the background.

'AFRICANISATION' AND THE KAR

The historian Timothy Parsons has suggested that 'the King's African Rifles was woefully unprepared for the transition to independence. Before Prime Minister Harold Macmillan signalled Britain's intention to withdraw from Africa in his famous "winds of change" speech in 1960, military authorities had little inkling that the colonial era in East Africa would soon draw to a close.'[4] It may seem strange that the leaders of the colonial army were unaware of what seemed fairly obvious to many people back in Britain, including many who were far less concerned with African affairs than the KAR commanders. No doubt wishful thinking played a part, as did a lack of interest in what was happening in African political circles. The British government had set up a consultative 'Legislative Council' for Ugandan leaders in the 1950s, but the southern kingdoms had long had a degree of autonomy and the Buganda kingdom, especially, had a complex political culture, with political parties split largely along religious lines, mostly Catholic versus Protestant, with the bulk of the aristocracy in the latter camp. National politics, too, was very concerned with the future role of the Kabaka, in an independent Uganda that would be considerably larger than his historical kingdom. As Parsons summarises the situation, '[f]aced with the prospect of sharing power with their less-prosperous northern neighbours, the Ganda tried to ensure that their autonomy would continue into the post-colonial era. As a result the anti-colonial movement in Uganda was fractured and contentious.'[5] Writing while the independence negotiations were coming to their conclusion, the American political scientist and historian of the Baganda, David Apter, wrote that '[t]he way is now paved for Uganda's final steps towards independence, and it is up to the Baganda to choose whether or not, by their continued intransigence, they will continue to retard the pace or, further, promote internal difficulty.'[6] This problem would continue to dominate Ugandan public life long after formal independence was achieved.

The first significant African political organisation in Uganda was the Uganda National Congress (UNC), which, in the 1950s, brought together various Ganda political factions, but was not representative of the wider country. Partly as a result of these political debates, however, the Kabaka was deported by the British in 1953 (to be welcomed back to a newly independent Uganda in 1962). The UNC effectively collapsed in 1955 but its remnants, under different names, continued to dominate the colonial (advisory) Legislative Council. In 1958, Apolo Milton Obote, a leftist former Kenyan trade union official originally from Uganda's Lango area, became a Congress member of the 'Legco'. The Langi were (culturally and geographically) close to the Acholi, and had been fairly well represented in the army, though not so numerous among the *askaris* as the Acholi and the various West Nile tribes. Obote went on to form the Uganda Peoples' Congress (UPC) in 1960, taking over the remnants of the UNC together with a splinter group named the Uganda Peoples' Union. Obote, in Parsons' words, 'became increasingly committed to ensuring that Uganda achieved independence as a unitary centralised state',[7] with minimal autonomy for the Baganda.

The British, too, despite the powerful attraction many of the colonial officials had towards the Baganda aristocracy, were keen to prevent the different countries they had demarcated across East Africa from disintegrating along their ethnic fault lines. In Uganda, however, the Ganda dominated the national political scene. In 1959, their leaders made a crucial mistake in withdrawing from the committee established to plan for independence, due to the British refusal to guarantee either political autonomy to Buganda, or the Kabaka's primary authority within his kingdom. In 1960, the political leadership tried to declare Buganda an independent state, but were unable to sustain the move. The following year, Baganda leaders boycotted the national elections, held to establish internal self-government as a stage towards full independence. This absence of the Protestant aristocrats from the political scene facilitated the rise of the Democratic Party (DP) led by Benedicto Kiwanuka, a Catholic who did not come from the traditional Ganda aristocracy. In 1961, the DP formed Uganda's first African 'government' which had, in reality, very limited powers. The Protestant elite, realising their error in withdrawing from the transition bodies, formed a new monarchist party called 'Kabaka Yekka' or 'KY' (translated as 'the Kabaka Alone'). To resist the growing influence of the DP, the monarchist KY came to a deal with Obote's leftist UPC, and together they won the 1962 elections under Obote's leadership.[8] These were supposed to lead into full independence. Under the deal with Obote, the KY got federal status for Buganda and four other southern Ugandan kingdoms, and the UPC formed the government, with the Kabaka, Mutesa II, as a largely ceremonial president to Obote's executive prime minister.

Within the army, change was a lot slower in coming than in the political system. As the countries of East Africa gained independence one by one, the KAR was formally dissolved into its individual national components, with the 4th Battalion becoming the Uganda Army. It was entirely characteristic of 4KAR to respond to the political changes by reaching back to the past, reverting to its pre-KAR name, 'the Uganda Rifles'. Many of the white officers found the changes difficult to accept, and took a long time to grasp the implications of the Africanisation programme. Some only seem to have realised what independence would inevitably mean for the army when it actually occurred. One KAR officer (very unusually of Asian origin) told researchers for a 1979 Oxford University research project on KAR history that '[i]t became obvious in 1962 that only black Africans had good prospects in the new army and so in 1964 with great regret I transferred to the Royal Engineers.'[9] In later life, many ex-officers thought a major mistake was made by not accepting Africanisation much earlier. One senior officer told the Oxford research project:

I think that most of us in the battalion felt that Africanisation should have started as soon as the war ended. If less reliance had been placed on

British WOs [warrant officers] and NCOs in the succeeding years, and Africans had been given more responsibility, there would have been firmer foundation of knowledge and experience when Independence was imminent. ... In the end, it was left too late and had to be done too quickly. Nevertheless, in the light of subsequent events in Uganda, it would have made little difference, except that Idi Amin might have been more senior at Independence, and come to power sooner![10]

Another opined to the Oxford researchers that:

Africanisation should have been started on a low key much earlier, eg, at the end of the 1939–45 war. Instead we had a 'crash programme' almost coinciding with the notorious 'wind of change' speech made by the then Prime Minister. ...

I think the failure of Africanisation of the K.A.R. in Uganda resulted from the excessive speed with which it was carried out for reasons of political expediency. Any African with personality and intelligence saw that the road to wealth and power was through politics. Obote and his successor Amin prove this point, and neither they nor any other African would be particularly scrupulous in their methods.[11]

Idi Amin, together with his comrade and rival, Shaban Opolot, were finally given the Queen's Commission in August 1961, both becoming lieutenants. At independence the following year, the two were still the only trained Ugandan officers in the army (others were going through training at the Sandhurst military academy). On the very eve of the independence ceremonies, however, Idi Amin dramatically sailed into public view, as controversy arose over a military 'incident' in Kenya (nothing to do with Mau Mau). Of all the deaths laid at Idi Amin's door over the years, this is the only example we have in which his actions were thoroughly investigated and tried in a court. In addition, it was followed some years later by a secret Foreign Office report which carefully laid out the evidence for his part in the killings, based on the court records, official files, and interviews with several of the participants. As such, it is well worth looking at 'the Turkana incident' in some detail.

OPERATION UTAH AND THE 'TURKANA INCIDENT'

Although most of the popular books on Amin cover his activities in the anti-Mau Mau campaign, about which very little is really known, the most controversial incident he was involved in (as far as we know from the archives) came as part of a more everyday activity on the part of the colonial forces – an anti-cattle-rustling operation among pastoralist peoples in the north-west of Kenya. In the first week of March 1962, just seven months before independence, Lieutenant Amin and his platoon were carrying out a routine operation to disarm some pastoralist herders from the Ngwatella section of the Turkana tribe. For two years, the Kenyan Turkana, using some 800 rifles they had acquired from an earlier conflict with another (Ethiopian) tribe, had been raiding the Ugandan Dodoth people across the border. According to a later British report, 'from the beginning of 1960 to the end of January 1962 124 Dodoth, 118 Turkana and 51 others were killed in 157 separate incidents. Over 20,000 cattle were reported stolen. The security forces killed 63 of the 118 Turkana who died.'[12] Members of the Ugandan Legislative Council criticised the Kenyan authorities for failing to stop the raids and on 14 February the Kenyan provincial commissioner 'ordered the arrest of all the Ngwatella, the seizure of their property and their detention in safe custody'. 'Operation Utah', as it was known to the British, was a cross-border action involving both Kenyan (5KAR) and Ugandan (4KAR) colonial forces. As such, the later enquiry found, '[i]t was approved by the Treasury and Colonial Office and the Secretary of State, Mr Sandys, took a close interest in the incident'.[13] The order only covered the Ngwatella section, but 'the KAR were unable to tell them apart from other Turkana'.[14]

The later Foreign Office report, titled 'Operation Utah: Incident involving Lieutenant Idi Amin', was attributed to 'Africa Section, Research Department' (no named author), classified as 'Secret', and dated 25 March 1977. It was produced to brief the Foreign Office minister who had to respond to a parliamentary question from Lord Bruce of Donington, though the latter was given a very selective summary of the full report.[15] The report found that Lt Col. Hartley of 5KAR, the military commander of the operation, had interpreted the provincial commissioner's order in a way that 'exceeded what was necessary'. His own order had instructed the military, 'that his Units should arrest all the Ngwatella they could find and to place them in thorn enclosures (*Zarebas*). They were then to subject the men to "the imposition of pressure" in order to persuade them to surrender their arms. They were to be kept out in the burning sun and deprived of water for up to 48 hours to make them reveal where their rifles were hidden'. The Foreign Office report states that:

> Colonel Hartley stood by these orders in Court but an army doctor said that he would have advised against them as even the hardened Turkana might die after a week of this torture. There was much criticism of Col. Hartley's orders. Even Amin said that they were unprecedented though Major Rogers [Commander of 4KAR] thought that they had been used against the Turkana before.... It was alleged at the inquest that the phrase about the 'imposition of pressure' was simplified into 'catch the Turkana, bring them here, beat them' by Amin.[16]

The author of the 1977 report points out that the KiSwahili verb '*piga*', used by Amin, can mean *both* 'to pressure', and 'to beat'.

Operation Utah began on 20 February, and after a week, according to the report, Amin's platoon had rounded up 231 Turkana men, 313 women, 450 children and many cattle, and were holding them in a place named Loputhke. The later enquiry describes what happened, giving a vivid picture of what such punitive expeditions involved, even with independence looming very close:

> The men were put in a zareba of only 450 square feet which although it never held more than 183 men at any one time meant that they would have had to stand or lie on top of one another. Sometimes they were forced to lie on their backs staring up into the sun. They had no shade and were under intense heat. But Lt. Col. Hartley and Major Rogers who visited Loputhke several times did not question these arrangements and Hartley confirmed that they were in accord with his wishes.... Amin had his tent under the tree where also sat the Bren-gunner who guarded the Zareba. The women and children supplied the men with limited food and water twice a day. The Turkana headman commented afterwards that 'this was not a system to collect rifles but to kill men'. Only 7 rifles were surrendered by the Turkana ...[17]

The later Foreign Office report concludes that 'although much of the responsibility for the ill-treatment of the Turkana captives therefore lay with Lt. Col. Hartley Amin seems to have been responsible for the beating and kicking which actually caused the deaths of at least four of the 5 men [who were killed]'. Following complaints by Turkana leaders, on 9 April the acting Governor General of Kenya told the governor of Uganda and the secretary of state in London about the complaints, writing of 'allegations that deaths had resulted from beatings ordered by an African officer (Amin)'. The involvement of the Foreign Office at such an early stage shows how politically sensitive the affair had become, in the light of imminent independence for both countries, and the report states that 'the Secretary of State asked to be kept "very closely informed" and in particular wished to be consulted before any public announcement was made'. A row broke out between the British governors of Uganda and Kenya, the former was '"indignant" about the allegations', the latter 'continued to resist all attempts to have Uganda involved in the investigation'.[18]

The bodies of the five men were exhumed and an inquest was conducted by a (white) Kenyan magistrate, who 'found on 17 October 1962 that four of the five Turkana had died from the use of illegal force by unknown members of the 7th Platoon and that an offence had been committed by some person or persons unknown among the members of the 7th Platoon'. This was reviewed by the Attorney General, who decided there were insufficient grounds to press charges. On 27 October, the Ugandan government issued a statement from the Ministry of Internal Affairs 'deploring the use of illegal force by a soldier or soldiers of the 7th Platoon, C Company, 4th Battalion, King's African Rifles'. The statement suggested that a further military enquiry was being instituted to establish whether charges could be laid against anybody, but 'No action was however in the end taken against Lt. Amin and it appears that the Ugandan authorities felt that the findings of the inquest in Kenya would have prejudiced his chances of a fair trial.'[19]

In fact, the Kenyan inquest had itself been fixed in advance. According to the Foreign Office report:

20. The Attorney General first minuted to the Governor on 5 May criticising Lt. Col. Hartley's operation orders. He pointed out that the beatings (112 were beaten in all) ceased when Amin left Loputhke.

But he suggested that there would be insufficient evidence to bring charges of murder or manslaughter. Mr Webb [the Kenyan Attorney General] . . . also referred to the extreme unreliability of the Turkana whom he described as being of low intelligence and negligible memory. He thought that their evidence was unlikely to stand up in court. . . . He noted that the incident had caused considerable concern to the Governor of Uganda and the GOC [General Officer Commanding] East Africa. . . . But he thought that an inquest should be held 'in order to obviate any suggestion that the matter is being hushed up'.

21. On 2 August 1962 the Attorney General minuted to the Governor that the Magistrate (Kneller) had decided to hold an inquest. He continued 'I have seen Kneller and have put him in the picture as to the background of this operation and of the possible implications of the result of any findings he might make. I am certain that we can rely on his discretion. I think it is probable that he will find that the dead Turkana died from shock caused by multiple acts of minor violence; but I am confident that he will not be able to attach any criminal liability of any particular person.'[20]

The 1977 Foreign Office briefing notes that this was written before the hearings had even begun. When they were over, the author writes dryly, '[t]he Attorney General's prediction had been fulfilled'. The verdict was 'politically convenient for Uganda, which . . . became independent on 9 October 1962'. The report goes on to suggest that 'had the Magistrate not been briefed as to his verdict beforehand one may speculate that his findings might have been more definite. The Attorney General reported . . . how "the military witnesses were all most unimpressive and were clearly lying". . . . On 8 September Mr Webb reported how "the Turkana witnesses turned out to be very much better than expected". For a few days it seemed as though there might be a verdict against at least some soldiers, but it is clear from the 1977 report that the fix was in.

The 'persons unknown' verdict was aided by problems with witness identification of the 'effective' culprits, that is, the soldiers who actually carried out the beatings, rather than Hartley and Amin, who ordered them. This was perhaps unsurprising, given the nature of the identification parade: 'The

Turkana ... had to wait from March until June before seeing the suspects and then only among the 250 men who were paraded in Jinja.' Moreover, the magistrate's report also pointed to 'a particular soldier, Lance Corporal Eugenio, as being especially involved in the killings. But Eugenio was hirsute at Loputhke and clean shaven by June and Amin swore that he had not shaved. His distinctively prominent teeth were still apparent however.' According to the report, Amin's own evidence 'was shown up and he made a bad impression. The vagueness of some of the Turkana witnesses no doubt helped to save him and the Kenyan Police Officer explained that this was understandable in view of the conditions they had suffered at the time'. The officer seems to be suggesting that, *because* the Turkana prisoners had been tortured by the British forces, they were therefore too traumatised to be reliable witnesses to the torture. The report concludes that 'Amin was fortunate that his platoon's captives were so primitive and in such an exhausted state but they did not prove as primitive as had been expected by the Attorney General.'[21]

One of the key points about the case, so far as the British Foreign Office was concerned fifteen years later, was that Uganda had become independent while these enquiries were going on. Many in the Foreign Office and elsewhere apparently thought later that Milton Obote must have intervened to prevent one of Uganda's only two commissioned military officers being arraigned for murder. In 1975, the London *Evening Standard* alleged a cover-up by the UK authorities, and this article led to questions being asked in parliament, which is what triggered the 1977 Foreign Office report I have quoted here. On the Ugandan attitude, the report found that:

The Uganda Government issued a statement on 27 October [18 days after independence] deploring the use of force by a soldier or soldiers.... The Commander of the Uganda Rifles [Colonel Cheyne] was therefore 'personally instituting a further military enquiry'. ... Nothing much seems to have happened subsequently.... However, according to the then Second Secretary [in the Foreign Office], Mr Martin Reith, the enquiry foundered because although Amin was clearly guilty the proceedings in Kenya were held to have prejudiced his case.... [I]t seems likely that it was this rather than any pressure from Obote on the Governor General which saved Amin from prosecution.[22]

Concern about the case was even expressed in London. Two years before these events, a major controversy had broken out in the British parliament over the beating to death of eleven Mau Mau prisoners in the notorious 'Hola Camp' in 1956. This scandal has been described by David Anderson as 'the decisive event in Kenya's path to independence'.[23] The last thing the British authorities in Nairobi and London wanted in the year of Uganda's independence was a repeat, thanks to Lieutenant Amin, of the public condemnation that followed the uncovering of the Hola affair. The young Kakwa officer had now stirred things up as far away as Westminster and Whitehall. The 1977 report states:

> The Secretary of State [Duncan Sandys] was clearly worried about the case throughout. . . . Mr Sandys clearly did not want another Hola scandal which had done so much to sway British opinion against the Colonial authorities in Kenya. . . . Lt. Col. Hartley's orders gave particular cause for concern should the press seize on them. Mr Sandys seriously considered whether to order a further enquiry. But eventually he merely told the Governor and the Attorney General, who were visiting London in November 1962, that nothing similar must happen again and that the military must draft their orders more clearly.[24]

The report's conclusion summarises the evidence in a balanced, lawyerly manner but, unsurprisingly, it focuses largely on Idi Amin's part in the affair. Lt Col. Hartley is never even mentioned by name, though his role is implicitly singled out for condemnation. The report was, after all, commissioned specifically to look at Idi Amin's role, and was written while he was still in power in Uganda, at a time when his relationship with the British was probably at its lowest point. It concludes:

> Amin seems to have escaped prosecution because the Kenyan authorities did not wish him to be named and yet by holding an inquest which produced findings which prejudiced his chances of a fair trial prevented any further action being taken in Uganda. . . . Amin was lucky in that his victims were primitive people without political friends, that he was engaged in an operation in another territory on behalf of his own territory and that he was needed for the new Uganda army. But most of all he

was fortunate in that his superiors who were British officers were responsible for the orders to place the Turkana in a small enclosure under a burning sun and to 'impose pressure' on them to reveal the whereabouts of illegal arms. . . . For the present purposes it is perhaps fortunate that responsibility can be laid upon the Ugandan Government for the final decision, for a fuller investigation of the Kenyan side of the affair might well show that there was a cover up and that Colonial servants were correct in their assumption about the role of the army in the affair.[25]

The 1977 Foreign Office report provides the only detailed, evidence-based legal examination of any of Amin's killings. Some observations which spring to mind on reading it include:

- The report is saturated with British racial attitudes (for example regarding the 'primitive' nature of the Turkana herders) on the part of most of the people quoted, including both the colonial legal authorities in Kenya and the KAR military officers, as well as the writer of the report him/herself.
- There is clear proof, accepted by the Foreign Office in the report, that there was a cover-up in which the magistrate was, in effect, instructed in advance by the Attorney General of Kenya what verdicts to bring in.
- There is also convincing evidence, again explicitly accepted by the Foreign Office, that the KAR officers (including Amin) were extensively lying to the magistrate.
- Amin's role in the massacre seems to have been restricted to interpreting and transmitting Lt Col. Hartley's (at best) ambiguous orders.
- Despite the ambiguities in phrasing, Hartley himself confirmed that he had explicitly ordered the prisoners to be subject to what most people at the time (European as well as African) clearly considered to be excessive violence and torture.
- The actual blows that killed the five men seem to have been delivered by junior African *askaris*, especially Lance Corporal Eugenio.
- Despite the ambiguities of its conclusion, the report seems, quite rightly, to blame his superiors at least as much as Amin himself.

Idi Amin was clearly one of those responsible for the violence at Loputhke, but he does not seem to have carried out the beatings personally, nor was he the source of the orders to treat the Turkana in this way. There is no evidence of any sadistic personal pleasure from inflicting pain, and no reference to any previous killings involving Amin, for example the Mau Mau deaths described (and in one case apparently witnessed) by Iain Grahame. On the evidence, he seems merely to have sat in his tent and encouraged the troops to beat up the herders as instructed. He may well also have ordered specific acts of criminal violence by Eugenio and others, but we do not have any proof of this, largely due to the 'clearly lying' military evidence at the inquest. It *is* certain that Amin was present when the lethal beatings were carried out, and in charge of the platoon at the time, so in military terms he was probably responsible for how the orders were interpreted. However, both Lt Col. Hartley, who had given the order to apply 'pressure' or 'beatings', and Major Roberts, Amin's own senior officer, had visited the camp and clearly approved of what was going on there.

If Operation Utah demonstrated Amin's ruthlessness and lack of moral scruples, it showed precisely the same attributes on the part of his British superior officers. As we have seen, 118 Turkana people 'died' in Operation Utah as a whole, at least 63 of them killed by the security forces. In this context, the five men who were tortured to death at Loputhke might have been considered something of a side issue. However, if the story had come out, the other 113 deaths might have been looked at more closely. This is only conjecture, but it is obvious from the documents that the main concern of the authorities was not the legality or morality of the KAR's actions, but the political consequences of information about them getting to the British public. The minister of state, Lord Goronwy Roberts, concluded his letter to Lord Bruce, which very selectively summarised what the Foreign Office knew about Operation Utah:[26] 'Historians will of course pass their own judgement on all this. In the light of hindsight we might have acted differently. However the important point is to face up to the problems of the present day as best we can.'[27] This might be paraphrased as, 'nothing to see here; move along'.

THE ARMY AFTER INDEPENDENCE

As Uganda's independence ceremonies and celebrations went on, Lieutenant Amin must have worried that his meteoric career might be about to come to an end. Would he have to face a full enquiry into the Turkana incident, probably to be followed by disciplinary action? Would his British commanders leave him to take the rap, or continue the cover-up? Would the politics of independence, and the will of Obote, work to help or destroy him? As the conclusion of the 1977 Foreign Office report suggests, he was lucky on all of these points. Eighteen days after independence, an enquiry was announced but, as we have seen, it never happened. Amin resumed his steady rise through the ranks, in what was to become an increasingly fast-changing army: he was promoted to major in November 1963. However, he had increasingly to deal with a powerful new factor that had entered his military world: Ugandan national politics. According to Kenneth Ingham, the devoted biographer of Milton Obote, the latter had paid little attention to the army until independence was imminent. Ingham's account of the Africanisation process stresses Obote's efforts to speed up the process:

A number of senior warrant officers and NCOs were given a cursory training course and promoted to the rank of *effendi*. This did not put them on a par with British officers, nor were they ideal material for officer rank. Not surprisingly, this intermediate status did not satisfy the ambitions of the men involved, and Obote considered it a thoroughly unsatisfactory expedient. After independence he made urgent arrangements for younger, better educated recruits [i.e. from southern tribes] to be sent, belatedly, to the Royal Military Academy Sandhurst for full officer training. As an interim measure some of the *effendi* were given commissioned rank. The two most senior of them were ... Shaban Opolot [who] hailed from Teso District in the Eastern Province, but was married to the daughter of a former chief minister of Buganda. The second, Idi Amin, a Kakwa from the extreme north west of Uganda, had been a popular figure in the army as a champion heavyweight boxer. Neither, least of all Amin, had any serious educational qualifications, and their promotion was an act of expediency rather than of sound judgement.[28]

As usual, Ingham suggests that Obote's intentions were pure,[29] but Timothy Parsons believes the prime minister's motivations were more complex and manipulative than that. He argues convincingly that:

Milton Obote came to power in Uganda as the head of a coalition government. The Uganda Peoples' Congress was more of an amalgam of self-interested local branches than a popular national movement....Although it is by no means certain that he intended to use the Uganda Rifles to seize sole control of the government, the army had become an important base of patronage and influence in the first year of independence. Obote's continued reliance on apolitical expatriate British officers to run his army, as opposed to politically suspect southern Bantu-speaking African officers, ensured he could rely on the military to follow his orders. Yet the continued British presence in the country antagonised both Obote's political critics and the rank and file Askaris.[30]

In the months following independence and over the course of 1963, dissatisfaction within the army became increasingly apparent to both the military authorities and the Ugandan government. The continuing dominance of British officers was obviously part of this, but another factor was what Ingham calls 'the low level of pay for all African ranks'.[31] The Africanisation programme continued to grind slowly on, but many in Obote's government, particularly interior minister Felix Onama who was responsible for the army, wanted it to go faster. As Parsons puts it, 'the political debate over the rate of Africanization represented a struggle for the control of the Ugandan military'.[32] Two issues particularly rankled the government; Uganda lacked an air force, and they wanted a second battalion for the Uganda Rifles. The latter was easily agreed by the British, though it took some time to implement, but the former was something they were very reluctant to fund.

A potential solution to both issues presented itself; Golda Meir's Israeli government was prepared to train Ugandan pilots, sell planes cheaply, and train army officers for the second battalion.[33] Twenty officers were quickly sent to Israel, but the British officer in charge of the Uganda Rifles, Colonel (later Brigadier) J.M.A. Tillet, inconveniently refused to commission them on their return. Parsons says 'As they stood forlornly on the tarmac of Kampala's airport wearing Israeli uniforms, the *Uganda Argus* quoted one cadet as complaining: "We don't know what is going to happen to us.'"[34] Officially, the British at first welcomed, or at least tolerated, the increasing Israeli presence. According to a British High Commission report to London:

'Four Israeli Officers had been introduced into the Uganda Army during 1963 to help with the training of the 2nd Battalion. They had cooperated willingly with the British officers and, having limited functions, had not conflicted with the activities of the British personnel.'[35] Private memos, however, suggest a growing distrust between the British civil and military authorities and the Uganda government. As we will see later, the British suspected, with some justice, that Obote was trying to play the Israelis off against themselves for the supply of arms, ammunition and training facilities. It is worth noting that, in the arguments over training new southern officers, the British and Idi Amin found themselves very much on the same side, defending the traditional northern recruitment and promotion patterns.

THE 1964 MUTINIES

What finally ended this situation was not so much the growing Israeli presence in the army (though that certainly irritated the British), but a series of events across East Africa in early 1964, which were to have a lasting effect on the politics of the whole region, and indeed facilitated Amin's rise to power. Unsurprisingly, discontent with the continuities between post-independence military structures and the previous colonial ones, had been simmering, not just in the Ugandan army but also its counterparts in Kenya and Tanzania. In the last week of January 1964, this boiled over into outright revolt across the region. The American historian of the 1964 army mutinies, Timothy Parsons, summed up their immediate effects:

[B]oth Great Britain and the East African nations viewed the barracks protests as a serious crisis. Headlines and editorials in the local and inter-national press carried dire warnings that the military unrest would lead to widespread anarchy. In the United States, the cover of *Life* magazine showed a British marine rounding up surrendering Tanganyikan Askaris. Most of the alarm stemmed from the fact that the soldiers' mass insubor-dination threatened the peaceful transfer of power in East Africa. The widespread military unrest shook the foundations of civil authority in the region and sparked a crisis of confidence in Great Britain and the new African governments....

The seemingly coordinated nature of the unrest in each country led contemporary observers on both ends of the ideological spectrum to suspect a plot. British officers and diplomats were sure that communist agents had provoked the Askaris to discredit the expatriate officers still serving in command positions in the East African armies, thereby ending Britain's influence in the region.[36]

The mutinies began in Tanganyika, which had been independent since 1961 and whose population was becoming increasingly radicalised because so little had changed since *Uhuru*. Intellectuals espoused revolutionary, socialist or even communist ideas, as well as African nationalist ones. The bulk of the population, whose expectations of economic gains from independence were unsatisfied, became more and more discontented. On 12 January 1964, President Nyerere sent the bulk of the Tanganyika police to quell an uprising on the neighbouring island of Zanzibar[37] and 'a handful'[38] of *askaris* in the Tanganyikan Rifles took the opportunity to declare a strike. On 20 January, they imprisoned their British and African officers and seized government buildings in Dar es-Salaam. Some of the poorer citizens began to attack the Indians and Arabs who ran most of the country's commerce. In the absence of police, Nyerere and his government were unable to do anything but come to an urgent deal with the soldiers, granting big pay rises and the expulsion of British officers.

The Tanganyikan mutineers quickly returned to their barracks, but not before inspiring their counterparts in Kenya and Uganda, where insubordination broke out within the week. Colonel Tillet was warned that the unrest might spread, and immediately called for a speeded-up Africanisation of the Uganda Army. Obote cut transport links with Tanganyika and sent the police to take over key military sites. Parsons, stressing a relative lack of information on the Ugandan aspect of the mutiny, writes that: '[I]t is clear that Ugandan askaris began to plan their own protest immediately after learning of the pay increases won by their counterparts in Tanganyika. Once again, British officials interpreted the timing of their actions as evidence of a larger plot.'[39] Parsons suggests that the real reason was that *askaris* from all three countries were using the military radio network to communicate with each other: 'Signals Sergeants provided the coordination that officers and politicians suspected was the result of a carefully planned conspiracy.'[40]

On 22 January, the Uganda government promised to raise army pay but did not indicate when. At the main barracks in Jinja, the *askaris* began to protest and the officers called *barazas* (public meetings of the troops) to explain the proposals. At the *baraza* for the 1st Battalion headquarters:

> When Major Campbell, the company commander, produced a letter from Entebbe promising a pay rise, the men did not believe him. Private Orsino asked Campbell: 'Why are you asking me to salute you, this is not your country?' ... [T]he men declared they would not listen to Campbell because he earned over sh.1,000 [Uganda Shillings] a month. Unlike in Tanganyika, however, the African soldiery did not round up and expel their British officers. They simply ignored them.[41]

At the subsequent courts martial, according to Parsons, it was stated that most of the sergeants had stayed loyal while the mutineers were almost entirely privates and corporals. Interior minister Felix Onama came to meet the soldiers, and was force-fed the *posho* (boiled corn meal) they had to eat every day, while his police escort was beaten up and the *askaris* took turns to drive his official Mercedes around the camp. Obote responded by sending those regiments who were not involved to the far north-east of the country to keep them away from mutinous contagion. By this time, the British had massed some 500 Royal Marine Commandos on an aircraft carrier off Tanganyika, and flown a battalion of Scots Guards to Nairobi, in case of serious unrest across the region.

On 24 January, the new Ugandan minister for regional affairs, Cuthbert Obwangor, went to meet the soldiers in Jinja Barracks. By now, they had added a demand for all British officers and NCOs to withdraw from the Ugandan army. According to Kenneth Ingham's account: 'After Obwangor's departure, the situation became tense until Major Idi Amin ... persuaded the troops to disperse to their billets.'[42] Obote was forced to request British military assistance:

> British military authorities in Nairobi sprang into action as soon as they received Obote's formal appeal for aid. At 10.45pm on 23 January, just two hours after Obote made his request official, seven cargo planes carrying the four-hundred-man 1st Battalion of the Staffordshire regiment and a

company of the 2nd Battalion of the Scots Guards landed at Entebbe's airport. . . . The Staffordshires' commander had instructions that simply read 'Your task is to assist the Ugandan government to maintain internal security.'[43]

The British troops first secured the airport and important sites in Kampala; Obote then ordered them to retake the Jinja military base. They raided before dawn on 25 January, surprising the *askaris* and taking over without opposition. Amin himself had conveniently been away in northern Uganda on a 'recruitment safari', but he returned on 26 January when, according to Ingham, 'Major Amin . . . called on Obote and presented the demands of the soldiers. Obote agreed to the pay increases and to the phased withdrawal of British officers and NCOs. . . . He also decided to appoint Amin commander of the battalion stationed in Jinja.'[44] According to his son, Jaffar, Amin was instrumental in ending the strike: 'Dad . . . helped calm things down, restored order and he was held in high esteem. Massive increase in pay, spring beds instead of wooden ones were the concessions won by the soldiers. . . . Dad's promotion to the rank of Lieutenant Colonel in 1964 after he successfully stopped a mutiny in progress was purely on merit. It was because of his work related to stopping the mutiny that he was promoted to that rank.'[45]

In fact, despite the British intervention, the Ugandan soldiers remained mutinous and, on 27 January, Obote ordered the Staffordshires to disarm them. However, Obote was facing considerable parliamentary opposition for calling in the British troops, and was also criticised by the intergovernmental Organisation of African Unity (OAU). Refusing to call the unrest 'a mutiny', Obote described it as a 'sit-down strike', and quickly created a Censorship and Correction Board to suppress unhelpful press accounts of the protests. Obote blamed the British for Uganda having inherited a badly trained army. He promoted Idi Amin and Shaban Opolot to command the 1st and 2nd Battalions of the Uganda Rifles, keeping Colonel Tillet as overall commander. He also agreed to implement the pay rise Onama had been forced to offer, and to improve rations and barracks accommodation. The Ugandan army, according to Parsons, became the highest paid soldiers in anglophone Africa. Despite this, there were further incidents of insubordination throughout the

Ugandan forces, which Obote did his best to hush up,[46] but the Staffordshires left after a couple of weeks.[47]

Parsons describes the political choices facing the three regional leaders: 'Nyerere, Obote and Kenyatta ... needed to make an example of the "ringleaders" but they did not want to create the impression that the strikes were a serious challenge to their authority and legitimacy'[48] Obote went further than the others in trying to minimise the effects of the mutiny. Unlike Kenya and Tanzania, Uganda put only a few mutineers on trial for minor crimes, and gave them relatively lenient sentences. On the advice of Colonel Tillet, 429 *askaris* were dismissed, but this was on full pay and service benefits, and they were later allowed to re-enlist. Just eight 'ringleaders', all corporals and privates, were tried by a court martial presided over by Lt Col. Opolot, who dismissed charges against four of the accused for lack of evidence, and sentenced the others to between 18 months and 3 years imprisonment. A more senior officer, Lt Jack Ojera, was tried by Lt Col. Amin for publicly supporting the mutiny/strike. Amin found him not guilty despite what Parsons calls 'damning eye-witness testimony'[49] Parsons suggests that, by being so gentle with the soldiers, Obote had allowed them to become 'dangerously autonomous'[50] After 1964, the army became 'a powerful interest group that was willing to use force to protect its status and privileges'[51] Increasingly, soldiers began to assert themselves physically on the streets of Kampala and other towns, with little risk of serious consequences to themselves.

The danger for the historian here, as Parsons concedes, is the temptation to read the events of 1964 as a prelude leading inevitably to Amin's 1971 coup. Parsons himself comes close to blaming Milton Obote for setting in place the military structures and attitudes which enabled Amin's seizure of power. It is certainly clear that, in effect, the mutineers had won; they had achieved their demands in full, and the experience of exerting their strength and winning can only have encouraged a growing sense of their potential power and influence as a group, despite the many ethnic and other divisions within the forces. It may even have led Amin himself to wonder about the possibilities his own future might offer. It seems quite likely that he was aware from family stories of the pre-colonial power of the Sudanese slave-soldiers and the key role played by the Nubi in carving out the British

Empire in East Africa. Amin was born into a tradition of politically powerful soldiers.

Unlike Parsons, Kenneth Ingham suggests that Obote had little or no choice in how he dealt with the mutiny, but, like Parsons, he sees the events of January 1964 as a kind of precursor to Amin's coup:

> On the surface he had behaved impeccably, but his intervention could easily be represented, if he so wished, as a protest by the spokesman of the soldiers against a less than responsive government. There were rumours, too, that he had secretly promised the dismissed soldiers that he would recruit them again into the army when the opportunity arose. Whether or not Amin contemplated establishing a power-base for himself in the army at that point is not clear, but the stage was clearly set for him to do so.[52]

This seems to rest partly on speculation after Amin's 1971 coup, but it may also represent some of the rumours going round among Obote's supporters in 1964. Obote himself, according to Ogenga Otunnu, used the mutiny as an excuse to 'purge the army of officers whose loyalty to him was questionable'.[53] This had the effect of further concentrating the ethnic structure of military command, causing increased resentment in the south: '[s]ome anti-Obote soldiers were either dismissed from the army or were transferred to less sensitive positions. Most of these soldiers originated from Buganda and Ankole. The ethnic composition of those purged suggested that the regime, led by a northerner ... and protected largely by soldiers from the north ... had declared war against the south.'[54] Another of Obote's moves was to establish, at first in secret, a new paramilitary security service, known as the General Service Unit (GSU), under the control of his cousin, Akena Adoko. According to Otunnu, 'Most of its estimated 1,000 members were strong supporters of the Obote faction of the UPC. Their major assignments were to gather information on soldiers, politicians, students, civil servants and traders. Soon, the GSU acquired more power and resources than the army. This made some members of the army regard it as Obote's private army. This perception eroded Obote's credibility and legitimacy in the army.'[55]

The British had been considering their future in the Ugandan army even before the mutiny. On the day before the Jinja events, the defence advisor at the British High Commission, D.W.S. Hunt, wrote to Sir Saville Garner of the Commonwealth Relations Office: 'According to Tillet, there is a certain current of dissatisfaction in the Uganda Rifles at the continued presence of British officers in executive command.' Felix Onama, the interior minister, had warned him of the growing disaffection, and called for 'an accelerated programme of Africanisation'. Tillet was now proposing 'the complete replacement of British officers by Ugandans this year and the transfer of some (but not necessarily all) British seconded officers and NCOs to a British training team which would have no responsibility for command'.[56] In the light of the events in Tanganyika, Hunt backed this. Three weeks later, Tillet put a proposal to Onama for the Uganda Army to revert to a single battalion, as there were not enough Ugandan officers to staff two adequately. The Ugandans were unlikely to agree to the shrinking of the army back to a single battalion, and Onama duly rejected the idea, on what Tillet called 'political grounds'.[57] Tillet tendered his resignation to Obote on 13 February, on the basis that his military advice was being ignored, and it was accepted. In fact, Tillet had regarded his position as untenable since the Jinja mutiny, and was looking for a way out.[58]

In a telegram next day Hunt reported that, 'Tillet said he had spent a large part of afternoon trying to explain training team to Amin and (? Opoloto) [sic] but was doubtful whether they had really grasped it.'[59] Tillet also told Hunt that 'British officers are already fretting at being commanded by officers they regard as incompetent and having to carry out orders and policies which offend their military consciences eg promotion of wrong persons for wrong reasons.'[60] Obote had said to Tillet that the question was not whether Uganda wanted British military assistance to continue, but only what form it should take. The telegram states that:

Obote confirmed that he has no intention of double dealing and that he was not negotiating for an Israeli Mission as alternative to British. He did however say that Uganda's need was desperate and that she must take help from wherever suitable offers were forthcoming. He would turn to Britain first but could not guarantee Britain exclusive wrights [sic] to train Ugandan Army. This confirms my view that Israeli training would be purely supplementary to British and on minor scale as it is now … therefore no need for demarche.[61]

Tillet was immediately withdrawn 'for family reasons', rather than serving out his notice until a successor was chosen, but there was continuing dispute about whether his replacement should be commander of the army or just a British defence advisor. On 28 February, a Top Secret telegram from London told Hunt that:

> We learn from very delicate source[62] that Uganda Minister of Defence and Security has asked Ghanaians whether they would be prepared urgently to second a Brigadier to command the Uganda army with a Chief of Staff and supporting officers....
>
> We are prepared to swallow continuation of small Israeli effort but anything on the above scale from any other country would clearly be impossible to work with alongside our mission ...[63]

In March the British secretary of state for the Commonwealth, Duncan Sandys, visited Kampala for talks with Obote. He insisted that, if Britain was to retain a military presence in Uganda, they would not expect any other country to be providing training assistance and unless there was a British Commander in Chief 'it would be difficult for us to agree to British Officers continuing to serve on secondment'.[64] Following the visit, Tillet was replaced, initially by Colonel Groom, and the British presence was reduced to 16 officers and 10 NCOs, as advisors or on secondment. Despite this, the Ugandan army was to remain essentially a branch of the British one, and the promotion to senior military roles of Ugandans such as Amin was irrelevant to the real lines of command. Groom's orders were clear:

> Your task is to assist the Uganda Government to maintain internal security. ... You are to be under the direct command of the GOC [General Officer Commanding] British Land Forces Kenya. In matters of operational concern and in dealings with the Uganda Government you are to be guided by the advice of Colonel J.M.A. Tillet. You will have direct access to the British High Commissioner. ... You are to maintain the closest liaison with the Uganda intelligence authorities. ... You are to send SITREPS to Headquarters British Land Forces Kenya twice daily.... You are to inform Headquarters ... by the fastest means as soon as any of your force is deployed operationally.[65]

In other words, some two years after independence the new commander of the Ugandan army was to report to British superior officers rather than the Ugandan government.

In the meantime, the British grew suspicious of the interior minister, Onama, who they believed was favouring Opolot over Amin, because the latter was seen as 'strongly pro-British', while the former was 'less wedded to the British connection'[66] and believed to be closer to the Israelis. On the morning of Monday, 29 June, Opolot, now a brigadier, unexpectedly arrived at army headquarters and sacked Colonel Groom. Onama and Obote refused to discuss the matter with the British, and the rest of the British officers based at the army headquarters in Kampala were removed the next day. On 1 July Onama announced to the Ugandan parliament that 'Ugandanisation of Army Headquarters had taken place'.[67] Obote then travelled to London for a Commonwealth prime ministers' meeting, and met the British Commonwealth secretary on 6 July. He had a list of equipment he wanted the British to supply, 'with the inference that he would wish to have it as a gift or at least on very favourable terms'.[68]

Obote's boast that the Ugandanisation of the military had been achieved had some truth in it. Following the mutiny, the changes had come very fast indeed, both for the army as a whole and for Amin in particular. According to Omara-Otunnu's history of the Ugandan military:

> Whereas prior to May 1962 none of the full officers had been an African, and in January 1964 only 18 were Africans, by February 1964 55 out of a total of 95 officers in the Ugandan Army were Africans; they included 2 lieutenant-colonels, 3 majors and 14 Captains....
>
> In general, the period immediately after the mutiny was one of rapid upward mobility for African soldiers. The most outstanding examples of this trend are the careers of Shaban Opolot and Idi Amin. In the space of less than a year after the mutiny, Opolot rose from Temporary Major (Unconfirmed) to Brigadier. Similarly Amin was promoted from Temporary Major in January to Colonel in September. Of these two men, Amin was the more astute in creating a personal following in the army. In September 1964 he was appointed Deputy Commander of the Ugandan Army, with responsibility for recruitment and training in the Army and the embryonic Air Force. In his new capacity, Amin

115

immediately re-enlisted in the army almost all of the men who had been dismissed for taking part in the mutiny, and they felt indebted to him for being restored to their former employment.[69]

THE ISRAELI FACTOR

As the British had suspected, Onama and Opolot were in fact trying to do a deal with the Israelis. According to the British records, they visited Israel in early June and, '[a]lmost from the moment of their return a marked change in the relationship between the Ugandans and the Israelis became apparent'. A letter from the Defence Attaché on 23 June stated that:

> At present there are five Israeli officers helping the Ugandan army with continuation training of recruits. There are also several young officers who have been trained in Israel. The Israelis co-operate willingly with the Army Commander [Groom] and are doing quite a good job. On the whole, the Israeli influence in the army is significant but it has been suggested that past indiscipline has arisen from the Israeli concept of training in 'strong-arm' techniques.[70]

This seemingly positive, or at least neutral, British attitude towards the Israeli presence soon changed. On 29 June, an Israeli aircraft landed at Entebbe with a consignment of 120 mm mortars. Over the next few days, a new training team of six Israeli officers arrived in Jinja, and Onama withdrew three trainee pilots from their British training course, sending them to Israel instead. On 12 August, 'four Israeli aircraft arrived from Tanganyika and a number of Israeli Air Force personnel arrived with them – more are believed to be on the way'.[71] British army officers reported being 'cold-shouldered' by former Ugandan comrades, and the High Commission believed that 'the Ugandans had obviously been ordered to turn to the Israelis for advice and to ignore British personnel except when and where the latter were doing a job which no-one else, including the Israelis, could do. ... [I]t was evident that British personnel were no longer required – or even welcome – except insofar as they were individually irreplaceable'.[72] The Israelis were keen to gain as much influence as possible in a country which bordered the Arab world (i.e. Sudan), and occupied a strategic position at the centre of a decolonising continent, over which the Israelis hoped to wield a wider influence in the wake of imperial withdrawal.

The British reacted like a jilted lover, flouncing off angrily. On 15 July, the secretary of state told Prime Minister Obote that all British service personnel would be withdrawn as soon as possible 'and made it clear that it was a consequence of the evident switch to Israel'.[73] Both sides agreed a deadline of 24 August but, in the event, '[t]he last British officer attached to the Uganda Rifles left Entebbe Airport on 22 August 1964, thus ending a continuous connection dating back to 1895 between Ugandan troops and the British Army'.[74] It was indeed, as Acting High Commissioner Aston wrote, 'The End of a Chapter'.[75] Aston's tone in the report is somewhere between that of a rejected suitor and that of a disappointed parent; he expresses almost a sense of betrayal, combined with a hope that the infant will eventually come to its senses and return to the comforting support of the colonial father:

> There seems little likelihood that the Israelis will have any more inclination here than they have elsewhere to help with improving the administration of the army or the inclination and capability to fill the existing gaps in equipment stores. ... There are already signs that some of the Ugandan officers, particularly those who have served and trained with the British Army, are becoming resentful of the Israelis ...[76]

Aston suggests that there remained 'a fund of goodwill towards us' in both the army and the police, as well as in the cabinet. Even Onama himself, he suggests, 'may well have a lingering affection subdued by his present marriage of convenience to Israel'. There was also, he suggested:

> an almost naive assumption ... that we are always there and will always be ready to help if the need arises, however much we may have been spurned in the meantime. Our reaction to the treatment of British officers and to the 'hole and corner' arrangements with Israel may prove to be a salutary and necessary lesson. When it has been learnt – to the detriment of the efficiency of the army – we may well find the Ugandans more genuinely disposed than ever to look to us for help. ... I suggest that, in the meantime, it is in our wider interests to encourage the pro-British elements within the army.[77]

As far as the British were concerned, this category certainly included Amin. Aston clearly thought that Opolot and Onama had timed the policy shift towards Israel to take place while Amin was away in Britain, on a training course at the School of Infantry. When Amin returned at the end of August, it was to find Opolot now a brigadier and army commander, while he himself had been promoted to colonel and given the title of deputy commander. From the UK perspective, he was now the key pro-British figure in the military, who had played no part in the Israeli *démarche*. From Obote's point of view, he now had to rely on Amin who, unlike Shaban Opolot,[78] had strong links with, and popularity among, the rank-and-file *askaris*, the men who had mutinied at the beginning of the year and remained a persistent threat to the government. Overall, Colonel Amin seemed to have emerged stronger than ever from the 1964 mutinies and the subsequent abrupt end to British military dominance in Uganda. He continued to rise in the ranks, but he was no longer in a position to do any real soldiering; from 1965 onwards he was (despite many denials) above all a political operator, whose continued success, even survival, depended on his relationship with Prime Minister Milton Obote.

This relationship became considerably closer after the mutiny. A number of factors were involved in this. One was Amin's key role in calming down the soldiers and minimising the situation by first treating it as a 'strike' rather than a full-scale mutiny, and a second factor was addressing at least some of the troops' grievances. Another element involved the changing situation in the Congo (now named Zaire). A rebellion against the authoritarian rule of Mobutu Sese Seko had begun in the west of the country and, by mid-1964, Mobutu's forces were pushing the rebels hard towards the Uganda border. In February 1965, his planes bombed villages inside Uganda, in Amin's homeland of West Nile. Obote wanted to support the rebels, though not openly, and entrusted Amin with the task. According to the prime minister's private secretary, Henry Kyemba:

> Obote wished to support the rebels to the utmost, and assigned Amin, now Deputy Commander of the Ugandan Army, personal responsibility to assist them in and around Amin's own home area of Arua. Obote established a direct link with Amin, bypassing the Army commander, Brigadier Shaban Opolot. He did this first because he wished Amin's

activities to remain as secret as possible, and second because he regarded Opolot as a potential ally of Obote's old rival, the Kabaka [King of Buganda].[79]

This operation was to lead to yet another of the career-threatening events that characterised Amin's rise to power. Known as the 'Congo Gold Scandal', this will be considered in the next chapter.

Another factor in the changing relationship between Obote and Amin came as the result of Obote's increasingly authoritarian rule. The colonial legislation inherited by the new country allowed considerable room for anti-democratic and anti-human rights measures on the part of the government, and Obote used these as far as he could, changing the law when it was not draconian enough, in order to maintain his power against perceived enemies, particularly the Ganda elite. According to Samwiri Karugire's political history of Uganda: 'by 1965 all the politicians had given up even the pretence of appealing to the electorate and it was clear that it would be the army which would be decisive in the power struggle'.[80] In the battle between Obote and the Kabaka's supporters, the latter believed that the army, being largely northerners, would back the Langi prime minister. This assumed a much more coherent 'north' than actually existed[81] – in particular, Acholi and Langi soldiers often conflicted with their West Nile and Nubi colleagues. But to the southerners they were all pretty much the same. As the eminent Muganda lawyer George Kanyeihamba summarises it: 'Obote came from the North. Those who opposed him saw the fight as being between the Northern region and the South. This assumption led them to think that if Obote was removed from office, the army would intervene. There was thus a psychological fear that a fight with Obote meant a fight with the army.'[82] Amin became a key figure in the ongoing struggle, which was sometimes overt but often hidden, between the national government and the Buganda leadership.

FAMILY MATTERS

While political events moved fast in the first half of the 1960s, Amin's personal and family life was expanding alongside his power, social standing and wealth. His mother (according to Jaffar Amin) attended the Independence

Day celebrations and was 'ecstatic as she watched her son Awon'go (Captain Idi Amin Dada) stand side by side with Obote'.[83] It was around this time, Jaffar writes, that his father formally adopted his grandfather's clan name, Dada: 'During the "British Empire Days", Dad's name used to only read Idi Amin but by Uganda's "Independence" from Britain, he had added Dada and was now known as Idi Amin Dada'.[84] His rise also enabled Amin, after an eventful single life, to marry. He now had the money to pay the traditional bridewealth, and when one of his long-term cohabiting girlfriends gave birth to a daughter in January 1961, he married her. This was Sarah Mutesi Kibedi (a name which, to Ugandans, suggests Ganda aristocracy). As is the custom among the Nubi and many other Muslim groups, she was renamed after her first child, becoming known as 'Mama Malyam' (or Mariam). According to Jaffar:

> Mama Mariam ... is considered Dad's first official wife even though Dad had another wife and concubines before her, namely Adili, a Kakwa, Mama Taban, a Lan'gi, and many others....
>
> Dad cohabited with Bironi, an Acholi wife, while he was stationed in Nakuru in the 1950s. By the late 1950s he was cohabiting with Taban Amin's[85] mother, a Lan'gi and cousin to Obote. By the time in 1960 when Dad continued to reside at the King George IV barracks in Jinja, he had linked up with four women namely, Adili of the Nyooke-Bori Kakwa clan, my Great Aunt Nnalonmgo Nnabirye Lovisa, Nnamuwaya Kirunda and Mama Mariam (Sarah Mutesi Kibedi). The first to vacate was my Great Aunt ... leaving the other three to fight over their man.
>
> Sarah Mutesi Kibedi won with the birth of Aaliya Mariam on January 21 1961 hence the name Mama Mariam which she became known by from then on.
>
> The other two Adili ... and Nnamuwaya Kirunda gave birth to Uhurus ('Independence') in 1962.[86]

A very different, much more conventionally 'romantic' picture of Idi and Mariam's courtship and marriage is provided in an interview she gave to the British tabloid newspaper, the *Daily Mirror*, in 1979. According to the historian Alicia Decker, quoting the article in her ground-breaking book on the role of women in 1970s Uganda:

Sarah Mutesi Kibedi never imagined that her 'kind and compassionate' husband would become such a tyrant. The Idi Amin she fell in love with as a young woman was 'gentle and passionate' not the 'strutting, arrogant womanising killer' who emerged in later years. Sarah first met Amin in November 1961 when she was just twenty two years old and working as an apprentice dressmaker at the Singer Sewing Machine Company in Jinja. She remembered looking up from her work and catching the eye of a handsome young soldier who was standing across the room. After flashing a broad smile, he strode over to introduce himself. The two soon fell in love and decided to get married. The only problem was religion.... Sarah knew that her family would be opposed to the decision, but she was determined to marry the man she loved. She thus began a course of Islamic instruction and changed her name to Malyam. Despite her parents' bitter opposition, the couple wed in March 1962, just eight months before Uganda gained Independence.

After three or four years of 'blissful' marriage, their relationship began to deteriorate.[87] Malyam heard rumours that her husband was seeing another woman and she crafted a plan to catch him in the act...[88]

Jaffar Amin's version seems considerably more convincing than the *Daily Mirror*'s romanticised account of the courtship. In a highly polygamous society, it is unlikely that a Ugandan woman would have harboured quite such romantic illusions about her soldier husband, who was already well known as a promiscuous philanderer. But Decker and Jaffar Amin agree that Malyam was Amin's first official wife, and that they married around the time of independence, either in 1961 or 1962.

A GROWING FORCE

How 'resistible' was Amin's rise over the first half of the 1960s, a period which saw the end of British political dominance and then British military control in Uganda? The country at this time was moving towards the creation of an independent state, rather than achieving that status in a single moment of liberation. As the process rolled on, the increasing pace of events over 1964–65 led to Amin becoming, by the end of the period, the second most powerful figure in the country. He was certainly lucky in emerging unscathed from a series of controversies, particularly the Turkana massacre and the 1964 mutinies, either of which might easily have sunk anybody's career. But it is difficult to attribute *all* of this to pure good fortune, unless you believe in the power of the Kakwa omens Jaffar writes about. As this chapter has shown, as well as dealing with successive potential crises in his career, Amin at this time also navigated his way very successfully through the murky and racially charged process of 'Africanisation' in the army, as well as through the complex and fast-moving politics of post-independence Uganda. In doing this, he demonstrated a new ability to operate politically as well as militarily. He had somehow acquired the set of skills he needed in order to survive, and, for someone normally depicted as an ignorant buffoon, he had done so quickly and successfully.

One connecting factor between the periods before and after independence was the persistence of key aspects of the British military model, even after their soldiers had left. Perhaps Amin realised that some of the methods he had learned, and demonstrated in the course of impressing his British officers, could be carried over into the new era. His charm, even his sense of humour, his ruthlessness and eye for the main chance, his skills in 'dividing and ruling' and other ways of manipulating others (including especially those who considered themselves his natural superiors by virtue of birth or education): all these were what teachers call 'transferrable skills', which Amin got from the British Army. He was certainly fortunate, but at the same time he exemplified the old maxim: 'the harder he practised, the luckier he got'. It is extremely difficult, looking at the events discussed in this chapter, to credit the view that Amin was merely an illiterate fool who stumbled into success by accident.

The moment of independence saw the emergence into the historical record of a figure who was to become important in Amin's life. This was Robert (Bob) Astles, a most unusual English ex-army officer who had been for some time a supporter of anti-colonial movements, first in India, then Uganda. There will be more about him in subsequent chapters. At this time, however, he was involved in what became known as 'the Tank Hill incident', after the upmarket Kampala district many of the whites lived in. To mark the end of imperial rule in neighbouring Kenya, a number of European – mostly British – expats with Kenyan links held a 'fancy dress' party, involving blackface make-up and drunken capers. Grahame describes the events in a downbeat, rather careful way, minimising the offensive qualities of the event:

> During the Independence celebrations, a party was held in Kampala by a number of European families, the theme of which was the end of the 'White Man's Burden'. ... Many of those attending came dressed in full tribal regalia and, as the evening progressed, ribald impersonations of certain African politicians were performed.[89]

According to most accounts, Astles, horrified at what was going on, reported the incident, and its participants, to the new Ugandan government authorities, and 'subsequently several Europeans were deported'.[90] His own version of the events suggests that someone else was responsible for informing on the revellers:

> [W]hat a party it was, with even dogs dressed up to play their part. ... But the theme for some of the guests seems to have been more 'anti-independence' than 'independence' and songs were sung making fun of Jomo Kenyatta ... to which at least one of the guests objected. He was an American named Curry who was working for the Milton Obote Trust, an organisation sponsored by an overseas socialist group. The capers were reported to ... the CID. ... I had not been at the party but there were unexpected repercussions for me because I was blamed for reporting the incident.[91]

Whatever the truth about his role, after this Astles was permanently shunned by most of the British community, and held in some contempt at the British High Commission (though they continued to seek information from him about political events and personalities in the country). In consequence, he grew nearer to many Ugandan circles in Kampala, including people closely associated with Obote, married a Muganda woman, and in the early post-independence years worked in a confusing variety of roles, from aircraft pilot, to television operations manager, via animal protection work, as well as being active as an intelligence and security agent for the new government. His relationship with Amin was to become as multifaceted as his professional life.

As the decade moved into its second half, many people, including even some British officials, had good reason to revise their disparaging opinions of Amin's qualities and abilities. At the same time, the army itself grew fast. According to Omara-Otunnu,[92] it more than doubled in size between 1964 and the end of 1965. Meanwhile, Amin seems to have done what he could to encourage West Nile rather than Acholi recruitment. An entirely unintended result of Obote's foreign and domestic policies in this period was, then, a massive increase in the power base of Idi Amin. This was to become Obote's main problem over the next five years, and eventually the cause of his downfall.

4

AMIN AND OBOTE, 1965-69

From 1965, for the rest of the decade, Idi Amin's career, indeed his life, depended largely on one factor, his relationship with Milton Obote. His former British employers still mattered, but much less so. As the army became more of a Ugandan national force and less an arm of colonial control, the largely uneducated Kakwa officer had to learn quickly that his job was now a much more complex and very political one. To survive and thrive in the fast-changing post-independence world, he had to use all the manipulative management skills he had learned in the KAR, while also developing new abilities to adapt to developments. As we have seen, Ugandan politics in this era was extremely complex, and I can only give a rather simplistic picture here. Broadly speaking, political divisions ran through a range of different factors. Those of particular importance included: (1) *ethnicity*, especially the north–south divide, though there were also fissures between different northern groups (e.g. the West Nilers and the Acholi) and between the southern kingdoms (Bunyoro and Ankole, for example, having old, pre-colonial quarrels with Buganda); (2) *class*-based distinctions, particularly a struggle between the old tribal aristocracies built around the southern monarchies, and a new rising middle class; and (3) *religious* divides. These were mainly Catholic vs Protestant, but also sometimes involved the considerably smaller population of Muslims. They frequently mapped onto class positions; for example, most of the poorer Baganda – peasants and wage workers – were Catholics, while the British-educated elite were largely Anglican Protestants. In this context, the religious labels need to be seen more as social categories, linked to family background and education, than as personal belief systems.

There were also more shifting, but real, *ideological* differences – with left- and right-wing views aligning only roughly with class position, and an increasing divide between a centrist social democracy and a more radical left, which mapped onto the wider international background of the Cold War. In effect, all these opposing political identities overlapped in ever changing ways. For example, for a while the northerners were allied with the southern leftists against the right, which was associated with the Ganda aristocracy and the other southern monarchies. Political actors had to take sides along all these vectors simultaneously, so that one might say of a Ugandan politician that he operated as, for example, an Ankole aristocratic Protestant right-winger, or an Acholi Catholic middle-class revolutionary leftist. Obote himself was associated with the northerners, the Protestants and the moderate left. Amin's role now required him to negotiate these complexities, and especially to deal with Obote.

Apolo Milton Obote was born in Lango in northern Uganda, in 1925, son of a colonial-era 'chief'. He was educated in Lango, Acholi and Busoga before going to Makerere, then Uganda's only university. There, he won scholarships to both the USA (to read law) and the UK (economics), so he left Makerere to prepare to study overseas. However, the British provincial commissioner for Uganda's Northern Province refused to allow him to take up either of the scholarships, on the grounds, according to Ugandan social scientist Ogenga Otunnu, that 'studies overseas would not prepare Obote to be of use to the country'.[1] Obote dropped his studies completely and went to Kenya, where he worked as a clerk on a sugar plantation and became involved in politics via the trade union movement and the Kenyan African Union party. According to Otunnu, in this period he was involved in 'logistical assistance to the Mau Mau fighters', which led to his arrest and detention.[2] Released in 1957, Obote returned to Uganda and joined the UNC. He was elected to the pre-independence Legislative Council in 1958 and became instantly successful, largely (according to Otunnu, citing Ingham) due to the fact that the Baganda members saw him as one of the few northerners who respected their culture, their independent identity and their king. On becoming the UNC's leader in 1960, however, he formed an alliance with a small anti-Baganda party, to create the UPC. Having absorbed them, he went on to do the deal discussed in the previous chapter, with the Kabaka Yekka party of the Baganda monarchists, which led to the narrow UPC victory over the (Catholic) DP in the 1962 independence elections.

Ugandan historian Samwiri R. Karugire emphasises the difficulties of Obote, and the weaknesses of the UPC structures, in the face of these social/political divisions. He writes that: 'Obote had inherited power but he had not inherited the authority that had gone with that power. This was because there were other centres of institutional authority in the various components of Uganda and these centres commanded loyalty and conferred authority to a far greater extent than any new African government could hope to do.'[3] Karugire argues that the strength of the UPC lay not in its own ability to mobilise the Ugandan people, but in the fact that most of its educated leadership had been colonial chiefs in their local areas. This meant that they had their own power bases outside the party, which weakened Obote's position considerably. His response to this, Karugire argues, led to Obote's adoption of the colonial 'divide and rule' strategy, both intensifying the religious divide and deploying patronage to ensure a steady flow of opposition politicians across the floor of parliament to join the UPC. Elections were fixed by using the law to overturn opposition (DP) victories, refusing to call by-elections which the opposition might win and redrawing inconvenient electoral boundaries. A.B.K. Kasozi backs up Karugire's analysis with a scathing description of post-independence Ugandan politics:

> Where most political parties are governed by an ideology or ideas that represent the interests and views of its members, the leaders of the UPC were divided in their aims; they had different ethnic and religious loyalties; they were power hungry and, for the most part, unprepared to act honourably towards one another and the nation.
>
> Most of the UPC leaders were notables who derived their authority from colonial appointments as traditional chiefs or civil servants. Many were the lineal successors of chiefs or clan leaders, the majority were Protestant, and a number had gone to [Ugandan] boarding schools based on the British public-school system. . . . Obote's power did not rest on the popular vote[4].

Constitutionally, Uganda had been established broadly on the British model, with a parliament, the National Assembly, which was partly elected and partly nominated by the four southern kingdoms (Buganda, Bunyoro, Ankole and Tooro) together with the (non-monarchical) southern territory of Busoga. The north had no extra nominated seats. The executive head of government was the prime minister, who would be the leader of the largest party in the National Assembly (i.e. Obote). There was also a figure-head president, sitting as the ceremonial head of state, modelled on the British monarch, a position which was from 1963 occupied by the Kabaka of Buganda. Buganda was especially powerful within the post-independence constitution, due to the kingdom's reserved seats in the National Assembly and the legislative powers of its own parliament, the *Lukiko*. A long-standing bone of contention involved what Ugandans call the 'Lost Counties'. These areas had been part of the pre-colonial Bunyoro kingdom, but were handed over to Buganda by the British. In 1964, Obote organised a referendum in the counties, which Bunyoro won easily after Obote disenfranchised many of the more recent Baganda settlers in the area. This revealed a key tension in the post-independence constitution, between Uganda as a unitary state and at the same time (in the south only) a partly federal one. As the eminent Ugandan constitutional lawyer, G. W. Kanyeihamba, puts it: 'the Independence Constitution emphasized division rather than unity. It placed regional inter-ests above national interests and exalted regional leaders at the expense of national ones. ... [T]he Constitution was designed to cater for a historical Uganda where traditions and economic power in the hands of a few were guaranteed. ... [H]owever, it lacked political legitimacy, for it was not an expression of the will of the majority.'[5]

POLITICAL DEVELOPMENTS, 1964-66

As Obote moved increasingly towards a de facto one-party state, these constitutional contradictions began to play out within the UPC, between left, right and centre factions. At a party conference in April 1964, Obote backed Grace Ibingira, an Ankole aristocrat who was the right-wing candi-date for the powerful role of UPC secretary general. At this point he seemed to be filling the cabinet with people well to the right of his own political position, and some important Ganda political figures were also joining the UPC, including former DP leaders and key KY moderates. Many of these right-wing, pro-monarchical and federalist converts seem to have joined

Obote's party with the aim of subverting it from within. They strengthened the UPC right, and, as A.B.K. Kasozi put it: 'Most of those who crossed the floor realised that it was violence, not votes, that decided who controlled the distribution of resources in Uganda. ... By the end of 1964, the UPC had seventy-four seats [in the National Assembly], the DP nine, and the KY eight. It is doubtful whether these numbers represented the UPC's actual level of support among voters.'[6]

The main political contest in 1964–66 involved the two most powerful factions of Obote's party, pitting the UPC right against the UPC centre. These ideological positions seemed for a time, on the surface, to have made the old tribal and north–south distinctions less relevant. The leader of the 'northern' (or 'Nilotic') centrist faction was Godfrey Binaisa, who was actually a Muganda, while the leader of the right-wing, 'southern' (or 'Bantu') faction was Daudi Ocheng, an Acholi who was also a committed monarchist, owned land in Buganda, and had been secretary general of the KY. As for the left, A.B.K. Kasozi, who was sympathetic to their position, wrote that: 'The UPC left consisted of young, well-educated politicians and trade unionists who shared certain ideas with the centre [of the party] on correcting regional inequality, but disagreed with them on the kind of social transformation that should be implemented, as well as on Uganda's structural relationship with the Western economic system.'[7] In these ways, the political struggles in Uganda, and those within the UPC, reflected the contemporary global conflict between capitalism and communism, the USA and the USSR. As elsewhere in Africa, the so-called Cold War often became distinctly hot. Kasozi points out that: '[t]he first eruptions of political violence in [post-independence] Uganda were caused by the struggle among the different factions of the UPC for control of the ruling party, and, hence, the state'.[8] This context of barely suppressed, politically motivated violence was, of course, an environment in which Idi Amin was well able to thrive.

What was particular to Uganda in the Cold War was the way these ideological differences became increasingly mapped onto geographical, ultimately tribal/ethnic, distinctions. By the end of 1964, the various divides within the UPC had coalesced into two main factions, respectively under Obote (northern, increasingly left-wing) and Ibingira (southern and definitely right-wing). From Amin's point of view, the key issue was the way these splits played out in the army, by now highly politicised. Here, the ideological and geographical splits in the country translated into a struggle for supremacy between Amin (on Obote's side) and Opolot (on Ibingira's). Both UPC factions wanted very much to keep the military happy and, as we saw in the previous chapter, defence expenditure more than doubled between 1964/5 and 1965/6. A British report dated 22 June 1965 noted the rise, concluding that:

> It looks therefore that the increase in defence expenditure is putting Uganda into the red on current account as well as reducing the resources available for development. ... [S]ome of their arms purchases ... are extravagant luxuries. ... The fact is that for the past year the Army has been a law unto itself and the expatriate [i.e. British] Permanent Secretary of the former Ministry of Internal Affairs has admitted that not only was it impossible to exercise any Ministerial control whatsoever, but it was difficult enough even to obtain information on the commitments that the Army were gaily entering into right and left.[9]

The British may have withdrawn from command and control of the Ugandan army, but they were certainly keeping a close eye on military matters, carefully listing the amounts of arms and ammunition coming into the country and noting administrative and financial changes in the army, such as the creation of a third battalion in September 1964.[10] They also kept a close eye on the changing power balance between Amin and Opolot, increasingly gathering information on the political role of the armed forces and the behaviour of the army towards civilians. The British military advisor to the Ugandan government, Colonel V.J. Senior, wrote on 27 February 1965 that:

> Numerous incidents of irresponsible and truculent behaviour by detachments of the Uganda Army towards the general public continue to be reported throughout Uganda. There is an almost total lack of supervision and discipline in the Army, which now could scarcely be more unpopular with all sections of the community.
>
> The army is obsessed with an arrogant sense of security and 'spy mania' which has resulted in innocent bystanders being arrested on completely groundless charges ...[11]

In August 1965, in a long report titled 'Uganda: The Politics of Defence', the new British High Commissioner R.C.C. Hunt outlined the relationship between Amin and Opolot in characteristically contemptuous terms:

> The last year has not been an easy time for the army. . . . This situation would have taxed the ability of a more experienced commander than Brigadier Opoloto. He is an ex-effenci [*sic*] of practically no education, little experience of staff work, endowed with considerable arrogance, no charm and a great enjoyment of the power which his position gives him. The Deputy Commander, Colonel Amin, is of similar mould, but in addition he is a bully. Relations between these two have been strained for some time. . . .
>
> As a result of the hasty re-equipment programme, there exists a hotch-potch of weapons including British, Israeli and Chinese. . . . Israeli influence in the army has been declining since they arrived in strength one year ago. . . . The fact is that now the Ugandans firmly believe they can run their own show.[12]

Hunt went on to consider the likelihood of a military coup, concluding that 'the present senior officers have too little political flair and find their present jobs of trying to run the army too exacting to have the time or inclination for political adventures ... [and] the close interest Dr Obote takes in the army and the personal control which he exercises over it ... virtually precludes at present any other politician securing control to the extent of being able to engineer a coup'.[13]

Where were the British getting their information from? There were several pro-British officers in the army who were happy to pass on confidential information and plot with the former colonial masters. The aim was usually to persuade the British to regard their political opponents as communist stooges. Major Katabarwa, Ibingira's brother, spoke 'confidentially' to Colonel Senior on 21 October 1965, a conversation passed on to London in a memo which gives a vivid picture of the atmosphere of Ugandan politics in 1965:

> He said I must understand that there is a deep and fundamental split in the country. On the one side were the Northern group – Obote, Onama,

Nekyon and Col. Amin, who stood alone. All the rest of the country – including especially Ibingira ... and Brig. Opoloto, were opposing them. He said most emphatically that the Chinese are supporting the Northern group. ... Katabarwa said he came to Kampala on the 8th October. ... Staff officers ... told him that they had received information about a possible assassination attempt (perpetrated by the Northern group) on Opoloto. ... Nothing happened, because ... the opposition got cold feet. ...

I asked Katabarwa why, if Obote wished to get rid of Opoloto, he did not just dismiss him. He said, because if he did so it would bring all the Southern group into open opposition against him. The Northerners were trying to gain absolute Left Wing control of the country. Once Amin got the position of Army Commander all the Southerners in the Army would be sacked. ...

The Southern group are now virtually in open opposition and planning ways and means to oust [Obote]. ... Could the Southerners rely on Western military assistance if they took positive action? I hastened to tell him in the most unequivocal terms that they most certainly could not ...[14]

The high commissioner, Roland Hunt, wrote to the Commonwealth Relations Office the next day, downplaying the possibility of assassination attempts on either side. Rumours of coups and assassinations were frequent, he suggested, and they reflected the febrile political atmosphere rather than what was really going on. He summarised the present situation as:

Ibingira and those who share his views ... are clearly convinced that the Northern Ministers ... in league with radicals, helped by Communists and reinforced by a large section of the Army are working to entrench their position. ... [T]he Northerners' side ... includes some non-Northerners who are either radicals, 'wild men', or pure band wagoners, just as the Southern group includes people of conservative conviction from northern areas. ... Almost everyone seems convinced that Obote is with the Northerners, but he keeps his cards so close to his chest that I doubt whether anyone really knows which way he is likely to play them.[15]

As Karugire puts it: 'In the course of 1965 ... the struggle was given an ethnic complexion, the predominantly Bantu regions against the predominantly

Nilotic North. More ominously for the future of Uganda, each of these factions was also cultivating a section of the army to its own position, Obote siding with the deputy army commander, Amin, and Ibingira with the army commander, Opolot.[16] In the event, this quintessentially Ugandan political division, which had been bubbling away for many months, now came to the boil, as a crisis broke out over the murky issue known as the 'Congo Gold Scandal', an affair in which Idi Amin was centrally and crucially involved.

CONGO GOLD - UGANDA CRISIS

Obote had, for some time, been opposed to the Congo prime minister, Moise Tshombe, whom he saw, with some justice, as a Western puppet.[17] Between December 1964 and March 1965, Obote arranged for two Congo rebel leaders, Christopher Gbenye and General Nicholas Oleng, to meet other East African leaders clandestinely, and bought arms for them from Tanzania (whose leader, Julius Nyerere, a close ally of Obote, was also vehemently anti-Tshombe). The rebels arrived at the meetings in Uganda with quantities of gold and ivory to pay for the guns; as Jorgensen writes: '[i]t was during this period that the rebels entrusted Col. Idi Amin with money, ivory and eleven bars of gold, each weighing 20 pounds, to purchase arms. From the sale of the gold, Amin deposited Shs.480,000 in the bank [in his personal account] towards weapons purchases.'[18] The issue first came to light when, in May 1965, the Kenyan government seized 75 tons of Chinese weapons being transported through the country en route from Tanzania to Congo, via Uganda. The Kenyans were furious, and the anti-Obote press in Buganda had a field day supporting Kenya against both the Tanzanian and Ugandan governments. To the Ugandan right, the developing Congo scandal signified a decisive move to the left by Obote, who had to make a personal apology to the Kenyan government, calling in at Nairobi on his way to visit Yugoslavia, China and the Soviet Union.

In the Congo itself, Tshombe's US-backed forces were pressing the rebels back towards the Ugandan borders, especially near Amin's home district, West Nile. Obote and Amin stepped up their support for the insurgents, working together and cutting Onama, the minister of defence, and Opolot, the army commander, out of the picture altogether. Obote's personal secretary Henry Kyemba, later produced an account of the events in which he implied, as did the right-wing faction in the UPC at the time, that Amin took the opportunity to feather his own nest:

> I was closely involved with this operation. Obote and I had a personal radio link with Amin. ... The rebels often came to Entebbe, stayed in Amin's house, and saw Obote. Their greatest need was for arms and transport. They had no cash, but they did have truckloads of gold and ivory, seized as they retreated from towns they had once controlled. Amin, as the rebels' contact man, sold their gold and ivory and bought arms for them. ...
>
> In Amin's dealings with the Congolese gold and ivory, no records were ever kept. The goods came by truck to his house. He did not have to account for what he sold. He simply began to bank for himself very large sums, regularly and in cash – up to 300,000 [Ugandan] Shillings at a time – amounting to something like a million dollars in all. He also kept large sums in his house to avoid undue publicity.[19]

In all this activity, the British Obote supporter, Bob Astles, played a key role, flying regular plane loads of *materiel* and funds in and out of the Congo, and this was when he first got to know Amin well. His memoirs draw an interesting picture of the colonel at this time:

> I was called into the office of Akena Adoko, who was head of the intelligence service, and asked if I would take on flying duties in the war zone on the Congo border. ... Adoko then introduced me to the man he wanted me to pilot. It was the army chief of staff, Colonel Idi Amin.
>
> ... That morning in Akena Adoko's office he looked the embodiment of a first class soldier. He was tall, well built and dressed in a uniform starched and fitting like a glove. He had a reputation for loving danger and for refusing to rest, and he had none of the arrogance then being shown by other up-and-coming officers who were beginning to recognise their power. Later he impressed me greatly by his concern for those on duty with him, as well as by his attitude to the duty itself, which had to be completed no matter what the hazards. Certainly he was different from all other Africans I have ever met. He would never take his meal until his men and staff on other duties like me had been fed and

accommodated and as a result his men worshipped him. Later there was to be a different Amin. . . .

Obote had found in Amin an officer built on what he thought was the British model; a buccaneer, a Black Wingate. He was a fighter, a man of immense passions and a lover of great intrigues. That he was later to be seen by so many as a monster is a common fate of such men throughout history. Too much power unbalances such characters and they leave their mark on history with both good and evil deeds scattered along their path.[20]

Astles' role at this time came to the attention of the British High Commission. Tommy Newton Dunn, the British military advisor, reported a conversation with the Sudanese military attaché:

He told me that the Sudanese were worried about a man named 'Astles' – he seemed to have a lot of money and was involved with some secret organisation. Was he working for the British? I said I had only met Astles on a few occasions and thought he was with Uganda Television. He was not popular with the British community who shunned him completely but really I didn't know much about him. Babiker further said that Astles was believed to have taken photographs of airfields and dumps in the Sudan. I said I couldn't help at all on this as I didn't know him [a handwritten note here confirms 'I don't very well'].[21]

According to Jaffar Amin:

During the 'Congo Crisis', Dad developed a friendship with Bob Astles, an ex-Royal Engineer in Kenya on whom the fictional character of Nicholas Garrigan in the hit movie 'The Last King of Scotland' is based. Bob Astles had left the King's African Rifles in 1952 and became an employee of the Public Works Department in Uganda. He also worked as a pilot and was told by Obote to fly Dad to the Congo for operations in the Katanga region during the 'Congo Crisis.' . . .

Bob Astles was Dad's British-born right-hand man. There are allegations that Dad ordered Bob Astles' death whenever he got tired of his company but I remember Bob Astles well and I don't believe Dad ordered his death. They were chums.[22]

The UPC right saw an opportunity in all the undercover operations going on in the Congo. Buoyed by winning several internal party elections (including replacing Binaisa as UPC chairman in Buganda), they struck at both Amin and Obote over the Congo affair. On 4 February 1966, while Obote was away from Kampala on a tour of Northern districts, Daudi Ocheng moved a motion in parliament calling for Amin's suspension from duty and an investigation into what was happening with the Congo gold. Distributing photocopies of Amin's bank details, Ocheng named not only Amin and Obote in his accusation, but also Onama and Nekyon; it was, in effect, an all-out attack, by a confident, Baganda-dominated right wing, on both the left of the party and the centrist leadership. To the latter, it looked like an attempted parliamentary coup, which seemed at first to be succeeding as the National Assembly voted overwhelmingly for Ocheng's motion. Meanwhile, outside parliament, the two sides were manoeuvring for control of the army and police.

The 1966 Congo gold crisis was a key event in Ugandan history and, as such, is wrapped in many myths and stories. At its heart was the conflict between Obote and his supporters' primary allegiance to a unitary Ugandan state, and the Baganda position, which oscillated between an extreme federalism which would devolve maximum power to the Kabaka, and outright secession. Probably most Ugandans, including most Baganda, felt overlapping loyalties: to their clan, their kingdom or ethnic group, Uganda as a nation, East Africa as an interlinked region, and so on. People such as Amin, coming from frontier ethnicities that spilled over Uganda's borders, tended to feel differently to those from districts entirely contained within the nation. Long-centralised political units such as Buganda attracted different loyalties to the less hierarchical, more flexible, traditional societies of the north. Overlapping identifications with different-sized political and social units are globally the norm, but it is often easy for politicians and intellectuals (sometimes even historians) to portray them as mutually exclusive identities. In Uganda in the mid-1960s, Ugandan nationalism had become clearly opposed to Buganda nationalism, and this was loosely mapped onto 'left' and 'right', republicanism and monarchism.

The broader political aspects of the Congo gold story are the subject of a strange publication, a book-length epic poem in free verse, written by a brilliant young British-trained lawyer, also a US-trained anthropologist, named

Akena Adoko – the man who had hired Bob Astles to pilot the Congo flights. Adoko, a Catholic from Lango who was Obote's cousin, saw the events of 1966 very much from the inside. As well as being president of the Uganda Law Society, the versatile young poet also headed Obote's notorious, widely feared, security organisation, the GSU, of which Astles was a member. Adoko's poem, *Uganda Crisis*, lauds Obote and Amin for challenging 'Feudalism' (in the form of the Baganda monarchy) and opposing 'Imperialism' (in the form of support for Britain and the United States in the Cold War). He begins with the resounding declaration that:

> The Imperialist Forces
> And the Feudalist Forces,
> Were united together
> To fight nationalism![23]

The poem goes on to suggest that oppressive principles were at the heart of Ganda kingship, putting the following words into the mouth of the Kabaka:

> 'Take away people kneeling,
> Forbid any prostrations,
> Insist on equality
> Of all person [*sic*] before law –
> Or that the distribution
> Of the national income
> Be guided by equity
> And not by the principle
> Of giving the lion's share
> To the king, the Kabaka
> Who may then encroach at will
> On the shoulders of all others
> Then I am all but quite lost:
> A fish out of the water,
> A square peg in a round hole,
> A mermaid without a tail,
> A garden without flowers,
> A bird without the feathers.'[24]

Adoko tells his readers that:

> We have learnt one great lesson
> All hereditary rules
> Are indeed rule by Corpses.
> No dead man has any right
> To rule over the living
> Directly through his own ghost
> Or indirectly through his heirs.[25]

Obote, he writes, was:

> Like Goliath among gentiles
> Like a giant among dwarves,
> Like a cyclops among men,
> Like Elgon or Ruwenzori
> In a big sea of ant-hills.[26]

The poem covers the Congo debate in parliament and subsequent events in detail, speech by speech and act by act. The evidence that Amin gave in March to the Commission of Enquiry into the Congo gold allegations is described thus:

> And Amin had this to say:
> 'The account produced by Ocheng ...
> Was indeed my Bank Account.
> On the seventeenth of March
> The year nineteen sixty five
> In a letter to Opolot
> Commander of the Army
> I admitted that Nyati
> A revolutionary
> In the neighbouring Congo
> Gave me twenty four thousand Pounds for their revolution.' ...

Summing up the evidence,
The Commission's lawyer Rankin
Said 'Amin never denied
The receipt of the money.
It was manifestly clear
From what Mr Nyati said,
That Amin discharged his trust
To the full satisfaction
Of those who reposed that trust
In Amin and Uganda.
There was no doubt on that point'. . . .

Obote and his ministers
Did not get Congo money;
Amin did get some money
Which was perhaps the proceeds
From the sale of gold and tusks
But he used it for the Congo,
Never did he in person
Benefit from the money. . . .[27]

This is perhaps enough of the secret policeman's poetry. However, Adoko's summary of Amin's evidence and the commission's findings seems a fairly accurate one. The report of the commission of enquiry, set up by Obote immediately after Ocheng's speech, was not published until 1971, but the commission held its sittings in public and the broad outlines of the report became known almost immediately. The commission consisted of three independent judges; Sir Clement de L'Estang of the Court of Appeal for Eastern Africa was the (British) chairman, Mr H.E. Miller of the High Court of Kenya and Mr A. Saidi of the High Court of Tanzania were the others. The commission was itself represented at the enquiry by Mr John Rankin, a London barrister who more or less ran the proceedings. Evidence was taken from Ocheng, Amin, Obote and other ministers, as well as from Amin's bank manager and representatives of the Congo rebels. A London QC, John Wilmers, represented Obote and the ministers, and a Kampala lawyer, Dr Anil Clerk, represented Amin. In the end, the commission found Ocheng's allegations to be without justification, exonerating Obote and Amin much as Adoko's poem describes.

Obote is often regarded as having been a rather indecisive and prevaricating leader, always anxious to balance one faction against another while keeping his own views hidden as long as possible, the better to play one side off against the other. In February 1966, however, on his return from an extended trip to the north, he struck quickly and decisively. In short order, he sent Amin on two weeks leave and appointed the commission of enquiry. By then, Kampala was buzzing with rumours of a planned coup by the UPC right and Felix Opolot. Obote called a cabinet meeting and arrested key figures including Ibingira and four other cabinet ministers. The British High Commission followed events closely, receiving detailed reports of private discussions between the lawyers. It was clear to all involved that behind the Congo allegations lay the larger matter of a Baganda revolt against Obote's government. Back in London, John Wilmers told Richard Posnett, then head of the East Africa desk at the Commonwealth Relations Office,[28] that 'Obote had no option but to act as he did in order to pre-empt an imminent move against him by the Kabaka and the five ministers [who had been arrested].'[29] Posnett sent a detailed account of their conversation to Peter Forster in Kampala, and the high commissioner replied cynically that Wilmers 'certainly seems to have followed the official propaganda hook, line and sinker. He was of course well paid to do so.'[30] The upshot of the Congo gold rumours was a revolutionary change in Ugandan politics, described as such by both Ibingira[31] and Obote himself.[32]

THE 1966 REVOLUTION

Obote then arrested Opolot, suspended the constitution and the National Assembly, and assumed all state power for himself, sacking the president (i.e. the Kabaka, Edward Mutesa) and the vice president, William Nadiope, accusing them of plotting with 'foreign governments' (presumably the British and the US) to overthrow him. The Kabaka described his own role a year later, from exile in London. He wrote that, in early February, while Obote was away in the north:

In my capacity as President, I talked with the Chief Justice and with the Brigadier [the British military advisor] about the danger of the situation, and it was at this stage that I sounded out the British High Commissioner and some African ambassadors as to whether it would be possible to fly in troops if the situation got out of hand. I did not invite a foreign force to invade Uganda. I had in mind something similar to the successful intervention by the British which Obote had authorised two years before [i.e. calling in the Staffordshire Regiment to help put down the 1964 mutiny].[33]

In the event, the planned coup *against* Obote became a coup *by* Obote, and in this Amin's role was central.

The ground had been well prepared for Obote's action, and the army and police, together with many urban workers (and all the left-wing intellectuals), backed Obote. On 15 April, he presented the parliament with an interim constitution, which, he said, provided for 'one country, one parliament, one government, one people'.[34] This was, of course, a direct attack on the Baganda aristocratic leadership, and on all the kingdoms possessing federal powers under the 1962 post-independence constitution. Their land-ownership systems, their courts and legal institutions, all were banned, and traditional monarchs and heads of districts were barred from holding other public positions. Virtually the only matters left to the kingdoms to decide were their laws of monarchical succession. When the Baganda parliament, the *Lukiko*, tried to respond by kicking the central government out of Buganda, Obote and Amin launched a military takeover of the kingdom and drove the Kabaka into exile in Britain, after which Buganda was divided into four districts. Henry Kyemba, himself a Muganda, described the events of the 'revolution' from inside Obote's close circle:

On May 22, 1966, Obote arrested some of the chief supporters of the Kabaka. As news of the arrests spread, government cars were stoned and the Kabaka's people threw up barricades on the roads leading into the capital from the Kabaka's palace just outside Kampala. . . .

The same day, Obote called a meeting in the President's Lodge in Kampala. . . . After some discussion, Obote told us that the disturbance was no longer a civil matter but a military one. He would ask Amin to move in on the palace. . . .

Very early the next morning, Amin's troops attacked. The Kabaka must have been warned, for his supporters had arms and put up an unexpected resistance for several hours. At 3.30pm, Amin went to the President's Lodge in his open jeep, with its six foot long 122mm gun, to report to Obote and to ask for permission to shell the Kabaka's main residence. He was in a jolly mood and obviously enjoying the fight. Permission was granted....

Within a few minutes, there were two large explosions. Shells punched holes in the Kabaka's main official residence. Smoke billowed up. Then, as if this was a signal to the heavens, it began to rain, torrentially. The fighting stopped. After the storm, the troops moved in quickly to find the Kabaka. At about 5.30, Amin came back to the Lodge bearing his trophies: the Kabaka's Presidential flag and the ceremonial cap that marked him as Commander in Chief of the Uganda Army. He did not know, he said, whether the Kabaka had been killed or escaped. The Kabaka had in fact seized the opportunity during the storm and had escaped through a side entrance into one of the nearby houses. From there he eventually made his escape to Burundi and then to Britain, where he died three years later.

The Kabaka later claimed that thousands had died in the assault; the official toll, based on Amin's own figures, was put at forty-seven; it was in fact much higher – certainly several hundred, perhaps as high as four hundred.[35]

As usual, Jaffar Amin gives a very different story, in which his father secretly saved the Kabaka from Obote's onslaught:

Dad told us that in the thick of battle he threw a smoke screen which shielded the Kabaka and the Kabaka escaped amidst a heavy shower by taxi where he and his ADC [aide-de-camp] Captain Katende drove away to the Congo and then to ... Burundi. From there the Kabaka flew by an American plane to Brussels and by the BOAC [a British airline] to London where he lived in exile until his demise in 1969....

Dad regularly told us that his action was in memory of the close relationship between the Buganda Royal Family and his mother in the past.[36]

The reader might think that this is mostly fantasy, but the storm, the taxi getaway, and the escape route through the Congo and Burundi are all confirmed in the Kabaka's own memoirs.[37]

The aftermath of the so-called 'Battle of Mengo' (the name of the Kabaka's palace complex) has been described by Phares Mutibwa as 'the first major bloodbath in independent Uganda'. For many Baganda, it was seen as the key turning point in post-independence Ugandan history. As Mutibwa put it:

> Following the flight of the Kabaka and the capture of his palace, Amin's men ... on Obote's orders – unleashed a savage and unprecedented slaughter of Baganda who ... put up a determined resistance against the regular army. Scores of these civilians were loaded onto army trucks and disposed of, many of them still alive, either by being thrown into Murchison Falls or by being buried alive in common graves. ... Thus, a precedent had been set for violence, murders and atrocities, which occurred on an even greater scale later. Violence appeared to become institutionalised in Ugandan society.[38]

The exile of the Kabaka did not end Ganda opposition to Obote. The British High Commission learned of several coup plots later in the year, one of which was mentioned in a letter to the Commonwealth Office dated 8 November:

> We have heard from an expatriate Bank Manager here that about a week ago, Paulo Kavuma [a Ganda politician] visited him and told him that the Baganda were obtaining rifles and automatic weapons and that only a few nights previously some of the ringleaders had come to Kavuma and had told him that they were planning to assassinate Obote. Kavuma had pointed out that this would only lead to more bloodshed as Amin would take over and would be utterly ruthless. Kavuma had therefore urged the ringleaders to kill Amin first, for then, in his view, Obote would not necessarily have the support of the army.[39]

By this stage, then, Amin was already being seen as a likely candidate to succeed Obote if he was killed. In October, he had officially replaced Opolot as head of the army, and was promoted to brigadier. It is clear from the

British note that, in the minds of many people, Obote now depended on him for the support of the army.

Amin's personal life also took a new turn around this time, when he married his second official wife, Kay (or Kaysiya) Adroa. She was a Lugbara from West Nile, and may have known the young brigadier from childhood. Jaffar Amin says that she was considered, in local kinship terms, as his 'cousin', and therefore the marriage would not have been allowed under traditional law, so they married in a Registry Office. Kay was an educated woman, from a very respectable family. According to Decker, she had been 'one of the first Lugbara women to study at Makerere University'.[40] Her father was a senior Anglican clergyman (an archdeacon), who strongly disapproved of the match. Many sources also suggest she had been Amin's lover for some time. According to Decker,[41] Amin's first wife Malyam knew nothing about their marriage plans, though she had caught them *in flagrante* some months earlier, while Amin was keeping his head down over the Congo gold allegations. Decker's account of this is similar to that of Bob Astles, who seems to have been very fond of Malyam, describing her as 'a very beautiful, stately woman as tall as Amin but with a gentle voice and quiet movements and without the arrogance of other military wives'.[42] He gives an intriguing portrait of the Amins' home life before Kay came along:

Before Amin started drinking it was a delight to visit the Entebbe house. He could be full of fun and he still played rugby and jogged along the lakeside in his tracksuit. I would often find him in the house polishing the furniture or the floor. Malyam told me that he frequently brought her breakfast in bed having cooked it himself, and certainly I never saw a cook there. He seemed a remarkable man to all of us who met him....

I am convinced to this day that the meeting between Amin and Kay was arranged by the politicians. ... The one person who was not aware of the coming marriage was Malyam but she suspected that Amin was having an affair. She managed to persuade him to let her travel to her relatives ... but when she got there instead of staying the night she returned to her house. There she found her husband in the living room and rushing past him into the bedroom she found a naked young woman on the bed. There was no escape and pouncing on the girl she took a good grip on her hair and dragged her towards the door before Amin could collect his wife. Malyam really had the initiative that night. The naked girl was Kay and later they became firm friends and stood together against his philandering.[43]

The wedding to Kay took place in Arua, the West Nile capital. Astles described it as 'a spectacular affair' writing that it 'was clearly being seen as an important occasion for the politics of Uganda'.[44] The reception, according to Jaffar, was a party that 'attendees remembered and talked about for a very long time'.[45] One of these was Henry Kyemba, who recalled that 'Kay was wearing a white Western-style bridal dress ... and Amin was in full army uniform.'[46]

Within a year, Amin married again. His third wife, Nora, came from Obote's home area. Kyemba says that their marriage was 'one of political convenience. ... To marry a Langi would reassure Obote that their tribal differences were insignificant, and thus allay his suspicions.'[47] In Decker's account, however, it is described more as a passionate affair that had been going on for some time. She cites Maylam's 1979 interview with the British tabloid *Daily Mirror*, when she was seeking asylum in the UK, to support a story that, before the wedding, Malyam and Kay had joined forces to confront Amin over his relationship with Nora, and he beat them both up as a result.[48] Uganda, of course, was (and to an extent is) a polygamous society, for men rich enough to afford more than one wife, and Muslims regarded this as sanctioned by Islamic law. It is unlikely that the appearance of another spouse would be unexpected, although polygamy is, unsurprisingly, often a source of antagonism within families. Moreover, by all accounts, including his son's, throughout his adult life Amin had had a large number of more or less acknowledged 'girlfriends', usually at the same time. Malyam's consternation and sense of betrayal over successive further marriages, as portrayed in the *Daily Mirror* article, may have been a case of tabloid journalistic licence rather than a truly first-hand account of events. This is not, of course, to deny that Amin was violent towards his wives. Even given that the sources are contradictory and unreliable, it would perhaps be more surprising if he had *not* hit his sexual partners, both in terms of prevalent social norms, and from all we know of his background and personality. Once again, however, the new bride was eventually accepted into the growing family; Astles writes that Nora 'joined Malyam and Kay in the Command Post [Amin's house] and all three became interested in dressmaking, selling dresses from the house to earn a little money as none of them was given any money of their own from Amin's income, which at that time was not large'.[49]

In 1967, Obote replaced the interim 1966 constitution. The new one abolished all traditional rulers and local government legislatures, and made him the executive president. UPC members believed to be loyal to Ibingira were expelled. Obote went on to introduce a range of seemingly radical economic measures, including a nationalisation programme and measures intended to prefer Ugandan workers over migrants. This became known in Ugandan politics as 'The Move to the Left'. The 1966 crisis, as Jorgensen wrote, provided 'both the impetus and the means for the Obote regime to restructure its basis of power. ... [T]he economic policy of the regime evolved into a "commanding heights" strategy in which the state assumed control or direction of leading [economic] institutions'.[50]

The relationship between Amin and Obote had also dramatically changed, or perhaps it simply emerged into public view for the first time. According to Henry Kyemba:

Amin was now Obote's undisputed favourite. Obote had little civilian political support left and would have to rely heavily on the army. ... It seemed safe to trust Amin. He was, after all, nearly illiterate and showed no signs of political ambition. Indeed, Obote foresaw a danger, not from Amin, but from some of the younger officers who had been trained by the British and Israelis. Obote believed that Amin would act as a first line of defense against their ambitions. ...

In the space of just a few months, Uganda had gone from a peaceful democracy to something very close to a military dictatorship.[51]

'THE PIGEONHOLE CONSTITUTION'

Between 1967 and 1969, Obote and Amin, working together, increasingly monopolised political power in Uganda. Complex federal structures were replaced with a single, centralised state. Local government elections were cancelled, and internal democratic structures within the UPC withered away. The new constitution became known to Ugandans as 'the pigeonhole constitution', because Obote ordered members of the National Assembly to pass it unread, saying they would find copies in their mail pigeonholes later.[52] As they voted, Amin's soldiers surrounded the National Assembly building and helicopters hovered above. Ugandan political scientist Akiiki B. Mujaju describes the symbiotic relationship between Obote and Amin at this time:

> The intrigue within the UPC [in 1966] ... not only made Amin a towering figure in the coalition of forces that emerged after the crisis ... they also made Obote and the presidency centres of concentrated power ... [and] linked Obote's political survival to Amin's, while Amin's security within the army was made ... dependent on Obote ...[53]

But for many Ugandan commentators, with the benefit of hindsight Obote's 1966 'revolution' led inexorably to the eventual military takeover. According to Karugire:

> [B]y 1965 all the politicians had given up even the pretence of appealing to the electorate.... [T]he two factions into which the ruling party had divided each hoped to get the support of some section of the army and in the end, in May 1966, it was the Obote faction which won. From that date it could be said that Uganda had a quasi-military government because the basis of Obote's abrogation of the 1962 constitution ... was based on nothing but force – force provided by the army ...[54]

Henry Kyemba broadly concurs with this, writing that: 'For three years, Amin remained indispensable [to Obote]. At the same time, as Obote himself saw, he posed a steadily growing threat. Their nascent rivalry erupted into open enmity in December 1969.'[55] The leader of the defeated UPC faction, Grace Ibingira, agreed, writing that: 'Although the Uganda Army did not overthrow Obote until 1971, in actual fact it had been deeply involved in Ugandan politics since 1966, for Obote used the armed forces to overthrow the established order of constitutional government and they were the means by which he maintained his increasingly unpopular regime.'[56] These conclusions were, of course, written after Amin's coup.

By the second half of the 1960s, however, the key issue for most Ugandans was probably one we have hardly looked at, because Amin seems to have had little interest in it. This was the Ugandan economy and its structural weaknesses, together with the effect these had on Obote's ability to deliver his policies. The situation is neatly summarised in Richard Reid's history of Uganda:

> [I]n 1963, Uganda's first full year as an independent state, the country could safely be depicted by a contemporary economist as 'the textbook description of a low-income country'. Its GDP was £176.1 million, which means that output per head amounted to £24.5 per annum, 'among the lowest per capita income figures in the world'. Nearly 27 per cent of GDP was derived from subsistence activity [i.e. small-scale peasant farming and herding] and agriculture alone accounted for more than 50 per cent of monetary GDP. National income was heavily dependent on export earnings, accounting for over 46 per cent of GDP. Most Ugandans were 'self-employed' – as farmers and herdsmen, operating at small-scale, subsistence level – while less than 6 per cent of Ugandan adults were classified as wage- and salary-earners. By sharp contrast, Asians and Europeans – constituting 1.4 per cent of the total population – were in receipt of approximately 26 per cent of monetary incomes.[57]

There was very little manufacturing industry, and Obote's economic strategy at first attempted to prioritise industrialisation and reduce the country's dependence on agricultural exports. After the events of 1965–66, however, Uganda's economic policies took a turn to the left, 'in the belief' as Reid puts it, 'that only a statist approach to the economy could bring about "Africanization" and enable the country to realise its full material potential'.[58] Reid points out that, at the time, belief in the efficacy of centralised state planning and state-controlled industrialisation was widespread economic orthodoxy, and had become an approach which 'was common across numerous newly independent nations across the continent'.[59] Obote's policy, which became known as his 'Move to the Left', was aimed at implementing just such a strategy:

> This was the rationale behind the nationalisation programme across the financial and commercial sectors, and the beginnings of a re-examination

of the status of the Asian community in terms of citizenship rights and their role in the economy. But it also led to greater interest in rural development. ... Much-derided consequently, it nevertheless represented an attempt to constitutionally enshrine a batch of entitlements and protections for the 'ordinary citizen'.[60]

Against this economic background, however, Obote's hold on power became increasingly fragile. Rumours of coup attempts proliferated, and Amin's standing within the country grew. He himself openly boasted of his power over Obote, and sought to boost it through strategic international alliances, especially with the Israelis and the British. The defeat of the Baganda elite in 1966 was probably the closest Amin and Obote ever got. Their falling out can be dated at least as far back as February 1967, when the British high commissioner, Roland Hunt, noted that, 'relations between Amin and Obote are badly strained.... Amin is aware of the latter's wish to get rid of him.'[61] Hunt went on to consider the likelihood of Amin either launching a coup on his own, or being used by other opponents of Obote, specifically Onama and/or Nekyon, to help them to overthrow the president.[62] The British certainly believed later that he actually attempted to overthrow Obote in 1967.[63] In any case, as the 1960s drew to a close, rumours of coups, assassination attempts and other plots increasingly dominated both Ugandan political life, and probably Amin's own.

Some sense of the intricate diplomatic dance being performed by the British officials is given in a 1967 High Commission memo which suggests that Amin was, at the time, working to gain British support against Obote. It is worth quoting at length for its detailed portrait of Amin's home life and his relationship with British officials. On the evening of 17 August 1967, Mr M.C. Oatley of the High Commission visited Amin's house to take him to a party for a visiting British army unit. He wrote:

I had a long and quite intimate conversation with Brigadier Idi Amin during the evening of 17 August....

2. Earlier in the day, Tommy Newton Dunn [the British defence advisor] and I had accompanied our Imperial Defence College [IDC] visitors to a very successful display and reception given for them by the Ugandan Army.... Much good will was generated and ... Newton Dunn

was able to extract Amin's promise to attend the supper party which he was giving.... The party duly began, and about an hour later Amin telephoned to say that he had been unable to find the right house. I therefore went to fetch him.

3. Amin now lives in the house on Prince Charles Drive which was formerly occupied by his predecessor, Shabani Opoloto, and which has been the scene of previous 'incidents'. Despite the telephone conversation, I thought when I arrived there that I was about to be involved in another one for, on pulling up, I was challenged with hysterical ferocity by a sentry and ordered out of my car at the point of his carefully aimed gun. It was not until one of Amin's children called to him from the house that he remembered that I was an expected visitor and agreed to let us in. Amin himself then appeared on a darkened balcony and called down that he would join me in a few moments but after five minutes I found my way upstairs to the main living room, drably furnished and containing a large television set, a cup for the East-African inter-Army football competition and a prominently displayed portrait of Chairman Mao. I was there entertained by two small dirty but cheerful Swahili-speaking sons of the house and eventually Mrs. Amin came in to explain that her husband was speaking on the phone to President Obote in Zambia.

4. In due course Amin appeared and apologised for the delay occasioned by the President's telephone call. He showed no inclination to move on, however, and called for some beer. I had the impression that he was still summoning the courage to attend the party; he seems diffident about his poor command of the English language. We talked a little about sport – he was a notable boxer – and discovered a mutual friend from his earlier days in the Army. He explained that he had been unable to find his way to the party earlier in the evening and had similarly failed to find the High Commissioner's Residence in time to attend the previous evening's reception.

5. I began to speak about our visit to Jinja earlier in the day and told him that some of the I.D.C. team had felt that it would have been more appropriate if they had worn their uniforms but that it had not been entirely clear to us that such a gesture would be appreciated from a political point of view. Amin said 'They could wear them. I would give an order

that they should wear them and no-one can argue about it. The President knows that he can only rule because of the army so I can do what I like.' The unexpected force with which this remark was delivered suggested that the principle could be taken to include more than the wearing of uniforms and Amin's manner implied not so much that the President relied on assistance from the Army but that he ruled by permission. And he seemed anxious to take the opportunity of making this point.

6. I congratulated the Brigadier on the performance by the Army Band which we had watched Beating the Retreat during the afternoon and said how impressed the I.D.C. team had been by their visit to Jinja and by the warmth and kindness of their reception. I thanked him for the hospitality which he had extended and said how very much it had been appreciated. Amin said 'This was nothing, just a small party which I ordered because their time was short. They did not see what they should have seen. They should have stayed here for several days. We would like to show them more. And you know we can make a real party, something big: you would not find anything better.' (I hope the sense of this dialogue is apparent in this verbatim reporting: Amin speaks very simply but I do not want to interpret for him.) He also said that relations between us should be good, 'I am the only one who can do this. You can do anything through me.'

7. He went on to express his admiration for Britain and particularly the British army, its methods and the training which it had given to him and to others. He said 'I feel this so much that in the Army they say "You are British, you belong to them."' And then, 'You know that there is hatred in the Uganda Army for you British because you were coming here to fight us last year because they know [the Kabaka] Mutesa asked for British troops to come here. This is the only cause of hatred. I know it because I go round and I speak to them and they hate you for this. This is the only thing. And now Mutesa has confirmed in his book that it was true. This is why I do not see you and why, though you invite me many times to parties, I do not come. . . .' He repeated the main points of this several times.

8. Taking a deep breath I began to explain that none of these things were true. . . . [W]e had told Mutesa categorically that we would not even begin to consider sending troops to Uganda without a formal request

151

from the Government of Uganda which meant the Prime Minister and his Ministers. Amin replied 'but we know that you had troops standing by in Mombasa to come here'. 'How do you know?' 'From Army intelligence sources. They know this and they have told me. This is why there is hatred in the army....'

9. I told Amin again that this was all quite untrue, that his sources of information were false....

10. At this point I felt that I might have made some impression on him but was unlikely to get much further.... Here he and I now were having a completely frank talk but it was the first time this had happened. How could we ever sort things out if we never met? Did he not think it a pity that the President would not let him see us. He said quickly that the President had no power to control his movements he could see whom he wished.

11. By this time we had been joined by the present Mrs. Amin [Kay], an intelligent, poised and friendly young woman in her very early twenties who was at Gayaza High School with one of Amin's sisters, speaks excellent English, and intends to study for a Diploma in Education at Makerere next year. I suggested that we should go out and join the supper party. Amin asked who would be at it and whether Michael Emojong (acting Secretary for Defence) would be there. I said that he had been invited....

12. As we left the house I told Amin that while all I had told him was true I did not necessarily expect him to take the word of a diplomat from the High Commission.... I therefore wanted him to put the same questions to Brigadier Blair (a member of the I.D.C. team who commanded the 4th Battalion, K.A.R. from 1958–1961) whom he knew well – 'Yes. He recommended me to become an officer'....

13. We then at long last left for Newton Dunn's house. (Amin, incidentally, drives himself at night in a large unmarked Chevrolet so perhaps he really did get lost at the first attempt.) On arrival we herded him together with Brigadier Blair and he duly took up the point about our intentions last May. Blair, who is a forceful and charming person played up well and, appealing to their previous comradeship, denied absolutely any intention to interfere in Uganda's affairs.... Tommy Newton Dunn then made a similar statement and later on Amin sat at supper with

General Fitz George-Balfour who doubtless had a soothing effect on him for, by the end of the evening, Amin was considerably mellowed and had invited the General to act as an Umpire in an important Inter-Battalion exercise to be held in September.

14. It was my distinct impression that Amin's decision to attend Newton Dunn's party and to bring into the open the suspicions which he voiced represented an important personal initiative on the part of this key figure. . . . I also felt that if he could only be persuaded to leave the door ajar it would not be difficult for us to establish a useful relationship with him. I hope this may justify the length of this account.[64]

Oatley seems to see Amin's approach as gauche and innocent, suggesting that the brigadier was hampered by his poor English, and socially insecure at the prospect of attending a party with *muzungu* senior officers. However, it might instead be seen as a carefully prepared attempt to get a clear message across to the British – that Amin was a British-friendly Ugandan leader, at least as powerful as Obote and maybe more so, but, unlike the president, also keen to strengthen the ties between his country and its former imperial master. Amin's 'verbatim' words here serve to reinforce the image of the blunt, not very bright, but totally reliable soldier which, I have suggested, he had sedulously cultivated over his years in the KAR. He seems to have charmed the British senior officers while, I suspect, seeing through Oatley's unctuous praise of the Ugandan army and its hospitality. He may also have kept his own views about the extent of British military support for the Kabaka the previous year. It seems likely that Oatley, like so many other British officials, fell into the trap of underestimating Amin's intelligence; the brigadier may not have been exhibiting social anxiety so much as manoeuvring for support in a power struggle.

Two months later, he gave an interview to the government-supporting newspaper, *The People*, headed 'Army doesn't want to take over – Amin'. According to the reporter:

Brigadier Idi Amin told me yesterday in an exclusive interview that he had told his senior officers this week . . . that they should set an example of being the only soldiers in Africa who have no ambition of taking over the government. . . .

He described it as 'alarming' to hear about armies in various parts of Africa taking over governments from good and efficient civilians.

The Ugandan armed forces were wholeheartedly behind President Obote and his government, he declared. Their only ambition was to become one of the toughest and most disciplined army [*sic*] in Africa.[65]

Obote would have had to be very innocent indeed not to see such assurances as an outright threat.

The portrait of Chairman Mao mentioned by Oatley is a particularly interesting feature of Amin's domestic environment. Chinese influence was clearly growing throughout the country, and especially in the army. In July, a disaffected Muganda officer, Major Senkooto, told the British defence advisor, Tommy Newton Dunn, that 'there were six Chinese in the Training Team at Jinja and another 4/5 at Mbarara. The former were trying to foist Mao doctrine on the students but he had forbidden them to do this'.[66] The next month, Newton Dunn reported to the Ministry of Defence about a meeting he had had with the Sudanese military attaché in Uganda, who 'mentioned that he and Amin frequently had conversations together. Amin and his officers appeared to be friendly with the Chinese. He wanted to know the names of some of the officers recently promoted (he had met several at the Chinese embassy) and he asked me could I give him the names of the officers who had been kicked out. I was able to be of some assistance to him over this'.[67]

August 1967, the month of Newton Dunn's conversation with the Sudanese military attaché, also saw the arrival in Uganda of a man who was to become one of Amin's close foreign allies, the Israeli Colonel Baruch 'Burka' Bar-Lev. On taking up his post, he was described by Colonel Newton Dunn in glowing terms:

Colonel Bar-Lev was the Chief of Staff of Central Command and based in Jerusalem. He is an Armoured Corps man and was enthusiastic about the 105mm gun on the Centurian [tank; *sic*]. He came to Israel from Lithuania and claims that his first language is Russian.

He is a very intelligent man and far more pleasant than [his predecessor, Colonel] Bar Sever. He is fond of music and of reading; he is a keen horseman and likes swimming. He is married with, I think, three children and his wife, who is the director of one of Israel's banks, will be joining him . . .[68]

Bar-Lev's posting to Uganda is a demonstration of the importance Israel attached to the country, partly perhaps as a customer for arms but, more important to Israel, as a potential supporter in the UN and other international forums.

As the Ugandan military now increasingly relied on Israel rather than Britain for arms and training, Bar-Lev became one of the British High Commission's main sources of information on what was happening in the army, and on Amin himself. In January 1968, Newton Dunn reported that the Israelis feared being supplanted by Chinese and Soviet bloc military suppliers. In a memo full of facts and figures on the Ugandan army culled from Bar-Lev, he wrote that the latter: 'told me that he had been having trouble with the Ugandan Air Force'. Israeli technicians had been replaced with 'eight Czechoslovakian Army officers who had come from Syria', six pilots had been receiving training in Russia, and Bar-Lev understood that Uganda would be receiving six Soviet MIG 17 planes 'as a gift'. In the army, there were 'five, possibly six, Russian artillery instructors at Masindi', and a considerable number of Russian artillery guns, mortars and anti-aircraft guns had been supplied. The Israelis themselves were providing Uganda with more infantry instructors as well as, according to Bar-Lev, some eighteen military aircraft with associated armaments. According to Newton Dunn, Bar-Lev told him that Amin was 'not too well, his leg was causing a lot of trouble, but he understood that he was receiving treatment from a British doctor. I hadn't heard this.' By this stage, then, the British were even learning about their own nationals from the Israelis. Bar-Lev informed Newton Dunn that:

He had told Amin and Onama that their policy of taking arms from the Russians and Chinese was foolish and would not pay off as they would be unable to get spares or ammunition, but apparently they would not listen to him – even now they are short of ammunition. Bar Lev said that he had seen the Chinese rifles, they were badly made and of poor quality. They very quickly get rusty in Uganda.[69]

Shortly afterwards, Newton Dunn wrote to the British Ministry of Defence:

> you will be interested to hear that when I saw Col. Bar Lev in the street today he told me that … [a]pparently six or eight Migs, believed to be Mig 17s, have arrived in large crates at Gulu. To look after the Migs, a Russian major has now arrived and the Czechoslovakian lieutenant colonel has been made subordinate to him. The lieutenant colonel has told Col. Bar Lev that he will not stand for this sort of thing and is protesting to his government. Bar Lev has promised to keep me informed of any developments.[70]

A couple of days later, Bar-Lev warned the British defence advisor that 'if at any subsequent voting at the U.N. the Ugandans voted against Israel … the Israeli training team would be withdrawn.' Passing on the details Bar-Lev had given about the Chinese and Soviet arms, Newton Dunn, who was shortly to be replaced by Colonel H.N. Crawford, reported the Israeli as saying that:

> During this coming year, Brig. Amin intends releasing many of the old soldiers who are married and have families because of the accommodation problem. No plans to recruit many more soldiers. Bar Lev has also been told by him that he is trying to get back some of the old soldiers who served with him in the K.A.R. and had heard that Amin had recently promoted to officer rank one or two truck drivers (because he knew they were really good fellows). Bar Lev says these men … need a really long course as they are such poor material but he is only allowed to give them three months training. … Brig. Amin is still having a lot of trouble with his joints which are swollen and stiff and will probably be going to Israel in the very near future to receive treatment.[71]

The new military advisor, Nigel Crawford, wasted little time in meeting Bar-Lev and getting his briefing on Amin. He visited the Israeli military attaché on 20 June and was told that General Amin:

> was completely loyal to Obote and had no political ambitions. He recognised his own good fortune to have reached General rank and also that he did not have the intelligence to be a politician. Bar Lev added that

Amin was happy to talk on minor tactics, weapon training, platoon company matters but immediately said that he was busy and changed the subject if Bar Lev tried to raise more 'general officer' like subjects of organisation, logistics or technical training.[72]

Avoiding such topics in conversations with an Israeli military official might be seen as prudent caution, rather than ignorance or lack of confidence, on Amin's part, but it is also possible that Bar-Lev was simply selling the line Amin wanted to project to the British. Many of Bar-Lev's later statements to the British certainly seem to fall into the latter category, and perhaps he rather enjoyed the position of go-between in the relationship between the Ugandan state and its former colonial master.

In September, Crawford told the Ministry of Defence that, as a result of a visit by a 'Mr Knott', to review Uganda's rather old stock of British Ferret armoured cars, 'my relations with General Amin and the army as a whole improved considerably'. At a cocktail party hosted by Amin for a dozen British representatives (including Crawford and Knott), together with 'Seventy to a hundred' Ugandan officers, the general was in bonhomie mode, and seemed keen to please his guests:

> During the party I spoke with General Amin for some fifteen minutes and found him in a relaxed and happy mood. He made several jokes and proudly showed me his 4th KAR tie which he was wearing. I said that since I saw he wore a KAR tie I must start wearing my 11 KAR tie, which I had hesitated [to do] up to now in case it offended anyone. He assured me that I must 'always' wear it and then went on to say that he owed much to the KAR and the British. He added that it was a great pity that we did not train his air force but it was our fault because we had quoted 15 years as necessary to do this, while the Israelis had said 2 or 3 years.

Amin proposed more British training for the air force, and Crawford promised to investigate the possibilities, then:

> We discussed types of aircraft and when I told him about the Harrier he came out with the startling question of whether it could bomb Cairo if he had it. I said that no plane of that size ... had the range to do this and in

any case surely he did not contemplate this ever being necessary. He replied that a small war was a very good way of training....

He also added, partly as a joke I think, that British soldiers were very tough and very rough off duty whereas his were very well behaved. I said I had heard of a few people being roughly handled by his soldiers whereupon he said 'well that is for the politicians' and laughed....

Towards the end of the party Amin made a speech in Swahili which was translated accurately into English for our benefit. He...told everyone how much Britain did and had done for the Ugandan Forces and how valuable they found the training and Courses [sic] they attended in the UK. He went on to say that the British were reliable and honest people and he trusted them in spite of what some people said....Amin continued to praise the British and his long experience of them and ended his speech by calling for four shouts of 'MOTO' (Hot) for the British and two shouts for the Uganda army and Air Force. This is the equivalent of three cheers.[73]

The question of whether, when and how Amin was joking was a regular refrain in British responses to his statements. Was his idiosyncratic sense of humour, as some believed, the result of social and linguistic ineptitude, or did he find it a useful way of creating confusion and doubt in the listener's mind, which he might then be able to exploit? Had he learned the usefulness of jokes in the army, as a way of dealing with his British officers? As with so much about the man, it is impossible to tell. He would not be the only politician ever to use humour as a distraction tactic.

Whatever the case, Amin's overtures to the British were noticed with enthusiasm in some quarters and scepticism in others; some diplomats at least were beginning to realise that the brigadier's motivations and moves might be more complicated and sophisticated than had previously been thought. The deputy high commissioner, Nigel Wenham-Smith, who was also at the party, poured cold water on the defence advisor's enthusiasm for Amin's apparent anglophilia. He wrote to R.G. Tallboys at the East Africa desk that:

It is possible that part of Amin's object in the exercise was to bring his own officers round to his friendly view of the British; and it may be that this point could best be got across when the actual presence of the British would require some friendly gestures. But it is hard to believe that this was the whole story. ... One might speculate that Amin was keen to establish a favourable relationship with us against the day of his coup.... This may be going too far, but what is certainly clear is that Amin must be a great deal more sure of himself than he was previously to take in public a line so much more favourable to us than anything the President or Foreign Minister have seen fit to propound.[74]

The high commissioner, Forster, who did not attend the party, also had some doubts about Crawford's enthusiasm for Amin's moves, telling Tallboys of:

my feelings that we need to be pretty cautious in our reactions to Amin's sudden burst of anglophile friendliness. As you well know, it is very hard in this country to guess accurately whether suggestions by someone like Amin will necessarily be endorsed by, say, Onama or Obote. Indeed Amin may well have some personal motive not shared by, or even opposed by, his theoretical political masters.

Although I certainly do not intend to discourage the closer relationship which Nigel Crawford has established with Amin and the Army ... I am convinced that all this should be kept on a tight political rein and I have accordingly told him not to take any further action....[75]

Tallboys' boss at the East Africa desk, Scott, noted in response that 'it occurred to me ... that Amin might have a more ulterior motive for this sudden sign of warm friendship for the British and my thoughts were running very much along the lines of Mr Wenham-Smith's speculation, mainly that if Amin ever has it in mind to stage a coup he would certainly hope very quickly to secure HMG's [Her Majesty's Government] recognition of his government....'[76]

At this time, the British went so far as to send recent reports on the political situation in Uganda to Washington. The US State Department's Country Director for East Africa [sic], Nick Feld, told the British ambassador to the USA that the US believed dissatisfaction with Obote in the army and civil service 'had not yet reached a level where Obote's position was seriously threatened (except possibly by assassination)'. He thought that 'the army officers (more interested in pay than politics) were still loyal to Obote'. According to the British ambassador:

> Feld agreed that, however unscrupulous some of his methods, it is very much in our interest that Obote should remain in control. If he were overthrown, Uganda would almost certainly succumb to serious tribal dissention. . . . All the possible alternatives to Obote looked considerably worse. Amin would be a disaster and Nekyon's unscrupulousness made Obote appear almost white.[77]

It is not entirely clear whether the racial slur was a direct quote from the American or a British gloss on his remarks, but it looks like the former. Tallboys commented that: 'It is not clear whether the Americans would consider Amin a "disaster" because of personality or lack of ability and intelligence, or because he would be another military leader replacing a civilian government.'[78]

In 1969, further reverberations from the Congo gold crisis of four years earlier presented a new problem for the British, with Amin at the centre of it. This concerned a legal case against Bob Astles. A memo from Le Tocq to D.C. Tebbit, the head of the Commonwealth Office, explained:

> A certain Robert Astles, a United Kingdom citizen who has been in Uganda Government service for some years, is being sued for slander by an Assistant Commissioner of the Uganda Police. The case arises out of the fact that Astles, who appears to have been in the pay of the Uganda Secret Service, reported (whether accurately or not we do not know) a meeting at which the plaintiff in the present suit, a Mr John Odongkara, took part at which a plan to overthrow the Uganda Government was discussed. The Commissioner of Police confronted Odongkara with this report, with the result that Odongkara is trying to clear his name in the courts.
>
> The complications arise because it is believed that a number of prominent Ugandans, including President Obote and General Amin, and probably Mr Felix Onama as well, are extremely anxious to get rid of Astles because of the knowledge which the latter is thought to have which would incriminate them, or at any rate damage their reputations; the notorious case of the 'Congo gold' is thought to be the subject.

Astles has been in Uganda for some years and ... it may well be known to some Ugandans that he has from time to time offered his services to the High Commission and attempted to convey information. Moreover, he appears to claim to be 'Ugandan', or even a 'Ugandan citizen', though ... the High Commissioner does not believe that he has renounced his U.K. citizenship, which would have been necessary before he could acquire Ugandan citizenship....

I do not want to be alarmist, but the affair is potentially messy; perhaps our best hope is that the belief that Astles is in possession of damaging information may induce President Obote to play the matter quietly.[79]

Wenham-Smith, the deputy high commissioner, explained to Tallboys at the East Africa desk that:

[t]he allegation states that Astles on or about 17 December 1966 falsely and maliciously spoke of Odongkara to and or in the presence of the then Colonel (now Major-General) Amin. Astles is supposed to have said that Odongkara and a group of other persons were meeting in the Uganda Club in Kampala to work out a plan to cause chaos and overthrow the constitutionally established Government of Uganda.

A source in Uganda Television had apparently suggested to Wenham-Smith that Obote was behind Odongkara's allegations because he wanted to 'put the squeeze on Astles' to prevent him saying what he knew about 'Uganda's internal affairs'. Wenham-Smith himself suggested that:

It is of course possible, despite what we have been told, that Astles is not himself the real target in this case. He may be no more than a stalking horse in an operation being mounted against Amin; this would fit in with some current rumours to the effect that Amin and Obote had fallen out. However, the scene is at present so murky that it would be misleading to suggest that we can at present give a plausible account of the play, or be sure that the manoeuvring is more than usually determined....[80]

In the event, the tangled case came to a low-key denouement. When the allegations came to trial in December 1969, it transpired that Amin himself had not, contrary to press reports, been directly involved. Astles, having admitted using the words (to someone else), was fined a small sum for defamation. The British correspondence about the matter clearly demonstrates the Shakespearian atmosphere of conspiracy, plotting and treachery that characterised Ugandan politics at the end of the 1960s. But the rumours were right; Obote and Amin were indeed beginning to fall out, and the consequences for Uganda would be immense.

What must have been even more important to Amin, however, was the death in August 1969 of his mother. From Jaffar's account, she seems to have been the one fixed, reliable point around which his hectic life had revolved. She had, in her grandson's version, brought up the young Idi almost single-handedly, and passed on to him some of the determination and strength to challenge authority she had demonstrated after his birth, by jumping the KAR rifle. There seems little doubt that she was by far the most important woman in Idi Amin's life, and her death must have affected him strongly, but the historical record gives us no information on this. Bob Astles attended her funeral:

> I once met Amin's mother. She was indeed deeply religious and respected by her community. I saw this at the funeral in Arua, West Nile, when a rift occurred between Amin and all her family. ... Amin, who was then army chief of staff, was not welcome ... during the initial funeral rites. He took it quietly and went off to pray at his mosque on the other side of the town. His mother's funeral, in fact, became one of the issues between him and Dr Obote. It had turned out to be one of the most expensive and lavish funerals during which the Israelis had flown over the burial ground and with great precision had dropped a wreath by parachute directly onto the grave. It caused great excitement among the tribe but when Dr Obote heard about it he angrily demanded to know who had paid for the services of the aircraft.[81]

In fact, Amin's 'issues' with Obote were about to come to a head.

5

'MARTIAL MUSIC'
THE BUILD-UP, THE COUP AND THE AFTERMATH, 1969–71

Amin's seizure of power is, of course, central both to his life story and to his image and myth. For most, including many Ugandans, the 1971 coup represents *the* key moment in Uganda's post-independence history, at which the country began to slide downwards economically, socially and politically, towards a penurious despotism. In fact, as we saw in the last chapter, many historians of Uganda believe that both the slide to authoritarian, unelected rule, and the economic decline, had begun considerably earlier, with Obote's 1966 'coup'. At the time, Amin's own coup was analysed by most Ugandan and other African intellectuals, as well as many in the West, either in Marxist terms or through conspiracy theories. The overthrow of Obote either represented shifting class forces, specifically a fascist victory of the petit bourgeoisie and reactionary peasants against a nascent working class, or else it was covertly organised by Western intelligence agencies (sometimes it was seen as both at the same time). Surely the stupid, uneducated soldier could not have done this by himself? Burka Bar-Lev or Bob Astles must have been behind it and, behind them, the British and/or Israeli intelligence services. When I was a young, left-wing investigative journalist in the 1980s, it was *de rigueur* to believe that, as Bloch and Fitzgerald put it: 'The British government now holds joint responsibility [with the Israelis] for installing one of the most savage regimes of recent times.'[1] The word 'savage' is symptomatic: it is a noun as well as an adjective. Amin was clearly a primitive savage, an ignorant Othello who needed a (white) Iago to guide him towards the bloodbath.

Unsurprisingly, there are widely differing accounts of the actual events of 25 January 1971, even among those who were there at the time and knew many of the participants. Basic factual details are disputed. At the time, Amin's seizure of state power was widely welcomed in both Uganda and the West. This chapter covers a considerably shorter period than the others and includes more direct quotation from primary sources. British archive material from the period and later Ugandan analyses of the coup are shown, not as opposed discourses, but parallel interpretations of events which interacted with each other. While we cannot know for sure, the evidence suggests that the British High Commission knew little about what was going on, while the Israelis certainly seem to have had greater involvement, and Bar-Lev may well have advised and assisted Amin before and during the coup. This does not, however, mean that the Israelis were 'behind it', rather than simply trying to steer and take advantage of events that were unfolding anyway.

PRELUDE TO COLLAPSE

Towards the end of the 1960s, as we have seen, Uganda was boiling with political unrest. Plots, and rumours of plots, were everywhere. Ugandan commentators tend to agree with the British assessment of early 1969; the question was when, not if, the coup would come. Plans for Obote's assassination were continually being uncovered, or invented until, in the last weeks of the decade, a serious attempt took place. It was (and is) not clear who was responsible: some thought it was Amin, others that it was a belated 'right-wing' Baganda response to the 1966 coup.

The background was the UPC annual delegates' conference, which opened on 14 November 1969, attended by presidents Jomo Kenyatta of Kenya, Julius Nyerere of Tanzania and Kenneth Kaunda of Zambia. On the agenda was a further move to the left in economic policy. The policy was laid out in a government paper written by Obote, titled the Common Man's Charter.[2] In this, the president announced that '[t]he Move to the Left is the creation of a new political culture and a new way of life, whereby the people of Uganda as a whole ... are paramount. It is therefore, both anti-feudalism and anti-capitalism.'[3] Explicitly socialist, though closer to the programme of the contemporary British Labour Party than that of the Soviet Union, the Common Man's Charter called for government control of industry, commerce and finance (possibly, but not necessarily, through nationalisation) and a major focus on education, as well as the establishment of a social security system and a civilian national service programme for public works. Its analysis of the country's economic problems is succinct and accurate:

> The structure of Uganda's economy is characterised by: an excessive dependence on agriculture as a source of income, employment and foreign exchange; a heavy dependence on exports based on two major export crops [coffee and cotton]; heavy dependence on imports, particularly of manufactured products, and the limited participation of Ugandans in the modern industrial and commercial sectors of the economy.[4]

The last point was addressed in an appendix to the Charter, consisting of a speech given by Obote on an issue which would lead to one of the most notorious actions of Amin's regime, the expulsion of Uganda's Asian population. The speech makes it clear that this policy was originally not Amin's, but Obote's. He wrote:

> Regarding the non-Ugandans who are also non-Africans, the majority of whom are British citizens of Asian origin, a comprehensive exercise is now being undertaken in a two-pronged dimension. First, in accordance with the provisions of the Immigration Act, passed by this House last year. This involves the documentation of all non-citizens living in Uganda. Secondly, a detailed documentation of persons now popularly known as 'Asians holding British passports' is being made. Government will issue an appropriate report on this matter in due course. For the moment, I wish to emphasize that as far as Uganda is concerned, these people are not Ugandan citizens and are not entitled to remain in our country at their own will or because they cannot be admitted to any other country. They have never shown any commitment to the cause of Uganda or even to Africa. Their interest is to make money, which money they exported to various capitals of the world on the eve of our Independence. They are, however, human beings and much as they have shown every sign of being rootless in Uganda, we would like their departure not to cause either them or others dear to them, or even ourselves, any human affliction. Government, when the two exercises are completed, will arrange for a systematic manner through which these persons are to disengage themselves from their hold on and continued residence in our country.[5]

It is clear from this that the expulsion of Uganda's Asians, almost universally believed to have been a crazy idea of Amin's, was in fact Obote's openly announced policy two years earlier. Amin simply implemented it after taking over, probably at around the same time Obote would have done.

Later in 1970, Obote expelled from Uganda a large number of migrant workers from neighbouring countries. Most of these were Kenyans from the Luo tribe, whose expulsion, unlike that of the Asians, is now forgotten, despite the fact that there were more of the former. As Ali Mazrui later explained:

out of 295,000 people employed in the wage-earning sector in Uganda at the time, 80,000 were non-Ugandans. The largest single group of these non-Ugandans were Kenyans, among whom the Luo were heavily predominant. Their precise number was not easily ascertainable, but one popular estimate at the time was that there were more than 20,000 Kenya Luos in the country. ... [T]here were enough of them [for their expulsion] to put a serious strain on relations between Uganda and Kenya.[6]

The 1969 UPC conference had ended with a bang. According to WodOkello Lawoko, a Radio Uganda journalist who reported the meeting:

Amin continued parading in UPC party uniform until the last day of the conference when suddenly, he did not show up. That day, after the president ... had delivered his closing speech and was leaving the hall, he was struck by an assassin's bullet. ... [P]andemonium replaced fanfare. ...

Because we were broadcasting the event live on Radio Uganda, the whole country also got to know at once that the president had been shot. Senior officers of the army started trying to reach their commander Major General Idi Amin so as to receive orders. ... Amin was also wanted by members of the cabinet and senior officials of the police, but was nowhere to be found ...[7]

It transpired that Obote had suffered only minor injuries to his mouth from the shooting. The police evidence, probably obtained by dubious means, pointed to the (Muganda) leader of the DP, Benedicto Kiwanuka, as the person who had commissioned the shooting, and he was duly arrested on 20 December 1969. The next day, the DP was banned as a political party.

Although the evidence is unreliable, Kiwanuka's involvement is now widely accepted in Uganda.[8]

At the time, the British seemed unclear about who might be responsible and what their aim might be. Mr Scott, from the High Commission, telegraphed the Foreign and Commonwealth Office (FCO) on 22 December to tell them:

1. It is still not easy to give a coherent explanation of who was responsible for the attempt and whether it was intended as prelude to a political coup.

2. Perhaps the most significant aspect of the whole affair is what has not repeat not happened. If a coup was intended, then it is difficult to understand why there should be no sign whatever of any follow-up....

3. There does, however, seem to be some evidence that army personnel may be in some way involved. General Amin, who was present at the congress with a large number of his officers, did not leave the stadium in his own car, but is reported to have hitched a lift back to his own house and to have lain low there ever since.... [A]n Israeli army officer who reported for duty at Jinja barracks ... says that no repeat no officers were present at all and the barracks were being run entirely by NCOs.

4. One possible explanation ... is that a group of middle ranking officers, who are known to be discontented and to have been allowed little responsibility ... may have decided to kill the President in preparation for a coup.... When they saw that the President was only wounded ... they got cold feet and simply faded away among their colleagues. Otherwise, it is extremely difficult to understand why the person who fired the shot should not have been arrested.[9]

In the wake of Obote's shooting, military and security forces set up road-blocks throughout Buganda, where, as Obote's biographer Kenneth Ingham puts it, they 'frequently acted with unprovoked brutality. ... It was some time before it was known that the president was alive ... and in the period of uncertainty a pattern of repression was quickly established.'[10] In early January, the fully recovered Obote chaired a meeting of the Defence Council, at which Amin's deputy, Brigadier Okoya, accused his boss of cowardice and desertion during the assassination attempt. The meeting was abandoned in disarray, intended to resume on Monday 26 January. On Friday 23 January, however, Okoya and his wife were gunned down by unidentified killers near his home in Gulu, the Acholi capital. Amin quickly came under suspicion but the police investigation seemed to go nowhere.[11] Throughout 1970, theories flew around concerning who was responsible for Obote's shooting and Okoya's death, with Amin an obvious suspect. Later that year, a group of men who had been arrested for an armed hold-up confessed to the murder of Brigadier Okoya, claiming that they had been paid to do so by an air force officer acting on Amin's instructions. Their trial was scheduled for February 1971.

Within the army itself, there were increasing tensions. As Mutibwa puts it: '[F]rom the beginning of 1969, Obote had divided the army into two factions along ethnic lines. As president and the Chairman of the Defence Council, he relied on the Nilotic soldiers, largely from Acholi and Lango, while for his part, Amin built his support on his fellow West Nilers.'[12] Some of Obote's moves, however, seemed calculated to anger the soldiers, particularly the massive growth in 1969 of Akena Adoko's GSU. Adoko, the poet and Obote's cousin, was seen by many soldiers to be building up the GSU as a Langi-dominated force that could challenge the army. Mutibwa writes that: 'In a series of moves Obote threatened the existence of the regular army by attempting to create armed organisations that were seen to be acting in rivalry to it.'[13] This included, as well as the GSU, an armed wing of the police named the Special Force. This and the GSU both seemed to the military to be favoured over them in the purchase of arms, equipment and manpower. The real issue in all this, however, was the growing rift and rivalry between Obote and Amin.

The Israeli military attaché Colonel Bar-Lev was by now, as we have seen, the British High Commission's main source of information on both the Uganda Army and the doings and thoughts of Idi Amin, though he was not always an entirely trusted one. In a letter to the East Africa desk of the FCO in February 1970, the deputy high commissioner, W.N. Wenham-Smith, suggested that 'Bar-Lev is of course very well informed and I think we must accept as true most of his observations, particularly about internal army matters; but do not rely on the conclusions he draws from his facts.'[14] In a conversation with the new British defence advisor, Colonel Crawford, in February 1970, Bar-Lev suggested that there had been a plot against Amin by Onama, the defence minister, and Okoya, and that Obote was worried that this would weaken his own position: 'The President must be aware of Amin's loyalty to him and would have reason to fear the result of his removal if Onama were to obtain a more direct control of the Forces.' Crawford also reports Bar-Lev as saying that it was 'probable, though he had no proof, that the attempt on the President's life in December was organised by Onama'. As far as Okoya was concerned, Bar-Lev told Crawford that 'both Amin and the President himself would have had good reason to order his liquidation but of course he had no direct evidence to support this. The day after the murder, Amin went to Gulu to visit the body. His only recorded remark to his Israeli pilot was to the effect that the murderer was a very good shot . . .'[15]

Bar-Lev went on to outline a number of changes in the senior ranks of the army planned by Amin, which would have the effect of strengthening the position of West Nilers vis-à-vis the senior Acholi officers. The deputy British high commissioner, passing on Crawford's memo to the East Africa desk, disagreed with Bar-Lev's analysis of events because it emphasised individual animosities, whereas the British preferred tribal explanations. Bar-Lev, wrote Wenham-Smith:

> is inclined to be too definite in his assessment of the personal relationships affecting the situation and to take too little account of the tribal factors which will certainly be affected by, even if they are not the mainspring behind, the personal rivalries. In particular we think that Bar-Lev takes too simple a view of the Obote-Onama-Amin triangle. Their mutual relationship, like other relationships in Uganda, is constantly shifting.[16]

R.N. Purcell of the East Africa desk, on receiving Crawford's and Wenham-Smith's accounts of the conversation with Colonel Bar-Lev, summarised the situation in a bullet point memo, his conclusions being:

(a) that Onama may have been in some way involved in the attempted assassination of Obote;

(b) that Gen. Amin probably arranged that Okoya should be murdered;

(c) that Obote will continue to support and retain Amin;

(d) that any Acholi tribal reaction to Okoya's murder is now highly unlikely.

He concluded with some psychological speculation, and a prediction:

> It seems clear that Obote's effectiveness as President has been considerably reduced since the December attempt on his life.... The effect of fear and uncertainty on Obote's mental make up, which I believe has never been particularly tranquil, may be of real significance. However this may be I would guess that Obote's authority will survive more or less intact during 1970 and that the Army, which seems to be increasingly the real basis of his country-wide authority, will remain on the whole loyal to him – assuming that Amin can retain his own position.[17]

The factor Purcell could not have foreseen was the deepening disagreement between Obote and Amin over a key regional political issue known as 'the Anyanya affair'; another item in the list of scandals that characterised Amin's rise to power. For David Martin, this represented 'the critical point' at which the potential for a coup attempt tipped over into the necessary conditions for a successful one.[18] Sudan, like Uganda, had national borders which had been drawn by the British to unite the very different north and south of the country. Unlike Uganda, however, this mirrored both a religious split (the north was predominantly Muslim while the south was a mix of traditional religions with some Christian influence), and a perceived *racial* divide between the dominant 'Arab' northerners, and the 'African' (i.e. 'black') southerners. In the 1960s, the south rose up in a struggle for independence that was to last the rest of the century before succeeding. The first stage of this uprising, known as 'Anyanya 1', gave Israel an opportunity to wage a proxy war against their enemies in the Arab world, and this probably accounted for much of their initial interest in Obote's Uganda. The Ugandan political scientist Mahmoud Mamdani summarised what was happening at the turn of the decade:

> The Israelis did not simply have economic 'aid' projects in Uganda; their officers also trained the police, the intelligence and the army. After 1969, Uganda occupied a central place in Israel's Arab-African policy. Northern Uganda was the base that Israel used to materially assist the southern Sudanese (Anyanya) guerrillas. But events took a decisive turn following

the May 25, 1969, coup in Sudan that brought General Nimeri to power. Relations with Uganda improved visibly. Talks began on a formal treaty between the two. The Israeli use of northern Uganda as a base to supply the Anyanya guerrillas was in imminent danger. When, in August 1970, the Israeli chief of the central intelligence organisation, General Zamir, sought refuelling rights in Uganda for the arms ferry to the Anyanya, Obote refused. At the same time, the [Ugandan] cabinet's security committee ruled to terminate Israeli training of the police force.[19]

Amin, however, continued to help the Israelis to supply arms and ammunition to the south Sudanese rebels, many of whom were from ethnic groups very closely related, linguistically and culturally, to the West Nile tribes. Some of them, like Amin, could also claim a hereditary association with the slave-soldiers of the nineteenth century.

In August 1970, a West German mercenary fighting with the Anyanya forces, Rolf Steiner, came over the border to make contact with the Ugandan army, and was arrested by the police. The Uganda police seized Steiner's diaries, which recorded, 'two meetings that had taken place between General Amin, an Israeli military officer, and the Anyanya commander, General Joseph Lagu, in the southern Sudan'.[20] Steiner's own, not entirely reliable, account claims that in 1969 he had learned about a British plot to overthrow Obote and replace him with Amin; 'he was their first choice because he was the stupidest and the easiest to manipulate'.[21] Steiner himself thought that Amin was loyal, but he passed on the information to Obote's people. In October 1970, he returned to Uganda where a 'top Ugandan minister' asked him to 'speak out against Amin ... by publicly confirming that he is the man the British are using to prolong their colonial hold'.[22] When he refused to testify, he was arrested and threatened with being sent to Khartoum. The minister offered money, and Steiner claims he replied: 'You bastard, do you think I'm going to sell my friends out? A punch in the mouth would be too good for you.'[23] In the event, Obote indeed had Steiner deported to the Sudanese capital, where he was scheduled to be tried in early January 1971, a trial which seemed likely to reveal more details of the extent of Amin's involvement in the Sudan civil war. Obote's supporters were closing in on the General.

Bob Astles' account emphasises the role of the Israelis in the Steiner affair:

[A] white mercenary was arrested by the police at Moyo after crossing the border from the Sudan. It was soon established that this was the notorious Steiner. ... He admitted that he was an instructor for the Anyanya fighting in the Sudan. When arrested, he demanded to see General Amin but this request was denied. There was some difficulty with his notebook that he was found to have with him. It was written in German and in code and at first he was not prepared to cooperate in translating it. But we [i.e. Ugandan intelligence] needed to have a positive identification of the Ugandan and Israeli personnel responsible for his recruitment and presence in Uganda. Steiner was clever, or had been briefed while under arrest, and at first he intimated that it was I who had flown him into the Sudan with weapons for the rebels. However, my movements were always logged daily and Obote, never a man to act on rumours, knew how far to believe that story. Investigations showed that the dates of most of the landings in the Sudan were when Amin was out of the country and his acting chief of staff was in hospital. The matter was never cleared up because the investigations were still going on when Amin seized the country. Eventually the notebook was translated and produced evidence that Amin, Uganda's own chief of staff, was not only operating against his government but had become a tool of Israel fighting the Arabs of the Sudan.[24]

OBOTE ATTACKS

With the West Nile presence in the military growing, and Amin's dominance strengthening, Obote ill-advisedly made an attempt to seize control of the army. This is seen by many Ugandan commentators as the main immediate cause of the coup, as Wycliffe Kato put it, '[w]hat led to Obote's fall was his involvement in the reorganisation of the army'.[25] As A.B.K. Kasozi explained:

Although Amin was not educated, he was attuned to the game of Ugandan political survival; use of violence at the right time decided who would rule the country. This Amin learned from Obote.... His simplicity and ability to talk to the common man at the grassroots level in Luganda and other local languages helped him reach out to many in the former kingdoms.

By mid-1970, Amin seemed to have a more popular base than Obote, especially in Buganda. The Baganda began to see the very man who stormed the palace of their king, the man who ordered his soldiers to rape, loot and vandalise their property, as their saviour . . .[26]

Obote waited until September 1970, then sent Amin as his representative to the funeral of the respected Egyptian president, Gamal Abdel Nasser. With his rival temporarily out of the way, he moved to reorganise the army, promoting every officer by one grade, and appointing chiefs of staff for the army and the air force, reporting to the President's Office rather than to Amin, who was to become a purely nominal overall head of the armed forces. Officers thought to be loyal to Amin were moved away from key army roles, while others were moved to civil service positions. On Amin's return, according to Mutibwa:

Obote and Amin were no longer on speaking terms and each camp was working out plans for the elimination of the other. Scenes of open quarrelling between the two men became more frequent; Obote blamed Amin for not disciplining his unruly soldiers and Amin blamed Obote for the hardship the ordinary people, including soldiers, were experiencing when he and his close associates were enjoying the rich booty of corruption . . .[27]

According to Kasozi, 'Now extremely alert to the possibility of arrest, [Amin] lived and moved with his trusted security men.'[28] Mamdani notes that at this point Amin shifted his religious allegiance, from the UPC-backed National Association for the Advancement of Muslims (NAAM), of which he had been co-leader, to the Uganda Muslim Community (UMC), the main Baganda Muslim organisation, a move which strengthened Amin's support in Buganda.[29]

Obote clearly anticipated the possibility of a coup at any time. In January 1971, he was due to attend a Commonwealth conference in Singapore. According to Nabudere, Obote did not want to go but was persuaded by the cabinet, because the meeting was to discuss sanctions against apartheid South Africa. Mutibwa, on the other hand, says that it was Obote's own decision 'because of the importance he . . . attached to the liberation of

Southern Africa. [Also] Julius Nyerere and Kenneth Kaunda ... strongly urged him to go.'[30] Obote's personal secretary, Henry Kyemba, wrote that 'Obote ... felt secure enough to go to Singapore. ... I was certain that he was not as secure as he felt and acted accordingly. I moved my more valuable personal property out of my residence, together with my car, a BMW, and took them to Jinja.'[31] As Obote flew off (with Kyemba) to the conference on 11 January 1971, he left Amin a memorandum in which, according to Mutibwa:

> there were two important matters to attend to and explain. One concerned the report of the police investigation into the murder of Brigadier ... Okoya ... and his wife ... which connected Amin with that murder. Equally important, Amin was requested to account for a large sum of money ... which the Ministry of Defence (or rather the army) had spent and which had not been accounted for. ...
>
> Obote's accusation that Amin had misappropriated defence funds and his directive that they should be accounted for had a ring of irony, but all the same this must have hurt Amin in a special way; to him it was a dishonest accusation. ... It was clear to Amin, although less so to those ignorant of the inside story, that the accusation was a pretext, a trick intended to tarnish the General's name and reputation.[32]

For Jaffar Amin, the falling out between his father and Obote was preordained; it represented the working out of his grandmother's predictions about her son's future:

> Unbeknownst to Obote, the rift between him and Dad was to be the ... fulfilment of the pronouncement made by Grandma Aisha Aate way back when Dad was an infant. A 'friendship' gone terribly wrong would in effect be the force that would aid Dad's ascent to the 'highest position in the land' of Uganda, as pronounced and predicted by Grandma Aisha Aate after the Deadly 'Paternity Test' Dad endured as an infant. The survival of the ordeal Dad endured on the slopes of the Kakwa Legendary Mountain Liru as an infant seemed to have become the norm as Dad survived one 'liquidation plot' after another![33]

BUILD-UP TO THE COUP

The coup, then, seems to have been multiply over-determined. Many of the long-term reasons were legacies of colonial policy, including the borders of the state itself, the exaggeration of 'tribal' differences (especially the north–south distinction), the unequal economic structure of the country (particularly Asian and European dominance of the formal economy), and the role and ethnic composition of the military. Postcolonial factors included the long-standing Ganda opposition to Obote, public discontent with the lack of economic growth since independence, increasing ideological splits within the UPC, and opposition outside the party to the lack of democracy and human rights. In sum, freedom had not brought the benefits many had expected. The immediate, short-term issues leading to the coup included the Okoya case, the Anyanya affair, the army reorganisation and Obote's enquiry into 'corruption' in the use of the defence budget. Finally, there were the international factors, particularly those associated with the Cold War and the Middle East conflict, including Israeli opposition to Obote's closeness to Numeiri, and British and American concern over the 'Move to the Left' plus the increasing Eastern bloc influence in the military. Mutibwa suggests, however, that the growing British animosity towards Obote was primarily because '[e]ver since, early in 1970, Obote's government resolved that all Asians holding British passports should leave Uganda, there had been considerable anxiety in London'.[34]

Ugandan commentators have emphasised different aspects of these factors, but there is broad agreement over the way things were going.[35] By the end of 1970, a coup was more than a distinct possibility; it was definitely going to happen soon. The only questions were exactly when, and who would do it. In 1969, Africa had seen military coups in Sudan, Benin, Libya and Somalia. It now seemed to be Uganda's turn. At the Singapore meeting, British Prime Minister Edward Heath, faced with a hail of criticism over arms sales to South Africa, reportedly asked the assembled African leaders: 'I wonder how many of you will be allowed to return to their own countries after this conference', a remark which has since been used as circumstantial evidence of British involvement in the coup.[36]

Many intellectuals at the time, including Mamdani and Nabudere, produced Marxist analyses of the coup, raising questions about how the military could be analysed in class terms. Michael Lofchie believed, with Mazrui, that 'the Uganda army can be best understood as a kind of economic class'.[37] Mamdani rejected this because 'soldiers do not *form* a social class, they *serve* social classes'.[38] As Amii Omara-Otunnu later wrote:

> contrary to claims that the coup was a class action staged as 'a corporate means of defending army interests' ... which would imply that the army was a cohesive social group with homogenous interests – the military was in fact far from united on the eve of the coup ... [which] succeeded because Amin's personal interests and those of the groups most affected by Obote's political tactics, particularly his Move to the Left, converged.[39]

These groups included the Baganda political leadership, as well as the Israelis and the British. It is a step further, however, to suggest that any of these was responsible for the coup itself, though many contemporary commentators thought this. As Lofchie wrote shortly after the coup, 'conspiracy theorists argue [that] Israel was compelled to depose Obote, in order to prevent growing military opposition along its major battlefront with the Arab world'.[40] However, Uganda had only a very limited ability to intervene in Sudan, while conspiracy theories are unfalsifiable and thrive on lack of evidence. There is, he suggested, 'something hauntingly paternalistic about any such conspiratorial explanation of the Uganda coup. This somehow implies that Ugandans were not in control of their own political destiny ... [and] severely underestimates the monumental importance of antagonistic social forces within Uganda society ... which led to the downfall of the Obote government'.[41] Mamdani also concluded that 'favourable as was the external environment for the coup, the conditions for its realization were most certainly internal'.[42]

Both British and elite Ugandan commentators tended to think that Amin was intellectually incapable of mounting a coup; he had to be the puppet of Western intelligence services, or at least of a British-educated southern Ugandan such as Felix Onama. But, whereas British left-wing commentators thought their own state was behind the coup, Ugandans have tended to stress an Israeli involvement. According to Mamdani:

> Bar-Lev ... said that [on hearing of Obote's plan] Amin had approached him, saying that his loyal supporters were outside Kampala and the

President would be able to arrest and kill him before they could rescue him. Bar-Lev advised Amin to bring to Kampala those soldiers who were from the same tribe as Amin and to make sure he had paratroopers, tanks and jeeps. So equipped, explained Bar-Lev, 600 men could over-power 5,000. These forces, which had been trained by the Israelis, played a key role in the defeat of Obote's army.[43]

Bar-Lev may seem, in many ways, a likely candidate for the role of Iago, but his boasts about his role in the coup came later, at a time when Israel had good reason to smear Amin's reputation. Immediately after Amin's seizure of power, the British high commissioner, Dick Slater, assessed the role of the Israelis as follows:

> The Israelis were of course accused by Obote (and others) of giving assis-tance to Amin before and during the January coup d'etat. The accusation looked plausible enough at the time. Colonel Bar-Lev ... was very active on the day of the coup and it was to his house that the former Inspector-General of Police fled, subsequently to be persuaded to throw his hand in with Amin. Bar-Lev ... certainly enjoys the confidence of Amin. Nevertheless ... it is unlikely that the Israelis had forewarning of the coup or were actually involved in mounting it.
>
> The Israelis have for a long time been close to Amin personally: he received his parachute wings in Israel and is known to admire Israeli military prowess. Amin is a Kakwa ... a tribe which is also found in the southern Sudan. This accounts for his sympathy with the Southern Sudanese rebels, a sympathy the Israelis have been careful to foster ...[44]

The evidence for external involvement in the coup is very circumstantial. Ogenga Otunnu believes that '[d]uring the Commonwealth Conference, Obote criticised the British policy of selling arms to ... South Africa and ... supporting ... Southern Rhodesia. In response, the British prime minister, Edward Heath, declared that "some of the fiery leaders sitting around the table would not return home". Heath was right; Obote was immediately toppled in a coup.'[45] Omara-Otunnu on the other hand concludes that: 'In January 1971 the southern Sudanese Anya Nya, the Israelis, and the British in Uganda, all wished to have a leader more friendly to themselves than was

President Obote.... The collusion of these forces in the overthrow of Obote was continued in intimacy with Amin's regime, at least in the early years.[46] Collusion is a vague word and we have seen that most of 'the British' were more doubtful about Amin's value to them than this suggests. In any case, Amin was quite capable of asking for, and taking or rejecting, the advice of Bar-Lev or anyone else. This is not the same as being a puppet of the Israelis, or of the British.

MONDAY 25 JANUARY 1971: AN ACCIDENTAL COUP?

The events of the coup, and the ways in which they have been represented, are significant for understanding Amin's myth, as well as his life story. Contrary to the conspiracy theories, British archives strongly suggest that the high commissioner, deputy high commissioner, and defence advisor all had very little idea of what was going on at the time of the coup. This does not mean for sure that there was no British intelligence involvement; it may, for example, have been undisclosed to the diplomats and/or kept out of the archives.[47] But unless the conspiracy included wholesale fabrication of the archival material, a British plot looks unlikely. The telegrams sent by the High Commission to the FCO on the day of the coup give a contemporary account of what happened as the day rolled on, whereas, as we shall see, later memories of the coup vary considerably, even over basic 'facts'. The diplomatic messages give a vivid picture of how a military coup unfurls, or at least how this one appeared to the British. They reveal the high commissioner's lack of knowledge about what was going on, and convey something of the atmosphere of that eventful day.

The first telegram from the High Commission on the day of the coup that I have been able to find in the archives is numbered 'TELNO 56 of 25 January 1971' – so there were earlier ones, giving a degree of credibility to the conspiracy theories. Number 56 was sent by the high commissioner, Dick Slater, to the FCO and copied to the Ministry of Defence and the British high commissions in Nairobi, Dar es-Salaam and Khartoum:

> There was sporadic firing in Kampala between 1 am and 3 am this morning, at times heavy.
>
> It has resumed since dawn in a desaltory [sic] way.

1. General Amin as commander of the Ugandan army and air force, proudly displaying his Israeli parachute wings, *c.* 1969–70. His first biographer, Judith Listowel, who met him around this time, wrote: 'I looked into the smiling face of a tall, muscular officer with shrewd eyes' (Listowel, 1973: 7).

2. Major-General Amin gives his first press conference as president of Uganda on Wednesday 27 January 1971, two days after the coup. His astute use of print and broadcasting media was a key factor in his political survival throughout the 1970s (see Chapter 5).

3. Immediately after the coup in January 1971, Amin released a number of political prisoners from the regime of his predecessor, Milton Obote. Here he is driving past cheering crowds to attend a ceremony for the newly liberated politicians. As president, Amin often insisted on driving himself.

4. Amin meets Golda Meir during his 1971 visit to Israel. This was his first overseas visit as president, but the following year he broke diplomatic relations, closed Israel's embassy in Kampala and expelled Israeli nationals from Uganda (see Chapter 6).

5. President Amin pictured with King Faisal of Saudi Arabia on 11 November 1972. This was during Amin's second visit to the kingdom, following his expulsion of the Israelis from Uganda. After his overthrow, Amin lived in retirement in Saudi Arabia for more than two decades (see Chapter 8).

6. Amin showing off his young son, in military uniform like his father, as he releases the imprisoned English writer Denis Hills (right) to British Foreign Secretary James Callaghan (left), 12 April 1975. Hills had been jailed for insulting Amin as 'a village tyrant' in his memoirs (see pp. 267–269).

7. President Amin arrives at JFK International Airport in New York on 1 October 1975 with his wife and two sons, to attend the United Nations General Assembly meeting. This was his first visit to the USA. The British ambassador to the UN walked out of the meeting (see p. 269).

8. Amin attends Kenyan President Jomo Kenyatta's funeral in Nairobi, 31 August 1978 (see p. 282). The two had frequently disagreed. By this stage, a UN Human Rights Commission enquiry into abuses under Amin's rule was under way, and international support for the regime was fast dwindling.

9. Amin in a tracksuit, 1970s. Throughout his life, Amin loved sports of all kinds. His British commanding officer in the army, Iain Grahame, wrote: 'His physique was that of a Grecian sculpture, and no matter to what form of athleticism he turned his hand, he excelled and he conquered' (see p. 71).

10. In the ring, December 1973. Amin had been a national amateur boxing champion in his colonial army days, and maintained a particular interest in the sport as president. Here he is seen taking part in an exhibition bout, as a curtain-raiser to the all-African amateur boxing championships.

11. Warming up before a basketball game with Ugandan soldiers near Kampala, 7 March 1977. This was the day after Amin had expelled the last white Anglican bishop, and just before he flew to Cairo for an Afro-Arab summit (see pp. 279–280).

12. Amin happily accompanying the Uganda Air Force Band on his accordion, 10 April 1972. He later played the instrument at length on the soundtrack to the French director Barbet Schroeder's 1974 documentary film, *General Idi Amin Dada: A Self Portrait* (see pp. 268–269).

13. Al-Hajji Field Marshal Dr Idi Amin Dada, VC, DSO, MC, President of the Republic of Uganda, looking at ease in his uniform. As his rule went on, he wore a growing array of self-awarded medals and honours. He was much mocked for this internationally, but may have copied the practice from the British royal family, whom he strongly admired.

14. Amin at a press conference in 1973. It was quite unusual for him to wear a formal pinstripe suit; he normally preferred military uniform or a safari suit. The intensity of Amin's expression here perhaps reflects the importance he attached to media appearances.

15. Amin in his role and robes as chancellor of Makerere University, at a degree ceremony in October 1976. Amin was an active chancellor, frequently issuing instructions to students on their behaviour. The vice chancellor of the university had been one of the first Ugandan notables to 'disappear', in late 1972 (see p. 236).

16. Amin pictured riding a bicycle ambulance during festivities in the Acholi region town of Kitgum, late 1970s. Amin's exhaustive programme of visits to every part of the country – even areas which consistently opposed him, such as here – continued to be a feature of his rule to the end.

17. British and other white residents of Uganda pledge loyalty to Amin, September 1975. His British friend and advisor, Bob Astles, can be seen kneeling apart from the others on the far right. 1975 saw something of a peak in Amin's efforts to embarrass and annoy the British (see Chapter 7).

18. Amin at Entebbe airport, 27 February 1977. Following the killing of Anglican Archbishop Luwum, Amin announced his intention to visit the UK, causing the British government to draw up elaborate plans to exclude him (see Chapter 8). On the right of the photo is Bob Astles.

19. Amin pictured with his first official wife, Maryam, whom he divorced in 1974. When they visited the UK in 1971, the British high commissioner to Uganda described her as 'tall (I would guess about 5ft 10ins) and ample. She is handsome and nice . . . an imposing and pleasant woman' (see p. 206).

20. Amin in exile in Saudi Arabia, holding his youngest son. From 1979 to 2003, Amin largely spent his retirement in relaxation (especially sea bathing), shopping and prayer. He and his large family subsisted on a generous Saudi government pension, and he made no political statements (see Chapter 8).

21. The major policy statement of Milton Obote's previous regime, the Common Man's Charter, looked like a British government White Paper. Under Amin's rule, however, official publications used colour and photography, together with sophisticated layout and typography, to get the message across (see p. 302).

Troops are much in evidence in the city.

Shops and offices are closed and the streets largely deserted.

Radio Uganda is said to be surrounded.

It is transmitting no news.

Parliament building is sealed off by troops.

We have had no reports from British subjects of injury to persons or property.

We are advising enquirers to stay home.

Neither I nor any of the colleagues I have consulted have been able to raise any body in authority.

Telephone operator at Ministry of Defence claims that ministry is virtually deserted.

The President has not yet returned from Singapore and I have no firm information about his movements other than that reported in my TELNO 51.

He is said to be due to arrive in Nairobi at 10pm tonight.

I will keep you closely informed of developments.

Slater[48]

The National Archive files suggest that the first thing the high commissioner did that morning was to send the defence advisor to ask Bar-Lev what was going on:

My Defence Advisor has been informed by Israeli Defence Attache that in the course of last night General Amin caused to be arrested all officers in armed forces sympathetic to President Obote.... Purpose of this operation was to anticipate move to arrest Amin himself allegedly planned by Obote to take place after latter's return from Singapore. It appears that Amin is now firmly in control of all elements of army which controls vital points in Kampala. Israeli Defence Attache discounts any possibility of any moves against Amin by army units up country. Inspector General of Police, Oryema, is according to Israeli informant, in the hands of Amin and police have been instructed by their own officers to co operate [sic] with army.

According to Col. Bar-Lev, Amin has in fact moved against President who will presumably be arrested if he returns. Reports from two independent sources state that army took over Entebbe airport within last hour and a half.[49]

Later that day, the high commissioner telegraphed London that there had been an announcement 'at about 4pm local time ... by an unidentified army officer over Radio Uganda'. This was the proclamation of what became known as the 'Eighteen Points', put forward to justify the coup; the speaker was Warrant Officer (Class II) Sam Wilfred Aswa (spelt Waswa in some accounts). According to the later published version of the statement, Aswa began by stating 'I have a special message for you from my fellow soldiers. It has been necessary to take action to save the situation from getting worse.' The Eighteen Points listed were 'examples of matters which have left the people angry, worried and very unhappy':

1. The unwarranted detentions without trial for long periods of a large number of people many of whom are totally innocent. . . .
2. The continuation of the State of Emergency for indefinite period over the whole country. . . .
3. The lack of freedom in airing of different views on political and social matters.
4. The frequent loss of life and property arising from almost daily cases of robbery with violence and kondoism [armed robbery]. . . .
5. Proposals for national service which will take every able bodied person from his home to work in a camp for two years. . . .
6. Widespread corruption in high places especially among ministers and top civil servants. . . .
7. The failure by political authorities to organise any elections in the last eight years whereby the people's freewill [sic] could be expressed.
8. Economic policies have left many people unemployed and even more insecure and lacking in the basic needs of life like food, clothing, medicine and shelter.
9. High taxes have left the common man of this country poorer than ever before. . . . The big men can always escape or pass them on to the common man.

10. The prices which the common man gets for his crops like cotton and coffee have not gone up and sometimes they have gone down....

11. A tendency to isolate the country from East African unit, e.g. by sending away workers from Kenya and Tanzania, by preventing the use of Uganda money in Kenya or Tanzania, by discouraging imports from Kenya and Tanzania, by stopping the use in Uganda of Kenyan or Tanzanian money.

12. The creation of a wealthy class of leaders who are always talking of socialism while they grow richer and the common man poorer.

13. In addition, the Defence Council of which the President is Chairman has not met since July 1969 and this has made administration in the Armed Forces very difficult. As a result armed forces personnel lack accommodation, vehicles and equipment....

14. The Cabinet Office, by training large numbers of people (largely from the Akokoro county in Lango District, where Obote and Akena Adoko, the Chief General Service Officer, come from) in armed warfare has been turned into a second army. Uganda, therefore, has had two armies....

15. The Lango Development Master Plan, written in 1967, decided that all key positions in Uganda's political, commercial, army and industrial life, have to be occupied and controlled by people from Akokoro county in Lango District, at the expense of other areas of Uganda.

16. Obote, on the advice of Akena Adoko, has sought to divide the Uganda armed forces and the rest of Uganda by picking out his own tribesmen and putting them in key positions in the army and everywhere....

17. From the time Obote took over power in 1962 his greatest and most loyal supporter has been the army.... It is, therefore, now a shock to us to see that Obote wants to divide and downgrade the army by turning the Cabinet Office into another Army....

18. We all want only unity in Uganda and we do not want bloodshed. Everybody in Uganda knows that. The matters mentioned above appear to us to lead to bloodshed only.

For the reasons given above, we men of the Uganda Armed Forces have this day decided to take over power from Obote and hand it to our fellow soldier Major-General Idi Amin Dada and we hereby entrust him to lead this our beloved country of Uganda to peace and goodwill among all. . . .

For the moment a curfew is necessary and will be observed by every-body between 7.00pm and 6.30am every day from now, every day until further notice.

Power is now handed over to our fellow soldier Major-General Idi Amin Dada, and you must await his statement which will come in due course. WE HAVE DONE THIS FOR GOD AND OUR COUNTRY.[50]

The British high commissioner reported that, following Aswa's announce-ment, first General Oryema, the chief of police, and then Amin spoke. Oryema said it had been agreed that 'Uganda would be run by the armed forces', and he pledged his support for Amin. Amin himself then said that he had assumed power reluctantly and:

He had always believed the forces should support the popular elected civil power.

His would be a quote thoroughly caretaking administration pending return to civilian rule unquote.

Free and fair elections would soon be held when security situation permitted.

Political exiles were free to return.

Political prisoners held on unspecified and unfounded charges would be released forthwith.

All people should report to work as usual.

Further directions would be issued as need arose.[51]

In Kampala, according to Slater these announcements were followed by enthu-siastic celebrations:

A wave of hysteria has swept the town. There are wild demonstrations apparently in favour of the army. A maelstrom of traffic is seething round the High Commission, but no interest has yet been taken in us. It looks as if chaos will prevail until curfew time at 7pm. . . .

I see no immediate threat to UK citizens as such. We will continue to advise them to keep their heads down: most will anyway. The extent to which they should respond to Amin's appeal for resumption of normal activities will have to be guaged [*sic*] in the morning.[52]

As Kasozi put it, however, it may be that, '[t]he Baganda rejoiced and applauded the change not because they loved Amin but because they hated Obote.'[53]

The tone of the high commissioner does not suggest in any way that he had prior knowledge of the coup, and the language of the radio announcement does not suggest that it was written by a Westerner, though it may not have been written by the person who spoke it. It reads very much like the language and concerns of a Ugandan army officer – specifically a West Niler worried about the position of the Langi in the military. George Kanyeihamba seems to be the only person to have claimed that, 'the first voice to be heard on Radio Uganda after the coup was that of an unidentified non-African male person';[54] everyone else thought the first voice was the African one of Warrant Officer Aswa.

In such circumstances, memory is often unreliable, and people had very different memories of listening to Radio Uganda that Monday. The BBC's International Monitoring Service at Caversham House reported at the time that Ugandan radio was 'transmitting non-stop Western-type music with no announcements or time signals'.[55] According to the writer Yasmin Alibhai-Brown, a student at Makerere at the time, 'on 25 January 1971, to the tune of "My Boy Lollipop" [a mid-1960s international hit by the Jamaican artist, Millie Small], which was played the whole day long, a sombre voice of a soldier announced that there had been a coup in Uganda and General Idi Amin Dada was now President....'[56] In a later version of the story, she repeats that 'The radio played "My Boy Lollipop" all day interspersed with horrible warnings and announcements about the new order....'[57] On the other hand, the judge Sir Peter Allen, who was in court that day in the Ankole capital, Mbarara, wrote that:

I finished the hearing by 3.50pm and, soon after, one of the advocates came into my chambers with a small battery radio. He said there had been a coup in Kampala this morning and switched on his radio. There was just martial music playing. At 4pm, it stopped and a man speaking poor English said he was Sergeant Major Wilfred Aswa and he then read out an 18-point announcement explaining why the Army had taken over and removed Obote from power.[58]

'Martial music' was also heard by others listening to Uganda Radio that day. According to Dan Nabudere: 'There was nothing from Radio Uganda except martial music. . . . At 3.45 pm the martial music stopped. Then a hesitant voice of a soldier made an announcement to the effect that Obote's regime had been overthrown.'[59] Bob Measures and Tony Walker, British telecom engineers working in Kampala, later wrote that 'the radio station played martial music, another requisite of a military coup',[60] but they are alone in remembering Aswa's announcement as being on Uganda Television rather than the radio. Heather Benson, a teacher from New Zealand working in Kampala, was told by her school caretaker about the coup: 'Teacher, why are you here? Something is up. The radio told us to stay indoors. . . . They've been playing military music for hours.'[61] Some heard both martial and pop music. Mallory Wober, a social psychologist based at Makerere, wrote in 1973:

On Monday, we knew that a coup was in progress, with the radio playing the martial music that seems to be inevitable on such occasions. At tea-time, a corporal read out a manifesto justifying a military take-over. There followed the sugary strains of the 'Missouri waltz', an old-time American minstrel song with the refrain:

The sandman is calling
And shadows are falling
So sweet and low.[62]

So was it 'My Boy Lollipop', the 'Missouri Waltz' or 'martial music'?[63] The issue is unimportant in itself, but it demonstrates the essential unreliability of memory in times of crisis.[64] People's memories of Idi Amin frequently suffer from such problems.

What *did* actually happen in the night? Once again, we cannot be sure. Amin himself later claimed repeatedly that he had not intended to seize power, but had been forced into it, at gunpoint, by low-ranking soldiers who had launched the coup in protest at Obote's changes in the army. More convincing perhaps is something like the version of events given in 1975 by the British anthropologist of West Nile, Aidan Southall:

> When Obote got to the Commonwealth Conference in January 1971.... he took the extraordinary course of telephoning one of his loyal officers at Jinja barracks to arrest Amin and his clique and, by arming the Lang'o and Acholi, to eliminate all officers of other ethnic groups from the army. The message was overheard by Sergeant Major Mousssa, a Kakwa loyal to Amin, who went on to inform him, and the coup d'etat occurred the next day.[65]

A detailed, near contemporary, analysis of the coup is that of James Mittelman, a US academic working at Makerere University. Using Amin's own statements in newspaper reports, he usefully distinguishes between three versions of what happened: the 'Spontaneity' theory, the 'Double Coup' theory and the 'Tripartite Coup' theory:

> In his first press conference after the coup, General Amin accused Obote and presidential aide Akena Adoko of hatching the 'Singapore plot'. ... The general maintained that when he returned from a hunting trip to Karuma Falls, a tank and a personnel carrier were waiting for him outside his residence in Kampala. A wounded soldier told him that pro-Obote elements had been instructing soldiers of the Lango and Acholi tribes to arm themselves and arrest members of army units drawn from other tribes. Asked by the soldiers to take control of the government, Amin 'could not let them down'.[66] He explained 'The soldiers and I did not plan a coup. It happened spontaneously. The Acholi and Lango officers were half way to victory when the ordinary soldier, seeing the dangers, took the initiative.'[67]
>
> Proponents of the double coup theory accept some parts of Amin's story but argue that planning is necessary for a successful coup. According to this theory, Amin got wind of a plan prepared by Akena Adoko before Obote's departure for Singapore, which provided for the arrest and murder of Amin and other leaders during Obote's absence. The Amin-led coup thus headed off the Obote coup. ...
>
> The tripartite coup theory goes one step further. The chief villain in this dramatic version was Akena Adoko. ... Under his plan, the president

would return from Singapore only after Amin had been eliminated. Then, when Obote stepped off the plane, he and the ministers waiting at the airport would be shot down, whereupon Adoko ... would install himself as president.[68]

It seems impossible to judge which of these three accounts is the more plausible – in fact, they do not differ very much in their analysis, apart from for the question of whether the primary responsibility for the coup lay with Obote, Adoko or Amin himself. It seems likely that all three played some part, and possibly the actions of a few West Nile NCOs and junior officers did too. Others may have also been involved; WodOkello Lawoko, who escaped to Gulu in the night after being chased by soldiers out of the television studios where he worked, was surprised to find Felix Onama and Bob Astles drinking together in the town's best-known hotel, 'The Acholi Inn'. The hotel manager, he recounts, told him: 'I am sure you know there has been a coup in Kampala and Amin has taken over power. Your friends out there are the masterminds. They commandeered the hotel's communication system. . . .'[69] The Inspector General of Police, Erinayo Oryema, apparently later told Lawoko (a fellow Acholi) that he had been forced into his role in the coup, broadcasting alongside Amin on the afternoon of the 25 January and then joining the government. According to Lawoko, Oryema had been seized by soldiers five days earlier and 'brutally tortured' in the presence of Amin. Like many other Ugandan writers, Lawoko here takes on board the British/Israeli conspiracy theory, with an additional role for the USA: 'At one point, Amin wanted Oryema killed, but, the American and British Ambassadors, as well as an Israeli commander of the airforce Colonel Barlev [sic], opposed this and prevailed over Amin.'[70]

Amin insisted that he had been forced to assume the presidency by junior army officers, and had played no part in the coup per se, but this does not seem to be the version of events he passed on to his son. According to Jaffar, Obote, in Singapore:

had eventually moved forward with his plan to get rid of Dad, so he had relayed orders to his loyal Lan'gi officers to arrest Dad and his key Army supporters.

Over the years, Dad had bittersweet memories of his coup against Obote, and it is to Mama Sauda Nnalongo of the Babito of Bunyoro that he owed his personal survival because she was the one who leaked word of the impending 'plot' and plan to arrest Dad to him. Mama Sauda Nnalongo ... was one of Dad's women and at the time of the coup she was expecting twins. ... She got word of the telegram from Singapore and without hesitation secretly informed her man.

Unbeknownst to the 'arresting team', Dad then instinctively swung into preemptive action....

Dad relied on the Crack Team of Israeli and Sandhurst trained Junior Officers who had their training in the Jewish Holy Land and Great Britain to secure the key installations and garrisons across the country. On hindsight Dad didn't realise that the preemptive move would turn into a counter coup....

On January 25 1971 at 2.00am, while most of the residents of Uganda were sleeping, Dad ascended to the 'highest position in the land' of Uganda as pronounced and predicted by Grandma Aisha Aate after the Deadly 'Paternity Test' he was subjected to as an infant ...[71]

Rather than Amin having been forced into the coup by junior officers in the first place, Jaffar describes their persuasive role as taking place *after* the coup itself:

Realising that in his haste to defend himself against Obote's Master Plan, he had incredibly taken over ultimate power, a certain reluctance came to Dad's heart and he was sincere enough to voice his doubts to his trusted men.

One Juma Oka ... was so infuriated with Dad's doubt in destiny that he pulled his gun and placed it on his Commanding Officer's temple. Then he demanded that Dad strengthen his resolve and realise their achievement of successfully bringing about change in Uganda or he would shoot him.[72]

The planned Acholi/Langi coup is also suggested in an interesting first-hand account by a southern Ugandan army officer, Lieutenant Jack Bunyenyezi of the parachute division, sent to the East Africa desk from the FCO 'Research Department' in April 1971:

> On returning to barracks ... in the early evening of Sunday 24 January, Lt. Bunyenyezi was roughly challenged and pushed about by the sentry on duty. On penetrating to the officers' mess, he found his fellow officers gathered together in a state of extreme unease. He was told that the Acholi C.O. had ordered them to remain in the mess until later, when he would have an important announcement to make. The Acholi and Langi rank and file were summoned to a briefing by the C.O. The other rank and file, unhappy about their exclusion from the briefing and evidently nervous of what might be afoot, took matters into their own hands, broke up the C.O.'s briefing and locked him up, and then attempted to overpower the Acholi and Langi soldiers, who had the keys both to the armoury and to the vehicles. Firing broke out. The soldiers told the officers not to interfere and to remain in their mess. Sergeant-Major Musa, of the mechanised division, emerged as the leader of the rank and file in the fracas which followed. Having gained the upper hand over the Acholi and Langi, the troops set off for Kampala, some in armoured personnel carriers, led by Sergeant-Major Musa, in tanks.[73]

Idi Amin's own account of the coup appeared in an interview in the Kenyan *Daily Nation* newspaper. It fits with Lieutenant Bunyenyezi's story, minimising the role of Amin himself and expanding on the spontaneity version of the coup:

> On that fateful day, it was a bright and sunny morning. Unsuspectingly, I went out hunting. While I was hunting and doing my duty to my country, my people and my President, my death and the annihilation of Uganda was being plotted. . . .
>
> I returned home at 6pm and all was quiet. I did nothing special and I did not sense anything at all. At 7.30pm, there was a tank on my front doorstep and the men in it were shouting almost hysterically and, like a tale, they told me that there had been an attempted coup. But they had countered it.

I want to make one thing clear. The soldiers did not plan a coup. It happened spontaneously. The Acholi and Lango officers were halfway to victory when the ordinary soldier seeing the danger took the initiative. One man, Sgt. Maj. Mussa did it.

By 6pm the Acholi and Lango officers had acted effectively and precisely. All non-Acholi and Lango officers had been disarmed or arrested.

Then it came to the all-important Mechanical Battalion [based in Kampala]. . . . It was here that Sgt. Maj. Mussa acted with precision and faultless efficiency.

He made for the armoury and at the same time warned the other soldiers in the battalion. Single-handed he overpowered the guards at the armoury and thus armed his fellow soldiers. He took charge of the situation and commanded a counter-coup.

Then he made a bee-line for my residence atop a tank. He told me what had happened and asked me to take command of the situation. I acted without a moment's hesitation. I took charge.

Meanwhile, another hero was being born to Uganda. While I was left without a single officer, only with NCOs and soldiers, another man was in the process of putting his life in danger. He was Second Lieutenant Maliamungu. The name incidentally means 'God's property' in Swahili. Atop a tank, he raced to Entebbe Airport where the airforce was ready and all set to follow Obote's orders. The planes were loaded with rockets and bombs. Second Lieut. Maliamungu stopped them with his tanks and other tanks that assisted him later. Otherwise Uganda might have seen genocide. . . .

I was in radio communication throughout the night until morning. I was ready and willing to die for my country. I fear nothing. I felt no remorse. Only one thought nagged my mind – 'Save Uganda, Save Uganda'.[74]

Many subsequent Ugandan accounts also stress the role of Musa/Mussa and Maliamungu. Regardless of the accuracy of the story, the interview gives a good example of Amin's new rhetorical skills. The soldier had finally become the politician.

THE AFTERMATH

Wild celebration of the coup in Buganda (and West Nile) began on 25 January, and continued for several days, while Amin's supporters set about rounding up and killing potential opponents in the army, particularly Acholi and Langi soldiers. On 26 January, Dick Slater telegraphed London to describe the situation:

> There was sporadic small arms firing during the night near Mbuya barracks but otherwise Kampala had a peaceful night, the curfew being strictly observed. Further small arms fire followed end of curfew this morning but the city is now returning to normal. Troops are in evidence but there are few, if any roadblocks. Shops and offices have re-opened.... Streets are as busy as on a normal working day and mood of celebration persists. Troops are cheered when they pass. ... There have been no repeat no reports of loss of British lives, injuries or damage to property. However two Canadians reported missing ... are now known to have been killed.[75]

The FCO prepared a briefing for British military commanders, which reiterated the prevailing Whitehall view of Amin as an ignorant puppet, open to manipulation:

> General Amin has risen from the ranks. He lacks education and has probably only a muddled political philosophy. The timing of the coup was probably dictated more by Amin's fear that his own downfall was imminent than by any real desire to save his country from Obote. He is not particularly pro-British but claims to be so if it suits his book. If he remains as President, he is likely to be influenced and manipulated by the present Minister of Defence, Mr Onama. He might prove more amenable to Israeli than to any other influence (because of his affinity with the people of Southern Sudan).[76]

Back in Uganda, Bar-Lev invited the British high commissioner and the defence advisor for a 'talk' on the morning after the takeover. He told them Amin was anxious that the British should know he intended to restore civilian government 'as soon as he had been able to get the army properly organised. He mentioned a period of three to five months.' Bar-Lev said that he had advised Amin that 'given the importance of the UK and the US as sources of public and private money, Amin should avoid doing anything "silly".... He should try to restore confidence and, in particular ... he should go slow on nationalisation and if possible de-nationalise ...' Bar-Lev told the British officials that 'we now had a thoroughly pro-Western set-up in Uganda of which we should take prompt advantage'. Slater seemed unsure of the degree to which Amin was really in charge; he told the FCO that 'Bar-Lev is well informed but clearly partisan and his assessment of the degree of control exercised by Amin needs careful checking.'[77] A follow-up telegram added that:

> Bar-Lev went into considerable detail to show that all potential foci of resistance, both up-country and in Kampala, had been eliminated. This had involved the shooting of a number of pro-Obote officers. The situation in Kampala was under complete control, the Baganda were all for Amin, if only because they knew Obote had been gunning for him.
>
> According to Bar-Lev, Amin's original plan had been to let Obote return and shoot him on arrival at the airport, together with a number of those who had gone to meet him. This plan was abandoned because of the difficulty of synchronising it with the liquidation of pro-Obote elements in the army.
>
> Bar-Lev added that the Inspector General of Police, Oryema, was lucky to be alive. Amin knew... [Oryema] had written instructions from Obote to arrest him and gave... instructions [for Oryema] to be shot. Oryema took refuge in the house of Bar-Lev, who claims to have persuaded Amin to accept him as an ally.[78]

In his final telegram to London that day, Dick Slater sums up the mood in Kampala: 'shops and offices have re-opened but the atmosphere in Kampala is one of carnival rather than work as usual. Obote Avenue [a major street in Kampala] has been full of cheering crowds and hooting cars all day. Banks closed this afternoon, but merely because the bank clerks had been dancing on the cashiers' counters.'[79]

On 26 January, Amin gave a press conference at his house in Kampala, broadcast on Radio Uganda, which confirmed, if anyone doubted it, his political dominance following the coup. He said that there had been a plan, 'arranged from Singapore', to 'congregate' Acholi and Langi soldiers in Kampala in order to 'seize the armoury'. He promised to bring back the body of the exiled, now deceased, Kabaka of Buganda, who would, Amin said, 'be buried with full military honours. I myself will command the ceremonies.' He also promised to release all detainees, including (mainly Baganda) government ministers detained in 1966, and to hold elections 'open to all parties, including the UPC. . . . I do not want a one-party system.' The army must be recruited country-wide, 'every tribe must be in the army and airforce; they all pay taxes'. He warned unnamed other countries, especially those bordering Uganda, not to harbour dissidents or interfere in the country's internal affairs.[80] In a telegram combining the condescending British view of Amin with the respect owed to a new ally, Slater described the broadcast:

1. Amin finds English difficult. His delivery was very slow but not hesitant. It conveyed well the impression of the bluff and honest soldier. Despite his limitations, he has considerable dignity and more of the air of a leader than Obote.
2. The underlying message was clearly that bygones should be bygones, no recriminations and no discrimination.
3. The Bantu [southern] tribes, and particularly the Baganda, for whose support the General seems to be making a bid, will be delighted with the reference to the former Kabaka and to a new pattern of army recruitment. But many northerners will dislike these passages. We must expect a request for Sir E. Mutesa's body at some stage.
4. The inference that the coup was not premeditated, but an instant reaction to a plan to split the army, is a new twist. It is not entirely irreconcilable with the story given by Colonel Bar-Lev (my telno 57). Obote might well have given orders for some such measures in order to neutralize the reaction to Amin's planned arrest . . . but I doubt if the measures had been put in train on Sunday; they were more probably intended to co-incide [sic] with Amin's arrest.[81]

The British press celebrated the coup. According to a telegram from the FCO to Dick Slater on 26 January, 'No reports are sympathetic to Obote'. The

Times headed its account 'Army Leaders Seize Power from President Obote in Successful Uganda Coup', while the *Daily Telegraph* had an editorial headed 'Good Riddance to Obote'. The tabloid *Daily Mirror* described Obote as the most violent African critic of British arms sales to South Africa, and called Amin a 'new strongman', adding that 'In London it is confidently expected that the new regime will be friendlier [to Britain] than that of Obote.' The liberal *Guardian*'s correspondent, more suspicious of Amin than the others, wrote that 'Obote was ruling over a police state', but added that 'It is hard to see Big Idi changing things for the better with no political guidelines to work on, his policies are bound to be opportunist and wavering.' The next day, *The Times* quoted Obote saying that the army had struck to prevent him from arresting Amin over 'disappearing military equipment and two murders'. Obote told reporters in Dar es-Salaam that the insurrection was backed by foreign forces 'specifically Israel', and that he was still president and would return to Uganda.[82]

The conspiracy theorists continued to suggest that Israel and/or Britain, and at the individual level, Astles and/or Bar-Lev, were responsible for the coup, using Amin simply as a puppet. The Pan-Africanist writer Horace Campbell, a student at Makerere University in the early years of Amin's rule, smuggled out of the country a pamphlet titled *Four Essays on Neo-colonialism in Uganda*, which was published in Canada in 1975. This combines the coup conspiracy theory with classic anti-semitic tropes, claiming that Astles was Jewish, for which I can find no evidence. Campbell wrote:

> Bob Astles, who is a Jew ... has been a principle [*sic*] link between the independent Ugandan army and the British government [this would have been news to the High Commission]. ... Someday, after Amin is overthrown, Astles true role in aiding the Israelis to overthrow Obote will probably come to light. ... Even after 1972, when the Israelis were expelled from Uganda, Bob Astles, a Jew and a known Israeli supporter, was allowed to remain in Uganda. ... As a close advisor to Idi Amin, this European Jew is taken on many foreign trips by Amin ... even when Amin goes to the most militant of the Arab states. ... Up to 1975 Astles remained a close friend, advisor and sometimes speechwriter for Idi Amin. He knows it is difficult for Amin to deal with him for he is one of the few people who hold the secret as to how much gold and ivory was

stolen by Amin from 1965–1968. With this belief, Astles struts around confidently with his [pet] monkey on his neck. . . .[83]

Campbell concludes that: 'Very few people in Uganda know of the influence of Astles over Amin. . . . [T]his story sheds some light on why the British have always maintained "we have first hand information of what is going on in Uganda."'[84] He is not clear whether it was the British or the Israelis Astles was really working for; probably he thought it was both (and the US as well). In fact, as we have seen, the British were if anything even more suspicious of Astles than they were of Israel's motives in Uganda. However, Britain and Israel did quietly work together in 1971 to help Amin establish his rule: while Campbell's analysis was paranoid and anti-semitic, the conspiracy theory certainly captured elements of went on *after* the coup.

Astles' own account of the coup is vague and confused – perhaps that was how he experienced it. He suggests that the key figure was one Captain Ochima, described at one point as a Kakwa[85] but later as a member of another West Nile tribe, the Alur.[86] Astles says little about him, but describes him as 'the man who organised the coup and who at first was much more powerful than Amin'.[87] Like others, he also sees the Israelis and British as being in some unclear way behind the coup but, uniquely, he also blames the *Greek* government. Astles' curious version is given in his privately published memoir:

Greece. . . needed support at the United Nations, so they had offered . . . to train soldiers of underdeveloped countries. As the offer had not gone through the president's Defence Council but had been made directly to General Amin, the soldiers who went off to Greece before the coup were Kakwa from Amin's tribe and Madi from the tribe of the defence minister. Their training, unfortunately for Uganda, was similar to that of the secret military police who were then plaguing Greece and from all accounts it was one of torture and violence. . . . When they returned to Uganda they became members of the new military police force and staffed the State Research Bureau, becoming the nucleus of Amin's 'secret army'. . . .

[I]n the early days of Amin's military government . . . all Greek-trained troops were brought into one unit under the command of Captain

Ochima.... The unit received orders to use their Greek training to purge all politicians from Obote's former government. Three Greek officers were flown in from Athens to draw up a programme and within a few days Ugandan military and police officers were also brutally purged by the Greek trained soldiers. I was arrested ... and taken to Mbuya barracks where I found scores of Ugandan officers.... Our discussions and fears revolved round Captain Ochima and his 'Greeks' and none of us expected to survive the increasing violence. Late that afternoon most of the officers I had seen ... were marched into a military school room for what they thought was a lecture and were blown up by explosives placed under the floor. It was indeed a purge. While all this was going on Amin was being acclaimed in the Western press and in Buganda as a hero, and ... the influence of the malevolent Greek military government went undisclosed.[88]

Lacking a direct line to Amin (which Horace Campbell supposed to have been Astles), the British attempted to influence the new president by working 'unobtrusively' through the Israelis, rather than approaching him directly. In a memo in May, Dick Slater made clear the favourable view both countries took of Amin's regime in its first few months, and their collaboration in supporting him at this time:

Amin's accession to power was a windfall for the Israelis, coming as it did when Obote was intent on mending his fences with Khartoum and keeping the Israelis in their place.... The Israelis are clearly delighted to have an old friend in power at this juncture and their co-operation with the new regime has been wholehearted.

Provided that the Israelis do not push their Sudanese schemes too far, this is in no way prejudicial to British interests. We too would like to see Amin's regime consolidated. Nor, in the process of helping him do we and the Israelis tread on each others' toes....

My Israeli colleague [the ambassador to Uganda] is leaving in July. We have been unobtrusively in fairly close touch since his return after the coup.... Our analyses of the strengths and weaknesses of the Ugandan regime are much the same.... We tacitly recognise that Britain and Israel have different reasons for wanting to see the regime survive: that any attempt at close co-ordination of efforts would be liable to draw attention embarrassing to both countries: but that it is important for each to have a fairly clear idea of the fields in which the other is giving, or prepared to give, help to Uganda. . . .[89]

The British and, probably to an even greater extent, the Israelis, were fully aware of the means by which Amin was ensuring his regime's survival. Only a week after the coup, on 1 February, Slater informed the FCO that: 'All the signs are that the Acholi and Lango tribes have been subjected to considerable victimisation in the aftermath of the coup and that their morale is at a low ebb. Since the Acholi account for about a third of the army and a large part of the police force . . . [t]his fact has implications for the efficient operating of the security forces and is clearly worrying the authorities.'[90] Later that day, he reported that shooting had been heard in Moyo town (near the West Nile/Acholi border area), at Karuma Falls (south of Gulu) and in Kitgum (the capital of Lango). 'All these incidents are probably due to rounding up of individual Acholi or Lango soldiers,'[91] he concluded.

Two weeks later, Dick Slater produced a thoughtful analysis of the coup for the Foreign Secretary, Sir Alec Douglas-Home, which shows how the British view of Amin had changed. Previously an illiterate buffoon, he was now a potential statesman:

Major-General Idi Amin Dada, then Chief of Defence Staff of the Ugandan Armed forces, seized power in the early hours of 25 January in order to save his skin rather than his country. But the result could be a healthier society in Uganda. . . .

Amin is not really a political animal, but Obote had so firmly entrenched himself in a political system of his own devising that the army offered the only hope of dislodging him; and, whether he liked it or not, Amin was inevitably drawn in. . . . I am sure that Amin would not have acted for purely ideological or patriotic reasons. He moved against Obote because he knew that Obote was going to move against him. . . .

My Defence Adviser has reported details of the fighting in so far as they are known to us. All that need be said here is that by mid-day on 25 January the Kampala situation was under control. . . . In the rest of the southern part of the country there seems to have been hardly a ripple. Up north the situation developed less favourably. Hundreds of Acholi and Langi soldiers disappeared into the bush, and ... a considerable number are still in hiding....

Spokesmen of the military government have foolishly claimed that this was a bloodless coup. It was not. The number of lives lost must run into hundreds rather than scores. In particular, there is evidence that Langi deserters are being shot on sight. But a great deal of salt should be added to reports from outside Uganda, notably those emanating from Dar-Es-Salaam, about heavy fighting, rivers of blood and stacks of corpses. Reliable information is hard to come by, but negative reports from our network of consular correspondents up-country do at least establish that, if there has been bloodshed on any considerable scale, it has been well away from urban areas. By African standards, I am told, this has been a kid-glove affair....

Once relieved of the more worrying external distractions, I think Amin has the wherewithal to provide a satisfactory administration. His assets include his own personality. He has shown greater qualities of leadership than I had expected and a marked flair for public relations. One has tended in the past to look at him as a figure of fun: large, ungainly, inarticulate and prone to gout. He is still slightly comic, but power has added a measure of dignity and the earthy directness of his public utterances touches cords [sic] left silent by the didactic harangues of his predecessor. He has earned a great deal of popularity by mixing freely among the people, driving his own jeep and ignoring security precautions – again in marked contrast to his predecessor....

Amin has promised to get back to barracks as soon as he can. Though he appears to be enjoying himself as Head of State, I believe him to be sincere in his wish to hold elections and restore civilian rule before long.... Externally, Amin will maintain Uganda's non-aligned position while making himself rather more agreeable to the West than was his predecessor and a little less agreeable to the East....

Anglo-Ugandan relations can only take a turn for the better. There is nowhere else for them to go: I had reached the end of the road with Obote. Amin's pro-British sentiments may not be deep-seated, but at least he is not anti-British; and for the moment he needs us. He is deeply grateful, as am I, for the promptness with which Her Majesty's

Government recognised his regime. [However] Uganda will not be able to fall behind her neighbours . . . in reacting to any sale of British arms to South Africa. Nor will Uganda become noticeably less impatient to get rid of her unwanted Asians. . . .

The Second republic of Uganda, as it is now called . . . has been launched all right, but there is a very rough passage ahead. . . . But Amin is nothing if not resilient, and my impression is that his government are becoming infected by his self-confidence. The Second republic has a sporting chance.[92]

For the first few weeks following the coup, Amin focused on internal affairs, declaring the Second Republic, establishing his position through the ethnic purges in the army, and making gestures calculated to please the Ganda and other southerners. In external affairs, his main worry was an Obote-inspired invasion by Kenya, Sudan and/or Tanzania. He set up a new government packed with former civil servants and many of Obote's former supporters, including Henry Kyemba, who snuck back into Uganda assuring Amin of his loyalty. As Omara-Otunnu put it, Amin 'co-opted some of the elite to important positions in the regime. . . . [W]ith characteristic opportunism they gave their backing to Amin in the hope of ensuring the continuance of their good fortune. Many regarded Amin an unsophisticated man, whom they felt they could influence if not exactly manipulate.'[93] In Ogenga Otunnu's account, the regime's new minister of health claimed that 'the present government is called a military government, in reality it is a professional government'[94] and, '[i]mmediately after Amin appointed the "professionals" he sent them on a nation-wide tour to acquire legitimacy and support for the regime'.[95] The new ministers held meetings across Uganda, blaming Obote for all the country's ills and praising Amin.

Shortly after the coup, on 28 January, Amin released fifty-five political prisoners from Luzira Maximum Security Prison and paraded them in central Kampala. They included senior Ganda politicians such as the former prime minister, Benedicto Kiwanuka (widely believed to have organised the assassination attempt on Obote), and eight former cabinet ministers, as well as Amin's old rival Brigadier Felix Opolot. In February, more than 1,500 other political detainees were freed – according to Otunnu, 'the overwhelming majority were Baganda monarchists'.[96] The former prisoners campaigned vigorously for the new president, holding a large pro-Amin demonstration in Kampala in early March. The majority of the Asian population, too, supported the coup, having feared Obote's 'left-wing' economic policies and his announced intention to dispossess their assets and deport them from the country. A prominent Asian Muslim, Manzoor Moghal, later wrote that the Asians:

> heaved a great sigh of relief after the coup and joined the Africans in hailing Amin as the great hope of Uganda. Obote's regime had become alarmingly hostile to the presence of Asians in Uganda and ... [they] hoped that the change of regime would give them some respite from the unrelenting harassment they had been suffering, and would perhaps enable them to maintain their stay in Uganda. ... So the Asians joined the Black Ugandan civilians and armed forces in a massive demonstration of loyalty to Amin, and assured him in many ways of their fullest cooperation.[97]

Above all, the new president endeared himself to most of the Baganda by arranging (with the help of the British) for the body of the former Kabaka, who had died of alcohol-related illness, to be flown back from London for a ceremonial burial in April, amid ecstatic celebrations throughout Buganda. The Ganda historian S.M.S. Kiwanuka wrote that: 'By promising the return of the body of Sir Edward Mutesa, Amin cemented the love of the Baganda, which he had already captured by the overthrow of Obote.'[98] Otunnu underlines the importance of Mutesa's funeral in sustaining Amin's position:

> [A]t every stage, Amin demonstrated the highest level of respect for Buganda's traditions. This earned him more respect and cooperation from Buganda. Second, the presence of hundreds of foreign dignitaries during the burial provided the regime with symbolic international recognition and acceptance. These were reinforced by the overwhelming popularity Amin enjoyed in Buganda during the burial. To many foreign dignitaries the popularity was an indication of Amin's popular legitimacy in the country. Thirdly, as soon as preparations for the funeral began, some Baganda killed, raped and terrorised some Acoli [a variant spelling of 'Acholi'] and Langi. ... [T]he regime, which had eliminated

thousands of Acoli and Langi soldiers, assumed the role of a conflict manager and provided some protection to the Acoli and Langi in Buganda. These incidents suggested to some Acoli and Langi that the Baganda were worse than Amin.[99]

The funeral led to a succession dispute in Buganda, splitting the monarchist faction, reinforcing the republicans, and allowing Amin to quash any moves towards the restoration of monarchical powers. In addition, he was able to persuade the young new Kabaka to continue his studies in Britain, conveniently out of the way of any recidivist influence from his advisors.

It is hard to believe that Amin's first actions in domestic politics were suggested to him by British or Israeli agents (or even Greek ones). They were all clever moves, clearly devised and carried out by someone with a deep understanding of Ugandan politics and an acute sense of the balance of internal political forces, as well as the ability to use sophisticated, flexible, divide-and-rule tactics to control them. His early actions did not come from some generic Western intelligence textbook of 'How to Stage a Military Coup', as Hebditch and Connor suggest,[100] but needed considerable local political knowledge and skills, not simply military ruthlessness and tactical capability. The eye-catching political spectacles – the release of the detainees, the Kabaka's return and funeral – distracted attention from the continuing killings in the army, and also from Amin's biggest political error in these early months: his failure to convince other African leaders to recognise his government. Obote flew round the region gaining support from Uganda's neighbours, and Tanzania was particularly strong in its condemnation of Amin, Nyerere declaring three days after the coup that '[t]he government and people of Tanzania unequivocally condemns the purported seizure of power by Maj Gen Idi Amin ... [and] continues to regard President Milton Obote as the President of Uganda'.[101] Obote was seen by African leaders as having the better political position on two key international issues: the Middle East conflict and the white settler regimes in southern Africa. Amin worsened the situation by his open ties to Israel, and some unfortunate initial overtures to South Africa. Jorgensen suggests that this 'Ultra-right Phase' of the regime, with its dependence on Britain and Israel for external support, was 'a reflection of the regime's political, military and economic weakness in its first year'.[102] Overall, Amin's early days in power were marked by a combination of domestic political sophistication and international clumsiness, which is what might be expected of someone with local political knowledge and little international experience, but would be surprising if Western intelligence agents were really in charge.

Holger Hansen clearly summarised the initial consequences of the coup, from the hindsight of 2013:

The political power was no longer with the independence elite, the group of leaders who by education were rounded of [sic] the western Christian tradition. It was with a new stock of people who had worked their way through the ranks, and who were Swahili speaking with strong roots in a Muslim tradition. . . . The difference in style and behaviour appealed to many Ugandans. This factor accounts also for the popularity in which Amin was held by many people beyond Uganda's borders. The fresh language he used against the colonialists and his at times absurd behaviour had a resonance with many people around Africa. . . .

The new military actors did not come to power after a revolutionary coup and with a socio-political reform programme. The coup . . . did not touch the underlying problems and tensions. It means that the new regime was faced with the same problems as the previous one. . . . Hence the agenda and challenges from the Obote years were carried over to the following period. . . . The common denominator . . . between the two periods is primarily the ethnic dimension.[103]

6

A HONEYMOON AND FOUR DIVORCES
THE FIRST TWO YEARS OF UGANDA'S SECOND REPUBLIC, 1971-73

The coup had been expected for years but, when it came, happened so quickly that it was almost a surprise, perhaps even to Idi Amin himself. His first few days were, unsurprisingly, largely spent in mopping up the opposition within the army. The killings that were to characterise his rule started right away, possibly even before Amin himself was aware of the pre-emptive coup. In this phase most of the deaths were Acholi and Langi soldiers; officers and junior ranks were killed or imprisoned, with the aim of consolidating Amin's power base within the army. While he probably ordered many of the deaths, others occurred as individual soldiers, especially the victorious West Nilers, took the opportunity to settle old scores. Despite these immediate killings, however, the early months of his rule are described by many writers[1] as Amin's 'honeymoon period'. In fact, all the different groups that welcomed the coup – the British and Israelis, the Baganda and other southerners, the Asians – were to be disappointed at different points over the first two years. By the end of the period, both the Israelis and the Ugandan Asians had been expelled from the country, Amin's relationship with Britain was virtually destroyed, and his fellow Ugandans, especially the southerners, were thoroughly disillusioned. For all four groups, the honeymoon was quickly followed by divorce.

Amin at this period was a man who had grabbed power in a military coup, without having fully planned or entirely intended it, and with absolutely no idea of how to rule, what to do and say. He learned pretty fast. The new president faced two immediate problems. The first was the risk of an invasion by neighbouring countries – particularly Sudan (due to his support for the southern rebels) and Tanzania, where Obote sat plotting return under Julius Nyerere's supportive protection. The second priority was to gain support, or at least acceptance, for the new government within Uganda itself. Amin embarked on an exhausting programme of local visits, travelling around the country by helicopter being greeted with adulation wherever he went. Everywhere, he promised devolved power to local chiefs and elders, and back in Kampala he set up a ministerial cabinet of civil servants and professionals, together with several of Obote's former ministers, which was greatly approved of by the British. At the same time, however, he made sure to concentrate real power in his own hands. On 2 February, the government issued a Proclamation appointing him Military Head of State with the power to rule by decree. On 20 February, 'the soldiers' invited him to assume the rank of full general and the presidency. Externally, Amin moved quickly, with British support, to get international recognition for the new government, especially from other African states. Ethiopia seems to have been the first country to recognise it, followed by Britain, then Ghana, then Malawi. At an Organisation of African Unity (OAU) Council of Ministers meeting in Addis Ababa in the last week of February, two rival Ugandan delegations turned up, one headed by Obote's foreign minister, the other by Amin's; the meeting was postponed. Throughout March, April and May, there were minor military clashes along the Sudanese and Tanzanian borders but, by June, Amin's delegation was able to take its place unopposed at the resumed OAU council meeting. Internally, military opposition arose, and was stamped out, at one southern garrison after another, in Buganda, Ankole, Tooro and Bunyoro. A stream of British military advisors descended on the country, and it seemed to many, inside and out of the country, that the former colonial power was trying to get back in the driver's seat.

With extensive advice and support from the British and Israelis, Amin began a series of moves designed to increase his popularity in the country and abroad. Early on, he promised to hold 'free and fair elections', asserting that his would be a 'caretaker administration.'[2] He lifted the State of Emergency which Obote had proclaimed in Buganda in 1966 and extended to the rest of the country in 1969. He released more than 1,500, mostly Baganda, political prisoners. Above all, from the Ganda monarchist point of view, he arranged for the return and burial of the late Kabaka's body from the UK. In addition, he announced the reversal of Obote's partial nationalisation programme, reducing government share ownerships from

60 to 49 per cent. As Omara-Otunnu remarked, '[t]his move pleased the Ugandan professional classes, the Asian traders and the multinationals'.[3] All these groups were very shortly to be disappointed.

At the beginning of February, Amin produced that Western fantasy of approved dictatorial rule known as a 'government of technocrats'. According to Omara-Otunnu:

> Many of the politicians who might otherwise have criticised his seizure of power believed Amin's promise that his rule would be transitional only, and they therefore began to jockey for position in order to be well-placed to bid for high posts in the anticipated civilian administration. They lent Amin their support and political expertise in the hope of later favours. Accordingly, he was able to form the new Council of Ministers ... from the top-ranking politicians, civil servants and professionals with a wide range of skills and talents.[4]

However, as we shall see, the realities on the ground were very different.

AMIN VISITS ISRAEL AND BRITAIN

Despite the political environment he had been embroiled in since the mid-1960s, Amin was always first and foremost a soldier. In order to defend the new regime against its many internal and external enemies, and to strengthen his personal power base, the new president's priority was to increase the capability of the armed forces. The problem with this was the poor state of the economy, but Amin thought he had the answer; his friends in Israel and Britain would pay for it. On 2 July, he summoned the acting British high commissioner (Slater was on leave) and announced that he would 'like to visit Britain for 4 or 5 days between 8 and 14 July. ... The purpose of his visit was primarily to discuss military matters but he would like after his initial discussions to go outside London (he specifically mentioned Scotland and sea-bathing) and to meet former British officers who had served in Uganda with the armed forces.'[5] It is not hard to imagine Amin's excited anticipation of meeting his former commanding officers as a head of state. However, he told the acting high commissioner, Booth, that the main reason for the visit was to get a promise of help from the British in the event of a Tanzanian invasion (which might well be supported, Amin suggested, by Soviet and Chinese troops).[6]

According to the acting high commissioner: 'He emphasized several times that he wanted to visit Britain first before going to any other foreign country. He mentioned however that he might stop off in Israel either on the way to Britain or on the way back.' Booth suggested that a week's notice was rather short for an official visit to be arranged and that, 'any suggestion of an official visit at such short notice would arouse undue speculation'. He proposed it could be called a private visit, to which Amin agreed, concluding by saying that 'he would be grateful for an opportunity to pay his respects to the Queen'.[7] Later that day, Booth reported that 'Amin began by saying that he would like to travel by BOAC, but later spoke of the possibility of his flying by a US Jet Commander aircraft which he is now buying and which he expects to be delivered today. In the latter event he might need to refuel in Israel where in that case he hoped to have short talks with the Israeli Minister of Defence.' This sounds like Amin's old trick of trying to play the two Western states off against each other in order to get more military funding. Booth concluded that:

Amin has certainly set his heart on making this trip. In spite of all the inconveniences of the short notice.... I hope it will be possible to meet his wishes to some extent. He is clearly determined to show the world that Anglo/Ugandan relations come first with him. Moreover the talks... might also provide an opportunity to nail agreement on immigration matters [a reference to the ongoing discussions on the return of British passport holders of Asian descent] if we cannot do so earlier here.[8]

Foreign Secretary Sir Alec Douglas-Home personally replied to Booth on 5 July, demonstrating the British government's enthusiasm for a visit from Amin. Despite being given only a week's notice, the British state had scrambled into action and the silverware was being polished, though some opposition was anticipated from Uganda's neighbours:

We will be happy to welcome President Amin for a short private visit next week.... We would suggest that he and his party arrive on the after-noon of Sunday 11 July. The Minister of Defence could have a talk with him and give him lunch on Monday 12 July. The Prime Minister would be willing to give dinner that evening. The Queen has offered lunch on Tuesday 13 July. I could fit in a talk that afternoon. The rest of the week could be spent outside London as suggested, though we would be grateful for some further indication of the President's wishes about visiting Scotland and sea bathing. . . . We hope the President will agree that there should be no publicity for the visit from either side without previous agreement. For your own information, we are particularly concerned about the presentation of the visit publicly. . . . Also terms in which we should present the visit to Presidents Kenyatta and Nyerere require careful thought. . . . May we assume that no wives will accompany?[9]

A few days later, just before both parties made their official announcements, Amin told Booth that he would be asking the UK for economic advisors to be attached to the Ministry of Finance, for increased financial assistance, and for debt relief from previous assistance packages, especially defence equipment contracts. He also requested that a VC10 aircraft be standing by, in case he needed to return to Uganda in a hurry and, in addition, he told the acting high commissioner that he would, 'like to buy some brown shoes in Scotland, size 12'.[10] On 11 July, Amin, his senior wife Malyam ('an imposing and pleasant woman, we know little about her',[11] according to Booth), their 3-year-old son, two military aides and a nanny left Entebbe in Amin's new Jet Commander plane. A dozen Ugandan ministers, military officers and civil servants followed by scheduled airline flights. While they were in the air, Booth telegraphed a hasty last-minute memo for Le Tocq of the FCO East Africa desk:

The following random thoughts may be of help:

2. Although Amin was formerly a heavy drinker he now seems to be a teetotaller. Reason is, I think, health (incipient gout) rather than religion and he has no objection to others drinking in his company. He likes smoked salmon. He is a devout Muslim.

3. At 6ft 6ins and heavily built an ordinary bed is likely to be too small for him. Mama Malyam is also tall (I would guess about 5ft 10ins) and ample. She is handsome and nice. She wants to shop in London.

4. Kibedi [Amin's Ganda brother-in-law, the new Foreign Minister] is not a teetotaller but likes Red Barrel beer best. He has a wandering eye for a pretty girl and has, possibly significantly, left his wife behind.

5. Although the visit is private Amin has taken uniform and will, I suspect, be tempted to wear it on military and possibly other occasions.[12]

In the event, Amin's first overseas presidential visit was actually to Israel, en route to London, and after the British visit he flew back to Jerusalem again from Edinburgh. At his British press conference, Amin said that he had had 'very interesting' talks on the way out with Israel's minister of defence, General Dayan, who was 'a personal friend', and that he had seen military weapons in Israel and was 'very happy' about the visit.[13] He held talks with the president and prime minister (Golda Meir) as well as the defence minister, telling a press conference in Tel Aviv that Uganda's relations with Israel were 'very good' and that his reception had been 'very friendly'. The British ambassador was told by the head of African and Asian affairs in the Israeli foreign ministry that, 'the Israelis were never in any doubt that General Amin intended to ask for an increase [in] Israel's military aid', and that they had reached no specific agreements; 'Ugandan requests for increased Israeli assistance in military training ... would need further detailed discussion. There was no question of supplying more sophisticated weapons such as tanks and aircraft. Ugandan requests for more civilian technical assistance would likewise require further study.'[14]

The considerably longer British trip, although it was portrayed to the Western media as a 'private visit', was calculated to flatter Amin's ego while taking advantage of several long-planned military and ceremonial events. It was the climax of Amin's long love/hate affair with the British state, the most important relationship in his life. The British government pulled out all the stops. According to the official programme, on arrival on Monday 12 July, Amin would be met by Lord Mowbray Seagrave and Stourton (one person), Lord-in-Waiting to the Queen, and by the minister of state for defence in charge of the Royal Air Force. That evening there was a formal dinner hosted by Prime Minister Edward Heath at 10 Downing Street. The following day, Amin would go to Buckingham Palace to meet the Queen for lunch, then call on the secretaries of state for foreign and home affairs, followed by a dinner hosted by the Ugandan high commissioner. On Wednesday, the minister for overseas development would call on Amin at his hotel, and he would then meet the secretary of state for defence, and visit Sandhurst, the British army officers' training academy. At 6 p.m., he would fly to Edinburgh on an aircraft of the Queen's Flight, where he would be met by the General Officer Commanding, Scotland. The next day the Ugandan party would enjoy a bit of tourism – a visit to Edinburgh Castle and the Scottish National War Memorial followed by a 'scenic drive' and a swim in the sea. That evening, Amin was to attend the Ceremony of Beating the Retreat by the Pipe Band of the King's Own Scottish Borderers, followed by the Headquarters Scotland Officers' Mess annual cocktail party. The following day, he was to return to London before leaving the country.[15]

The ministers and civil servants who were meeting their Ugandan counterparts, as well as Amin, for the first time, were provided by the Foreign Office with brief biographies of the Ugandans. Amin's own profile was considerably more flattering than previous ones produced by the British authorities; this honeymoon portrait of the president says that he:

Joined KAR about 1945 as a private soldier and worked way up through the ranks. One of first Ugandans to be commissioned. ... Popular and a natural leader of men, but simple and practically illiterate; a man of the people. An imposing presence, 6′ 3″ in height; once a good heavyweight boxer and rugby player. As Head of State, has shown an engaging lack of formality and a disregard for his personal safety. Benevolent but tough. Well-disposed to Britain; perhaps to an extent damaging to him in the African context. Speaks passable English. God fearing and deeply religious. A Muslim with four wives and seven children.[16]

The official timetable for Amin's visit has an interesting gap, the morning of Tuesday 13 July. Draft timetables in the archive files also have a hole during this part of the day. According to a letter by a Mr McCluney to P.J.S. Moon of the Prime Minister's Office dated 16 July, 'you said that the Prime Minister felt it would be useful if we could provide General Amin with some information about the Chinese threat to Uganda from Tanzania and Rwanda. A briefing [some words redacted] was arranged on the morning of 13 July.'[17] Similarly, the Briefing Note for the meeting with the secretary of state (Douglas-Home) later on the Tuesday says, 'General Amin will, we hope, have been briefed [words redacted] . . . during the morning about our assessment of the threat.'[18] Probably the censored phrase in both documents is something like, 'by MI6' – the hole in the official programme was to allow for Idi Amin to be briefed by British Intelligence.

The trip was widely welcomed by the British establishment, happy to have found a friendly leader in Africa who was not a white settler. The conservative *Daily Telegraph* newspaper editorialised that Amin:

> provides a welcome contrast to those African leaders . . . who bring African rule into discredit in their own countries. . . . Dr Obote who . . . was justifiably ousted by Gen. Amin was in that category. . . . Gen. Amin, always a staunch friend of Britain, has been quick to express this in his country's policy. His request now for the purchase of equipment for the re-building of Uganda's defences deserves the most sympathetic consideration.[19]

The trip was dominated by Amin's perception of the Tanzanian/Chinese threat to his regime, and Uganda's consequent need for more arms, despite many British attempts to convince him that he was mistaken. The MI6 briefing was probably no different from what he was told by other civil servants, ministers and military officers. The line was that the British knew precisely how many Chinese troops were in Tanzania and what they were doing, and they were no threat to Uganda. Tanzania itself had no plans to invade on Obote's behalf. Nor had the Sudanese.[20] Amin seemed unimpressed by these assurances. At the sole press conference of the trip, he told the media that he had come to Britain to buy arms for Uganda's defence and to discuss aid and development matters. He claimed that, shortly after he had left Uganda, Tanzanian guerrillas and Obote supporters, together with three Chinese soldiers, 'had attacked the Ugandan army at three places, including Moroto and Jinja', killing seventeen soldiers. This, he said, brought the number of Ugandan soldiers killed by Tanzanian-trained forces since the coup to 1,000. Amin declared he was going to write to the Chinese government and President Nyerere, as well as the OAU, the UN and the Commonwealth Secretariat, about this 'interference in the internal affairs of Uganda.'[21] If Amin seems rather paranoid here, we should remember all the rumours and conspiracies leading up to the coup. The late 1960s and early 1970s were obviously a paranoid time in Uganda, but also around the world, as the Cold War heated up. The journalist Francis Wheen's history of the 1970s is subtitled *The Golden Age of Paranoia*[22] and this was very much the tone of the times. It is also worth noting that Amin *was*, eventually, overthrown in an invasion by the Tanzanian army along with Ugandan exiles, all trained by the Chinese, and manipulated politically by Obote. As the old joke goes, just because you're paranoid doesn't mean they're *not* out to get you.

Amin's meeting at the Home Office presaged future trouble in the relationship between the two countries. It was to discuss his plans to implement Obote's policy of expelling the Asians ('UK passport holders', as the two governments referred to them) from Uganda. The British were prepared for this and discussions were well advanced by the time of Amin's visit. According to the notes of the meeting,

> The Home Secretary referred to discussions in Uganda about United Kingdom passport holders ... which ... should be brought to a speedy conclusion in the interests of both countries.... President Amin said that a committee had been appointed to look into the question of Asians in Uganda. It was a major exercise to assess the numbers involved, particularly as many of the Asians who might be Ugandan citizens had not obtained proper documentation.[23]

The British wanted the Ugandans to move on with this, and proposed to introduce a voucher system on the model they had previously agreed with Kenyatta for Kenyan Asians with British passports.

The president was largely unsuccessful in his proposed military purchases. The British noted his request for debt relief on previous arms deals, and were unsure about the Ugandan economy's ability to pay for the expensive weaponry Amin wanted. He was particularly keen to buy Harrier Jump Jet fighters, extremely costly and technically advanced planes with vertical take-off and landing capacities, which were very expensive to maintain and extremely difficult to fly. The British were less pleased about his interest in these than they might have been, because they had information 'from secret sources' that the Ugandan defence minister, Oboth-Ofundi, had been in France the previous week to place orders for six Mirage jets. This not only ignited British rivalry against the old enemy, but also indicated that Ugandan state finances would be even tighter than previously thought. Duggan of the FCO's East Africa desk wrote that: 'Such purchases would seem to make nonsense of the request ... for a postponement of financial commitments, debt repayment etcetera, particularly on defence contracts.'[24] The British were agreeing to as little as possible on arms sales or debt repayments, until they got an anticipated report on Uganda's public finances from the International Monetary Fund (IMF).[25] Selling arms to poor countries was fine, but only if one got paid for them. The British were also evasive about aid and development assistance, publicly announcing a £10 million 'project aid loan', but telling Uganda's finance minister to wait until the IMF report was published so the British could decide what projects the money should be spent on.[26]

While the Ugandan minister of finance was meeting the overseas development minister, Amin himself was in Scotland, mixing shopping with ceremonial activities. According to one of the organisers, Seton Dearden:

The army put on a magnificent show which went, apart from the President's constitutional incapability of keeping any appointment on time, very well indeed. . . . The President was delighted with his reception and the military honours done him in Scotland where he took the salute (with his little son, Moses) at the Beating of the Retreat. . . .

The tour of Edinburgh Castle was made in a high and fairly cold wind, and the ceremony of the Scottish National War Memorial was held in the open with coats provided for the chilly Ugandan ladies. We were all glad to see that though arrangements had been laid on for it, there was no mention of sea bathing that day. Instead the President went shopping in Princes Street with the General's ADC.[27] He spent over £700 on purchases which included 10 pairs of shoes size 12, and 14 kilts. He apparently intends to start a pipe band in Uganda. . . . [S]o much personal shopping had been acquired that one person had to be turned off the President's private plane and returned to London.[28]

On leaving, Amin told a journalist that: 'The reason for my visit was to thank Her Majesty the Queen for the assistance that has been given to Uganda by the British government ... and also for allowing the body of

Uganda's first President to be returned home. I decided that before I went anywhere else in the world I must come to Britain first to thank the queen personally . . .' His stop-over in Israel had, it seems, been forgotten. About the trip to Scotland, he said: 'This has been a great pleasure for me. I have been very impressed with everything I have seen, including the colourful military ceremonies.'[29] It is good to hear an African talking about British 'colourful ceremonies', but the irony may have been deliberate; quite possibly Amin knew very well that he had been fobbed off with all the royal flummery, gaining no concrete financial support from his visit.

On his return from the UK, Amin again dropped in on the Israelis. According to the British embassy in Tel Aviv, 'At the luncheon General Amin said that Uganda would shortly open an embassy in Jerusalem as a sign of friendship with Israel. He was convinced that Israel wanted peace and he would raise his voice in the OAU on Israel's behalf.' He was also reported to have presented the Israelis with 'a long list of requests for military and economic aid, to which the Israel government undertook to give sympathetic and thorough examination.' Amin went on to Jerusalem, where he visited the Al Aqsa Mosque and the Dome of the Rock, meeting what the British diplomat described as 'a group of Arab notables'.[30] All the high-level meetings in Tel Aviv and London, however, and all the military pageantry in Scotland, did not hide the fact that Amin had returned more or less empty-handed from his first international trip, after pleading for assistance from his two closest allies. Uganda's economic problems, and the gaps in its military capacity perceived by Amin, remained unchanged: so did the worsening repression in the army and elsewhere.

Amin returned to Uganda on 19 July, to a disorganised army, split by internal ethnic conflict. He was greeted by the British high commissioner, Dick Slater, and an Israeli embassy representative. In Slater's account of Amin's return, we can clearly see the first glimmerings of the end of the honeymoon, as far as the British were concerned:

1. General Amin's homecoming . . . was a sombre affair. . . . The President himself looked grim, made no speech and departed almost at once to lay a wreath on the grave of one of the Ugandan soldiers who lost their lives allegedly fighting against guerrillas. He then gave a press conference in the officers' mess.

2. This was on predictable lines. He spoke of the success of his visits to Britain and Israel and uttered a fresh warning to Tanzania. But there was one significant feature. He admitted that dissident Ugandan soldiers had supported the guerrillas and been partly responsible for the fighting in Jinja and Moroto.

3. It is hard to find anybody here who is really convinced that Ugandan guerrillas, let alone Tanzanians or Chinese instructors, were involved at all. ... It seems quite clear ... that the fighting during Amin's absence was the product of tribal rivalries within the Army.[31]

The trip to Israel and the UK was the premature climax of Amin's international credibility in the West, and it took place at what may have been the highest point of his popularity in Uganda itself. He returned from being feted abroad to find Uganda's domestic problems as bad as ever, especially in the army. He also returned to his first major international problem. This involved two Americans, a Makerere University lecturer named Robert Siedle, and Nicholas Stroh, a freelance journalist. In early July, they had travelled to the town of Mbarara to investigate rumours (which were true) of mass killings of Acholi and Langi soldiers in the local barracks. Siedle and Stroh then simply 'disappeared', among the first of many people to do so over the next few years. After nine months of pressure from the US government, Amin set up a Commission of Enquiry, headed by a (British) Ugandan High Court judge, David Jeffreys Jones. The commission encountered many difficulties, particularly a reluctance by army officers to testify. In the end, Jones had to rely to a large extent on testimony from junior officers who were in exile in Tanzania. After resigning as a judge and leaving the country, Jones posted his report to the authorities: it found that the Americans had been killed by members of the Uganda Army's Simba Battalion. A government White Paper was issued criticising the judge, but this was soon followed by an official statement that the government accepted his findings. In 1973, Amin's government took responsibility and paid compensation to the men's families.[32]

ETHNICITY, CONFLICT AND THE MILITARY

One of the paradoxes of military coups is that they are often very bad for the armed services themselves. The seizure of political power detracts in so many ways from the military mission; soldiers turn into politicians, entre-preneurs, bureaucrats and gangsters, while the army risks splitting into factions on political (and therefore often religious or ethnic) lines. In the case of Uganda, the situation was complicated by the fact that the survival of Amin's coup in the early months depended on the elimination of the mili-tary power base of both the army's largest ethnic group, the Acholi, and what had been (under Obote) its most powerful one, the Langi. Writing in 1976, former Makerere lecturer Nelson Kasfir contrasted the president with his predecessor: '[b]y casting political action in ethnic terms ... [Amin] imme-diately created a threatening situation for people – both inside and outside the army – who were easily identified as Acholi and Langi. From the start, therefore, he reversed Obote's policy of avoiding all public reference to ethnic units as political actors.'[33] Kasfir noted that: 'In his speeches, Amin tends to discuss people as if their ethnic identity were the most salient feature of their personality. In doing so, he reinforces ethnic self-definition much as the colonial ... governments did.'[34] Kasfir concludes that 'Amin's actions and speeches have certainly increased the relevance of ethnicity for Ugandans, both in categorizing people and in explaining their conduct.'[35]

Throughout 1971, then, Amin's domestic policy focused on dealing with the Acholi and Langi in the armed forces, and elsewhere in the state machine. In March, in order to give retrospective justification for the army purges already under way, Amin released what he claimed was Obote's 'Master Plan' to place his fellow Langi in key positions. Hundreds of northerners were rounded up, imprisoned and killed, but the killings were not primarily moti-vated by any deep ethnic antagonism (traditional or otherwise) between the West Nilers and their fellow northerners. As Otunnu writes: 'The continued elimination of the Acoli and Langi was influenced largely by the perception that the two ethnic groups were determined to topple the government. This perception was enhanced by the numerous rumours about impending armed invasions by Acoli and Langi refugee warriors. ... [T]he elimination of members of the two ethnic groups was a direct response to the perceived threat they presented to the regime.'[36] Amin was, once again, not being entirely paranoid. By early 1972, at the latest, small groups of armed men – the 'refugee warriors' – were indeed infiltrating across the Tanzanian border and attacking military posts. Within the army, there was mass disaffection among Acholi and Langi soldiers, who in many cases simply refused 'to acknowledge the change of leadership'.[37] This came to a climax in a series of mutinies in Jinja, Moroto and Mbarara barracks, while Amin was away in Britain and Israel. These gave Amin all the reason he needed to increase the levels of collective punishment and political violence towards the Luo speakers in the army.

As we have seen, Amin came to power in part on the basis of ending Obote's ethnic bias towards the Luo-speaking Acholi and Langi, especially in the army. In the '18 points' justifying the coup, it was suggested that Acholi soldiers, as well as the West Nilers, had been victims of Langi plotting under Obote. Clearly, however, the Acholi, with their majority in the army, were much more of a threat to Amin, and he quickly turned his fire on them, especially after the July mutinies were followed by a series of armed incursions by pro-Obote forces. As Phares Mutibwa summarised events:

> Most of the killings in the army during the first twenty months took place in four phases or incidents. The first was when a coup was attempted in July 1971 and Acholi and Langi soldiers were massacred at Jinja, Moroto and Mbarara barracks; the second was at Mutukula on the Uganda-Tanzania border in February 1972; the third was during another attempted coup in June 1972; and the fourth ... occurred after the invasion in September 1972....
>
> Thus, although the public did not know it, this early period of the Amin regime witnessed unprecedented organised violence.... Foreigners as well as Ugandan civilians tended to see these killings as no more than the normal 'mopping up operations' that follow a coup. But the murders of the military officers were never reported, nor were they believed by Western diplomats.[38]

This is not quite true; the British may not have publicised it, but the archives show that they knew quite a lot about what was going on, although they seemed largely unworried by it. According to the British High Commission's Annual Review for 1971 (written in January 1972, and still broadly pro-Amin):

> The first half of the year was dominated by anxiety about the army. ... Suffice it to say here that the circumstances of the coup d'etat sparked off tribal feuding in the army, which reached a climax in the shooting

matches in June and July ... and led to the murder or removal of most of the senior officers, whose places were taken largely by men without experience or qualification promoted from the ranks. The result was a breakdown in discipline and organisation and a considerable amount of victimisation and even killing of civilians as well as soldiers.[39]

Within the army itself, the anti-Luo policy, through sackings, desertions, imprisonment and killing, got rid of a very large proportion of Uganda's trained troops over the course of 1971. This led to massive recruitment drives including signing up large numbers of non-Ugandans from south Sudan, Zaire and other neighbouring countries.[40] In particular, West Nilers were widely recruited, and quickly promoted up the ranks. Omara-Otunnu, citing Ugandan army records, writes that:

> If it had not been for the large numbers of new troops enrolled under Amin, the deaths and desertions would have threatened to reduce the army to a fraction of its pre-coup level. During the year 1971, recruits alone accounted for 19,742; had none been killed, the total army strength might have been expected to be around 27,000. Instead, the army comprised only 11,409 men by the end of the year, leaving 15,764 unaccounted for; of those ... only 3,083 were recorded by the army as being missing. ... A breakdown of the total recruited shows ... some 4,000 were former Sudanese Anya Nya and Zairean rebels [i.e. closely related to the West Nilers] and most of the rest were from ... West Nile district. ... Many of the recent recruits (154) were enlisted straight away as officers of the rank of Second Lieutenant or above.[41]

One outcome of all this was a narrowing, from 1972 onwards, in the ethnic base of the military, and thus of Amin's rule itself. The army became increasingly based on Kakwa and Nubi recruits, and even other West Nile groups began to face the kind of treatment previously meted out to the Luo speakers. Kasozi outlines the process, concluding that Amin's:

> political fortunes began to decline when he narrowed his base by gradually trimming the large West Nile support in the army. ... After the 1972 invasion of Uganda by Ugandan exiles ... Alurs were removed from most

strategic positions. The turn of the Madi came in late-1972. Amin accused all Madi of drunkenness and removed them from sensitive positions. He then called in Madi elders to explain to them the crimes of 'their sons'. Pruning of the Lugbara began in early 1972. Their 'son', Obitre-Gama, was dismissed in March as minister of Internal Affairs, brought back in a minor portfolio and again dismissed in mid-1973. Another Lugbara, Lieutenant-Colonel Ondoga, the Ambassador to Moscow, was recalled and made Minister of Foreign Affairs. He was later publicly dismissed and his body was found floating in a river. Many Lugbaras were killed at this time.[42]

Kasozi assumes that Amin directly ordered the killings, but the situation at this time was complex, and it is unlikely he had full control over the army.

Clearly, the increasing ethnic repression in the armed forces was officially inspired, but the many unofficial acts of violence probably had a greater impact on most people's lives. The military takeover, and ensuing changes in the composition and structure of the army, led to the growth of an increasingly ambitious, untrained and uncontrolled soldiery. As Omara-Otunnu sums it up:

[T]he conduct of his [Amin's] soldiers soon began to tarnish the relationship between the public and the regime. The soldiers were divided . . . and undisciplined, and they took advantage of the situation to engage in indiscriminate harassment of the civilian population for their own ends (something which they continued to do throughout Amin's regime). . . . As far as the troops were concerned, the inauguration of military rule gave them licence to get rich quickly, often by use of the gun.[43]

At the end of 1971, however, British Acting High Commissioner Harry Brind was still optimistic about the state of the Ugandan military: 'In the latter part of the year, there were signs that the army was beginning to pull itself together, though it has a long way to go before it becomes a disciplined and effective force.'[44] It is clear that what was happening to public security in Uganda at this time was not the result of an authorised, controlled and disciplined military operation, but a much more chaotic process. As Kasozi recounted: 'Amin told his soldiers that the gun was their breadwinner, their mother, their father, their great protector. Many who heard this speech thought that he was giving licence to the security forces to get whatever they wanted from civilians by violence.'[45]

Amin's need to appease the army, together with his military-minded notion of what government itself involved, had other consequences. Obote had left the economic condition of the country in a poor state, including a massive public deficit. After the coup, according to the British, Amin's arms shopping spree included 36 armoured cars from the UK, 15,000 rifles from France, 7 Sherman tanks and 'a large number' of trucks from Israel, 9 helicopters from the United States and the same from Italy, together with 'numerous smaller items'. He also spent a large amount on military construction projects, including a number of new air bases. At the same time, world prices for Uganda's major exports (coffee and cotton) fell and there was also a 'serious fall' in tax receipts, as Uganda's mostly Asian businessmen got as much of their money out of the country as possible. Amin's government borrowed $20 million dollars from the IMF, which then refused to extend any more. British banks lent another $6 million. By the end of the year, according to the British high commissioner, 'the Government has been almost without funds, even for day-to-day business', while 'the cost-of-living index for the lowest group is said to have risen by 20 per cent in the first nine months of 1971, and the man in the street or the village is already feeling the pinch'.[46]

Harry Brind, at this stage still largely pro-Amin, summarised the main problems with the president's first year, acerbically but accurately, as arising from his 'style of government':

> Amin's ... personal rule denies responsibility to Ministers and paralyses initiative in the civil service. To obtain a decision on even a minor matter frequently takes weeks, and often has to be raised with the President himself. The President's background does not make him the ideal person to take these decisions. He has little understanding of economics or finance, and no grasp of the implications of some of his policies. Hence decisions are often taken in haste, after inadequate consideration; frequently they have to be reversed; sometimes they should be reversed but cannot be because of the loss of face which would be involved. A further complication is that the President, accompanied by a full court

of Ministers and senior officials, spends so much of his time touring the country and performing ceremonial functions. Even day-to-day business, therefore, languishes, waiting for the attention of the President or Minister who is not there to deal with it.[47]

DOMESTIC POLICY IN THE FIRST TWO YEARS

Some of the most interesting primary documents on Amin's first two years are the colourful booklets produced by his government, outlining its policies and activities and containing verbatim accounts of the president's speeches, with plentiful photographs and pull-out diagrams. Mostly undated, although the year can be deduced, they were published by the Government Printer, and usually began with a foreword by the president himself. No one would suggest that he wrote them (which head of state really writes what is issued under their name?), but Amin was very concerned indeed with his public image, and looked closely at everything written about him that he could find. In several cases he took strong action against writers he believed to have insulted him. It would be surprising if he had not been closely involved in preparing and producing these propaganda pamphlets. They included *Uganda, the Birth of the Second Republic* (on the coup), *Achievements of the Government of Uganda during the First Year of the Second Republic*, *Uganda, the First 366 Days of the Second Republic* and *Uganda, the Second Year of the Second Republic*.[48] They list the exhaustive and exhausting itineraries of his many national and international trips, together with (supposedly) verbatim transcriptions of his main speeches, and they give us a valuable picture of his chief political concerns over the period. In short, these booklets provide the nearest thing we have to Amin's own account of the early years of his regime.[49]

In the first year, 1971, his domestic strategy was fairly clear. As with most new leaders, it involved blaming all the country's problems on his predecessor and their supporters, while actually implementing many of their policies. Its key element was to mobilise support from two key groups which Amin believed (rightly) were very widely respected among the general public: local chiefs or elders, and religious leaders.[50] Amin's initial appeals to the Ugandan people are outlined in *Uganda, the First 366 Days*,[51] with a foreword by the president. He is presented throughout as a man of action who could get things done, as opposed to the effete and incompetent politicians who had previously run the country. According to the presidential introduction,

> The first 366 days of the Military Government of the Second Republic of Uganda have been gone through at a breathtaking speed. As soon as the new Government was established, it acted on the motto 'government by action'. Our aim in adopting this motto was to make Uganda move once again after she had been lagging behind for the last nine years....
>
> For a whole year I have been engaged in district tours to learn at first hand all the problems the ordinary Ugandans are facing.... I have toured the whole country, county by county, so there will be no-one to claim that I do not know their problems.[52]

In fact, the relevant section does not show that he had visited all of Uganda's several hundred counties, though it repeatedly states this. According to the booklet:

> From the start, General Amin announced that his was going to be a 'Government of action' as opposed to a government of mere discussion, the type of discussion that never solves anything.
>
> President Amin, therefore, embarked on an energetic policy of getting the country moving again. But he had first to learn the sources of the ills, and the problems the country was facing. He had to learn the problems first-hand. And this is what he did. In less than six months, General Amin accomplished the seemingly impossible task of touring all the 20 districts in Uganda, visiting some of them on more than one occasion
>
> A comparison of the military and the politicians' government in this respect shows how Obote was completely left out of the picture for, in his nine years of government, he did not tour even half the country; and yet this was the same man who had written saying that 'the military cannot do as well as the politicians'.[53]

The 'chronological list of the Presidential tours' in the document actually includes eighteen of Uganda's then districts. Amin opened institutions ranging from cement, jute, sugar and tea factories to new military installations, addressed rallies and spoke to Elders and chiefs around the country. The official account continues:

> Characteristic of the President's visits were the spontaneously cheerful crowds and their eagerness to shake hands with him. Nearly everywhere he went crowds approached him to thank him for delivering them from what they called the 'devil's teeth'. At Mubende Town, there was an old woman who politely insisted that the President accept a fifty cent piece of money as her way of saying 'thank you'.
>
> Also characteristic of the visits were the memoranda presented to him. They all expressed views very frankly, as opposed to the submissiveness of the Obote days where one always said whatever would please Obote.[54]

In August, he addressed Langi Elders, warning them not to heed 'guerrillas' and telling them that:

> I would very much like to discuss the points concerning the development of the country rather than guerrillas. . . . You the people of Lango, you must not be confused politically. You have very good people with good brains and they are well-educated, they should continue because there is no interference at all. Even there is nobody who is going to interfere with Obote's family. You should not live in fear. . . . I decided not to fear the people from Lango, why is it that my wife, who comes from Lango, is still with me and I have not dismissed her from my house?[55]

The same idiom of relatedness was deployed in an optimistic bid to win over the Acholi, after 'their sons' in the army had been thoroughly persecuted for eight months. On 23 September, he told a group of Acholi Elders in Padibe County:

> you listen very carefully to what I am saying. I do not fear you at all. I know very well the people who recommended me to be promoted in the Army were the Acholi. I know also very well that when I was wounded in the war and was in hospital the people who looked after me were the Acholi. I know also that my third son is an Acholi from

Padibe.... You the people of Acholi should not fear me. Tell me the truth. If there is anything against the Government or the Army, also tell me. I have come to try to solve your problems.[56]

The next day, he told another group of Elders in West Acholi that, '[y]ou Elders of Acholi are responsible for controlling and advising the people in East and West Acholi. You are responsible for advising them day and night. If something went wrong, I know the Elders are responsible. If my Government and members of the Armed Forces caused confusion, it is your responsibility to tell me so I can take disciplinary action against them.'[57] He concluded with the words: 'I am going to address Army Officers tomorrow morning starting from the headquarters. I am going to tell them to co-operate completely with the people of Acholi and no harm will be done to the people of Acholi. You should not fear at all, but you must be co-operative.'[58] It seems unlikely that the listeners were reassured.

Amin's bid to win over religious leaders was not much more convincing or successful than his charm offensive towards the Acholi and Langi Elders. Noting the fragmentary tendencies of both the Protestants and his fellow Muslims, he seemed above all to want the various religions and denominations to be streamlined into military-style organisations with chains of command which could issue, and take, orders. As Kasozi says, 'Amin wanted uniformity in religion and could not understand groups that differed from the main church of Uganda, the Roman Catholic Church, or the main Sunni sect of Islam (as interpreted by the organisation he set up to streamline Muslim organisations, the Uganda Muslim Supreme Council).'[59] Amin clearly understood the importance of belief systems, their ideas and values, and he wanted to mobilise faith leaders to support the regime. Kasozi sums it up:

Amin, like Obote, desired to wield ideological power. He seems not to have understood the power of educational ideas. But he turned his attention to religion and the media instantly. ... The moment he grabbed power, Amin began to portray himself as an impartial God-fearing religious man, an 'ecumenical mediator' who would see that there was complete religious tolerance and noninterference in the affairs of religious organisations.[60]

AFRICAN NEIGHBOURS AND 'REFUGEE WARRIORS'

In foreign affairs, Amin's main aim from the beginning (apart from his relationships with the British and Israelis) was to get support from other African countries and convince them that he was not just a tool of the West. In 1971 he visited the heads of state of Ethiopia, Liberia, Ghana, Zaire and Nigeria. His major obstacle was the opposition of Tanzania and Sudan. Nyerere solidly backed Obote, who became an exile in Dar es-Salaam after being rebuffed by Kenya's President Kenyatta. Together, Obote and Nyerere established a growing base of armed Ugandan opposition to Amin, and engaged in a propaganda campaign. In the first couple of months after the coup, Obote gave 'a series of press interviews in which he held the Israelis and the British responsible for destroying the "socialist" project in Uganda. He also held them responsible for the deaths of tens of thousands of innocent Ugandans during and after the coup.'[61] His rebels quickly began to infiltrate Uganda and attack symbols of Amin's power. As Otunnu says: 'This led to the first wave of cross-border invasions by refugee warriors from Sudan and Tanzania. In an attempt to confirm to the international community that the government had a severe crisis of legitimacy, Obote appealed to UPC supporters to mobilize and destabilize the regime. ... However, the only objective Obote's strategy achieved was to provoke more state terror.'[62]

Amin's hopes of wider African recognition were frustrated, at least in part, because of his continuing close relationship with the British and Israelis. This brought him up against two firm pillars of foreign policy for the OAU and the vast majority of African states: opposition to the white minority regimes in South Africa and Southern Rhodesia, and support for the Palestinians against Israel. Instead, Amin repeatedly compared South Africa's apartheid policies favourably with Sudan's attitude towards its southerners, while his Israeli affiliations were well known. In February 1971 he gave an interview to the *Uganda Argus* (the main Ugandan newspaper, not yet nationalised), in which he said:

> Some African leaders such as Obote were unable to solve problems in their own countries and went on to talk about South Africa and Rhodesia. I disagree with people like Obote. ... Everybody is talking about South

Africa but we have another South Africa in South Sudan where Catholics and Protestants are not allowed to go to church. When worshippers went to church in the Sudan, they were machine gunned and their houses burnt. This must be solved first before we talk of arms to South Africa.[63]

Addressing Acholi Elders in September 1971, the president told his listeners that:

You know very well that the Arabs are killing more black Africans than in South Africa. The Sudanese Government is worse than South Africa in the way the Arabs treat the black Africans and Christians in Southern Sudan. You have never seen Arab refugees from Sudan fleeing to Uganda except black Africans from the South. Therefore, there is no difference between the Sudanese Government and the South African one.[64]

There was an obvious tension here between Amin's religious identity as a Muslim and his ethnic identity as a black African. Amin's early positions on Sudan and southern Africa had 'isolated the regime in Africa and the Arab world'.[65] In October 1971, according to Otunnu, '[t]his prompted the regime to change its position by denouncing colonialism in southern Africa and Zionism in Palestine. . . . In fact, the new position made the regime quite nervous about what Britain and Israel might do. . . . The result was that the regime began to search for new allies.'[66] The contradictions were unsustainable, and something would have to give. However, as we shall see, many other factors were also in play.

1972: THE EXPULSION OF THE ISRAELIS

From the beginning of 1972, Amin began a series of far-reaching changes in both his international and domestic policies. These amounted to a 180-degree U-turn. The contrast is vividly expressed in the British High Commission's annual reviews for 1971 and 1972. The former began '1971 was Amin's year'[67] and, as we have seen, the overall tone was very positive. The second was vehemently negative. Its first sentence was '1972 was a bad year for Uganda and saw a spectacular decline in its standards.' The report went on, 'Until the beginning of the year it was still possible (though becoming increasingly difficult) to regard Amin as a simple soldier who was doing his elephantine best to clean up Uganda and to play an honest broker role in world affairs. It became apparent in the course of 1972 that this interpretation could not be sustained.[68] What had changed?

The first indication that Amin might not be going in the direction the West wanted came in his relations with the Israelis. Already by the beginning of 1972, the British were beginning to feel that at last they were getting the edge on Israel in their influence over Amin. On 3 January, Acting High Commissioner Harry Brind told the East Africa desk:

> You will know ... that the Israelis are far from popular in many quarters here, and that the feeling has been mounting that their influence is detrimental to Uganda's interests. I was told over the weekend by a highly reliable source that the President has now come round to sharing this view, that there are to be no more orders or contracts placed with the Israelis, that some existing contracts are to be cancelled, and that Bar-Lev, one of the more sinister members of the Israeli embassy, and several Israeli officers engaged in training Ugandan military forces have been, or are being sent back to Israel.[69]

A week after Brind's letter was received in London, P.N. Forster of the East Africa desk spoke to 'Mr Shalev, Head of the Africa Division of the [Israeli] Foreign Ministry' about the matter:

> I got on to the subject of Uganda, asking him if he was aware that there had been growing irritation among Ugandans over Israel's influence on Amin, particularly his relationship with Col. Bar-Lev. I added that I had also seen a report that the Ugandans felt they were pushed too hard by Israel during the Middle East debate at the United Nations. I asked whether the Israelis were not perhaps over-playing their hand a bit, adding that I was speaking entirely personally and that we feel no schadenfreude over Israeli difficulties in Uganda or elsewhere. . . .
>
> Shalev took this in good part. He said that the Israelis knew that they had come under criticism in Uganda. But this was natural enough. Colonel Bar-Lev's personal influence had probably been exaggerated. But it was true that the Ugandans had leant on them to a considerable

extent. Their policy had been mainly directed to promoting stability and
restraining Amin as far as possible . . .[70]

No *Schadenfreude*, indeed! But the British were right, Amin was preparing
to ditch the Israelis, his most enthusiastic international supporters.

In part, this can be seen as an attempt to shore up his rocky position
with Uganda's neighbours and the OAU, and to ingratiate himself with
fellow Muslims, especially the increasingly powerful and wealthy rulers
of the Middle East. It also served to counterbalance Amin's previous
reliance on 'the West', moving Uganda towards a 'non-aligned' position
which allowed the president to balance between East and West on the Cold
War tightrope. The international context for the break with Israel was propitious; as we have seen, Amin first came under Israeli influence in their
joint cause of supporting the southern Sudanese against Numeiri's northern
Arab-dominated government, but, in February 1972, Numeiri reached a
deal with the Anyanya rebel leader Joseph Lagu, ending the (first) Sudanese
civil war. From then on, Israel was, from Amin's point of view, no longer
needed in Africa. Acting British High Commissioner Harry Brind had pres-
ciently remarked in his 1971 annual review that: 'The Israelis have . . . been
chivvying Amin, as they used to do Obote, over co-operation at the United
Nations over Middle East matters. There have recently been some signs that
Amin, like his predecessor, is beginning to tire of this. . . . [T]his forward
policy could well backfire and already Israeli influence on Amin is generally
regarded as baneful by Ugandan Ministers, officials and some senior
officers.'[71] According to Mutibwa: 'Amin found the Israelis high-handed,
especially since they knew they had played a significant part in his rise to
power and continued to believe that his survival depended on their support.
Certainly, during the first months of the coup, they behaved as if Amin was
"in their pocket", an attitude which awoke all Amin's resentment against
"white racist arrogance".'[72]

Most writers link the break with the Israelis to Amin's first visit to the
Arab world. In February 1972, he flew to Colonel Ghaddafi's Libya, issuing
on his return a strongly anti-Zionist communiqué. Over the next six weeks
he moved fast, expelling the Israeli 'military instructors', reducing the size of
the embassy to four officers, and banning Israeli contractors from working
on Ugandan government projects. By the end of March, the embassy was

closed down, its diplomats expelled. Harry Brind concluded that: 'While the Israelis had over-played their hand here, their expulsion was maladroit and it appears that Amin burnt his boats with the Israelis before he was sure of any help from the Arab world.'[73] Ali Mazrui, on the other hand, believes, I think rightly, that Amin had thought the matter through:

> It has been suggested ... that Amin became anti-Israeli as a result of visiting Libya. The sequence and causation were probably in the reverse order. Amin visited Libya because he was already calculating to expel the Israelis. But if he was going to expel the Israelis, it made good economic and diplomatic sense to extract advantages from Israel's enemies. The causes of Amin's rejection of the Israelis did not lie in the Arab world, they lay in the history of southern Sudan, the personality of Idi Amin, and the fear he had that those who made him could so easily break him.[74]

According to Jaffar Amin, his father's attitude towards the Israelis had always been influenced by the words of his prophetess mother (born a Catholic, later a Muslim convert, always a Kakwa healer and initiate of Yakan): 'Do not forsake the children of God, my son, never forsake the children of God.'[75] Jaffar writes that Amin later regretted not having heeded his mother's advice; in retirement, he 'would lament this point ... even whilst continuing to show staunch support for the Arab Islamic cause'.[76] In Jaffar's account, '[i]n February 1972, Dad went on a pilgrimage to Makkah, which turned out to be a glorious occasion in Saudi Arabia following a mystic rainfall that Muslims in Saudi Arabia remember to this day'.[77] The Saudi king presented Idi Amin with a new private jet, and told him to get rid of the one he had been given by the Israelis the previous year. The king offered him 'the key to unlimited assistance ... from the Saudi Royal family', awarding him 'the highest Islamic order – a Palm Tree medal he would begin to wear to every occasion'.[78] As Jaffar put it:

> Dad's requests for armaments were rejected by supposed allies Israel and Great Britain. ... Deep down, Dad felt an overwhelming sense of betrayal from those he felt intimately loyal to, namely Britain and the Jewish Nation. So, despite his mother's plea to 'never forsake the children of God', at this critical juncture, Dad was all ears to the illustrious group of

Arab League Heads of State. He was convinced that they would honour his request for armaments, after his supposed allies Israel and Great Britain rejected the request.[79]

All the evidence suggests, however, that Amin's decision to expel the Israelis was taken some time before his trip to the Middle East, and both domestic and international factors were involved. From a personal point of view, his friend and supporter Baruch 'Burka' Bar-Lev announced in January 1972 that he would be returning to Israel in May. He told his British counterpart that he was retiring, having reached his maximum pension level,[80] but there may have been other reasons, too. Bar-Lev seems to have been under some strain in the months following the coup. In a report to the Foreign Office in July 1971, the (British) principal of Uganda's Institute of Public Administration, Michael Davies, wrote:

> It is known as a fact that Colonel Bar-Lev genuinely believes and has publicly stated that he thinks the United States of America should end the Vietnam War by dropping an atom bomb on Hanoi. It was while pursuing this line of argument with officers of the American Embassy in Uganda at a public reception that he nearly brought about a physical confrontation between himself and one of the American Embassy officers; both were sober at the time.[81]

None of these reasons for the president's move against the Israelis – the end of the Sudan civil war, Bar-Lev's retirement, Amin's increased interest in his Muslim faith, the need to counterbalance his previous dependence on Britain and Israel, the promise of arms – contradicts any of the others. They may all have been partial causes and, from Amin's point of view, together amounted to a compelling list of arguments for expelling the Israelis. By the end of March, in theory at least, all Israeli citizens had left the country.

THE EXPULSION OF THE ASIANS

The British lack of 'Schadenfreude' towards the Israelis was shortly to be followed by their own discomfiture. On 17 October 1971, Obote's planned census of 'British Passport holders' was carried out under Amin. The count was always to have been a preliminary to expulsion, and this was the inevitable result. Brind, disingenuously, wrote in his annual review for 1972 that, 'Amin first announced this – quite casually after one of his dreams – on 4 August.' As we have seen, however, the move had been planned since Obote announced it in April 1970, and was discussed at some length during Amin's 1971 visit to Britain. The myth that Amin came up with the idea by himself after a mystical dream is nonsense, though it is certainly what Amin told the Ugandan public. Western rationalists might have regarded such prophecies as superstitious symptoms of Amin's intellectual inferiority, but the divine inspiration of dream predictions is widely accepted in many societies. As Ali Mazrui wrote, 'Some ... Ugandans might dispute the validity or authenticity of this or that particular dream claimed by Amin, but perhaps the great majority would not dispute the proposition that some dreams are intended to be guides for action, and that supernatural forces might at times be in communication with such a leader.'[82] In the context, the public announcement of the dream was Amin taking ownership of Obote's expulsion policy, claiming it had been ordained by God. This suited the British, as they could then blame the expulsion on Amin's impetuosity and anti-Asian racism, rather than the Asian presence being a legacy of imperial rule which the UK had been happy to negotiate away just a few months earlier. Many Asians, too, found it easier to believe that their forced exit from Uganda was the irrational action of a depraved lunatic, rather than a policy nurtured by successive governments as a gesture of independence, a step towards shaking off the economic handcuffs of colonialism, and an attempt to gain more control over the economy. Almost all writers on the Asian expulsion tell the dream story, and ignore Obote's publicly announced policy and the long-standing negotiations with the British over the issue.

As Obote had done with the Kenyan Luo, Amin deliberately conflated those Asians with foreign passports and those who were legally Ugandan. In both cases, the confusion over what was going to happen to whom, together with widespread intimidation and bullying, led to the result the government desired – the creation of a hostile environment, leading to many more leaving the country than were legally compelled to. Mahmoud Mamdani, himself expelled, described the process as beginning more than a year before Amin's dream of 4 August 1972, though he omits Obote's policy statements on the issue:

On June 28 [1971], the General assured the African traders that his government would do anything in its power to place the economy in their hands. On October 7, a census of the Asian population only was ordered, and every Asian was required to carry a 'green card'. On December 7, following the 'Asian census', Amin put a stamp of finality on the non-citizen status of many Asian traders by cancelling the application of over 12,000 Asians for Ugandan citizenship. At the same time, he called together a conference of 'Asian community leaders' and accused them of economic malpractice, of sabotaging government policies and of failing to integrate into the community. ... Threats to the commercial bourgeoisie, articulated in a racial form, continued. On January 5, 1972, Amin warned thirteen representatives of the Asian community that 'Uganda is not an Indian colony'. A week later he said he would like to see Ugandans owning businesses on Kampala's main street.... On May 9, the minister of finance was instructed to tell the Bank of Uganda to give available money to Africans and not to Asians.[83]

Five days after the 'dream', a decree was issued requiring all non-citizen Asians (mostly British passport holders, some with South Asian nationalities) to leave Uganda within 90 days. Ten days later, on 19 August, a public announcement was made to the effect that *all* Asians, including Ugandan nationals, should leave. Shortly afterwards, this was amended so that even non-citizens, in specific professions, could stay. As Mamdani wrote:

In the first few days after the [9 August] announcement, Amin vacillated between expelling all Asians or just Asian commercial capital. Publicly, this was articulated in his indecision over whether or not to exempt professionals from the expulsion order. Another issue was legal. An expulsion confined to noncitizens would leave the bulk of big Asian capital untouched. ... The citizen Asians, asked to queue in order to confirm the validity of their citizenship, found their passports and certificates torn up.[84]

As late as December 1972, the British were still looking for any possibilities other than allowing their own passport holders to come to the UK. A.A. Ackland of the FCO wrote to the Prime Minister's Office on 13 December:

Our colleagues have expressed interest in the possibility of settling Asians on a suitable island in the dependent territories. Various possibilities have been examined.

Generally the remaining territories are small islands or island groups overpopulated in relation to their limited economic potential and their natural resources. In the Pacific territories under-employment and population pressures are already an increasing problem. The same is true of the Seychelles and the West Indian islands.

... None of the island territories, apart perhaps from the Falkland Islands and its Dependencies, and one or two offshore islands in the West Indies in private ownership, could offer space for resettlement on any significant scale. ... Those islands which have no permanent indigenous population, such as Ascension and parts of the Seychelles ... have already been reserved for Anglo-American defence use.[85]

Eventually, however, the British accepted responsibility for their passport holders, and hurried to register them with the High Commission in time. Civil servants were sent from London on a temporary basis to process the applications, although, according to Brind, 'the numbers involved turned out to be considerably smaller than estimated'.[86] Non-British Asians were processed by the UN High Commissioner for Refugees, and resettled in several places including the UK itself and, in particular, Canada. According to the British High Commission, around 24,000 British passport holders and their dependants left for Britain, some 2,500 other passport holders to India or Pakistan, and 1,500 to Canada, plus 'a handful' to other destinations. Brind wrote in 1973 that:

The Asians were in most cases allowed to take only a small amount of money and possessions with them – £60 and 200kg. of unaccompanied baggage per family. Their assets and bank accounts in Uganda have been frozen. No announcement has yet been made as to how the Asians will be compensated for the property they left behind.[87]

It is rarely mentioned[88] that around 500 Asians remained in Uganda after the expulsion. Brind thought this was because of their 'professional or technical skills',[89] but they also included several Asian families well known to

Amin himself – his friends, in effect – including the biggest market traders in his home town of Arua, the Chawda family, who never left and were still there in 1996.[90]

The consequences of the expulsion took a while to work themselves out.[91] Brind's annual review for 1972 said that:

> The expulsion of the Asians was undoubtedly a popular move. They were heartily disliked by many Ugandans and even those who foresaw the economic consequences of their expulsion were not prepared to shed any tears for them. . . . At present, many of their shops stand empty, trade is at a standstill and many of their commercial enterprises have ground to a halt. The government is finding it much more difficult to hand over their businesses than it had expected. On the other hand, the Ugandan economy has not collapsed, the growth in unemployment has been less evident than anticipated, and Ugandans are not starving.[92]

The key missing word in this assessment was 'yet'.

Throughout the country, the expulsion of the Asians was indeed very popular. The expellees' bank accounts were expropriated by the state, while abandoned homes and businesses were quickly seized by local people, the servants of the previous owners, or passing soldiers, as well as by the government itself. This led to the rise of a class of illegal entrepreneurs – thieves, smugglers and black marketeers – known as the *mafuta mingi*,[93] translated by Reid as 'men dripping with oil'. Many of them were serving or former soldiers. This urban criminal element was doubtless part of what Mazrui, Mamdani and other African intellectuals at the time were talking about when they used the word 'lumpen' to describe Amin's social base. According to Mamdani, the Asian expulsion was:

> the fascist regime's way of rewarding its supporters and expanding its ranks. The property expropriated from Asian capitalists and small proprietors was distributed to big business and military circles. Committees formed to distribute the loot were headed by military officers and opportunists. . . . Thus was born a new social group, the *mafuta mingi*, a class of persons for whom fascist terror provided a framework for quick enrichment. These were the main local beneficiaries of the Amin regime.[94]

For him, this all marked a transition period 'when the military regime was evolving into a fascist dictatorship'.[95] According to Moghal:

> The magnitude of this loot was beyond the wildest dreams of the recipients, and for this sudden change in their fortunes these people were deeply grateful to 'Big Daddy'. They lavished praise on him and lionised him wherever he went. Amin's stupendous success in driving out the thousands of Asians and effectively handling the crisis enhanced his personal reputation in the eyes of the whole of black Africa, and his name became one of the best known in the world.... [H]e had demonstrated to his black African brothers all over the world that the once mighty Britain could be bullied and publicly humiliated with impunity.[96]

For most British people, this was the first they had heard of Idi Amin. In Uganda itself it heralded the beginning of what was called 'the Economic War'. Phares Mutibwa wrote that:

> The initial distribution of confiscated Asian property had its comical aspects. Men who had recently had nothing had become rich bosses overnight. Former cooks in Asian households moved into their former masters' bedrooms.... Even professors and lecturers at Makerere abandoned their ivory towers and joined the great scramble for businesses, or in other words the loot left behind by the hardworking self-made Asians....
>
> The Economic War of the Amin era was primarily an exercise in wealth redistribution at the expense of the Asian community who, as a result of the colonial system ... were the richest group in the country. The beneficiaries were the holders of power, Amin's ministers, army personnel, Nubian and Muslim communities and their supporters and potential allies. The poorest income groups in the country – including peasants, pastoralists and the urban proletariat – did not benefit, except for those who looted the property of the fleeing and harassed Asians.[97]

The expropriation of the Asians, and the wider Economic War, had another consequence: the increasing strain on, and eventual severing of, relations with the UK. Jaffar Amin writes that:

With the expulsion of the Asians, Dad started 'behaving very badly' towards the British, Uganda's former colonial masters. Armed with his agenda for the Emancipation of Africa and its Diasporas, he stopped 'listening' to the British and began 'taunting' them in unthinkable ways including 'insulting' the Queen. This was the very same Queen Dad had bragged about before and had a warm conversation with when he went on the Official visit to England in July 1971.[98]

The popularity of the Asian expulsion within Uganda was only partly due to their economic role in the country; it was also perceived as a blow against British colonialism. The British Empire had forcibly brought the ancestors of many of the expelled Asians to the country as indentured labourers, and had then privileged them over the Africans in many ways, telling them that they were racially superior to the local people, though of course inferior to the Europeans. The satisfaction many Ugandans felt at their downfall may have been due to the Asians' associations with the imperial *ancien régime,* rather than any anti-Asian feeling per se. The economic outcomes of the expulsion were important, but there were other aspects, too.

Amin's ejections of the Israelis, and then the Asians, were followed by a number of related measures. Many foreign Christian missionaries were expelled and, on 18 December 1972, a decree was announced taking over several British and other foreign companies. Uganda's foreign policy shifted radically. As Harry Brind summed it up, rather contemptuously, in his 1972 annual review:

In the realm of foreign affairs Amin's Government have attempted to get back into the mainstream of African foreign policy. All the right noises are made, in strident tones, about the iniquities of racist regimes in Southern Africa, colonialism, imperialism, with Zionism thrown in for good measure. These mouthings have paid dividends in that Uganda is no longer ostracised by African countries as she was in the early days of Amin's regime. ... The Government has also established relationships with some of the Arab Governments.[99]

As far as the British themselves were concerned, the Asian expulsion signified a marked deterioration in relations. According to Brind:

Relations with Britain have taken an uneven, but steadily downhill path over the year. Amin's speeches are still scattered with references to the British people being his best friends, of loyal remarks about Her Majesty and of flattering references to the Prime Minister. . . . At the beginning of the year relations were still cordial. We had reasonable working relations with the President. . . . I suspect, however, that it was already beginning to dawn on Amin that Her Majesty's Government were not prepared to foot the bill for his extravagances and that we were not going to write cheques and reschedule debts out of love for him.[100]

This was compounded by Amin's belief that the high commissioner, Dick Slater, had been conspiring with British journalists sympathetic to Obote. Brind noted that the strength of the British reaction to the Asian expulsion 'came as a genuine surprise to Amin and as usual he took it in a personal way. By this time Amin had probably come to the conclusion that the British government was incorrigibly hostile to him and that he would have, as he so frequently said "to teach Britain a lesson".'[101] In August, the British suspended the loan of £10 million tentatively promised during his 1971 trip. The next month he claimed Britain was planning to invade Uganda and expelled the military training team, which he said was to spearhead the invasion. Many Britons were arrested and several expelled. In October, he ordered Slater to leave the country 'with the last Asian'.[102] By the end of the year the British community had shrunk from 7,000 people to under 3,000.

REBELLION, AND ANOTHER DIVORCE

The claims of a British invasion followed an actual incursion, on 17 September 1972, by some of Obote's 'refugee warriors'. In Brind's annual review and elsewhere[103] this is presented as a non-event, used by Amin as an excuse to eliminate more of his potential opponents. However, Mutibwa gives a convincing account which suggests a more consequential invasion attempt:

Plans to remove Amin were mounted right from the time of the coup. An invasion of Uganda from Tanzania was considered in August 1971, but the plan was vetoed by Tanzania's military leaders who did not consider the chances of success good enough. Apart from spasmodic cross-border exchanges of fire between Ugandan and Tanzanian soldiers, no serious invasion was mounted from Tanzania until September 1972. This time was chosen because it was believed that ... the chance of success was high. The international community, particularly the Western powers, was hostile to Amin, and it was not expected that he could count on assistance from outside....[104]

The invaders amounted to 'a little over 1,000 men'[105] under two senior Acholi officers. They came from various exile groups, including an obscure Maoist organisation called FRONASA (Front for National Salvation) led by a young man from the south-west of the country named Yoweri Museveni. A two-pronged attack was planned, with the main force crossing the border and heading for the south-eastern town of Masaka while a smaller group of commandos would be flown by the Tanzanians into Entebbe, before moving to Kampala to capture the radio station and other strategic targets. The invasion failed, according to Mutibwa, because it was badly planned and the guerrillas were in poor shape; because Amin was ready, having had advance warning; and because, in Mutibwa's words, 'Amin ... still had the support of the civilian population of the invaded areas.'[106] To get to the capital, the rebels had to pass through Buganda, and at this time most of the Ganda were still supporting the president.

In the aftermath of the failed invasion, however, this quickly changed. Amin moved decisively against those he believed were in cahoots with Obote, most of whom were senior Muganda leaders. The first to be killed was the respected Chief Justice, Benedicto Kiwanuka; others included the vice chancellor of Makerere University, student leaders, military officers and former ministers in Obote's government. At the end of Amin's first two years, according to Mutibwa, out of Obote's final cabinet of twenty ministers, eight had been killed and four were in exile. It was not long before many of the Baganda regretted their opposition to the rebel invasion. Mutibwa concludes that: 'By the beginning of 1973, Amin's true nature was emerging. ... The marriage between Amin and the population had not yet collapsed; no one was talking of divorce, but certainly the honeymoon was over. The hard realities of the regime were clear.'[107] Even Amin seems to have been aware of these strains, and of some of the problems likely to affect the regime in future years. In his foreword to the official account, *Uganda, the Second*

Year of the Second Republic, published in January 1973, Amin warned the Ugandan people, using a soldier's language of war:

> The year 1972 saw the departure of the Israelis, the non-Ugandan Asians and the Government take-over of some key British firms in the country. This was part of the economic war declared by us to put the economy into the hands of our own people. The country had to be rid of suckers who were milking the country of its wealth and investing it elsewhere.
>
> We have just ended another phase of the war which involved allocating businesses left by the departed Asians to African traders; you can now walk proudly along Kampala Road here in the capital and in other towns and will find shops open, being successfully run by Africans. The African is now truly master of his own country.
>
> But that is not the end of the economic war. Recently we announced that 'operation mafuta mingi' will soon be launched. This operation is to fortify the new businessmen and to equip them completely for the final assault in this war. . . .
>
> But as we enter the third year and the new era, let us remember that the going will not always be easy. We shall suffer some hardships, but then these always exist in any war situation. The important thing is not to be distracted by such temporary hardships. Let us fix our minds on the goal ahead, for it is a noble goal. . . .
>
> So as we celebrate the second anniversary of the Second Republic, let us resolve to fight to the end for economic independence.[108]

Richard Reid gives a shrewd and balanced summary of Amin's economic policies at this point:

> There was considerable continuity between Obote and Amin in economic terms. . . . Amin's was not itself a ludicrous economic programme; he was addressing – in the expulsion of the Asians in 1972 – an issue of long-standing importance in Uganda, ie, economic inequity and a chronic imbalance in commercial opportunity, around which grievances had been crystallising since the 1930s. But it heralded two decades of economic disorder, not least the result of Amin's short-termism and highly emotional approach to deep-rooted structural problems. When Amin declared his

'economic war' in August 1972, his declared enemies were those non-citizen Asians who owned too much and contributed too little, who sent their savings abroad ... and had for too long stood haughtily apart from (even above) Ugandan Africans. For sure, these were the politics of envy; but it is also widely accepted, again, that the Asian community harboured often ill-disguised racial attitudes towards Ugandans. In the 'New Uganda' – which for Amin was all about African economic empow-erment and liberation from the increasingly arthritic grasp of greedy foreigners – there would be, could be, no place for such people.[109]

To sum up, by 1973, Amin had carried out a total *volte face* in his foreign policy, from a pro-West, pro-Israel position to a pro-Arab and increasingly anti-British one. In Uganda itself, he had carried out Obote's policy of getting rid of the Asians who ran most of the formal economy and redistributing their assets, thereby – in theory – 'empowering' black Ugandans. Both internal and external policy shifts were brave, in the event probably fool-hardy, moves but, in the context of the times, they seemed far from irra-tional, and were certainly very popular in Uganda itself. Amin's polygamous honeymoons, with the Israelis, the Asians, the British and the southern Ugandans, were all over, and the real violence and oppressive nature of the regime were building up underneath.

7
THE CENTRE CANNOT HOLD
PRESIDENT AMIN, 1973–76

Most of the killings, 'disappearances' and other human rights abuses we associate with Amin occurred in the central years of his rule: a time when, it was said, '[p]ower rides naked through Uganda under the muzzle of a gun'.[1] It was also then that Amin's eccentric behaviour and statements came to worldwide attention and the first books about him were published; in effect, it was the time in which his myth was created, and he became Africa's icon of evil. However, this period was also one for which we have little primary evidence. Between 1973 and the end of Amin's regime, contemporary sources of information increasingly fade away. Gradually, almost all Uganda's academics, journalists, writers and other intellectuals left the country. Some joined the exile groups based in Tanzania, Kenya and Zambia,[2] others went to the UK or North America. The British High Commission, whose records are, despite their bias and prejudices, by far the most important source of contemporary material on Amin's Uganda, was operating under severe limitations from 1973 onwards, with frequent expulsions of key staff, and restrictions on travel outside Kampala.

Above all, though, it is important to focus on the severe human rights violations that took place in this period. In writing about these, I want to emphasise three things: first, that questioning the evidence base of some of those who have written about Idi Amin is not the same as justifying his actions; second, saying that a myth was created around Amin is not to imply that any of the very real atrocities which occurred were somehow imaginary or didn't happen; and third, critically examining the nature and degree of Amin's culpability for what happened is not to suggest his innocence. In short, I am not a pro-Amin revisionist, but I do aim to assess the evidence for and against what Amin did and didn't do.

1973: NEW DIRECTIONS

Having cut himself, and Uganda, adrift from their major Western supporters, Amin spent much of 1973 thrashing around, looking for new directions and playing with novel possibilities. His policies veered dramatically and frequently went into sharp U-turns. In February he addressed the nation in a major speech, which even criticised the army. A week later, Amin accused 'the Luos' (i.e. Acholi and Langi) of 'plotting with Obote', and the next day he withdrew this, blaming instead Imperialists and Zionists.[3] At the same time, he announced the replacement of Uganda's five colonial-era 'regions', by nine 'provinces', with military officers (including some Sudanese ex-Anyanya fighters) as governors. He also increased the role of the 'Defence Council', the composition of which was secret at the time and is still unknown; it probably changed frequently at the president's whim. Phares Mutibwa describes what little is known about this shadowy organ of Amin's state:

> [T]he Defence Council . . . though originally meant to deal only with major military matters, increasingly encroached on the powers and duties of the Cabinet. It had been created soon after Amin's take-over in January 1971, but only around February 1973 . . . did it assume greater importance and begin to replace the Cabinet as the major decision-making organ. . . . [M]ajor policy and security decisions . . . were being taken by the Defence Council and then communicated to the Cabinet by the President, so that to all intents and purposes it was the supreme authority in the country. Its precise composition was never established, but it certainly included the Chief of Staff, the Commander of the Air Force, the Minister of Defence and the most trusted army officers commanding major units. . . . It was of course chaired by Amin himself.[4]

The increased role for the Defence Council had an immediate effect on civilian politicians. In early 1973 Amin's Ganda brother-in-law, Wanume Kibede, resigned as foreign minister and Edward Rugamayo stepped down as minister of education. Both sent in their resignations from the comparative safety of Kenya, and Kibede joined the pro-Obote exiles. They were not alone; from 1973 onwards, many 'prominent people ... went into exile and wrote damaging accounts of Amin and his regime'.[5]

Amin's rule was effectively that of a sole dictator. His cabinets never had much authority, and senior posts were switched around at his whim. Following Kibede's and Rugamayo's resignations, Amin ordered all government ministers to take a month's leave, making senior civil servants acting ministers. Uganda also saw its first public executions, of suspected 'guerrillas' and armed robbers, known as 'Kondos', who had plagued Ugandan society since Obote's time. In March, the ministerial leave was extended to 60 days, and widened to include some senior army officers.[6] As the extension ended on 7 May, Amin summoned the former ministers and new acting ministers to his 'Command Post' at 6 a.m. The ex-ministers were given token posts on committees, while the former civil servants were confirmed as the new ministers. In July, he banned various Christian sects, including the Mormons and Seventh Day Adventists; at the same time, several senior army officers were sent on leave. There were further ministerial reshuffles in August but, in October, he criticised his new ministers for not 'solving the problems of the people'.

However, Amin spent most of 1973 focused on foreign affairs. His relations with Britain worsened further, as he continued to expropriate UK assets and expel British visitors and High Commission staff. Amin and Uganda became notorious in the Western media, and Amin made frequent attacks on the British press for misrepresenting him. However, he greeted the appointment of a new substantive high commissioner, J.P.I. (Jim) Hennessey with his habitual warm words about the UK, confirming his willingness to pay compensation for the loss of the Asians' property. It was these payments, rather than the human rights violations, which were the main problem the British had with Amin at this time. The president insisted that before he paid any compensation, the British prime minister would have to visit Uganda for talks, which ensured that payments would not begin any time soon. In December, Amin launched his 'Save Britain Fund', a deliberate tease based on the serious economic problems the UK faced at the time.

This followed major campaigns against Amin in the serious British media (especially, he felt, the BBC and the *Observer* Sunday newspaper), and a sustained attack of mockery in the less serious press. This included a weekly column by the journalist Alan Coren in the humorous magazine *Punch*, which mimicked his accent and outrageous statements. Written as if by Amin himself, it continued for several years. Today the articles may seem crudely racist, but they were very popular at the time. The first year's columns were published in book form as *The Collected Bulletins of President Idi Amin*,[7] which had three reprints in six months. Its nature can be seen from the first paragraph:

> Lotta people gonna be wonderin' about how de cornerstone o' Ugandan literature gittin' laid. Lotta people gonna be walkin' about over de nex' few centuries and quotin' de ensuin' tome at one anudder an' mutterin', 'How dis great talent kickin' off? History recognisin' where he de fust-class military genius, also de dipperlomatic giant o' his generation, not to mention bein' a dab hand at de five card stud, but how it comin' about dat de great Idi Amin also wipin' de floor wid Wilfred Shakespeare an' Edward de Gibbon an' sim'lar?' [8]

More positive, from Amin's point of view, was his first biography, by Judith Listowel, the Anglo-Irish aristocrat Jaffar Hussein called 'Dad's Official biographer'.[9] As we have seen, Lady Listowel was fascinated by Amin and drew a largely positive picture of him, all the more valuable to the historian because it was written before the myth of the psychotic monster was fully formed. Milton Obote hated the book, and successfully sued Listowel for libel. Her biography heralded an avalanche of books, articles, TV programmes and movies, which gradually formed the accepted picture of the icon of evil we know today.

Internationally, the biggest change in this period was Amin's shift away from the former colonial power towards a strategy of building up Uganda's relations with other Third World countries, while exploring the potential advantages of realigning the country towards the Soviet Union. International financial support was vital to Amin, not least to keep the army ready for the next attack from Tanzania. Having spent his first couple of years in power exhaustively touring Uganda, Amin now began a whirl of foreign trips and diplomacy. In January, he established diplomatic relations with East Germany. In March, the Saudi government gave Uganda Sh. 53 million, and the next month a Russian military delegation arrived. In May, Amin attended an OAU summit in Addis Ababa. No longer seen as a British puppet, his position was now firmly established with most African governments, and he even signed a reconciliation agreement with Nyerere. In June, he went on a ten-day tour of Libya, Somalia and Ethiopia, July saw visits to Uganda by the presidents of Gabon and Rwanda, as well as the Burundi foreign minister. President Mobuto of Zaire also visited, and lakes Albert and Edward were renamed Lake Idi Amin Dada and Lake Mobuto. Over the rest of the year, Amin visited 'Congo-Brazzaville', Gabon, Rwanda, Burundi, Kenya, Guinea, Guinea-Bissau, Zaire and Senegal. Back in Uganda, he was visited by heads of state or senior ministers from Gabon, Zaire, Burundi, Somalia, Tanzania, North Vietnam, West Germany, Rwanda and Sudan.

The new British high commissioner's annual review for 1973 was strangely positive about the overall situation in Uganda. The summary read:

Amin retained considerable support, even outside the army. He kept his finger on the nation's pulse. A man of the people. . . .

His growing confidence – security and law and order improve – harassment of foreigners practically ceases. A few tourists and Asians return.

. . . [T]he economy, founded in peasant proprietors growing their own cash crops and food, is basically resilient.

Twin aims of foreign policy: support for the Arabs in return for economic aid and help in the liberation of Africa; and good neighbourliness. Neither did him much good. His policies did nothing to endear him to his fellow leaders; many felt humiliated by his actions. But his influence on the masses probably caused him to be treated with wary respect. . . .

Anglo/Ugandan relations continued chilly. But threats against British companies and the British community diminished. Active harassment eventually almost ceased. Tension was reduced. . . . The British community continued to decline in numbers. . . .

Amin's love/hate relationship with Britain. His growing isolation recognised. He would now welcome any move to improve relations.[10]

In the main body of the report, Hennessey explained his 'love/hate theory' of Amin's relationship with the British:

It is doubtful . . . whether he ever really understood why Britain continued to cold shoulder him – had he not promised compensation to the Asians? Thus, mixed up with his oft expressed deep seated regard for the monarchy, the British people and British traditions and institutions, there was considerable resentment, too. The picture of Her Majesty in his office; the Remembrance Day parades; the military bands playing British Army tunes; and the many professions of undying affection for his best friends, the British; all this was perfectly genuine – but it was the obverse of the coin of his deeply complicated love/hate relationship with the British.[11]

What Hennessey, and other British diplomats who made similar points, never seem to have admitted to themselves was the extent to which this dynamic worked both ways. British diplomats were alternately horrified and fascinated by Amin, hating while at the same time admiring him. It was the response of Mary Shelley's Dr Frankenstein to the monster he had created.

In retrospect, Amin's move away from the Western powers at this time looks foolhardy, another crazy self-destructive gesture like the expulsions of the Asians and Israelis. However, there seemed good reasons for his shift towards the Arab and Soviet blocs. The year 1973 saw a serious oil crisis in the West, caused by a Saudi embargo in response to Israel's Yom Kippur War. This ended the long post-Second World War economic boom, and seemed for a while as if it might cripple the American economy and seriously weaken its international power. Many people believed this assertion of strength by recently decolonised Third World oil states heralded the eclipse of US power. Amin was not alone in thinking that global capitalist dominance was on the way out, and the future lay in Africa aligning itself with the Middle Eastern oil producers. This view now seems misguided, but at the time it seemed by no means crazy, or even particularly unusual.

1974: 'IT IS NOT MUCH USE TRYING TO ARGUE WITH A GUN'

The year 1974 saw a continuation of the erratic policies of the previous one. Again, Amin spent much of his time on foreign affairs, touring the Middle East in January and receiving a Japanese trade delegation in February. In March, Colonel Ghaddafi of Libya made a state visit to Uganda, and Amin met an Italian trade delegation in May, followed by a South Korean one in July, and signed a loan agreement with West Germany in November. The Arab states continued to be generous, and the president received a 'donation' of Sh. 35 million from Saudi Arabia in March, and a 'loan' of $5.6 million from the Arab League in October . 'It is difficult,' Jim Hennessey wrote in his annual review, 'to discern any pattern or coherence in the policy followed by the government in the field of foreign affairs.'[12] The main exception to this was the continued enmity with Tanzania, which ebbed and flowed but steadily worsened over time. In July Amin accused Tanzania and Zambia of planning an invasion of Uganda, and in December he very publicly stepped over the internationally recognised border with Tanzania, telling Tanzanians not to fear Uganda. By that time, he was suggesting that the Sudanese, rather than Zambians, were plotting with Nyerere to invade.

The other constant was the increasingly erratic Uganda–UK relationship. Amin's attitude towards Britain (and vice versa) became even more of a switchback ride between Hennessey's poles of love and hate. In January 1974, he sent a telegram to the prime minister, Edward Heath, sympathising about the state of the UK's economy, and 'the people of Kigezi'[13] offered a consignment of fruit and vegetables to the apparently starving Brits. In February, a 'Military Spokesman' condemned the UK, after the Foreign Secretary had omitted Uganda from a tour of East Africa. The biggest bone of contention remained the question of compensation for the losses of the expelled Asians. On 13 February Amin agreed to meetings between British representatives and a 'Ugandan Compensation Board', only to withdraw this the next day 'on the advice of the Defence Council'. March saw more eccentric telegrams to the prime minister and the Queen, but at the end of April Amin payed an unscheduled visit to the British High Commission, spending the afternoon in and around Hennessey's swimming pool and chatting at length about his love for the UK. In May, he sent another telegram to the British prime minister and the Foreign Secretary 'saying he still admires them', followed by a telegram offering to mediate in the British conflict in Northern Ireland. Many of the lowest moments in the relationship arose from British media reports, to which Amin became increasingly sensitive. In July, he once more dangled the carrot of compensation, telling Hennessey that he was ready to hold talks, and again inviting the prime minister to visit in order to start the process. Later that month, he agreed to meet a British team of officials in September to discuss the issue. However, before the meeting could take place, Uganda's new foreign minister, Princess Elizabeth Bagaya of Toro, denounced Britain at the UN, in what Hennessey described as a 'vitriolic speech'. Things really blew up in November, after more hostile British press reports. With very short notice, Amin ordered the reduction of British High Commission staff to five, and expelled the defence advisor along with some development consultants. In December, however, he repeated his promise of compensation for the Asian expulsion.[14]

Ever the optimist, Hennessey summed up Anglo-Ugandan relations in his annual review for 1974:

[R]elations started on a hopeful note. The President sought a rapprochement, despite continuing personal attacks in the British media. With a hiccup or two, he got to the point of making an offer on compensation. The jilted lover. Angered beyond control by a series of events [mostly items in the UK media] in early November he ordered the expulsion of most of the High Commission UK staff. But he kept his respect for the British. Their esteem was desired above all. ... Amin wanted nothing better than a return to his old relationship with the British. ... [I]n a number of intimate conversations I had with him ... he waxed sentimental about the good old days in the army at Warminster. Certainly, he found some odd, even crude ways of expressing what was in his heart – the outrageous telegrams were only one example – but it did not need a psychologist to explain his actions.

What he appeared not to comprehend was the lack of response. The British, he felt, should have known him better. It took much hard work ... to explain ... why we had adopted such a firm line towards him. But gradually ... he seemed to understand. The verbal attacks almost ceased. The earlier violent reactions to British press criticism became much more muted. The British community was left in peace. ... Official contacts became frequent. ... [T]he crucial question of compensation was at last recognised as being the key that could unlock the door to better relations. ...[15]

Relations again worsened following a series of BBC reports on Uganda. On 5 June, Amin threatened to expel the entire British community within

48 hours unless the broadcasts stopped. The Foreign Office apparently intervened with the BBC – Hennessey's annual review says that 'the BBC was left in no doubt by your Department of their responsibilities in the matter'.[16] The high commissioner believed that Amin's agreement to compensation talks was 'a mark of Amin's single-minded determination to continue to work for an improvement in our relations. . . . Not many African leaders would have been as prepared as he was to risk losing face.' However, there was no response from London, and Amin felt 'badly let down'. Then, in November, the *Observer* newspaper published allegations that Amin had murdered his wife and driven his father into exile. It was, wrote Hennessey, 'the end of the courtship'. The defence advisor was thrown out, followed by most of the other embassy staff. Of twenty-nine British diplomats in Kampala when the high commissioner had arrived in 1973, only two were left. Hennessey wrote:

> Perhaps Westerners underestimate the strong feelings aroused in Africans by such personal attacks in the British Press. Amin was not alone in Africa – and perhaps other parts of the developing world – in thinking that it went too far. . . . Not only did it seem to show the contempt of white for black, but a complete disregard for the sensibilities of the people. No African leader could afford the loss of face entailed by a failure to respond. . . .[17]

Throughout this report, Hennessey uses terms like 'intimate', 'sentimental', 'jilted love', 'love/hate relationship' and 'end of the courtship'. He had developed an interesting theory about Amin's attitude to the UK. The president did not want a business-like, diplomatic relationship with the British, but something more like a marriage, with mutual affection and support and, if not love, then at least a return to the days when his KAR officers admired and respected him. Once again, however, Hennessey was unable to turn the mirror round and see how far Amin's emotional ambivalence was reciprocated by the British.

Internally, 1974 saw more constitutional reorganisation, political repression and economic decline. In January, Amin appointed eight new provincial governors, and the Defence Council awarded him three British-sounding medals: the 'Victory [not Victoria] Cross', 'Military Cross' and 'Distinguished

Service Order'. In February, he banned women from wearing trousers or wigs in public. In March, a senior army officer, Lieutenant Colonel Ondoga, was stopped by military police in central Kampala, shoved into the boot of a car and driven off. Three days later Amin told a meeting of the new provincial leaders that Ondoga's body had been found in the Nile. Two weeks after this, fighting once again broke out between different army units in Kampala. The Chief of Staff, Brigadier Arube, was reported to have committed suicide, and Amin took over the role himself.

Amin also divorced three of his (by now) four wives in 1974. It has often been noted that they were all from Christian backgrounds (though Malyam had converted to Islam),[18] whereas his later wives were Muslims by birth. The president's divorces have therefore been associated with Amin's move towards a pro-Arab foreign policy. Jaffar, however, attributes it to his father being swept off his feet by a new Baganda Muslim sweetheart. At their wedding in 1973, he writes, 'Dad was in a "honeymoon mood" with his new flame Mama Madina – the undertone reason for the three simultaneous divorces he gave to his other wives that was waiting around the corner in 1974.'[19] That year, she succeeded Malyam as Amin's official senior wife, and Decker says she 'willingly took up the mantle of "mother of the nation"'.[20] The next year, he married Sarah Kyolaba, described by Jaffar as 'a so-called go-go dancer from the Suicide Mechanised Unit Jazz Band in Masaka'.[21] She seems to have been the last of his official wives as president, but he continued to have many relationships with women, some of which became long-term.

In May, Amin announced the setting-up of an independent Commission of Enquiry into 'disappearances' since the coup (considered below), which held its first hearings on 1 July. In September, he denounced the budget delivered by the finance minister in June, and cancelled its proposals. On October 19, it was announced that Amin and 'all available ministers' were beginning a 15-day leave, later extended to 30 days. On 23 November, the president revoked his ban on women wearing trousers and, six days later, he again reorganised Uganda's political structure, this time splitting it into five military commands, each under an army cabinet minister.

Economically, the country looked to be in a complete mess. The British high commissioner reported that Uganda's 1973–74 budget deficit was four times higher than estimated, and the overall balance of payments deficit for

1974 was three times the projected figure. Agricultural exports, vital to the country's economy, crashed sharply – sugar down 75 per cent and cotton down 50 per cent, while coffee and tea became difficult to export at a reasonable price. The cost of living went up by 65 per cent. All these, however, were official statistics, applying only to the formal economy. The *real* economy of the country[22] depended on small-scale peasant farming, both for subsistence and for exchange or informal sale, almost none of which was officially recorded. As Hennessey remarked in his 1974 report, 'the country's natural wealth will remain. In this Garden of Eden no one need ever starve.' The illegal '*magendo*' system also grew over this period, coming to dominate much of the cash economy until long after Amin had gone. Like subsistence agriculture, this was invisible to the official statistics. Amin's attempts to run Uganda like a military unit led inexorably to the development of a parallel economic system; as Hennessey wrote, 'the campaign to reduce prices ... amounted to a threat to shoot any shopkeeper who failed to sell his goods at a price arbitrarily set by the government. As the figure was usually well below the level at which any profit was possible, shops were quickly cleared of goods.'[23] In this context, rather than being the parasitic criminal counter-economy portrayed in most of the literature on Amin's Uganda, *magendo* became an important survival strategy for a large part of the population.

Hennessey concluded his 1974 report with a vivid picture of the president:

[A] visitor to the country today may be forgiven for asking whether the picture of Uganda presented in the Western Press is not just another example of 'hostile propaganda'. ... [T]owering over everything he sees, the huge, charismatic figure of President Amin: joking, dancing, talking, always talking to his people in the slow, soft voice that still fascinates so many. The picture he sees is not one of widespread discontent, of a country verging on the edge of economic chaos.

... The President runs things as he was taught by his British COs to run a battalion. The cleanliness, the tidiness, the spit and polish, the smart police – even the flowers around the petrol stations – these are the result of direct, personal orders from the top. Nothing is too small to escape his attention: the length of the women's dresses, the importance of boiling the drinking water, the need for personal hygiene – there is no argument, Ugandans are naturally submissive. They repress their feelings, stand patiently in queues . . . aware that it is not much use trying to argue with a gun.

. . . [I]f one ignored the black moods, the violent temper, the ruthless determination to have his own way – and tried to understand his constant desire to put himself and his country first, with Africa and all black men a close second . . . what is certain is that leaders like Amin will always be with us – if not in Uganda then somewhere else. He typifies a type of post-colonial African dictator that is likely to be around for a long time to come.[24]

Unpleasant, then, but hardly the figure of supernatural evil portrayed by later writers.

HUMAN RIGHTS AND WRONGS

The year 1974 is a suitable point to stand back from the chronology for a while and consider Amin's overall human rights record, as the year saw the establishment of two very different enquiries into human rights in Uganda. The International Commission of Jurists (ICJ) produced the first detailed international report into the killings and 'disappearances' since the coup. Perhaps aware this was coming, Amin set up an independent Commission of Enquiry into the disappearances; surprisingly, this is now recognised by historians of human rights as the world's first Truth Commission. The two reports considered broadly the same topic, in very different ways. It is usual for writers on Amin to dismiss the Ugandan Commission as a fraud, and accept unquestioningly the findings of the ICJ report, but each had its strengths and limitations.

From the coup onwards, Amin's rule was characterised by growing numbers of 'the disappeared'. People, especially those who might be considered enemies of the regime, seemed to just vanish. Sometimes bodies turned up, sometimes they didn't. Hiding corpses is not too difficult in a country with a lot of overgrown, unsettled land, criss-crossed by hundreds of rivers heading into the massive Nile, and containing many carnivorous animals only too happy to hoover up any remains. Amin probably knew, and cared, about only a small proportion of all the killings, but military activity – essentially, violence and killing – had been Amin's whole career. As Iain Grahame said of the President's KAR days 'he was known to be ruthless, which good soldiers are; you've got to be'.[25] My purpose here is not to minimise or exaggerate Amin's responsibility; probably a final reckoning is impossible but he certainly deserves a large part of the blame, even for deaths he knew nothing about. Amin created a state which allowed and encouraged violence, especially on the part of its military and other coercive forces. Some of the disappearances were more closely linked to state or presidential purposes than others, but there is a good argument for laying all the deaths at Amin's door, as well as another good argument for suggesting that he was not *directly* responsible for most of them. As A.B.K. Kasozi, no supporter of Amin, suggested: 'Hundreds of innocent people were trapped in a vicious circle of violence. All the members of these paramilitary units used violence for their own selfish motives: the demarcation between officially sponsored and private violence was very thin.'[26]

An influential summary of the violence, killings and torture during Amin's rule was published after his overthrow in an Amnesty International report on *Political Killings by Governments*. It concludes that somewhere between 100,000 and 500,000 people 'were killed by the security forces'[27] in Uganda during the Amin period. These figures, especially the larger one, are often cited, but the 500 per cent variation indicates the limitations of the estimate. Even so, a very large number of people had clearly been killed, in a country with a population of just over 10 million at the time. According to the report:

> Systematic and deliberate killings by government forces began in the first month of President Idi Amin's rule in Uganda. . . . Those who were not killed outright or shortly after arrest were mostly tortured by the army, the intelligence service or a special police unit, and then killed. . . . The victims included members of particular ethnic groups, religious leaders, judges, lawyers, students and intellectuals, and foreign nationals. The impunity with which the security forces were permitted to kill political opponents and criminal suspects created the conditions in which many other people were killed by members of the security forces for criminal motives or even arbitrarily.[28]

The Amnesty report describes the setting-up of new special military and police units, the Public Safety Unit and the State Research Bureau, which replaced Obote's GSU. It recounts the growth of legislation allowing the security forces to arrest, injure or kill anyone 'suspected of armed robbery' ('Kondoism'). The report goes on to conclude that '[t]he possibility of obtaining a fair trial, undermined by a 1973 decree empowering military tribunals to judge certain cases ... [was] further reduced by the killings of judges, lawyers and defendants'.[29] Addressing the issue of the 'disappeared', Amnesty stated that '[p]olitical killings by government agents in Uganda were generally carried out in secrecy ... as it became understood by the government that a practice of causing suspected opponents simply to "disappear" enabled a semblance of normality to be maintained in the country. From 1971 onwards many people were arrested by the security forces and made to "disappear" with the authorities denying any knowledge of them'.[30] The report lists multiple allegations of torture and killings. It claims that 'whole villages were massacred' in the Acholi and Langi areas, a rather vague charge for which I have been unable to find any reliable evidence, though it is certainly possible. The report noted that, '[d]uring the entire period of President Amin's government, no security official was charged, fairly tried, convicted and punished for any act of arbitrary arrest, detention, torture or murder'.[31] It was published just as killings by Milton Obote's second government were beginning to reach levels Amin's regime had never attained but, of course, its authors did not know that at the time.

Jan Jelmert Jorgensen, in his *Uganda: A Modern History*,[32] was suspicious of the number of killings attributed to Amin. His analysis seems carefully balanced and coherently argued, and he was certainly no supporter of the dictator:

It would be a mistake to attribute all violence in Uganda under the Amin regime to agents of the state. The Amin regime provided a perfect cover for private individuals who wished to settle the score with personal enemies. In some cases, it was only necessary to denounce one's rival to the State Research Bureau or Military Police; in other cases, personal murders might be staged to implicate the State Research Bureau or Military Police. Even in such murders the regime should bear ultimate responsibility for the breakdown in law and order....

But how many did die. . .? Estimates range from 80,000 in the first two years of the regime, to 300,000 to 500,000 by the end. If so many died, why did so few flee? Even the 80,000 deaths estimate must be treated with some scepticism. Such a figure represents 0.8 per cent of the total population of Uganda. Carnage by the state apparatus in such a short period at that magnitude should have resulted in massive emigration. . . . [But] the refugee totals appear low. Ordinary peasants tended to remain in Uganda. . . .

Certainly many did die under the Amin regime, but the high estimates appear to be the result of treating peaks of violence as averages. . . .

I estimate that the total number killed at the hands of state agents under Amin ranged from 12,000 to 30,000 (1,500 to 3,750 per annum).[33]

My guess would be that this is a serious underestimate, but the main point here is that we simply cannot know. The highest figure in the Amnesty document, derived from the ICJ report mentioned above, is 500,000, often quoted as 'the' definitive number of deaths for which Amin was responsible. This is 41 times larger than Jorgensen's lowest estimate of 12,000. With that kind of variation among informed analysts, it is hard to see any of the figures as truly reliable. Moreover, it could be argued that 12,000 deaths are as bad as 500,000; if the overall death toll is what matters, Mao Zedong would always be judged the worst dictator in history, simply because of the size of China's population.

Stung by media criticism of his human rights record, particularly in Britain, in 1974 Amin set up the world's first Truth Commission. The Commission of Enquiry into the Disappearances of People in Uganda since 25 January 1971 took evidence between 1 July 1974 and 2 January 1975, and the report was written and presented to Amin, but not published, later that year. Many at the time, including the British high commissioner, thought it a whitewash, but in retrospect human rights experts have tended to give a more positive picture. Richard Carver has written that:

In view of the considerable practical difficulties it faced and the highly unfavourable political climate in which it operated, the achievement of the Commission on Disappearances was remarkable. It heard the testimony of 545 witnesses and succeeded in documenting 308 cases of 'disappearance', although it stated in its conclusion that these were only a fraction of the total number. The Commission concluded that the Public Safety Unit and the State Research Bureau, special security bodies set up by Amin, bore the main responsibility for the 'disappearances'.[34]

Carver says that the commission's conclusions were 'reported in a distorted version on the state-owned radio',[35] and then brushed under the carpet. It is a testimony to the independence of the commission that its members did not fare very well after the report was produced. The Chair, Mohamad Saied, a Pakistani judge, did not have his Ugandan contract renewed, and returned to his country. The Ugandan members were two police superintendents (one of whom was later framed for murder and sentenced to death, while the other left the country to avoid arrest), and an army officer who seems to have survived.[36] The commission carefully listed all the evidence for each of its 308 cases, and its report and appendices cover more than a thousand pages of detailed painstaking investigation. Despite its limitations, it was, unlike all the other contemporary human rights reports, based on serious research inside the country, rather than the testimony of exiles. As Hayner remarks, however, '[t]he 1974 Ugandan Commission has been all but forgotten in history'.[37] Although widely seen as a cover-up, particularly by those who have not read it, the commission's report strongly criticised state and military bodies, laying the main blame for the disappearances on Amin's security organisations, though not the president himself. It is unsurprising that its findings were largely ignored and the report buried.

Apart from the deaths, Amin's forces certainly carried out innumerable beatings and tortures, though the details tend to blur into generic horrors, and it is usually impossible to tell what evidence lies behind most of the stories. I strongly dislike repeating torture tales, which are omnipresent in the popular books about Amin, but it is essential to give some account of them here, if only to avoid any suggestion of downplaying the president's atrocities. The Amnesty report, based on evidence from Ugandan exiles, says that:

Nearly all prisoners were severely tortured; most either died under torture or were killed in other ways.[38] Prisoners were sometimes ordered at gunpoint to kill other prisoners. In this method of execution prisoners were lined up: one was given a hammer and ordered to beat another prisoner to death with it; he in turn was then killed by another prisoner and so on, with the last survivor of the group being shot by a prison guard. Prisoners' bodies were frequently dumped in rivers or forests. Occasionally the bodies (usually mutilated) were returned to relatives by security officers on payment of large bribes.[39]

The use of hammers is mentioned by many commentators, which does not necessarily mean it is true, but it was certainly common currency among the exiles and is repeated in much of the literature on Amin.

Phares Mutibwa writes that, after the publication of the commission's report:

> things drifted on till the late 1970s. The violence and murders became institutionalised, and for the first time in the country's history, citizens lived in spite of and not because of, the existence of the state, and individuals and communities found themselves without protection against humiliation, molestation and dispossession. Life, liberty and property were at a discount. In such a state of chaos, many lives were lost, including those of leading personalities in the land.[40]

Mutibwa is no Amin supporter, but recognises that a single person could not have been responsible for all the killings and torture without the active assistance of others, who later had a powerful motive for blaming everything on the president:

> Amin was a killer, who ordered mass executions. The State Research Bureau was a state within a state, run by men who did not seem to possess the hearts and feelings of human beings. Amin's 'boys' had the licence to kill – but not all of his killers and supporters were 'boys'. Those who supported and served him for several years were men and women with whom we had been together at good schools ... at Makerere University and at Britain's ancient universities and Inns of Court. These well-educated and trained people ... may not themselves have signed the death warrants, but there is no doubt that it was to them that Amin turned for advice on the legal formalities that were used to give

legitimacy to his barbarities. . . . Who operated and served these organs which sent innocent men and women to their deaths on mere suspicion and over trivial rivalries. . .? They were the instruments he used to destroy Ugandan property and lives – although they may later have abandoned him and written sensational articles and even books condemning all his works . . .[41]

Mutibwa does not give any specific examples, but some of the best-known Ugandan writers on Amin were indeed his associates over a long period; indeed, that is what has given their books credibility. Probably the most widely quoted and influential book on Amin is *A State of Blood* [42] by Henry Kyemba, who had been Obote's private secretary before becoming Amin's principal private secretary and secretary to the cabinet, then permanent secretary, later minister, in the Department of Culture and Community Development. In 1974, he was promoted by Amin to minister of health, and remained in that post until he went into exile in 1977, by which time, as we shall see, the regime was obviously tottering. Kyemba's book was published shortly after he left Uganda, and must have done much to bring him back in favour with Obote. It is the earliest published source for many of the wilder stories about Amin, including his alleged cannibalism.

Nor was it only educated Ugandans who 'facilitated' Amin's abusive rule. Several British and other European people stayed on in Uganda to work for the dictatorship. A little known but fascinating figure of the era was an Englishman named Peter Jermyn Allen. A former colonial policeman in Hong Kong and later Uganda, at independence he was teaching law to trainee Ugandan magistrates. Under Obote, he became principal of the Makerere Law School in 1964, and was transferred to the judiciary in 1970 as chief magistrate. In 1973, Amin appointed him as a High Court judge, and he continued in that role for twelve years, throughout not only Amin's rule but the even more murderous 'Obote II' regime that followed. Allen was made Chief Justice of Uganda in 1985, under the military council which briefly replaced Obote. For three days, in 1986, he became, according to his own account, 'a sort of acting Head of State',[43] before swearing in the victorious rebel leader Yoweri Museveni, who promptly replaced him with a Ugandan. For his public service (to Amin and Obote?), he was knighted by Margaret Thatcher in the 1987 New Year's Honours List, and retired to the

Cayman Islands. Allen published two books about his time in Uganda, a rather uninformative memoir and what he said were his diaries of the time (which, however, do not read like diary entries, and contain much background information which the writer would have known well).

A much better known British figure of Amin's time was the notorious Bob Astles, whom we have met before in connection with the 1971 'Tank Hill incident'. Makubuya gives an account of his career:

In his eight-year rule, Amin relied on advice from an improbable source: Robert Astles, an ex-British soldier, veteran of the Second World War and a recipient of the British Empire Medal for his work in the Colonial Office. Astles' military unit had been sent to Uganda to quell the 1949 riots in Buganda. Following that assignment, he remained in the country as a colonial officer in the Ministry of Works. Astles, who later renounced his British citizenship and became a Ugandan citizen, was most notorious for his dealings with Amin, with whom he had a love–hate relationship. . . .

Astles worked for Obote's government as a civil servant, pilot and cameraman until the 1971 coup. Although he swiftly transferred his allegiance to Amin, his previous support for Obote brought him under suspicion, and he spent several weeks in Makindye Prison, where he was shackled and brutally interrogated. After denouncing Obote as 'almost a madman' on Ugandan television, he was released and almost immediately recruited by Amin as his advisor on British affairs. He was arrested again in 1976, but released after only a week and appointed Head of Amin's anti-corruption squad.

Astles was equally feared by Europeans and Africans. When Astles was not in Amin's jails for one misdemeanour or another – such as 'confusing' his ministers – he was a member of Amin's much-feared State Research Bureau. His zoo-like home, which hosted a python, an owl, a mongoose, a monkey, a dog and several crested cranes, was equally intimidating. . . . He always insisted that he had no blood on his hands. But he did not deny humiliating European expatriates by forcing them to kneel before Amin, which earned him the name, the 'White Rat'. For his anti-corruption work, Amin awarded Astles the Republic medal. Amin also appointed Astles' [Ugandan] wife . . . as a minister in his government.[44]

Other Ugandan writers draw a more complex and sometimes rather confusing picture of the man. Peter Nayenga wrote in 1979 that:

> Bob Astles, a British-born confidant of Amin since 1971, is generally regarded by many Ugandans as the uncrowned vice-president of that country. As he has no specific governmental responsibilities, others view him as the economic link with the western countries. In addition, some call him a 'double agent' who drives Amin to extreme courses of action in order to discredit the entire black leadership on the continent. ... Although any one of these views may be wrong, the crux of the matter is that Bob Astles is central to Ugandan politics.[45]

By the end of the 1960s, he was already very involved in Ugandan politics, having been first a supporter of the Kabaka, then of Obote (in his memoir he portrays himself as having been much closer to Obote than to Amin). According to his book, privately published after his death, Astles was a member of Obote's Police Special Branch, and then of Akena Adoko's GSU. In 1969, Astles claimed he had taken up Ugandan citizenship, but the High Commission believed he retained British nationality. However, his allegiance was always uncertain. In January 1969, the then head of the Foreign Office's East Africa desk, E.G. Le Tocq, wrote to his boss, the permanent secretary:

> [I]t is believed that a number of prominent Ugandans, including President Obote and General Amin ... are extremely anxious to get rid of Astles because of the knowledge which the latter is thought to have which would incriminate them....
>
> Astles has been in Uganda for some years and even during my time there rather fancied himself as a secret agent and tried to get himself recruited in this capacity by the High Commission. He used to feed us a certain amount of information, mostly of a somewhat pathological, anti-Communist nature, and we were unable to place much reliability on it.[46]

Astles, who died in London in 2013, seems (most of the time) to have been one of Amin's very few real friends, and it is a pity that we know for sure very little about him. Shortly before his death, the American historian Alicia Decker stayed for several days with Astles at his London home, while researching her book on women in Amin's Uganda. In this she writes that: '[s]ome of the most interesting information for the book came from Bob Astles, a British expatriate who was in charge of the anti-smuggling unit that was established in 1975. . . . Getting to know one of Amin's closest friends was an incredible opportunity, providing me with a wealth of information, only some of which made it into this book.'[47] Like Peter Allen, Astles wrote a memoir, privately published after his death but written in 1987–8, which I have quoted in several places. Like Jaffar Amin's book, it takes a very different line on events from most commentators (for example, on the role of the Greek government in the coup). Of the killings and 'disappearances', he writes: 'By 1972 soldiers all over the country were being paid to kill people because of land issues and personal jealousies. It was too simple. No serious investigation would be made because police could be bribed or were stupid or they could themselves be killed. Then the head of state could be blamed through rumour-mongering.'[48]

Much more influential than Amin's own Truth Commission was the ICJ's widely cited 1974 report, *Violations of Human Rights and the Rule of Law in Uganda*,[49] which came out first and was the first major international investigation to consider his crimes in detail. The report forms the evidential core of almost all subsequent accounts of Amin's human rights violations. As such, it has been immensely influential; most of the more convincing stories of the horrors of Amin's Uganda in the early years of his rule (such as the use of hammers) come from this document and were endlessly recycled by Western journalists. There are, however, serious problems with the ICJ investigation and report which have not been sufficiently considered. From the mid-1970s onwards, the closure of Western embassies and the exile of so many Ugandans, especially the literate minority, made it difficult or impossible to get accurate, first-hand information on the ground. The lack of reliable data grew as the decade went on, leading to the contamination of the historical evidence by rumour, guesswork and deliberate disinformation.

Over recent decades, international human rights organisations have developed sophisticated methodologies and techniques for finding out what is happening in places to which outsiders have little access. Satellite and other remote surveillance systems make it much more difficult to hide the evidence of widespread violence. More recently, social media have enabled continuous first-hand reporting from the ground in such situations. In the 1970s, however, none of these technologies existed. The ICJ report, accepted as neutral and balanced truth by later commentators, was in fact based very largely on evidence from friends and allies of Obote in exile. The report elides any distinction between what Amin himself did, what he was directly or indirectly responsible for, and what occurred as a result of the social chaos his rule created. One major source for the report was the testimony of Wanume Kibedi, Amin's former foreign minister and brother-in law, who has been called 'perhaps Amin's closest civilian associate'.[50] Like Henry Kyemba, he had his own reasons for attacking the man he had been so closely associated with, and in 1974 he badly needed to establish his credentials with the other exiles. Appended to the ICJ report is a 'letter' from Kibedi addressed to Amin himself, in which he writes:

> I want to personally confirm here and now that indeed you are person-ally responsible for the liquidation of all the people who have 'disap-peared' in Uganda ever since you came to power. People have 'disappeared' *either* because you have specifically ordered their liquidation as individ-uals or as a group, *or* because they have fallen victim to the murderous ravages of lawless elements who have thrived in the country as a result of your deliberate refusal to restrain the criminal activities of such elements, or to place any sort of discipline over them. You have in effect placed such thugs completely over the law, since they know that they can kill, maim and loot with impunity.[51]

The report itself is more ambiguous; it seems to both imply Amin's culpa-bility and to deny that it is doing so:

> It is understandable perhaps that many of the witnesses, especially among the Ugandan exiles, should seek to place personal responsibility for many of the violations which have occurred upon General Idi Amin. This study is concerned rather with describing the events than appor-tioning blame. Clearly, as head of state and as Commander in Chief of the Armed Forces, the ultimate responsibility for any violations of human rights must fall upon General Amin.[52]

The last two sentences here seem to contradict each other, and the implications of the first are not explored.

The report was written by a young American lawyer named Michael Posner, who went on to become a significant figure in US human rights circles, eventually being appointed Assistant Secretary of State for Democracy, Human Rights and Labor under the Obama administration. Apart from the testimony of exiles such as Kibedi, his report mentions two other sources of information. One of these was 'non-Ugandan and non-Asian sources who were in Uganda at the material time. Some of them were persons holding responsible positions.'[53] This may have included British diplomats and other expats who remained in senior positions in post-independence Uganda, but it is likely that one of these sources was the last US ambassador to Amin's Uganda, Thomas Melady, who left when the American embassy closed in 1973, having served slightly less than two years. Melady wrote the book *Idi Amin Dada: Hitler in Africa*,[54] which develops at length an unconvincing comparison between Amin and Adolf Hitler. He claims that Amin, like Hitler, was motivated primarily by anti-Semitic ideology:

> Amin's Uganda is the example of ongoing genocide. His rule must be placed in the same category of the recent Hitler and Stalin terror eras.... His early embrace of brutality was found in his statements and actions on Israel and the Jewish people. He endorsed the worst forms of anti-Semitism that included the Nazi genocide. He has continued to copy the man that he admires – Adolf Hitler.[55]

This analysis is not shared by Ugandan writers, and it is difficult to see Amin being motivated by any kind of ideology.

Two sources specifically mentioned in the ICJ report were the British journalists Colin Legum and David Martin, open supporters of Milton Obote with very good contacts among the exiles. The Preface to the ICJ report says:

> We have also been considerably assisted by having put at our disposal numerous statements by Ugandans and other information in the possession of Mr Colin Legum and Mr David Martin of the London *Observer*, and by seeing in proof a book shortly to be published in London by

Mr David Martin, entitled 'Amin'. These have confirmed much information already in our possession as well as providing us with additional information.[56]

Thus, a secondary account by a Western journalist, who was *parti pris* in the matter (and does not seem to have been to Uganda at that time), has become a key part of the primary evidence used by later historians, in the form of the ICJ report. A recent account by historians Derek Peterson and Edgar Taylor says that 'Journalists David Martin and Colin Legum regularly cited sources close to the deposed President Milton Obote. These informants had their own reasons for caricaturing Amin ... as unfit to rule.'[57] In a footnote, they point out that 'Colin Legum was a close friend and admirer of Milton Obote since the 1950s, while both he and David Martin frequently referenced accounts by recent defectors. ... He and the International Court of Justice relied on former Minister of Education Edward Rugumayo, who defected in 1973.'[58]

Many, possibly even most, of the killings listed in the ICJ report probably occurred, and the testimony of exiles, even diehard Obote supporters, is not necessarily untrue. However, both the human rights reports and the more popular books on Amin contain similar detailed but unsupported accounts of violence, phrased as statements of fact. These stories are often plausible, but there is little evidence either for or against them. Perhaps, as head of state, Amin was guilty in law of everything done by government agents, on or off duty, but I am no lawyer and am interested here in moral culpability rather than legal responsibility. I suggest there is a real ethical distinction between someone who consciously plans and carries out atrocious acts, and someone whose incompetence and carelessness about the consequences enables others to get away with such actions. This is recognised in British law by distinctions between murder and manslaughter, and in US law by the various 'degrees' of murder charges. I have attempted here to distinguish between different kinds of evidence, to examine the motivations of different witnesses, and to show as clearly as possible what we can and cannot know for certain. Amin was certainly behind many of the killings, for others the link is often tenuous. To many of the questions about Amin's human rights abuses, as well as other aspects of his story, the honest answer is 'we do not know', but this is not something most journalists or academics like to admit. Having looked carefully at all the available documents, and considered their methodologies and sources (which are often mentioned only in the vaguest terms), I confess I am unable to judge the truth. The number of deaths for which Amin was responsible is almost certainly somewhere between Jorgensen's 12,000 and Amnesty's 500,000, but I do not know where, and I am disinclined to believe anyone who claims greater certainty.

1975: THE SWITCHBACK RIDE CONTINUES

Uganda continued on its downward, chaotic path in 1975. Perhaps recognising that his oppressive tactics had failed to address Uganda's social, economic and political problems, Amin now increasingly turned his attention to the international arena. According to many Ugandan commentators, such as Kasozi, this was a year when the killings increased dramatically, and the country began to fall apart. Amin seemed at first to want to patch up his quarrel with the British, but increasingly appeared to be trying to humiliate them. He knew – not 'instinctively', but from long experience with the British – how best to distract their attention from Uganda's growing accumulation of human rights atrocities while, at the same time, getting under their skin and annoying them intensely. He deployed 'dead cat' distraction tactics brilliantly. A good example of this came in January, when Amin sent a long telegram to the Queen, announcing his intention to revisit the UK. This is a fairly representative example of his messages to world leaders, so I am quoting it at length to give an idea of the genre:

Your Majesty,[59]

You are, no doubt, kept abreast with the great strides in the economic fields Uganda has made since I asked your authorities to assume responsibility over your nationals of Asian extraction who had vowed to perpetually dominate and share the economic destiny of Uganda for their own selfish and situational aims. Since I gave the directive that non-citizen Asians of British nationality return to their motherland, Britain, so much has taken place and so much has been said. The economic war which we have been fighting tooth and nail has been honourably won. This is a fact, not a fuss. We have encountered a parade of intericate people's [sic] on our road to economic independence and the consolidation of our political sovereignty. Now the dust is settling, or should I say, it has settled.

I have now the time to relax a bit. Consequently, I have decided to spend my economic war honeymoon in England on the 4th August 1975.

Your Majesty, it is ardently hoped and expected that you will, through various agencies, arrange for me so I can see and visit Scotland, Wales, and Northern Ireland. I should like to use that chance to talk to these people who are struggling for self-determination and independence for [sic] your political and economic system. . . .

I shall also be obliged if arrangements are made for me to meet and exchange views with the non-citizen Asians of British nationality that I rooted out of this country in September 1972 because of our unequivocal determination to rid Uganda of economic slavery and loyalty to corruption. . . .

During my stay in your country, I shall have the chance to meet my old colleagues and friends. Now that Uganda is, beyond dispute, economically free and politically sovereign, my proposed visit to your country will be a good omen in the direction of normalising relations between us and the British. We are committed to safeguarding our political and economic independence jealously. Any tendencies, real or imaginary, distant or near, aimed at displacing the economic status quo in Uganda shall meet organised opposition from us.

As my former Commander in Chief of the King's African Rifles and Head of the Commonwealth of Nations, I wish you and the people of Britain on behalf of the people of Uganda and my own behalf, a happy and prosperous New Year, long life and a bright future.

I am sending this message early so that you may have ample time to help you arrange all that is required for my comfortable stay in your country. For example, that there will be, at least, during my stay, a sure and reliable supply of essential commodities because now your economy is ailing in many a field.

I look forward to meeting you, your Majesty. Accept, your Majesty, the assurance of my highest esteem.

Al-Hajji General Idi Amin Dada, VC, DSO, MC

President of the Republic of Uganda

c.c. Prime Minister Wilson Harold, 10 Downing Street, London

c.c. Mr Edward Heath, Leader of the Opposition, London.[60]

The telex certainly bears out Jaffar Amin's view of his father's strange sense of humour, and it is difficult to take it very seriously. Like so many of Amin's apparently crazy messages to world leaders, it seems to me obviously a deliberate wind-up. That was not, however, the view of the Foreign Office, nor the Prime Minister's Office. Jim Hennessey first learned about the message from Radio Uganda, and the next day sent his own telegram to the FO, copied to Buckingham Palace and 10 Downing Street:

> We had no prior warning, nor have we received a copy of the telegram (Amin would have known that I would be unlikely to accept it). . . .
>
> The telegram does not appear to call for a reply. It is in any case beneath contempt. . . .
>
> But you would probably prefer that I said only that we had not received the telegram and could not therefore offer any comment. I shall reply accordingly – if asked – unless instructed to the contrary.[61]

R.N. Dales of the Foreign Office wrote to Patrick Wright of the Prime Minister's Office later that day, attaching Hennessey's message, and 'offer[ing] advice on what reply might be sent' to Amin. He seems to have felt the need to denounce the message, perhaps in case Number 10 thought the FO was inclined to be soft on foreigners:

> As you will see from the text, the message is intemperate in language, its general tenor is insulting, and its content is unacceptable in that it indicates an intention to make contact with advocates of the secession of Scotland, Wales and Northern Ireland from the United Kingdom.
>
> There would seem to us to be some advantage in our showing General Amin that his presence here is unwelcome and in making our reply public. . . . Above all, it is just possible that if no reply is sent, he will turn up at Heathrow on 4 August, with embarrassments that are hideous to contemplate.
>
> . . . The Palace have been consulted. . . .[62]

By this time, the British media had got hold of the story. Patrick Wright sent a copy of Amin's telegram, together with Hennessey's response, to the prime minister, Harold Wilson, reporting that, '[i]n response to Press enquiries, Buckingham Palace are saying that the questions raised in the message are matters on which the Queen will need advice from the Prime Minister ...'[63] Wilson himself scribbled a comment on the memo about the wording of the reply. The following day, Number 10 agreed to the Foreign Office's response, as outlined by Mr Dales, and Wilson was told that 'Buckingham Palace have been consulted on the terms of the reply, and agree that, while it should be made clear to General Amin that Her Majesty has received his message, it would be inappropriate for her to become directly involved in an exchange on the subject.'[64] Hennessey, however, was concerned about the consequences of delivering the message. He telegraphed:

> Given Amin's general unpredictability and his present high blood pressure it is impossible to say that there would be no risk to the [British] community [in Uganda] or to our staff should a note on the lines proposed be delivered now.
>
> If the note were left until after the weekend the risk might well be less: Amin usually cools off quickly, and while I personally doubt if he would ever go so far as to expel us or the community there is no doubt in my mind that harassing action of some kind would be likely. He rarely if ever fails to react.[65]

A major problem was that the following weekend saw the anniversary of Amin's coup, a public holiday during which a number of foreign dignitaries were expected and, aside from the added insult to Amin of a rebuff on his big day, there would be no one around to receive the letter.

On Monday, Hennessey telegraphed again:

> I have spoken informally over the weekend to trustworthy colleagues, (particularly African), to ministers, officials and others.... The consensus appeared to be that the President's telegram would be best ignored. This would be the African way of saying that the visit would not be welcome....[66]

Dales informed Wright and the PM (who once again annotated the memo), that:

> our Acting High Commissioner in Kampala has recommended ... that, in accordance with the discretion given to him, he should not carry out the instructions in our telegram ... to deliver to the Ugandans our rejection of General Amin's proposal to visit the UK from 4 August this year. ... We have consulted the Palace who agree that a dignified silence at presence [*sic*] would be acceptable to them.[67]

By this point, Amin's letter had occupied much of the time of some of the most senior echelons of the British state for the better part of a week. It is only one example of the many times Amin was able to set a cat among the pigeons of Whitehall and Westminster. He cannot have known quite how successful his tactics were, in simultaneously annoying the English elite, distracting attention from what was really happening in Uganda, getting global publicity for himself, and boosting his image in Africa as an anti-colonialist and world statesman.

In April, a more serious conflict with the UK was to blow up, which Hennessey was less able to limit; this was the Denis Hills affair. Hills was a British schoolteacher and part-time lecturer at Makerere who, in April 1975, was arrested and charged with espionage and sedition. He had written a memoir, *The White Pumpkin*, the manuscript of which was brought to Amin's attention, infuriating him by the derogatory terms in which it described him. As Hills himself put it, '[t]he prosecution would have a dictionary and I could not hope to gloss over the phrase "village tyrant". My reference to the "Black Nero", if the prosecution had spotted it, or indeed dared to mention this insult even in closed court, was worse.'[68] As Makubuya writes:

> Following a military-style trial, Hills was found guilty and condemned to death by firing squad. Britain tried but failed to persuade Amin to pardon and release him. After failed diplomatic pleas, and with only one day left before his execution, Amin said that since Her Majesty the Queen of Britain was his friend, he would consider sparing Hills' life, but only if she interceded and apologised to him on Hills' behalf.[69]

The British instead sent Amin's former commanding officer, Iain Grahame, together with the distinguished head of his KAR Battalion, Lieutenant General Sir Chandos Blair. They carried a letter signed by the Queen herself, pleading for Hills' life. Amin met them in a traditionally thatched building (which the British called a 'hut') in West Nile. To get through the small entrance, they had bow down low, and Ugandan commentators have suggested they were made to crawl in.[70] Their appeal was at first refused, and Britain then had to send the Foreign Secretary, James Callaghan, with seven senior officials, to reinforce the call for clemency. Amin told Callaghan, as usual, that he had always admired the British people, who had educated and trained him, but this was precisely why the hostile and insulting attitude of the British media pained him so much. It seemed that Hills was suffering for the anti-Amin attitudes of the BBC, the *Observer* and other British news outlets. According to Makubuya's account:

> Following an exchange of views, Amin assured the visitors that he would release Hills to Callaghan and that the lecturer could return to London with him. At this point, a shaken and dazed Hills was shoved into the room and presented to Callaghan as a free man, having survived 102 days in Amin's jails. He flew back to Britain with Callaghan the same day.
>
> The 'Hills Saga' proved that Amin did not have any pretentions or fear in his dealings with Britain. The humiliation of the British Government seems to have been Amin's payback for their refusal to provide him with the military and other support that he had long yearned for, and that they had indeed promised when he ousted Obote.[71]

The Hills case reveals the importance Amin attached to his public image, and to public relations in general. It had been foreshadowed by events the previous year, when a French documentary film maker, Barbet Schroeder, made a documentary about Amin that remains one of the most interesting accounts of the dictator, showing him largely as he wished to be seen. According to some sources 'Amin and his subordinates worked to direct the camera, staging scenes and generating scenarios for the director to pursue',[72] while the president himself contributed the musical score on his accordion. There remained a few scenes Amin did not like and, when Schroeder refused to remove them, Amin threatened to detain all French citizens in Uganda until they were cut. Schroeder conceded, and thereafter subtitled the film *A Self Portrait*, declaring Amin was its real director, as he had 'the final cut'.

The Hills case kept the British Foreign Office busy for the first half of the year, but Amin himself was concerned with other matters. On 6 January, he attacked his ministers and civil servants at a cabinet meeting, blaming them for the country's economic situation; twelve days later, the finance minister, sensibly, fled the country. On 6 February, the foreign minister, Elizabeth Bagaya, followed him. In the same month, Amin again tried to organise Uganda's religious organisations, appointing military personnel to the Muslim Supreme Council and banning more Christian sects. He also survived an assassination attempt while driving along the main Kampala to Entebbe Road. At the end of March, in response to the rise of the *magendo* economy, Amin launched a national conference on overcharging, hoarding, corruption and smuggling. In April, a decree nationalised all 'unused land', and a number of senior police officers were 'retired'. The following month, the Defence Council discussed subversion by expatriate missionaries. In June, the Commission of Enquiry into the Disappearances published its report. In July, Amin attended two major OAU meetings, and as expected was elected chairman of the organisation on 28 July. In August he married one of his favourite girlfriends, Sarah Kyobala. He tried again to reorganise Uganda's administrative structure, announcing his intention to set up a National Forum (presumably to replace the abolished parliament) and a National Union of Uganda, which was to represent the different tribal groups. He also announced that Uganda would give land to the families of 'Palestinian freedom fighters'.

Towards the end of August, now chairman of the OAU, the indefatigable Amin embarked on yet another tour of African countries, beginning with Ethiopia (the first country to recognise his government after the coup) and including Libya, where he apparently had a tonsillectomy. September was devoted largely to yet more foreign travel: to Italy, Algeria, Somalia, Ethiopia again, Zaire and Congo-Brazzaville. In October, after visiting the United States for the first time to address the UN (the British ambassador walked out), he turned again to the Middle East, visiting Kuwait, Qatar, Saudi Arabia and the United Arab Emirates. At the same time, he tried as usual to deal with Uganda's worsening economic situation by reorganising official bodies and making vague public announcements; setting up new commissions of enquiry into problems at the Ministry of Health and Uganda Airlines; and announcing that military personnel harassing businessmen might face military tribunals. On 1 November, the president warned government officials against maltreating the population. Twelve days later, in a move to clamp down on ivory smuggling, he banned elephant hunting, and a month later started a drive against currency smugglers. None of this activity seems to have particularly improved the situation in Uganda, either economically or politically.

Internationally, he was playing his old game of setting potential opponents against each other. Having given a speech on 31 October praising Soviet assistance to Uganda and the Third World in general, Amin then spent much of the rest of the year criticising the USSR and its supporters. On 9 November, he threatened to break diplomatic relations with the Soviets, and the next day he sent telegrams to Angola's nationalist leaders criticising their struggles as 'useless'.[73] These messages were copied to US President Ford, British Prime Minister Harold Wilson and Chairman Mao of China. Two days later, he demanded the replacement of the Soviet ambassador to Uganda, and the following day he held a reception in honour of the Soviet embassy staff and military experts who had assisted him. This was more than enough for the Soviets, who (temporarily) broke off diplomatic relations with Uganda the same day. On 19 November, Uganda radio denied Radio Moscow reports of the break with the Soviet Union, while Amin warned Arab leaders not to support any of the factions in Angola. On 6 December, he declared he would 'never be against the people of the Soviet Union'. By the end of the year relations with the UK had improved, following another promise by Amin to pay compensation for the expelled Asians and, on the last day of the year, UK–Ugandan relations were upgraded again, with Hennessey's title changing from 'acting' to full high commissioner. The British seemed to care more about the compensation money than any symbolic humiliations Amin heaped on them.

1976: THE YEAR OF ENTEBBE

In 1976 came Amin's final break with Britain, and the West more widely, thanks to the famous 'Entebbe Raid' in July. This became the single event which, more than any other, came to dominate international opinion on Amin's government, although it had, originally at any rate, very little to do with Amin. In Uganda itself, other matters commanded attention that year. In January, Amin gave a cheque for $1 million to the Indian government in compensation to the Indian nationals who had been expelled in 1972; the British got nothing. In February, Radio Uganda broadcast the president's claims to parts of Kenyan and Sudanese territory, to go alongside his long-standing view that Tanzania's Kagera area should be part of Uganda. In March, he announced the setting-up of another commission of enquiry, this time into the killing of a Makerere law student. At the end of April, Amin had his old friend Bob Astles arrested (again) for 'rumour mongering', and 'using the President's name'. He was released a week later. On 20 May, the Voice of Uganda (Amin had nationalised and renamed the former 'Radio Uganda') applauded the country's appointment to the UN Commission on Human Rights. On 1 June, Amin's pamphlet, *The Shaping of Modern Uganda* appeared.[74] This was the only book ever to be published under the president's name, a tedious, semi-academic account of the colonial legal history of Uganda's borders. It is impossible to believe that Amin himself had anything to do with actually writing it, but it served to justify some of his claims on the land of neighbouring countries. On 10 June, there was another assassination attempt on the president, as he attended a military passing-out parade at Kampala's Nsambya barracks.[75]

Relations with Uganda's neighbours continued to deteriorate. Amin, having begun the year by laying claim to a chunk of Kenya's land bordering Uganda, went on to accuse the country of collusion with Israel. The Kenyans retaliated by imposing a blockade on Ugandan goods in transit on their way to Mombasa port, the primary route for Ugandan exports to the world. On 25 July, Amin had sent a telegram to the UN and OAU secretaries general complaining that Kenyan authorities had blocked the export of oil and other commodities. This was a serious threat to the Ugandan economy. On 6 August, however, Uganda and Kenya signed a Memorandum of Understanding which committed Amin to pay compensation to Kenya, to be monitored by the OAU. While the relationship with Kenya was worsening, that with Tanzania was improving slightly, and Amin went on being supported by the Eastern bloc – the USSR supplied weapons for the army, and the Cubans opened an embassy in Kampala – as well as the Arab states, which continued to supply money.

The 1976 British Foreign Office Report on Uganda, produced in 1977 by Martin Ewans in London, once again gives a useful summary from the

British viewpoint of the situation in the country. It well illustrates the complex and often contradictory attitude of the British authorities to the Ugandan president:

> Amin continued to run the country by personal dictate [*sic*] with the support of the rag-bag Defence Council, his tribal adherents in the Army and the bully-boys of the State Research Council [*sic*], whose continuing loyalty he purchased by increasing material privilege. Amin's one-time popularity with the public at large rested almost exclusively on his expulsion of the Asians and this by 1976 had worn very thin indeed. There can now be hardly a family in Uganda which has not suffered at some time at the hands of the regime. But although the widespread conviction persists that he must one day meet a violent death, Amin displayed no little personal bravery and a considerable talent for survival in the face of continuing assassination attempts, probably mounted by groups from Kenya and Tanzania. All serious opposition within Uganda has long since been crushed and most of the best men are dead or in exile. To this can be principally attributed the slight easing up of the mass repression that characterised the earlier years of the regime.[76]

In fact, at the time it was the British themselves who were seriously contemplating assassination. The then Foreign Secretary, Dr David Owen, wrote later, '[w]hen I was ... totally frustrated by the inability to stop Amin's massacres, I contemplated his assassination and discussed it with a senior diplomat liaising with MI6'.[77] Apparently, the intelligence service turned down Owen's suggestion, whether due to moral scruples or to a recognition that the British state was no longer in a position to just kill African leaders at will.

On 25 June, Amin was declared Life President of Uganda. Three days later, an Air France plane flying from Tel Aviv to Paris was hijacked by members of a radical Palestinian organisation, the Popular Front for the Liberation of Palestine, together with an extreme left-wing German terrorist group. The hijackers forced the plane to land at Entebbe, where they held the passengers hostage. The story of the Entebbe raid has been told many times, from the Israeli point of view, which was quickly established in a series of books published immediately after the events,[78] and has been continued in more recent accounts, such as Saul David's 2015 book.[79] These books inevitably portray Amin as simply a psychotic monster, in league with the terrorists. At the time, the Israel government called in Amin's old friend Bar-Lev, to attempt to gain useful information for the planned attack, under the guise of mediating with Amin. Shimon Peres, the minister of defence, had decided to send in special forces to free the hostages. He:

> determined ... to set up a telephone link with Amin as soon as possible in the hope that it would provide the military planners with the detailed information ... [to] enable them to form a more accurate assessment of the situation on the ground in Entebbe.
>
> The officer entrusted with this task was Burka Bar-Lev, a man once described as 'Amin's personal advisor'. He was asked by Peres to call Amin and say he was speaking for people 'close to the top policymaking echelon in Israel'. Peres added: 'Burka, this entire office, all the telephones, all the secretaries, are at your disposal.'[80]

On 3 July, Israeli paratroopers stormed the plane, killed all the hijackers for the loss of one Israeli soldier,[81] and released the passengers, except for an elderly woman with joint British/Israeli citizenship named Dora Bloch, who needed treatment at a Kampala hospital. British High Commission officials tried to visit Bloch on a number of occasions over the next week, but were not allowed to see her. It became clear she had joined the ranks of the 'disappeared'. Eventually, on 10 July, the high commissioner received a formal diplomatic note claiming that the Ugandan government had no knowledge of her whereabouts. Hennessey was immediately withdrawn as high commissioner, and Uganda–UK relations sank to a new low. Various members of the British High Commission staff were told to leave the country, accused of collaboration with the Israelis over the Entebbe operation, and on 27 July two British nationals were arrested for spying. On 28 July, Britain, finally losing patience with the president, broke off diplomatic relations with Uganda. It was the first time since 1946 that the British government had unilaterally cut all ties with a country, and in that case it was Albania rather than a member of the Commonwealth. The long-lasting, on-off, mutual love/hate affair between the Ugandan president and the British state had finally ended.

THE END OF THE AFFAIR

The British Foreign Office's Uganda annual review for 1976 was not, therefore, written in Kampala, but in Whitehall, by Martin Ewans of the East Africa desk:

> It was a difficult decision.... But it was done on the basis that enough was enough.... Events, or rather the lack of them, have shown that the decision was right. It took some time for it to sink home with the Ugandans that the break was not a short-term affair and Amin still seems perplexed by it. ... There has been the occasional anti-British outburst on the Ugandan media and there have been allegations about the harassment of Ugandans at London Airport. But Amin has sought essentially in the post-break period to cultivate an image of sweetness and light. There has been no further harassment of the British community....
>
> On the debit side, the break means that there can be no prospect of progress in securing compensation for expropriated British property, including that of the Asians expelled in 1972. Nor are we likely to find the Ugandans falling over themselves to pay their now considerable debts to HM government. But even when relations with Uganda were supposedly good, we had to doubt the likelihood of any progress on either score....
>
> The majority of Ugandans, including Amin himself, would very probably like to see a resumption in relations. But the present situation suits us very well and there is little inducement for us to contemplate a resumption while Amin remains in power.[82]

On 20 September, Amin appointed yet another commission of enquiry, this time into the disappearance of Dora Bloch; it duly reported on 16 November that the Ugandan government had nothing to do with this. Relations with Britain continued downhill; on 2 October, Amin summoned the French ambassador, who was acting on behalf of British interests, to complain about the mishandling of Ugandan ministers at Heathrow airport, and the UK blocking payment for business deals between the two countries. Two months later, two Ugandan soldiers were detained at Heathrow, pending enquiries into their reason for visiting Britain. Despite the deteriorating relationship between the two countries, according to Ewans British exports to Uganda totalled £8.3 million in the first 10 months of 1976, while Ugandan exports to the UK were 'up to' £29 million.[83] Trading relationships between Uganda and the UK would continue to the very end of Amin's rule, but political relations were never to recover.

8

DECLINE AND FALL
IDI AMIN AND UGANDA, 1977–79, AND AFTER

As we have seen, Amin had from the start attempted to control Uganda's religious communities by abolishing smaller denominations while supporting a single Muslim organisation, plus the Catholic and Anglican churches for the Christians. Within these terms, as Omara-Otunnu puts it: 'Religious leaders had remained relatively free to express their views, provided it was within a religious context and idiom. Increasingly however ... the Churches were coming under pressure from the state.'[1] In 1977, the pressure racked up. On 5 February, soldiers burst into the house of Anglican Archbishop Janani Luwum and interrogated him at gunpoint about a plot by exile groups to overthrow Amin. Uganda's Anglican bishops protested in an 'open letter' to the president, which went beyond the specific issue to criticise the overall state of the country, in what amounted to 'a serious indictment of the regime'.[2] A week later, Amin called a meeting of military representatives to discuss the conspiracy, and ordered the bishops to attend. There he claimed again that Luwum was involved in the plan, and the same day the archbishop was arrested and 'disappeared', along with two cabinet ministers, Erinayo Oryema and Charles Oboth-Ofumbi (both, like Luwum, northerners), who had bravely signed the churchmen's letter. A government spokesman blamed a 'motor accident'.[3]

For many Ugandans, regardless of religion, Luwum's death was a symbolically important moment, a tipping point in the nation's history. Omara-Otunnu described it as 'a climax in the unfolding drama of Uganda's suffering under the military regime'.[4] According to Mutibwa, the killing occurred because 'a coup was being organised by some Acholis and Langis based in Nairobi. When the Archbishop was asked to join the group, he declined. ...

What led to Luwum's death was the fact that he did not tell Amin of this plot.[5] The murder of the archbishop led to wide international condemnation, including 'from those who had hitherto been his friends,'[6] such as Ghana, Zambia and Jamaica.[7] It also galvanised the many competing opposition groups among the exiles. In Britain, they formed the 'Uganda Action Group' and the 'Uganda Group for Human Rights'; in the USA, it was the 'Freedom for Ugandans Movement', the 'Uganda Freedom Union' and the 'Committee on Uganda'. In Kenya, there was the 'Uganda Passive Resistance Movement', and in Tanzania, the 'Front for the Liberation of Uganda' and Museveni's 'Front for National Salvation'. In August, many of these organisations came together in Lusaka, Zambia, to form the Uganda National Movement, which was, however, boycotted by the largest and most influential body of exiles, the pro-Obote group in Tanzania.[8]

Two days after Archbishop Luwum's 'disappearance', Amin used his dead cat tactic again to distract the attention of the British from the crisis. As in 1975, he announced his intention to visit the UK, to attend a Commonwealth meeting in June. This time many more British officials were involved, over a much longer period. The UK National Archives hold hundreds of pages of official reports, memos, minutes, letters and telegrams produced over the following three months, as the British developed contingency arrangements to keep Amin out. 'Operation Bottle' involved the army, navy and air force, civilian air traffic control, several local police forces, the intelligence and security organisations, and many other official bodies. One memo, for example, was copied to more than twenty heads and senior officers of the armed services, together with the highest ranking civil servants in the relevant ministries. A vast swathe of the British state swung into action to prevent the Ugandan president from coming to the country. A detailed operational plan was produced, including 'Rules of Engagement' outlining the circumstances in which the British military could open fire on members of Amin's party. On 10 May, senior ministers, including the prime minister and the Foreign and Home Secretaries, met in the Cabinet Room to agree the outlines of the operation. A subsequent meeting on 19 May was attended by senior officials from the Cabinet Office, the FCO, the Ministry of Defence (an eight-strong delegation, mostly very senior military officers), the Department of Trade, the police (including six chief or assistant chief constables), the 'Scottish Home and Health Department', and the Security Service ('MI5'). Another meeting the next day involved many of the same officials, plus representatives of the Immigration Service, the government's 'Public Relations Branch', and a legal advisor.[9] A massive amount of work went into Operation Bottle.

By 26 May, a week before the Commonwealth Conference was due to begin, the plans were complete. A summary written by a senior Home Office official lists its key aims:

Our instructions are:

(1) to draw up a plan to ensure Amin's exclusion;

(2) to cover action to be taken if Amin lands without prior authority;

(3) to ensure that no hotel in London accepts bookings for Amin.[10]

Accordingly, Operation Bottle covered every eventuality. All scheduled flights from Uganda were to be diverted to Stansted airport and met by police, in case Amin was on board. If he used his personal plane:

it will be interrogated as soon as the aircraft approaches or is discovered in British air space. The pilot will be told that he has no clearance to enter British air space or to land in Britain and asked to declare his intentions. . . .

Once this procedure is invoked, NATS [the National Air Traffic Service] will notify the Metropolitan Police at Heathrow and the Department of Trade. The Heathrow police will be responsible for informing the Essex, Sussex and Thames Valley forces (who may all become involved, depending where the aircraft lands). The Department of Trade will inform Home Office . . . FCO, MOD and Cabinet Office. These Whitehall Departments will then arrange for Cabinet Office Briefing Room (COBR) to be activated as for a terrorist incident. . . .

Once NATS has informed the Metropolitan Police and Department of Trade, it will seek to maximise delays by keeping the aircraft stacked. . . . This will give the police more time to prepare themselves. . . .

If the aircraft insists on landing, NATS will . . . accept it and seek to control it. The police would prefer to handle a landing at a military airfield. . . .

Scout cars and armoured ambulances will be on standby. . . .

The first objective would be to persuade Amin to depart as soon as practicable in the aircraft by which he arrived. Only if he refused to do so should we wish to contemplate removal by the Royal Air Force, or by scheduled service or by chartered aircraft. . . .

If Amin arrives at Heathrow or another civil airport, he could be held there for up to six hours. If there were any question of holding him for appreciably longer, another place of detention would have to be found. . . . Once a decision has been taken as to where Amin is to be detained, the Home Office will make an order designating the site as a place of detention under the Immigration Act 1971. . . .[11]

The memo detailed further plans in case Amin chose to land in Scotland (which would have involved different public authorities and laws), and outlined how to keep the operation secret until the last minute. Of course, Amin never turned up, and probably never intended to. It was another perfectly successful wind-up, and if Amin had only known quite how much time and trouble he had caused the British government, he would doubtless have been very gratified indeed.

Back in Uganda, following the Luwum murder Amin announced that there had been a mutiny by 'an army battalion (of Langi and Acholi soldiers)'.[12] On 25 February, he summoned all Americans in Uganda to a meeting, banning them from leaving the country in the meantime; four days later the restrictions were lifted. International condemnation of the attacks on Christian organisations continued; at the end of February the All Africa Council of Churches called for an end to the 'despicable silence' over Amin's atrocities, while on 6 March the last white Anglican bishop was expelled. On 20 September, Amin banned a further twenty-seven religious organisations, including the Salvation Army and the Baptist Mission and, on 2 November, there was the 'beginning of a new wave of arrests of hundreds of Christians in Masaka . . . following the murder there of a Moslem businessman, known to be close to the President'. A number of prominent Ugandans escaped over the course of the year. On 1 April, Nairobi Radio announced that Uganda's minister of justice, Godfrey Lule, would not be returning to the country 'for health reasons'; on 2 July, he claimed asylum in the UK. On 5 June, minister of health Henry Kyemba also defected to Britain, publishing his influential book *State of Blood* three months later.

Several attempted 'invasions' of the country were reported; on 24 February, Radio Uganda claimed that Tanzanian troops were massing near the border and that the Libyans had offered 'to place all their armed forces at Amin's disposal'. On 2 March, Amin declared that 2,600 British, American and Israeli mercenaries were about to invade Uganda from Kenya. On 3 May, it was announced that thirty-seven Tanzanians and Ugandans were to be executed for being part of an 'invasion force' (they were later pardoned). On 20 June, there were 'reports that Amin has disappeared following an assassination attempt at Entebbe airport (on 18 June) and that a selective purge of the Army had followed'. On 23 June, Ugandan radio announced that Amin was alive and 'enjoying a belated honeymoon' with his wife, Sarah. On 23 August, the trial opened of sixteen men allegedly involved in the planned February invasion, and twelve of them were publicly executed on 9 September.

Relations with Britain reached a new low after Henry Kyemba's defection. Three days after he left, Amin announced a ban on Britons leaving Uganda. The next day, he asked the French embassy to close its British Interests Section, which they did on 15 June. Britain responded by asking for the withdrawal of the Ugandan Interests Section of the Saudi Arabian embassy in London. On 1 July, the ban on Britons leaving Uganda was rescinded. The president's narrowing international support base is indicated by the fact that he went on far fewer foreign trips in 1977 than previous years. He flew to Cairo for an Afro-Arab summit on 7 March, telling the conference that Uganda was 'under control and law-abiding'. On 22 April, he went to Kinshasa for discussions with Mobuto, and on 12 May to Cairo again to sign an agreement with the Arab League to send technical experts to Uganda. He also travelled twice to Gabon, to sign trade agreements on 1 June, and to attend an OAU meeting on 2 July. From 6 to 11 December, Amin was in Libya to sign economic, military and other agreements. Ghaddafi remained Amin's main financial supporter but, according to Martin Ewans of the FCO, '[t]he Soviet Union held the dubious distinction of being Uganda's largest and fastest growing national creditor', probably because much of Libya's financial support was given rather than loaned. Economically, the country continued to survive, thanks to high international prices for coffee (which at this stage represented 90 per cent of Ugandan exports), and the strong informal safety nets created by subsistence agriculture and the *magendo* economy. Amin even paid off some of his international debts and got a good report from the IMF. However, coffee prices peaked in April, and began to decrease, falling to half of the April value by the end of the year. Ewans concluded that:

> The lack of direction and co-ordinated stimulus to economic life contributed during the year to a continuation of the return to subsistence agriculture which characterises every run-down basic economy. Ugandans formerly engaged in the wage economy are increasingly obliged to desert it. Moreover, the cost of living is calculated ... to have risen by some 60 per cent during 1977.[13]

1978–79: A STICKY END

Amin began 1978 in his usual way, with a flurry of international activity and attention-grabbing statements. In early January, he visited Kuwait, and hosted representatives of a Zimbabwean liberation group ('ZANU-Sithole'), to whom he offered military training in Uganda. At the end of the month, he signed an Economic and Technical Cooperation Agreement with the USSR. In February, he hosted a Kenyan delegation and announced, yet again, his intention to visit the UK, to discuss 'misunderstandings'. But his international allies were deserting him. Between 28 February and 3 March, a closed session of the UN Commission on Human Rights finally agreed to launch a formal investigation of human rights abuses in Uganda.[14] This time, neither the Eastern bloc nor the Arab and African countries sought to stop the British and American proposals, though many of them continued to make friendly gestures towards Amin in public.

In March, the president of Rwanda and the crown prince of Swaziland visited to sign trade deals, Qatar promised $5 million for road building, and soldiers killed the chairman of the Uganda Industrial Court. On 3 April, Amin set up a Uganda Human Rights Committee. At the end of the month, the vice president, Mustafa Adrisi, was badly injured in an apparently genuine road accident, and a couple of weeks later, on 2 May, Amin dismissed his foreign minister, Colonel Juma Oris, taking over the role himself. This meant that Amin had now lost two key allies, both with strong personal bases in his home area of West Nile. In May, a number of senior police and prison officers were arrested for corruption, Uganda withdrew from the Commonwealth

Games, and a cultural and scientific cooperation plan was signed with the USSR. In June the Salvation Army was banned. July saw an agreement between Uganda and Kenya to reopen their High Commissions, and Uganda was given a $6.4 million loan by the Arab Economic Development Fund of Abu Dhabi. However, a sign of later troubles came when, for five days, the international oil companies stopped supplies to Uganda for non-payment of debts. On 26 July, Amin dismissed his finance minister, Brigadier Moses Ali, another West Niler with a strong following among the Madi people. He seems to have been trying to run the show largely by himself.

August saw a visit from the Liberian vice president, an Air Transport Agreement was signed with Sudan, and Amin attended Jomo Kenyatta's funeral in Nairobi. In September the vice president of the Soviet Union visited, as did Zaire's President Mobuto. On 10 September, Amin inaugurated his Uganda Human Rights Committee, and, between 14 and 18 September, a UN Commission on Human Rights representative made a first visit to the country. On 19 September, Amin went into hospital for a neck operation, and the next week he visited Libya and Egypt. The most significant event for Amin in September, however, happened on the other side of the world. The US administration seems to have been taken by surprise when Congress appended a ban on American trade with Uganda to a general appropriations bill. As a result, from the beginning of October, US companies supplying around 40 per cent of Uganda's oil suspended deliveries. French oil companies made up some of this, but British and Dutch suppliers refused. Amin tried to prioritise repaying oil debts, but they quickly built up again. 'Oil supply', A.G. Monroe of the FCO East Africa desk observed in the 1978 annual review 'is an Achilles' heel.'[15] The Americans also suspended imports of Ugandan coffee.

The US move followed hearings before the Senate Subcommittee on Foreign Economic Policy in June. These saw a number of familiar figures giving testimony, including Michael Posner and Thomas Melady. Posner seems to have been more aware than he had been previously of the problem of agency in assessing Amin's responsibility for human rights abuses, and he addressed this directly, if not consistently:

> Since the present regime came to power in 1971, there has been a complete breakdown in the rule of law. ... Government security forces

virtually control the country and have assumed practically unlimited powers to kill, torture, and harass innocent civilians.... On another level, there has been an almost complete breakdown in the institutional structures of the society. The effectiveness of the criminal justice system, for example, has been almost completely undermined, and the role of the judiciary usurped by military tribunals.

Primary responsibility for this situation must be placed directly in the hands of President Amin.... [I]t is clear that a substantial number of the killings in Uganda have been either directly on his orders or indirectly through the actions of officials he has placed in positions of authority and institutions he has created for that purpose.

However, it should also be pointed out that the security forces have now become so strong and the random violence so pervasive that it is unlikely that President Amin now has the power or the capacity to end this reign of terror.[16]

In response to questioning, Posner concluded that Amin:

is in a position now where he has fewer and fewer allies to trust and he is relying only on those who have been with him and who he is sure will go with him in any situation. Those tend to be some of the most violent people in the security forces.... While I think, as I have said, that he is personally responsible for what has gone on in the country, I think it has gone beyond him now, and, in fact, many of the atrocities are committed randomly by members of the security forces. He really has no control over that at this point. There has really been a basic breakdown in the structure of the society which goes beyond Amin.[17]

The chairman, the powerful Senator Church, called for stronger sanctions, saying: 'I am certainly going to do all I can to see to it that this committee begins to move in that direction and forces this issue. It is time that something be done.'[18] It may be that US sanctions would have had a real effect, but they came too late to seriously damage the regime. Other forces were to push Amin out before that happened.

Amin responded desperately to his many and growing problems, thrashing around looking for enemies and deploying the usual distraction tactics. In early October, he alleged several times that Tanzania was invading. On 13 October, he survived another assassination attempt. On 19 October, Amnesty International published another critical report on human rights in Uganda. Suddenly, at the end of the month, Amin moved. After renewed allegations of a Tanzanian invasion, and a reported mutiny among Ugandan troops near the border, Ugandan soldiers invaded Tanzania on 30 October, and on 1 November announced the capture of the 'Kagera Salient', a chunk of Tanzania bordering Uganda, which had previously been claimed by Amin, and which he believed held the 'refugee guerrillas' fighting against him. According to the British:

> Perhaps having convinced himself of a Tanzanian hand in the trouble [the mutiny] and perhaps also with a cunning view to rallying his own forces, Amin went on to occupy the whole of the salient down to the Kagera river. . . . Throwing prudence to the winds and in defiance of the almost sacred OAU principle of territorial integrity, he announced its annexation. The Tanzanians were completely unprepared and unable to offer effective resistance.[19]

Amin declared an unconditional withdrawal on 14 November, but announced another invasion two weeks later, claiming continued Tanzanian aggression. Numeiri visited him on 6 December to personally offer OAU mediation but, on 15 December, Amin again complained to the OAU and the UN about Tanzanian incursions. Trying, too late, to secure his home base, Amin appointed new ministers for internal affairs and defence, and announced an amnesty for all Ugandan exiles (unsurprisingly, no one seems to have taken up this offer).

The exiles were, in fact, desperately trying to put together a plan for the obviously forthcoming Tanzanian invasion. The factious opposition went through a number of alliances and splits before coalescing at the last possible moment. By the end of 1978, the Tanzanian army, with a considerably smaller number of Ugandan refugee fighters, had massed in force near the border. In January 1979, they crossed into Uganda. Mostly travelling and fighting on foot, the troops moved slowly through the country, despite little organised resistance. The Tanzanians had strong international support; their ammunition, for example, was paid for by the British (according to the then Foreign

Secretary) 'in a roundabout way'.[20] However, it was only in March, the war nearly won, that the Ugandan opposition groups got their act together. This time even the Oboteists joined the conference in Moshi, Tanzania, to assemble an umbrella organisation to take over once Nyerere triumphed. By early April the Tanzanians were in Entebbe, and on 11 April Kampala fell, and the invading soldiers moved north. According to the British, 'it was clear that Amin's troops were in no condition to make a stand, and by the first week of June the war was over'.[21] Amin's popular backing was not enough to resist the invasion, but it seems to have slowed down the military campaign, and there were no significant civilian uprisings in support of the Tanzanians.

In early April 1979, as the invading troops prepared to move into Kampala, Amin himself fled the capital with some of his family. Jaffar Amin wrote: 'I will never forget the last days of our stay in Uganda, due to the constant boom sound made by the ... rocket shellfire into the capital Kampala by the Liberators. ... [W]e set off in a convoy ... towards Entebbe ... to await the planned flight to Tripoli, Libya.'[22] Amin declared in a radio broadcast on 6 April that he would never leave the country, whatever happened. In his son's account, he was forcibly restrained and taken to safety by the Presidential Guard. 'They actually immobilised him in the process with straps and placed him in his ... car. On April 11, 1979, when his government was overthrown, Dad ... wanted to die in battle like a true soldier but several of his presidential guards would not let him. Then the convoy ... set off in a row for Jinja.'[23] There Amin made 'an emotional speech', before heading via Gulu to West Nile. His decision in 1972 to build a sizeable airfield in Arua town proved useful. On 23 April, according to Jaffar, a Libyan Hercules transport plane landed and took his father into exile, as his former soldiers fired aimlessly at nothing, and thousands of West Nilers, keenly aware that they were seen as 'Amin's people', scrambled to get over the borders.

The Tanzanians continued to push the remnants of the Ugandan army towards West Nile. When they reached the region, they unleashed atrocities quite up to the high standards set by the ex-president, forcing virtually all the local population into Sudan and Zaire. The West Nilers were not alone in being mistreated during the 'liberation'. According to Kasozi:

> [I]n their rejoicing, and taking their cue perhaps from Amin's soldiers, Ugandans did violence to the infrastructure of their country and to

sections of society that were perceived to have collaborated with Idi Amin. ... Whenever Tanzanian soldiers completed a task, Ugandans rushed to the scene and looted whatever could be found and destroyed what they could not take.... What took forty years to build was destroyed in less than one year....

The Muslims in southern Uganda suffered the same fate as the people of the West Nile ... [and] were persecuted after he fell....

The violence that accompanied the struggle to remove Amin and the destruction that followed have left a permanent mark on Ugandan society and on the country's physical structures.[24]

G.W. Kanyeihamba agrees:

Kampala city and other towns were raided by hoodlums and looters from rural villages. They carried with them any symbols of wealth which they believed or imagined had been owned by the Amin people or his supporters. Electric kettles, typewriters and adding machines and telephones ripped from their sockets together with toilet seats were taken to the villages where there was no electricity or modern toilets.... It was as if the whole country had gone crazy.

In addition, revengeful killings and assaults of anyone imagined to be an enemy, supporter or associate or relative of that enemy became common occurrences.[25]

This vengefulness bore particularly hard on the West Nilers. Ugandans had little sympathy for them, seeing them as having 'eaten' (enriched themselves) during Amin's presidency and believing they had all been supporters of the dictator, despite the fact that many had been persecuted under the regime. Lugbara and Madi people were treated the same as the Kakwa and Nubi. In 1997, I asked a Lugbara ex-soldier whether the West Nile region as a whole had benefited during Amin's rule. He replied:

Oh, nothing, nothing. During Amin's time here it was nothing. Because when he came here, what he did based here was recruit all the youths; even teachers were taken to join the army. OK, from the army you got ranks and so on. That is what they benefitted from. But there was no

tangible development here, not here, but people were enjoying themselves all over, all over the big shops in the city, everywhere, and so on.
[They became] directors of factories, ministers without qualifications
and what, what . . .[26]

Amin certainly bore considerable responsibility for what happened after he
fled. His regime had destroyed much of the social solidarity and national
feeling which had just about held the country together in the face of ethnic
rivalries under the first Obote administration. This became evident in the
chaos that followed the Tanzanian invasion, and especially under Obote's
second regime.

AMIN'S FALL: ETHNICITY AND THE MILITARY REVISITED

The Tanzanian invasion might have happened earlier, but Nyerere was
cautiously building up his forces to ensure success. In the event, the key
factor in the Tanzanians' victory was the overall weakness of the Ugandan
troops. As I have suggested, military coups are often disastrous for the army
concerned, military objectives inevitably giving way to the political and
economic aspirations of the soldiers, and this was what had happened to the
Ugandan forces. As we have seen, Amin's whole life had been the army and,
from the beginning of his rule, the military was the main focus of his attention. Perhaps he thought that if he could get the army right, the rest would
fall into place, or at least become more controllable. In the early days, it is
impossible to tell how far Amin had planned his first moves against the
Langi and Acholi soldiers, or if he was simply responding to a series of
attempted military uprisings and planned counter-coups. Whichever it was,
his actions in the weeks after the coup set a pattern which led first to an
increasingly narrow ethno-military base, and then to an army which, in the
excitement of power, lost all touch with its structure and purpose. Gradually,
the non-Kakwa, non-Nubi West Nile groups – the Lugbara, Madi and Alur
people – were removed, one way or another, from key roles, and Amin's military support base imploded into a small, hard, ethnic core:

By 1975, the Kakwa-Nubi-Anyanya core had closed ranks and was the
foundation of Amin's power machine. They held most of the strategic

positions, manned key institutions, and easily grouped whenever there was trouble. The other alienated West Nile groups did not fight Amin because they rightly judged that it was not in their interest to overthrow him. If he were overthrown they would be punished for their natural association with him. ... [S]ubsequent events have proved them right; the Acholi/Langi militia brutalized the whole population of West Nile in 1980–83 for being associated with Amin on ethnic basis.[27]

Writing in 1976, Ugandan political scientist Nelson Kasfir pointed out, using newspaper reports, how Amin's language was saturated in ethnic assumptions, perhaps especially when talking about the military:

In his speeches, Amin tends to discuss people as if their ethnic identity were the most salient feature of their personality. ... For example, he referred to the Obote partisans undergoing military training in Tanzania as mainly 'Alur, Acholis, and Bagisu. ... Lango [sic] are no longer in the majority'. ... In discussing rumours of another coup, Amin said 'Last year there was confusion among the Alur people, then among the Jonams and now it is the Lugbara'.[28]

This emphasis on ethnicity was, as Kasfir points out, one shared by the British authorities. The Foreign Office Africa experts and ex-KAR officers believed that tribal characteristics were at the root of Ugandan (in fact, all African) society, and so did Idi Amin. By 1977, the ethnic base of the army had narrowed dramatically. According to Omara-Otunnu's figures for that year, among those officers who had been commissioned before 1971, 37 per cent were 'Sudanic', 32 per cent 'Bantu', 17 per cent 'Lwo' and 13 per cent 'Nilo-Hamitic'. Among those who had been commissioned after the coup, the figures were 58 per cent, 24 per cent, 10 per cent and 5 per cent respectively.[29]

Many Ugandan writers, rejecting arguments around ethnicity as neo-colonial, have focused on the importance of class in the social role of the military, and in its recruitment strategy. Mahmoud Mamdani, for example, in his second book on Amin,[30] depicted the army as his main tool for establishing a fascist dictatorship. Using the model of Europe in the 1930s, he argued that 'the first step in the development of Amin's military dictatorship into a fascist dictatorship was the militarization of the state'.[31] For Mamdani, Amin had altered:

> the character of the army, giving it a predominantly mercenary and lumpen character. Much attention has been given to the recruitment of mercenaries from Southern Sudan and Eastern Zaire into Amin's army ... [but more] important than the recruitment of mercenaries from outside was the recruitment of urban riff-raff into the army. ... The fascist army was not just a neo-colonial army that functioned as a repressive arm of the state; it did not use terror simply to defend a class dictatorship. Individual members of the armed forces used terror to eliminate all obstacles that stood in the way of their search for wealth.[32]

There are, I think, two decisive arguments against this evocation of fascism. First, Hitler and the other Nazi leaders were motivated to a very large extent by an ideology of anti-Semitism, which embraced a whole theory of global history, economics and politics: it may have been mad and bad, but it was a relatively coherent worldview. Amin, on the contrary, was clearly not motivated by an intellectual ideology of this or any other kind. Second, Hitler's rule was based on a heavily organised, centralised nation state, using relatively advanced twentieth-century technologies of control and surveillance, and aiming at a mass mobilisation of the entire society behind the state. The Nazis may have come to power using street violence and thuggery, but they ruled a disciplined country which (until near the end) saw relatively little spontaneous interpersonal violence, or crime by state agents for purely personal ends. Again, this is all very different from Amin's rule. The term 'totalitarianism' is wholly inappropriate in the circumstances of Uganda in the 1970s; it was not a tightly controlled state so much as a buzzing anarchic mess. Amin had no intentions whatsoever of re-shaping human nature or world history in accordance with a set of political ideas. He did not care what his people *thought*, what mattered was what they *did* – specifically, whether or not they obeyed his orders. Apart from their ruthless use of violence, there is little in common between Amin, the highly un-ideological career soldier, and Hitler, the radical right-wing journalist and ideologue. It is true that Amin, in several of his telegrams to world leaders (especially the British government), declared his personal admiration for Hitler; but how far was this intended simply to wind up the recipients?

The notion that Amin's Uganda was dominated by a 'lumpen militariat' was originally developed by Ali Mazrui in a 1973 article in the journal *Political Studies*. He wrote that: 'The lumpen proletariat is a mass of disorganised workers and ghetto dwellers in the developed world; but the lumpen *militariat* is that class of semi-organised, rugged and semi-literate soldiery which has begun to claim a share of power and influence in what would otherwise have become a heavily privileged meritocracy of the educated.'[33] He suggested that postcolonial Africa might go through a phase of 'the political supremacy of those who hold the means of destruction' for 'two or three decades',[34] before reverting to the normal Marxist model, based on European history, of rule by those who control the means of economic production. The tone adopted by some of these Marxist intellectuals in writing about the 'lumpen' Ugandan poor – the use of phrases such as 'urban riff-raff' or 'rugged and semi-literate' – has an air of haughty disdain reminiscent of the British colonial officers. However, it is clear that, as Amin's rule went on and the ethnic base of the army narrowed, so the military's role in the wider society grew. As we have seen, the troops became increasingly responsible for state functions, from the legal system (through the expansion of courts martial for non-military offenders) to local government structures, where, from 1973, they were involved in 'selecting several thousand chiefs at village, parish, sub-county and county levels'.[35] For Amin, the answer to virtually every political, social or economic problem lay in the army.

By 1974, Amin's power rested almost solely on the military, which he himself now had to appease. As Omara-Otunnu writes:

> Amin continued to maintain his popularity with the military rank and file in a number of ways, first he allowed the various units to operate almost autonomously. They often engaged in 'clean-up' operations without prior authorisation from the centre, and the fact that they were not reprimanded for their excesses appeared to sanction them. ... [T]he troops enjoyed the power that their quasi-independence allowed them. It brought them certain economic advantages, since they were able to terrorise the people and to loot at will. ...

Secondly, Amin's standing with the servicemen was enhanced by skilful public relations; he was able to interact with them at their level, so that with him they felt appreciated and understood.... Far from being a professional military force, the Army's purpose had become to give personal support to the current incumbent of power.

Thirdly, while Amin allowed military units to operate independently in local areas, he maintained scrupulous control over the higher ranks. He changed commanders frequently, thus allowing no one besides himself the opportunity to get a grip on the army.... Amin also made sure that he alone had free access to the troops. He barred his officers ... from addressing the troops in his absence or without his permission.[36]

As time went by, it became increasingly obvious to most observers that much of what was happening was not the result of organised state oppression, but of non- or semi-organised chaos. As economic and social structures collapsed, so eventually did the army itself. An ex-soldier I interviewed put it very eloquently:

I was in the army, but personally I knew by 1977–78 there was no army. The situation we were in really showed militarily. There was no army.... Because at that time, all soldiers were now acquiring big shops, otherwise they had factories, in every town they were just celebrating. The military way of life, that way of life got lost completely, completely.... They were now living lifestyles, extravaganza lifestyles, and civil ones, not military at all. So when the war came, seriously speaking, there was no fighting.... Everyone protected their riches, how could they die? Everybody said 'I'm going home to take my car, to take my this, take my family that.'[37]

This was, I think, the key reason for Amin's downfall. Paradoxically and unwittingly, he had rendered impotent the force that had brought him to power and maintained his rule for more than eight years.

AFTER THE FALL

An interesting picture of Uganda shortly after the invasion is given by a Commonwealth Team of Experts who arrived in May 1979. As development economists, they focused on the collapse of the formal economy, treating the informal one as simply a criminal by-product of economic and political collapse, rather than a set of cultural resources which had kept Ugandans alive despite the social disintegration. However, the experts did try to distinguish between the effects of the war and the effects of Amin's rule, which few commentators since have done:

1. The Government of the National Liberation Movement inherited a country in ruins.
2. As a statement of physical damage this would be an exaggeration. It is the economy that has been ruined. . . .
3. Social conditions are of the same order. . . .
4. Much of Uganda has indeed been badly damaged by the fighting. . . . Several towns were almost completely devastated by artillery or aerial bombardment (or a combination of the two). In others, like Kampala, a proportion of houses, factories and public buildings was gutted or partly destroyed.
5. After the fighting came the looting; at first in selective reprisal against the supporters of the former regime, then spreading like an epidemic. The public hospitals lost almost all their beds. Not only were food, clothes and furniture appropriated from shops and houses, and tools from workshops; any objects which were immovable or valueless to the looters, such as laboratory equipment, were smashed. Thousands of cars and lorries were stolen.
6. But war damage is not the main problem. If it were ... [t]he economy would be functioning more or less normally within a few months.
7. In 1978, however, the condition of Uganda was by no means healthy. Years of arbitrary rule had demoralised the country (which helps to explain the mass looting). During the military regime, success had depended, not on hard work or thrift, but on acquiring the right contacts and seizing the opportunity for magendo. Many who refused orders were killed or forced to flee. ... [R]ecruitment and promotion to senior positions was determined far too often by personal favour rather than by professional standards. The financial controls necessary to any system of administration decayed. ...

> Improper practices were common, not merely in government, but throughout the large public sector.[38]

This implies that, before Amin's coup, the Obote government was *not* engaged in such arbitrary rule and improper practices. Many Ugandans and most historians of Uganda would disagree. As we have seen, in many ways, Obote's first government laid down the path his successor followed. Moreover, as the Commonwealth Team noted, much of the destruction was due to the invasion and its aftermath, rather than the military regime itself.

After the Tanzanians left, successive regimes lacked legitimacy and faced the lasting consequences of Amin's misrule, including the normalisation of economic looting, the impunity of ruling elites, increasing economic under-development, and the creation of what Otunnu terms 'a concentration-camp-like environment, where torture, arrests, incarceration, solitary confinement, disappearances and other degrading forms of physical and psychological torture became common practice'. The Amin regime, he writes, 'destroyed public trust in the state, its institutions, laws, political elites and political processes. Furthermore it promoted a culture of violence that not only reduced political contests to a zero-sum game but also gave dispro-portionate power and prominence to warlords in the political process. . . . Additionally, it promoted a culture of suspicion, piracy and distrust in the country'.[39] Many believe that the consequences of this have persisted to the present day: since Amin's time, no Ugandan ruler has taken power through free and fair elections.

After a couple of short-lived and fragile governments, Milton Obote took over again in December 1980, following Uganda's first elections since 1962. As Richard Reid puts it, the polls 'were rigged in favour of Obote. . . . A crit-ical turning-point, it effectively marked the end of even the pretence of serious electoral politics for a generation, and tilted the political scene in Uganda decisively towards violence as a means of resolution.'[40] He sums up 'Obote II' as follows:

> [Obote's] second stint arguably remains even murkier as an historical episode than Amin's period. . . . Obote II has received very little sustained attention, and is shrouded by the smoke of battle and obfuscated by a kind of collective stress disorder. . . .

In many ways, Obote represented continuity from Amin, and further utilised the role of the military in politics; the militarisation of political culture arguably reached its apex in the early 1980s. ... The consensus is that [Obote's] reign from the end of 1980 to the middle of 1985 was more brutal, and resulting in higher numbers of deaths, than the whole of Amin's.[41]

This is not a maverick view; the consensus among Ugandans and Western historians is that Obote's second government killed more people than Amin's, in about half the time. It finally ended in 1986, after a long, gruelling civil war against the National Resistance Movement of Yoweri Museveni. Like Amin, Museveni is a military man, who spent many years organising guerrilla resistance to successive Ugandan governments from his base in Tanzania. In 2021 he will have been in power for 35 years (longer than all other post-independence Ugandan leaders put together) and his regime perpetuates the dominance of the military established by Amin. However, Museveni's international image remains relatively unsullied, despite human rights abuses, violence against political opponents (sometimes fatal), rigged elections, and widespread corruption. 'At least he isn't Amin or Obote', Ugandans say, though most are much too young to remember the former dictators.

A 'MANIFESTLY DEVOUT EX-MONSTER': AMIN IN RETIREMENT

While Uganda remained in turmoil, the last twenty-four years of Amin's own life were spent in quiet retirement. There seem to have been no more telegrams to world leaders, no more grandiose public speeches. Perhaps his hosts prevented him from making such announcements, but if he had wanted to I suspect he would have ignored them. His eccentric statements had, it seems, been a weapon he used to stay in power rather than a symptom of mental illness. All that was now over, and he no longer had to pose as an international statesman. After an argument with Ghaddafi in 1980, he moved to Saudi Arabia and, according to his son Jaffar, became increasingly religious: 'once Dad fell silent on the world stage ... he refocused his energy into understanding further his own religion, Islam. For most of the 24 years he lived in exile until his death on August 16 2003, dad studied Islam in further depth and he was devoted to and strictly followed the teachings of Islam.'[42]

Jaffar, in exile with his father and siblings, gives us an account of everyday life in the Amin household, which sounds almost parodically mundane:

> On a typical day at our household in Saudi Arabia, we had morning prayers at 5.30. Then, at 7.00 am, Dad dropped our young siblings ... at the Expatriates' School, in the family's Caprice station wagon. Then he passed by the Safeway to buy groceries. After that, he would begin his extensive phone calls to 'dependents' [sic] cum political opportunists who kept the flame of his 'anticipated return' alive and the phone ringing off the hook in his skeptical ear....
>
> After the phone calls ... Dad would have lunch at his favourite Pakistani Restaurant and then he would drive off towards the Cornishe [sic] for a dip in the sea, having collected our young siblings from school. He would then check on friends like Abdul Rahman, a member of the group they referred to as Arua Boyz....[43] Dad had lots of associates with him in Jeddah.... Magrib prayers at 19.00 would find us back home with bags full of groceries for the sagging Freezer and the Frost Free Fridge for the delicate stuff.... Fridays would find us in a long convoy for the Holy City of Makkah Al Mukaramah for Juma Prayers ... and back to our Al Safa residence by 19.00 for Magrib Prayers.[44]

On his time as president, Jaffar says, his father was philosophical. 'He would put it this way, "The people will appreciate what I was trying to do for the Indigenous African".... I'd ask him what happened. He'd look at me and say: "People fought me, I fought them back, but I never killed innocent people", and then say again "God will be the one to judge me."'[45] Amin's retirement was very comfortable:

> Dad was given a monthly allowance that funded an opulent lifestyle, but life in exile was still hard.... We lived in luxury but it was not home. I was with Dad in Libya and Saudi Arabia and remember the luxury well.
>
> In Saudi Arabia, there was marble everywhere in our 15-room house but it was still not home. Dad was paid $30,000 per month by the Saudis. He had more than 30 of us [family members and dependants] with him.[46]

Occasionally, Western journalists would track him down. After Amin's death in 2003, a veteran British foreign correspondent, Tom Stacey, reminisced in the *Mail on Sunday*:

> We would drive up the coast in his white Chevy Caprice – an inexpensive conveyance by Saudi standards – some 17 miles to Obhor Creek. There he would strip off, displaying his formidable physicality, and streak away through the waters of the Red Sea in a powerful crawl ... and return, beaming, to greet the onlookers who knew him as 'Sheikh Amin' in a neighbourly way.
>
> We'd drive back, Idi at the wheel, to his villa in the south of the town where he lived with the youngest nine of his 43 acknowledged children who evidently loved him, and his recently acquired wife, a demure little Muganda girl called Chumaru – and his Saudi minder in the forecourt. Chumaru, 11 years ago, presented him with a new daughter, Iman, who at once became the apple of her father's eye. ...
>
> We all tucked in to roast chicken, mutton stew and isra (the millet-made flat bread of East Africa). Only I bothered with a knife and fork and we talked until prayer time. Idi was a manifestly devout ex-monster. To the very last, he dreamed of returning to Uganda to live in dignified retirement as an iconic figure from an era which history somehow got all wrong. ...
>
> Saudi Arabia ... provided him with a nice but not luxurious nine-room villa in the city of Jeddah, with surrounding high walls and enough of a stipend to pay his running expenses and a bit – but not a whole lot more. Unlike most of his fellow East African dictators, Idi never robbed his country's exchequer, such as it was. He came out with a dozen trunk-loads of personal kit, no more. When I first met him in exile, back in 1982, he was turned out like an elegant superannuated British general, with handmade shoes ...[47]

Stacey's obituary recounts many of the usual stories, demonstrating the familiar mixture of fact and fantasy, and the tone of racial superiority, characteristic of most Western accounts of Amin.

Another Western journalist who claimed to have interviewed Amin in Saudi Arabia was the Italian Riccardo Orizio, quite a collector of dictators. His book about seven of them, *Talk of the Devil*, published in 2004, begins with an account of trying and failing to track Amin down. It is well salted with the familiar tales, and consists mostly of the author's repeated failure to find Uganda's former president. Eventually, he gets a telephone interview, in which the conversation does not sound very much like the ex-dictator, though this may be a result of the translation from Italian. Amin tells the journalist that 'nowadays my only interests have to do with Islam. My sons are all grown up now and have left Jeddah. ... I've got a little daughter, Iman, and a young wife, but I am dedicated to religion and nothing else. I recite the Koran, play the organ, go swimming and fishing at a resort near the Yemeni border.' He misses Ugandan food, and his friends. Asked if he feels any remorse, Amin replied, 'No. Only nostalgia.' 'For what?' Orizio asks. 'For when I was a non-commissioned officer fighting against the Mau Mau in Kenya and everyone respected me. I was as strong as a bull. I was a good soldier in the British army. The terror of the Mau Mau. I was born in a very, very poor family. And I enlisted to escape hunger. But my officers were Scottish, and they loved me. The Scots are good, you know.'[48] Eventually, Orizio actually met Amin at home, but apparently the former president only wanted to show off his giant TV screens, and we get no more interview material. His nostalgia for the KAR seems very plausible; they may well have been the happiest days of his life.

THE PERSISTENCE OF IDI AMIN

Perhaps the most interesting question about the Amin regime is, how did he survive in power for so long? Most early writers saw this as a consequence of keeping the population in continual fear. More recent accounts have complicated this picture, showing quite how sophisticated some of his strategies were, while structural economic factors also played into his hands. As I have suggested, by and large people survived by juggling a variety of livelihood strategies outside the formal economy, including subsistence agriculture, barter exchange, and the various illegal economic activities known as *magendo*. As Holger Hansen summarised Uganda's economic situation in the late 1970s:

> People developed a number of coping mechanisms. The peasants scaled
> down the production of cash crops and turned to growing food stuffs

simply in order to maximise their food security and secure a livelihood. It had the effect that in this period of Ugandan history we saw little malnutrition and people in rural areas managed to keep their livelihood at a reasonable level. They diversified their production at household level, and service provisions, like settling of conflicts and access to land, became localized. In spite of their withdrawal to a household-based economy people made use of their customary institutions with regard to land issues and family matters. At the same time, we saw a considerable expansion of urban farming.[49]

Amin was also lucky in that world coffee prices stayed exceptionally high almost until the end of his rule, stabilising the formal economy and producing vital foreign currency. This was what kept the senior military and civilian figures vital to the regime well enough supplied with luxuries for them to stay on board. It enabled the infamous weekly 'whisky run' between Stanstead airport in the UK and Entebbe, which continued to the bitter end despite the efforts of the FCO to close it down.

To the economic conditions enjoyed by the regime may be added the paradoxical but important factor that, for many Ugandans, there seemed relatively little real threat from Amin's men. Drunk, or sober, soldiers might kill, rob and abuse people with impunity, but that kind of thing had happened under Obote as well, especially after 1966 (and happens today). Although Amin did indeed create a state of terror, particularly among the educated, Westernised Ugandan elite whom he persecuted consistently, less privileged Ugandans were often less hostile to their president. Apart from Acholi and Langi people, and army officers, ordinary Ugandans felt they had little to fear for much of the time. Amin's personality and style of governance also helped to sustain surprisingly widespread internal support for the regime. He seems to have been more popular than outside commentators suggested, and he worked hard to keep that public support. As I have suggested, it may have been boosted rather than depressed by his seemingly eccentric behaviour on the international scene. His grandiose public statements on world affairs, deprecated as stupid or insane by British writers and educated Ugandan exiles, were interpreted by many in Uganda itself as the behaviour of a strong, powerful man who could get away with offering impertinent advice to renowned world leaders.

A third element behind Amin's survival was the comparative success of his foreign policy (as opposed, for example, to Obote's). Throughout his rule, Amin set powerful members of the international community against each other, making sure that they competed for his attention and for Uganda's support in global forums such as the UN. In the early period of his rule, as we have seen, this included the Israelis and Arabs, later it involved also the Cold War opponents of East and West. The Americans were always suspicious of him but, as we have seen, the British constantly hoped he would come back on board with themselves and the anti-communist forces of the 'Free World'. On and off throughout the 1970s, both sides of the Cold War competed for his support. At different times, the British, the Israelis, the Soviet Union, Libya and Saudi Arabia tried to outdo each other in supplying the country with money and the army with weapons. Even Henry Kyemba wrote in 1977 that 'amazingly, Amin's foreign policy has worked'.[50] As I have suggested, throughout much of his life Amin's relationship with the British state was the most important one he had, but it did not stop him from being unfaithful with other international powers when it suited his interests. Moreover, within Africa itself, there was widespread support for his expulsion of the Asians, as well as his grandiose anti-colonial statements.

Perhaps the main factor behind Amin's survival, though, was his skilful use of public relations (PR) techniques and the use of mass media, especially to project his massive personality. His obsession with this was a comparatively new element in international politics. Amin may have been one of the earliest politicians to see its full importance. Although many leaders had extensively deployed PR techniques before (J.F. Kennedy and Adolf Hitler being contrasting early examples), Amin was perhaps one of the first to realise that all publicity can be good publicity. As I have suggested, he was particularly adept at the 'dead cat' tactic, distracting attention from some uncomfortable issue by making fantastical and newsworthy statements. He saw the need to dominate the news by all means necessary, even if it meant saying or doing ridiculous but dramatic things. In this, Amin was way ahead of his time; some of his utterances which seemed inexplicable at the time sound commonplace in today's Trumpian/Johnsonian era. In his use of the media, and the deployment of his own personality and 'sense of humour' to increase his power, Idi Amin might even be considered the father of modern populism. His jokes, his 'buffoonish' but very macho persona, together with the immense charm attested to by so many of those who met him, all helped to increase his popularity among the *wananchi*, as Ugandans refer to the ordinary people of the country. This was not a fake image; it was real enough. Unlike most political populists, Amin was not pretending to be 'the common man', he *was* one. He knew first hand, unlike Obote, that the vast majority of Ugandans were rural peasants with virtually no education; they were not urban, literate or widely travelled. The bulk of the Ugandan people appreciated that their background was his too, at least until his mismanagement put their lives and property at serious risk. As his sworn enemy Kyemba put it, Amin's 'remarkable personality ... is not ... to be underrated. True, he is nearly illiterate; he is politically naive; he is violently unpredictable; he is utterly ruthless. Yet he is also jovial and generous, and he has extraordinary talents – for practical short-term action, for turning apparent weaknesses to his own advantage, and for asserting his leadership among his gang of thugs.'[51]

Amin's public image also helped to boost what had always been one of his secret weapons: making people underestimate him. As we have seen, a key element in his amazing rise to power was the belief of the British and southern Ugandans (as well as Milton Obote) that he was essentially stupid and manipulable. Amin's jokes and eccentricities enabled him to survive for as long as he did, by leading clever people to constantly underestimate his intelligence as well as his ruthlessness. The same applies to the conspiracy theories of Ugandan intellectuals who believed he was simply a puppet, either of shadowy international forces (the British, the Israelis, global capitalism, etc.), or individual manipulators (Astles, Bar-Lev, Kibedi, etc.). He was seen as an ignorant peasant soldier who could not possibly have succeeded on his own, and these patronising attitudes were among the chief means by which he rose and thrived. But it was not only Amin's personal style and its projection into a PR image that attested to his interest in public presentation. Kampala, until near the end of his rule, was kept almost obsessively clean, as Western commentators often noticed. The army developed a public relations role, with endless parades and demonstrations of their skills, as well as involvement in cultural activities, from traditional dancing at ceremonial functions to the formation of the Suicide Mechanised Unit Jazz Band, one of whose members Amin married. But it was the deployment of PR, and particularly the mobilisation of his larger-than-life personality, that was his main weapon (alongside the real weapons) in ensuring the survival of his regime.

This is not an original argument. Derek Peterson and Edgar Taylor, in their introduction to a special issue of the *Journal of Eastern African Studies* in 2013, emphasise the importance of Amin's use of print and broadcast media. 'It was', they write, 'in the news media that government officers found a medium with which to address, exhort and summon the Ugandan public.'[52] Ugandan newspapers and radio were seen as the key way to influence, not only the population as a whole but quite specific constituencies. Students, city workers, women or local chiefs would be instructed by newspaper and radio what to do, even if few people in rural areas had access to these sources of information. Like so much else, Amin saw the Ugandan press and radio in a very military way, as a means of making civilians behave as soldiers do – you issue an order and it is obeyed. As Peterson and Taylor put it: 'The news media was more than a vehicle through which propaganda was disseminated. It was a vehicle by which populations were managed and a machine through which government worked.'[53] They give an example, quoting a *Voice of Uganda* journalist:

> On 5 February 1974 ... Amin's government summarily banned the wearing of wigs and trousers by women.[54] In the directive, announced in the pages of the *Voice of Uganda* and over the government radio station, Amin described how wigs were 'made by callous imperialists from human hair mainly collected from the unfortunate victims of the miserable Vietnam war'. . . . Amin's decree . . . came as a surprise. . . . One editorialist named C. Kakembo listened to the news broadcast on the radio at 8.00pm on 4 February, when no mention was made of the directive. It was only during the 10.00pm broadcast – and in the newspaper the following day – that the directive was announced. It brought many people up short. 'Those who heard the announcement and happened to be in public places had to pull off the wigs immediately to avoid being bullied, touched and embarrassed', Kakembo reported. For Kakembo and many other young women, Amin's dictates demanded the radical, rapid revision of their physical appearance. In the days following the Presidential directive women were obliged to find ribbons and cloths to tie over their heads in order to 'look respectable enough in public'.[55]

This is an interesting example, and Amin's attempts to control women's bodies were clearly a significant aspect of his rule,[56] but it is not clear how often – or where – Amin's radio edicts actually had any effect. Like most of his other attempts to make Ugandans act like British colonial soldiers, many of them seem to have been unheard or ignored. As Peterson and Taylor conclude, 'Rather than a monolithic dictatorship or anarchic mess, the Ugandan state under Amin was a field of action, in which officials struggled to exhort their subjects into compliance';[57] this probably included Amin himself. But Peterson and Taylor were by no means the first writers to suggest the importance of PR to Amin's rule. A.B.K. Kasozi wrote in 1994 that, 'Amin, like Obote, desired to wield ideological power. He seems not to have understood the power of educational ideas. But he turned his attention to ... the media instantly.'[58] Even official government publications were presented in a more stylish manner than before. The last major policy statement of Obote's first government, the Common Man's Charter (which contained his plans to deal with the Asians), looked like a British government White Paper, with a cover containing only title text. Under Amin, however, government publications used colour and photography, with sophisticated layout and typography, to get the message across.

Alicia Decker emphasises Amin's deployment of his larger-than-life persona – the performative aspect, as she calls it, of his ruling style. As her language suggests, she sees this as a conscious, deliberate tactic. Her index lists as 'performative aspects of his rule' the following features: 'to create a sense of normalcy ... to emasculate perceived enemies ... to foster national unity ... media, strategic use of ... political capital, cultivating ... [and] political theater'.[59] But I would argue that this theatricality was not so much a thought-out strategy as a central aspect of Amin's personality and style; one thinks of the public demonstrations of physical prowess during his KAR days, which Iain Grahame so loved describing, as well as the publicity photographs showing the president dressed as a soldier, a diplomat, a sportsman, or the vice chancellor of Makerere University; like an Action Man doll of the period, he had a dramatic outfit for every occasion. As Decker suggests, Amin's performative skills were vital in cementing his power: the constant touring, public addresses, international grandstanding – all these displayed his charisma and strengthened his support in Uganda, while intensely annoying the international community. He took a close interest in how he was portrayed, and was quick to respond angrily to any negative reports in the international press, or in books and films (as Denis Hills and Barbet Schroeder could attest). But while he seems in part to have performed from conscious deliberation, that was also just what he was like. Amin's ability to deploy his charismatic personality, and his other PR skills, came naturally to him, but had been developed and polished over his military career, and he could use this both through the mass media and more directly, as he tirelessly criss-crossed the country and toured world capitals.

'BAD OR MAD?' THE PSYCHOLOGY OF THE DICTATOR

If I am right to suggest that his personality was a key factor in his success, it is also an important element in any understanding of Amin and his regime. The problem here is that there are so many layers of fantasy and prejudice in the published (and unpublished) material on him, that it is often impossible to penetrate beneath them. Moreover, Amin himself had so many personae, and was capable of moving so rapidly from joviality to threat, relaxation to exertion, anger to happiness, that his real feelings, beliefs and tastes are almost completely hidden. This was no doubt deliberate; above all, he liked to keep people guessing. The British Foreign Office experts spent vast amounts of intellectual energy in trying to discover his true motivations, and how far his persona was 'real', how far 'fake'. They never got very close to succeeding.

People meeting Amin for the first time noticed above all his physical presence, charisma and sheer energy. He seems always to have dominated any room he was in. The soldier was huge, and seemed even bigger as a result of his massive personality, but his demeanour had some delicacy about it too. His first biographer, Judith Listowel, described meeting him in 1969, in Gulu, at the consecration of his future victim, Anglican Archbishop Janani Luwum: 'I looked into the smiling face of a tall, muscular officer with shrewd eyes, who invited me to a cup of coffee. He was a hulking figure of a man and I was fascinated by his hands – beautiful slim hands with long tapering fingers.'[60] Three years later, she met him again, this time as president of Uganda: 'He was smiling and charming, and diplomatically pretended to remember our meeting in Gulu. His manners were impeccable, and looking at this towering black general beaming at me, with his aristocratic hands and tapering fingers, it seemed almost incredible that this was the man who had ordered the ... executions.'[61] The fascination with Amin's hands seems to have been Listowel's personal thing, but the overall sense of an elegance amid his roughness, a strange sophistication alongside the crudity, is often expressed by others who met him.

Another trait, which people who spent any time around him noticed, was his weird sense of humour. It was always very hard indeed to tell when he was joking and when not – perhaps he himself was sometimes unsure. I suspect he developed this as a defence mechanism in his KAR days; many of his jokes have a barrack-room smell. His son, Jaffar, describes his taste for practical jokes, such as tipping excessive quantities of chilli into food before it was presented to his family and guests. On one such occasion, he records, while the children were gasping with pain at the heat, 'my father was engaged in one of his tearful earthquake laughs. ... My siblings and I were not amused by Dad's "African Chili Prank" at all.'[62] On another occasion Amin played the same trick on his ally, General Moses Ali, tipping tabasco into his drink when he turned away briefly.[63] Amin's sense of humour was also present in more subtle ways, as with his many attempts to annoy the British government such as the launch of the 'Save Britain Fund', which was supposed to send aid from Uganda to assist the mother country through its regular economic crises of the 1970s. Jaffar, otherwise largely uncritical of his father, writes that: 'Dad liked to crack jokes and laugh even though some of his jokes could be very annoying and in terrible taste. No one was exempted from Dad's jokes including us his children, family members, associates and foreign dignitaries. We just learned to take them as they came.'[64]

The close link between humour and aggression has often been noticed, not least by Freud, and Amin's 'jokes' were usually at least tinged with threats and the desire to hurt. In this context, it is relevant to raise the role of joking in military life; military memoirs from countries all over the world testify to the importance in army life of joking relationships. In 1970s Britain, this would have been termed 'piss-taking' or 'ribbing', now we would say 'banter' or 'trolling'. Perhaps many of Amin's actions and statements which puzzled outsiders were due, at least in part, to his aggressive (and also defensive) sense of humour. Much of this was directed against the British, from whom he may have learned his joking style alongside much else. His perceived ability to mock the former colonial masters did a lot to cement his popularity in Uganda, and Africa as a whole.

Amin's apparent irrationality probably also aided his survival. Being unpredictable can be a formidable weapon for a political leader and would-be international statesman to deploy. We have seen how his unexpected announcements of a visit could get the British state rushing around like a kitten chasing its tail. Being thought potentially insane can have distinct advantages for a leader; as Machiavelli wrote, 'it is a very wise thing to simulate craziness at the right time'.[65] Certainly Amin was lucky, which helped him to continue in power longer than many thought possible, but, as I have suggested, it is hard to believe that luck was *all* he had going for him. Unless his survival in power was pure chance, we have to accept that there was, as the cliché goes, 'method in his madness', and perhaps a keen, if unschooled, intelligence behind some of his moves. The British, aware that Amin's personality was a key factor in his success, tried hard to understand it. As his rule went on, the idiosyncratic announcements and policy shifts, together with international media speculation about his behaviour (often based on fictions), led many Western observers to suspect he might be mentally ill, a conviction which became increasingly widespread. As Otunnu shrewdly remarks, his apparently eccentric actions:

> were presented by many political commentators, including S. Kiwanuka, D. Gwyn, H. Kyemba, and T. Malady and M. Malady, as a clear indication that Amin was suffering from schizophrenia. According to them, what they presented as a series of confused orders, 'senseless killings', 'sadism' and involvement in 'blood rituals' by Amin confirmed their medical 'diagnosis'. . . . What the commentators, who . . . were not qualified medical experts in the field, failed to understand was the legitimation function of the drama. . . . [The apparently irrational statements] made Amin extremely popular in the country, because he had humiliated white men. To ordinary Ugandans, this was a payback moment.[66]

Western diplomats sought medical and psychological opinions on Amin's sanity, but the various professionals were usually guarded in their responses. In May 1972, a meeting took place between the FCO and a delegation from the US State Department. According to the British memo of the meeting, Mr Wendell Coote of the State Department:

> said that the American view was, quite simply, that Amin was a nut. They were, he said, beginning to think that he was mentally deficient, though they had not decided what form his deficiency took. I said that we also had concluded that he was dangerously unbalanced. We agreed that, despite this, we had no option for the time being but to keep alongside him and try to limit the damage.[67]

A couple of months later, the outgoing US ambassador to Uganda called at the FCO on his way home. From a memo of this visit, it appears that the Americans had failed to get medical confirmation of their views on Amin's sanity:

> The Americans have been observing Amin closely (they arranged for two of their psychiatrists to be present during a 3 hour public occasion at which President Amin was speaking). In their view, there are some signs that the President is slightly schizophrenic, but there is no clinical confirmation of this.[68]

The UK government also looked into the president's psychiatric state. During the stand-off over the arrest of Denis Hills, the British Foreign Secretary, James Callaghan, sought medical advice on how Amin might best be approached in the negotiations. Through the FCO, he contacted an eminent psychiatrist, Sir Denis Hill[69] of the Institute of Psychiatry and the Maudsley Hospital. Hill at first concluded that Amin seemed to have moments of insanity but, after further research, he changed his mind. In a fascinating letter to Norman Aspin of the FCO in June 1975, he wrote:

> I have now read the two books ... by David Martin and ... Denis Hills. I have also seen the interesting papers sent by Dr J.W. Wober and I have interviewed three psychiatrists who have worked in the University Department at Makerere, done research in the country, seen Amin in action on many occasions, and two of them have met him. ...

One of the difficulties is that there are really no standards by which to judge his personality. Had he been brought up in this country, whatever his position in life, one would have had no hesitation in saying that he had a grossly abnormal personality, but nearly all those pieces of behaviour such as awarding himself the VC, DSO and MC, wearing the Israeli Air Force wings, playing the harmonica or the banjo as part of a presidential television broadcast and making wild, grandiose statements about himself and his abilities, which might suggest something serious, become explicable in terms of his background, his achievement, and his need to preserve his position in the eyes of his countrymen. It was said to me that those who met him or listened to him, if they did not know he was a ruthless killer, would be attracted by his considerable presence, by his warmth and wit. He can hold a university audience and make them respond to him.

My own conclusion [is that] ... Amin normally has an elevated mood of exuberance and self-confidence which sustains him, but which is precarious and gives way now and again to the opposite mood. Psychiatrists would regard this type of personality as an abnormal one ... but it does not amount to psychosis or 'madness' as commonly understood. Such a view does however reinforce the idea that the maintenance of his self-esteem is all-important in keeping good relations with him. Such a person needs emotional support and the emotional reward of being accepted and highly regarded. Such a personality is sensitive to personal slights, is conceited and arrogant and tends to be suspicious from time to time.[70]

The 'Dr Wober' mentioned here was Mallory Wober, a former lecturer in social psychology at Makerere University who later worked in the UK and the United States, and published a book on *Psychology in Africa* in 1975. When he returned from Uganda in 1973, Dr Wober gave a BBC radio talk, later published in *The Listener* magazine. Titled 'An Attempt on the Mind of Idi Amin', it argues that Amin was in a postcolonial psychic condition characterised by an insecure dependency on the former imperial power. After taking power, therefore, he suffered from a split, or 'cognitive dissonance', between his self-image and the reality of his actions:

He ... seems to think of himself ... as a paternal embodiment of the national identity. He would have needed, then, to expunge the awareness of himself as responsible for eliminating so many of his new subjects; indeed many of his own army, to whom he had been psychologically quite close. To settle his mind, he had to develop the idea that his Presidency was a natural and necessary step in Uganda's national evolution. And to support this notion, he had to get foreign recognition.[71]

In Wober's analysis, Amin at first got this recognition from the British and other Western nations, but not from many respected African leaders, especially Nyerere. This 'fuelled Amin's mental dissonance'.[72] His authoritarian personality, caused by strict discipline during childhood, led to an unwillingness to acknowledge his 'anti-social impulses' and a compulsion to try to get rid of them by projecting them onto others, as well as 'a tendency to think in rather rigid categories and stereotypes'.[73] Somehow, he projected his anti-social urges onto the Asians: 'He now dreamt that he must expel his country's Asians. . . . So, we can see his scapegoating of the Asians as partly a projection of his own guilt onto others, thus trying to export feelings he could not comfortably contain.'[74] Amin's 'dependency feelings' had been fixated on the British, which meant that he 'found comfort for many formative years within British institutions'. However, 'For psychological and political reasons he strives to assert his own and his people's independence', leading to a contradiction which remained unresolved. As a result, 'Amin's personal struggle for independence and his authoritarian personality, have become a source of tragedy for his country.'[75]

More recent work on the psychology of dictators sounds more scientific than Wober's speculative analysis, but it does not get us much further in understanding Idi Amin. Fathali Moghaddam's book, *The Psychology of Dictatorship*, for example, was published by the American Psychological Association in 2013. It looks almost exclusively at European and Middle Eastern leaders – a narrow cultural focus for a book making universal claims about human nature and history. Moghaddam largely excludes political and cultural context, focusing on the key role of political ideology in the establishment and sustaining of all dictatorships everywhere. His only specific mention of Idi Amin compares him, oddly, with the Iranian revolutionary religious leader Ayatollah Khomeini, a man for whom ideology (in the form of Islamism) was all-important. In contrast, Amin, as I have suggested, barely knew what the concept of ideology meant; at different times he was pro or anti both West and East, the British Empire and anti-imperialism, Israel and the Arab world. Moghaddam writes that Khomeini's purges, 'continued until only those considered completely subservient and in line with Khomeini's thinking survived. The same mixture of egocentric and manipulative behaviour can be witnessed in . . . President for Life Idi Amin.'[76] But, to repeat myself, Amin had no desire at all to make everybody think like him, as long as they did what they were told. It is impossible to discern anything in Amin's rule which looks like the kind of rigid belief system that Moghaddam suggests is at the heart of all dictatorships.

Despite the doubts of the professional psychiatrists, for many Western 'rationalists', including those in the State Department and the Foreign and Commonwealth Office, Amin's eccentric public statements were clear signs of mental illness. When, for example, he said that the decision to expel the Asians had come to him in a dream, as guidance from God, they saw this as a symptom of his psychological problems. For many Ugandans, however, it was seen as a powerful justification for his actions, and a very good reason for carrying out what were evidently God's wishes, conveyed, as divine communications often are, in dreams. Amin having appropriated the Asian policy from Obote, the dream made it entirely his, so justifying both the policy itself and his legitimacy with supporters. Rather than a symptom of insanity, his talk of the dream can be seen as a rational political move, which helped strengthen his political support in the country. The disjuncture between Amin's real life and his image as an icon of evil rests on exactly this kind of misrecognition. The British (and the Western-educated southern Ugandan elite) failed to see what he was doing, were confused by his lifelong performance of buffoonery and stupidity, and simply didn't understand him. The inexplicable can very easily become the supernatural or the monstrous – and the charismatic, brutal soldier fitted so neatly with a certain Western idea of evil.

AFTERWORD

At the beginning of 1977, while Amin was still in power but after his final break with the UK, Martin Ewans, the experienced head of the FCO's East Africa desk, distributed what the Foreign Office calls 'a think piece'. Titled 'Dealing with Amin', this goes some way to explaining British diplomatic thinking, as well as wider Western attitudes towards him. Ewans wrote:

[W]hat manner of man is he? Theories – even books – abound. It is perhaps easier first to say what he is not.

He is not a joke. We have partly to thank the British popular press, plus Alan Coren, etc, for the impression most people seem to have that he is merely a figure of fun. . . . It seems traditional with us to make fun of those who kick us around (Boney, the Kaiser, Hitler, Gandhi, Mussadeq, Nasser), no doubt as some sort of psychological compensation. Colour, of course, also comes into it. And, of course, he plays to the gallery.

But Amin is nevertheless an unscrupulous mass murderer, an incompetent wrecker of his country and no way a force for reason and moderation in international affairs. Not really funny at all.

He is not mad. . . . [I]n all my dealings with him, I can say that I have always found a logic, and often a craftiness or even an astuteness, behind his actions. Naive the logic may sometimes be, as one would expect of a man who has had no formal education and little experience of the outside world. Often it is warped or perverted, but it is never wholly absent. I would never (or hardly ever) apply the word 'irrational' to his actions, however bizarre or maverick they may appear. There is a brain there, and it works.

To turn to the positive side, I would say that the two most important clues to his character are that (a) he is what I would call an 'unregenerate African', and (b) he is a former British soldier.

THE AFRICAN

We . . . have been used to dealing with men made in our own image. Their thought processes, their ideals, their political frameworks, their whole terms of reference, are to a great extent ours. . . .

Amin has no such background, and his behaviour and thought-processes are therefore very 'African'. . . . The figure Amin cuts is very much the figure which the African in the bush expects of 'the boss' – the pronouncements on world affairs, the messages to his equals, the travels and visits, the medals and reglia [*sic*]. The trouble is that all of them, the messages no less than the medals are 'putty' ones; this is not how the adult, responsible world behaves.

This also means that Amin has no respect at all for human life. . . . [He] was clearly wholly disconcerted at all the fuss over Mrs Bloch – what was one old lady? There can be no question about his responsibility for, and personal participation in, the blood-letting in Uganda. . . .

THE SOLDIER

All this, however, is qualified by Amin's training as a British 'other rank'. As the British army says, 'if you see something, whitewash it; if it moves, salute it'. To some extent, Amin rules Uganda like an army barracks.

First, the whitewash. Kampala, for example, is – or was when I last saw it – a well-run city. The hedges are cut, the verges trimmed, the road signs painted. Amin himself dresses immaculately, if bizarrely. Appearances are important. . . .

Not only in good order, however, but also military discipline. Ministers obey instructions, the Commanding Officer gives and receives 'briefings'. Affairs are run from a 'command post'. Wrong-doers are, so to speak, put on a charge and shot for desertion; if you need some serious law-enforcement, you have a court martial. The concept of hierarchy prevails over that of persuasion or consultation.[1]

For Ewans, Amin's lack of 'respect for human life, came from his being 'an "unregenerate African"' and again, because 'his behaviour and thought-processes are . . . very "African"', he therefore 'has no respect at all for human life'. His African-ness made him, not just murderous, but also childlike: 'this is not how the adult, responsible world behaves'. This was also not how the more 'white', less 'African', Western-educated leaders, such as Obote or Nyerere, behaved. Amin's lack of respect for human life did not, in Ewans' view, have anything to do with the two decades he spent in the British military, being trained to kill and taking part in internal repression in Uganda as well as the often unrestrained violence of the KAR's Kenyan operations in the late 1950s. Instead, for Ewans, the president's army experience had produced his best self – the one that liked keeping things clean and well painted, insisted on orders being obeyed, while himself obeying his superiors. The killings on the other hand were due entirely to his 'curious background', which made him a very *African* African. The trouble with Amin, in the eyes of the Foreign Office, was precisely that he was *too* African.

What is happening here, I suggest, is not just a denial of responsibility, nor merely a simple-minded racism. It is the methodical, if unconscious, invention of an 'other', designed to be the mirror opposite of the British (or at least, the Foreign Office) self-image. This exemplifies what Chinua Achebe called 'the desire – one might indeed say the need – in Western psychology to set up Africa as a foil to Europe, as a place of negation at once remote and vaguely familiar, in comparison with which Europe's own state of spiritual grace will be manifest.'[2] The psychic impetus for this, as I suggested in the introduction, is an instance of Freudian projection: the 'other' is needed precisely to prevent the 'self' from realising that the 'evil' comes from within, not from an external other. However, the repression of similarity never fully works; at some level, the self knows the ugly truth, and it is this that gives 'colonial desire'[3] much of its pleasure. As Conrad put it, 'What thrilled you was just the thought of their humanity – like yours . . . ugly.'[4] The British needed Amin to be other than themselves, so they could deny, to themselves as much as to other people, the fact that he had been taught by them, assisted by them in his rise to power, and was throughout, in many ways, very like one of their soldiers. We see this denial in Ewans' inability to see any link between Amin's violence and his military background; one might ask, what is the army there for? It is certainly not for painting fences. As I suggested in

Chapter 7, when Foreign Office diplomats repeatedly referred to Amin's 'love/hate' relationship with the UK, when they spoke of him as a rejected lover, the terms might be reversed. It was more the British who had the romantic ambivalence, and they who needed Amin to be as African, as Evil, as Other, as possible, in order to maintain their imperial illusions. The iconic image allowed them to avoid responsibility for making him the man he was.

But this is not the whole of the matter. As we have seen, Amin was by no means simply a puppet of the British. The story in this book is very much one of *self-fashioning*. Gradually, the young soldier, against all the odds, took control of his own life, manipulated the would-be puppet masters, and slowly rose in his society until he took over. This was an extraordinary achievement. Discussing the young Amin's sporting prowess, his KAR officer Iain Grahame wrote that 'he excelled and he conquered',[5] and he did the same in manoeuvring through the complex and often vicious politics of post-independence Uganda, which required mental rather than physical strengths. He was never simply lucky. The British could never understand this; perhaps prevented by the stereotypes of the warrior and the mission boy, they did not realise that Idi Amin was a fiercely intelligent (if unschooled) man, who had learned in the army a lot about bullying Africans and manipulating Europeans. Adopting these techniques had proved highly successful in his military career, and he rose to the top. They were successful in the first years after independence, in dealing with the intricate and violent struggles between Obote supporters and the Ganda traditionalists; again he rose to the top. They did not, however, work so well after he seized power, when it came to organising and controlling the Ugandan state and its relations with the rest of the world. His abilities enabled him to last a lot longer than most predicted, but gradually he lost control.

In telling this story, I have tried throughout to look at the myth and the reality together, and to tell the story by bringing together often conflicting accounts of what happened. This seems to me to be the best way of avoiding what, in the case of Idi Amin, would be the pitfalls of a conventional biography. As I have argued, Amin is by no means a typical historical subject, but one in whom the myth and reality are often impossible to distinguish from each other, and in whom the myth is often more important in determining events than the reality. If I had ignored all this, and written a conventionally omniscient summary of the material I have found in the archives, published books and interviews, it would have led to either another uncritical repetition of the legend, or a very short and boring recitation of the known facts. In contrast, the polyphonic approach has allowed me to dig out and expose the inconsistencies and inaccuracies of the accepted historical account. Amin was *not* put in power by the British (nor the Israelis, or even the Greeks). He was *not* a cannibal, and did *not* have his wives murdered, or keep heads in his fridge. He did *not* expel Uganda's Asians because of a dream he had, nor because of racist attitudes towards them. He was probably *not* responsible for half a million deaths, nor anything like that figure. On the other hand, he was personally capable of being violent and aggressive, and he ruled as a very nasty dictator who destroyed much of his country, even though he probably killed fewer people and was less destructive than his predecessor and successor, Milton Obote. Above all, Idi Amin was absolutely not, as he liked to present himself, a simple man, and nor was he stupid: he was, as I hope I have shown, a very complex character indeed.

NOTES

NB Minor changes of punctuation and capitalisation have been made to some of the quoted material in the editing process.

PREFACE

1. Edwards (1991: 407–8).

INTRODUCTION: IDI AMIN DADA, MAN AND MYTH

1. This was the full name he normally used (although he had several other family and tribal names), and there was some argument about whether 'Dada' was a birth name or given as an army nickname. In fact, according to Amin and Akulia (2010) 'Dada' is a clan name in the Kakwa tribe.
2. These are by Twiss (2002), Castleden (2005), Law (2006) and Montefiore (2008) respectively.
3. York (2005) and Clark and Scott (2014) respectively.
4. I have written elsewhere about Amin's image in the movie *The Last King of Scotland* (Leopold, 2013).
5. See Kiwanuka (1979) and Mutibwa (1992).
6. His sons Hussein and Jaffar both support this view (see Chapter 1, and Amin and Akulia, 2010).
7. See e.g. Smith (1980) and Harrell-Bond (1986).
8. Grahame (1980: 9, 12).
9. See Kyemba (1977: 109).
10. Hansen and Twaddle (1988) and Reid (2017).
11. See e.g. Mazrui (1979) and Mamdani (1995). The fact that the Luo and Banyarwanda were not expelled to a Western country, but neighbouring African ones, may be relevant to this. In fact, as we shall see, Amin inherited his Asian policy from Obote.
12. Amin and Akulia (2010: 430).
13. Nabudere (1980: 4).
14. Wooding and Barnett (1980) and Melady and Melady (1977) respectively.
15. See, for example, the summary in Reid (2017: 74–75).
16. Hills (1975: 333).
17. Coren (1974, 1975).
18. Ivory was important to Europeans not least because a growing middle class wanted the material for their piano keys, billiard balls, snuff boxes and cutlery sets, along with many

other luxuries. By the late nineteenth century, one major cutlery manufacturer in Sheffield was using up to 20 tons of ivory per year (Beachey, 1967: 288).

19. Achebe (1988: 261).
20. Moyse-Bartlett (1956: 50).
21. On the Nubi and the legacies of slavery in the region, see Soghayroun (1981), Johnson (1988, 1989, 2009). See also Leopold (2003, 2005, 2006). A key text on this from the colonial period is Stigand (1923, reprinted 1968).
22. See e.g. Pain (1975), Southall (1975), Mazrui (1975a, 1977b) and Kokole (1995).
23. Martin (1974: 14).
24. Quoted in Leopold (2005: 66).
25. Achebe (1988: 254), quoting Conrad.
26. Amin and Akulia (2010: 239).
27. *Daily Telegraph*, 22 July 2003.
28. See, respectively, Grahame (1980), Kyemba (1977), Martin (1974), 'Donald' (1978), 'Kamau and Cameron' (1979), Kato (1989), Smith (1980), Melady and Melady (1977), Benson (1992), Hills (1975), Hale (2009), Measures and Walker (1998), Lawoko (2005), 'Gwyn' (1977) and Allen (1987, 2000).
29. Nayenga (1979: 127).
30. Academic accounts of Amin are rarer than the popular ones, but they certainly exist and are used throughout this book. The most interesting contemporary intellectual debate about him was between the Kenyan-American political scientist Ali Mazrui and the Ugandan-Asian social scientist Mahmoud Mamdani. This was carried out primarily in Mazrui (1975a, 1975b, 1977a, 1977b, 1979) and Mamdani (1973, 1976, 1984, 1995). To simplify, while Mazrui celebrated Amin's 'warrior' image as an assertion of African nationalism and Black power, Mamdani criticised such an analysis as based on racist assumptions. The relationship between Amin's rule and that of his predecessor Obote has also been explored, for example by the Ugandan-Canadian academic A.B.K. Kasozi (1994) and by Samwiri Karugire (1988), then head of the History Department at Makerere University in Kampala. Omara-Otunnu's book (1987) is a fascinating military history of Uganda, while the political, economic and social consequences of the Amin period were analysed in depth in the trilogy of edited collections produced by Holger Hansen and Michael Twaddle (1988, 1991, 1998). More recent work is discussed later.
31. See Leopold (2009).
32. See: https://www.youtube.com/watch?v=2FPrJxTvgdQ.
33. Parkin (1985: 1, 2).
34. Southwold (1985: 131).
35. Taylor (1985: 27).
36. Quoted in Pocock (1985: 42).
37. Parkin (1985: 7).
38. Pocock (1985: 51).
39. Ibid. 56.
40. Ibid.
41. La Fontaine (1998: 14–15).
42. Martin (1974).
43. Ibid. 14.
44. Kyemba (1977: 15).
45. Ibid. 109–110.
46. Grahame (1980: 32).
47. Ibid. 12.
48. Ibid. 14.
49. Smith (1980: 33–34).
50. For example, Grahame and Kyemba were both interviewed (along with myself and other academics working on Amin) for the American PBS TV series *The Dictators' Playbook*, first broadcast 13 February 2019.

51. See Omara-Otunnu (1987), Mutibwa (1992), Kasozi (1994), Kanyeihamba (2010) and Makubuya (2018).
52. Otunnu (2016: 284).
53. Astles (2015: 143).
54. See Arens (1979). Zoologists, on the other hand, have pointed out that it is common in many other species, and have therefore tended, to a much greater extent than social anthropologists or historians, to credit at least some of the cannibal allegations that haunt many human societies (see e.g. Schutt, 2017).
55. Evans-Pritchard (1963).
56. See Behrend (2011).
57. A very literal inversion of the natural order of things, this is a good example of the reversal of norms attributed to evil monsters. Versions of this story are also told in Blandford and Jones (1994), Twiss (2002), Orizio (2004) and Montefiore (2008). Astles (2015: 153) suggests the body was dismembered by the terrified doctor who had accidentally killed her in a botched abortion, in an attempt to hide the corpse. The death of Kay was a central theme in *The Last King of Scotland*.
58. Law (2006: 147).
59. Twiss (2002: 185–186).
60. Blandford and Jones (1994: 15).
61. Ibid. 17.
62. Montefiore (2008: 283).
63. See Leopold (2009: 325).
64. See Southall (1975, 1977, 1980, 1988) and Mazrui (1975a, 1975b, 1977a, 1977b), as well as other papers in Mazrui (1977c).
65. Mazrui (1977a: 77).
66. Mazrui (1975a: 71, 73).
67. Mazrui (1975b: 149).
68. Southall (1975: 101).
69. Ibid. 85.
70. Ibid. 90.
71. He seems to be referring to the West Nilers here, but (as I have argued in Leopold, 2005) it is very difficult indeed to see how they could possibly be described as leading a life unchanged by history.
72. Southall (1977: 166–167).
73. Ugandan sources cited throughout this book include Omara-Otunnu (1987), Mutibwa (1992) and Kasozi (1994). Reliable twenty-first-century histories include those of Otunnu (2016, 2017), Kanyeihamba (2010) and Makubuya (2018). In the West, recent serious reconsideration of the Amin period began with a landmark issue of the *Journal of Eastern African Studies* (vol. 7, no. 1) in 2013, in effect beginning the systematic academic study of the period by Western historians. This work has continued with Decker's (2014) important book on women in Amin's Uganda, and more recently in Richard Reid's (2017) excellent, if rather Buganda-centric, general history of Uganda.
74. *Daily Monitor*, 11 April 2019.
75. Amin and Akulia (2010).
76. www.idiamindada.com

1 'WRUNG FROM THE WITHERS OF THE WESTERN NILE': BACKGROUND, BIRTH AND YOUTH, 1928(?)–46

1. Amin and Akulia (2010).
2. Ade Adefuye in Asiwaju (1985: 67).
3. Listowel (1973: 12). These 'tribal' distinctions are based primarily on linguistic distinctions. Until fairly recently, the Lugbara language was classified as a 'Sudanic' (not 'Nilotic')

language, while Kakwa *was* seen as a Nilotic tongue. More recent (known as 'Post-Greenbergian') historical linguistics classifies both as 'Nilo-Saharan' languages.

4. Martin (1974: 14).
5. 'Gwyn' (1977: 15)
6. Ibid. 24.
7. Smith (1980: 25).
8. Ibid. 42.
9. Melady and Melady (1977: 9).
10. Hale (2009: 33–34).
11. The Baganda are the dominant tribe in Uganda, from whom the country gets its English name. With British military help, they came to control virtually all of the south of the country in the late nineteenth century, and their ruling aristocracy worked closely with the colonial regime. The people are called *Baganda* (singular *Muganda*), sometimes abbreviated to *Ganda*, their land is *Buganda*, the language is *Luganda*, and the adjectival form of the name is *kiganda*.
12. Kiwanuka (1979: 13).
13. Kato (1989: 4).
14. Harrell-Bond (1986: 33).
15. Sembuya (2009: 32).
16. Southall (1975: 101).
17. 'Kamau and Cameron' (1979: 28–29).
18. Grahame (1980: 23).
19. See e.g. UKNA FCO 31/1055: Periodical Report of Defence Advisor, British High Commission, Kampala 1 January 1971–30 September 1971; UKNA FCO 31/1961: Brief for Secretary of State J. Callaghan's visit to Uganda, 9 July 1975; UKNA FCO 31/2667: Leading Personalities in Uganda, 1975.
20. Omari Kokole cited in Jorgensen (1981: 320).
21. Such as Decker (2014).
22. Amin and Akulia (2010). Interestingly, the highly imaginative 'Kamau and Cameron' account gives the same year as Jaffar, unlike most other versions.
23. Another variant is Emin, as in Emin Pasha.
24. Listowel (1973: 18).
25. Smith (1980: 64).
26. Amin and Akulia (2010: 39).
27. This was the Kakwa 'chief' appointed by the Sudanese authorities; at the time, West Nile was annexed to the Anglo-Egyptian Condominium of Sudan, before being transferred to British-controlled Uganda.
28. Tanganyika was a German colony in 1914, and so it was regarded as enemy territory by the British.
29. Amin and Akulia (2010: 42–43).
30. Ibid. 47.
31. Ibid. 60.
32. Ibid. 54.
33. In English literature, such stories range from Thomas Malory's *Morte d'Arthur* (1485) to Philip Pullman's *His Dark Materials* trilogy (1995).
34. Amin and Akulia (2010: 60–61).
35. Ibid. 63.
36. Ibid. 64.
37. Ibid. 62.
38. See e.g. Martin (1974), 'Kamau and Cameron' (1979), Smith (1980), Sembuya (2009), Dougherty (2010).
39. 'Kamau and Cameron' (1979: 29).
40. Smith (1980: 42).

41. Martin (1974: 14–15).
42. I have written about Yakan in this context in Leopold (2005: 82–107).
43. Listowel (1973: 15).
44. 'Kamau and Cameron' (1979: 29).
45. Smith (1980: 41).
46. Ibid. 42.
47. Ibid. 37.
48. Ibid. 43.
49. Ibid. 41.
50. 'Donald' (1978: 19–21).
51. Amin and Akulia (2010: 55).
52. Ibid. 56.
53. See Leopold (2005: ch. 5).
54. Jorgensen (1981: 41).
55. Ibid.
56. This is obviously a very brief account of a complex history. There is no space here to do justice to the story of British colonialism in Uganda, nor to the longer history of Uganda itself. This account is largely taken from Jorgensen (1981: ch. 1). A more recent, excellent if idiosyncratic, history of Uganda (focusing largely, as do most histories, on Buganda and the south) is Reid (2017). A very readable popular account of the building of the railway is Miller (1971).
57. Winston Churchill, quoted in Grahame (1980: 52).
58. This is, of course, something of a travesty of the complex historical relationship between the Baganda and the British, but the present book is not the place for a more detailed and nuanced account. The topic has been extensively covered, for example by Low (1971: ch. 3), Otunnu (2016: ch. 2), Reid (2017: ch. 5).
59. Listowel (1973: 12).
60. Kato (1989: 4).
61. Various terms for the East Africa desk – 'East Africa Department', 'East Africa Political Department', or sometimes it is referred to as a 'Section' – appear in the archival material as the official name changed fairly often (as did the name of the ministry). This book will use 'East Africa desk' in the main text and EAD in the notes; references in quoted material will remain as they appear in the original source.
62. UKNA FCO 31/2145: A.C. Stuart to M.K. Ewans, EAD.
63. I have written about the pre-colonial history of the region at greater length elsewhere. See Leopold 2003, 2005, 2006.
64. Middleton (1971: 17).
65. King (1970: 22) and Geria (1973: 77).
66. See Uganda National Archives (UNA) file A46/794:810: Northern Uganda Provincial Report for 1917.
67. See Rhodes House Library, Oxford, Mss Afr.s.1638: Weatherhead's diary for 4 March, 22 March and 13–30 May 1918.
68. See UNA file A46/811: Northern Province Annual Report for 1918–19 and RH Mss Afr.s.1638: Weatherhead's diary for 13–30 May 1918.
69. Driberg (1931) and McConnell (1925).
70. Middleton (1971: 13).
71. Driberg (1931: 420).
72. Amin and Akulia (2010: 56).
73. King (1970: 8).
74. UKNA WO106/253:112: Hogg to Chief Secretary, 5 January 1920. Most of the archival evidence we have on the Yakan Uprising is from this trial evidence, and it is the basis of most published accounts of Yakan (as well as Driberg's article, these include King, 1970; Middleton, 1971; and others cited in Leopold, 2005).

75. In my doctoral thesis (Leopold, 2001) I argued that Weatherhead's diary (which had not previously been cited by scholars) provides further evidence that Hogg was right, and that in fact Driberg had invented much of the uprising. He was later 'allowed to resign' from the Sudan Political Service for inventing another 'uprising' there.
76. King (1970: 15).
77. Amin and Akulia (2010: 63).
78. Ibid. 64.
79. Ibid. 70.
80. King (1970).
81. I have explored this theme at length in Leopold (2005).
82. Grahame (1980: 9).
83. Ibid. 12.
84. Kyemba (1977: 109).
85. Mazrui (1975b: 46–47).
86. Ibid. 76.
87. Asiwaju (1985: 67).
88. Martin (1974: 14).
89. Grahame (1980: 9).
90. Smith (1980: 34).
91. 'Gwyn' (1977: 24).
92. Kato (1989: 4).
93. 'Kamau and Cameron' (1979: 30).
94. Shaw (2013: 100).
95. Listowel (1973: 15).
96. Ibid. 19–20.
97. Martin (1974: 14–16).
98. Smith (1980: 45–46).
99. Amin and Akulia (2010: 66–67).
100. Ibid. 68.
101. Ibid. 69.
102. Ibid. 75.
103. Ibid. 76.

2 'HE COMES FROM A FIGHTING RACE': LIFE IN THE KING'S AFRICAN RIFLES, 1946(?)–59

1. Moyse-Bartlett (1956: 3).
2. This category included many, from both Sudan and the Swahili coast of East Africa, who were not actually Arabs (in the racialised terms of the time), but were African Muslims with strong links to aspects of Arabic culture.
3. These initially included many Indian soldiers.
4. Moyse-Bartlett (1956: 11).
5. Ibid. 123.
6. Amin and Akulia (2010: 45).
7. Ibid.
8. Ibid. 76.
9. See Atkinson (1994).
10. I have discussed this attitude, and other aspects of Uganda's 'north–south' divide, in relation to Ugandan press coverage of conflict in northern Uganda in the 1990s, in Leopold (1999).
11. Moyse-Bartlett (1956: 685).
12. References to this occur throughout the book, even in his discussion of the uniforms of the Uganda Rifles and then the KAR (in his Appendix A, ibid. 689–690).

13. Ibid. 686.
14. Page (2011).
15. UKNA FCO 31/1024: IRD Biographical Report on Amin (27 January 1971).
16. UKNA FCO 31/1026: Leading Personalities in Uganda 1971.
17. UKNA FCO 31/1055: Periodical report (30 October 1971).
18. UKNA FCO 31/2667: Leading Personalities in Uganda 1975.
19. UKNA FCO 31/1961: Briefing for Sec. of State's visit to Uganda July 1975.
20. Amin and Akulia (2010: 77).
21. Ibid. 78–79.
22. Ibid. 79.
23. 'Kamau and Cameron' (1979: 30–31). G.I. Smith, who also uses this quote, attributes it to the (British) *Sunday Times* newspaper, and names the sergeant as Jim Gregor. He joined the KAR in 1958, when Amin was a platoon commander with the rank of Warrant Officer, a slightly higher rank than Gregor (Smith, 1980: 48).
24. 'Gwyn' (1977: 25).
25. Rhodes House Library, Oxford, KAR Files. Mss Afr.s.1715, Box 18.
26. Rhodes House Library, Oxford, KAR Files. Mss Afr.s.1715, Box 3.
27. UKNA FCO 31/1624: A.H. Brind, Some Reflections on Leaving Uganda, 16 July 1973.
28. UKNA FCO 31/1624: Ewans to Hennessey, 13 September 1973.
29. Smith (1980: 48).
30. Mazrui (1977b: 131).
31. Grahame (1980: 14–15).
32. On the history of these markings, see Leopold (2006).
33. Grahame (1980: 20).
34. Amin and Akulia (2010: 81).
35. Listowel (1973: 20).
36. Amin and Akulia (2010: 84).
37. Listowel (1973: 21–22).
38. 'Gwyn' (1977: 25).
39. Smith (1980: 50).
40. In his earlier book, he says it was ten years (Grahame, 1966: 190).
41. Grahame (1980: 34–35).
42. Amin and Akulia (2010: 100).
43. Allen (2000: 61–62).
44. There is a photograph of Peach on parade, on Facebook, posted by his son. See: www.facebook.com/HIPUganda/photos/a.158607877548400.39687.154821697927018/797194547023060/?type=1&theater (accessed 4 June 2020).
45. Allen (2000: 88).
46. Listowel (1973: 23).
47. See the accounts by Anderson (2005) and Elkins (2005).
48. Quoted in Listowel (1973: 23–24).
49. Ibid. 24.
50. See Leopold (2009).
51. 'Gwyn' (1977: 26).
52. Martin (1974: 18).
53. Smith (1980: 51–52).
54. 'Kamau and Cameron' (1979: 32).
55. Ibid. 33.
56. Ibid. 34.
57. Ibid. 37.
58. Ibid. 36–37.
59. Martin (1974: 17).
60. Ibid.
61. Smith (1980: 49).

62. Amin and Akulia (2010: 81). The number is confirmed in the official 'Supplement to the London Gazette' when Amin was promoted to the rank of Effendi in 1961. See: www.thegazette.co.uk/London/issue/42461/supplement/6682/data.pdf (accessed 3 June 2020).
63. Grahame (1980: 22).
64. Grahame (1966: 199).
65. Ibid. 190.
66. See also the 1974 correspondence in UKNA FCO 31/1781.
67. Anderson (2005: 7).
68. Grahame (1980: 24).
69. Ibid. 23.
70. Ibid. 32.
71. Ibid. 33.
72. Ibid. 35.
73. The KAR had both African and British sergeants, who obviously could not eat and drink together.
74. Grahame (1980: 35).
75. Listowel (1973: 22).
76. This suggestive phrase is used by David C. Martin (not the David Martin who wrote the book on Amin) as the title of a book on CIA covert operations in the 1960s and 1970s.
77. In a footnote, Grahame explains that 'Sudi' is 'an abbreviation for Sudanese or Nubian' (Grahame, 1980: 39).
78. Ibid.
79. Brown and Brown (1996: 34).
80. Amin and Akulia (2010: 95).
81. Ibid. 97.
82. Vyner (1999: 43).
83. See Leopold (2009).
84. Grahame (1980: 40–41).
85. Quoted in Smith (1980: 49–50).
86. UKNA DO 213/50: Command Structure of the Uganda Army.
87. UKNA DO 213/50: G.G. Griffith to N. Aspin, Commonwealth Relations Office, 27 January 1964.
88. Amin and Akulia (2010: 103–104).
89. Hespeler-Boultbee (2012: 116–117).
90. Ibid. 118.
91. Ibid. 120.
92. Ibid. 121.
93. Ibid. 122.

3 A RESISTIBLE RISE? 1959–65

1. Quoted in Page (2011: 210).
2. Gikandi (1996: 15).
3. I have applied under access legislation to look at several 'closed files' in the UK National Archives. Of those which have eventually been released to me, none have been of any interest for my present purposes.
4. Parsons (2003: 53).
5. Ibid. 71.
6. Apter (1961: 468).
7. Parsons (2003: 71).

8. Around this time, DP supporters began to refer to the UPC as the 'United Protestants of Canterbury' for their somewhat cynical support of the Anglican aristocrats.

9. Rhodes House Library, Oxford, KAR Files. Mss Afr.s.1715, Box 10, Maj. Suresh Khanna (3KAR Kenya 1961–64) [sent Aug. 1979].

10. Rhodes House Library, Oxford, KAR Files. Mss Afr.s.1715, Box 3, Lt Col. H.K.P. Chavasse, MBE, Royal Irish Rangers (4KAR Uganda 1960–62) [sent July 1979].

11. Rhodes House Library, Oxford, KAR Files. Mss Afr.s.1715, Box 18, Maj. R.D. West (4KAR Uganda 1958–60) [sent Dec. 1979].

12. Most of the material in this section comes from the later Foreign Office investigation into the 'incident', undertaken to answer a parliamentary question on the degree to which Amin's activities had been known to the British authorities before independence. The quote above is from para. 4 of a briefing note headed 'Operation Utah: Incident involving Lieutenant Idi Amin', dated 25 March 1977, in UKNA FCO 31/2145.

13. Ibid. para. 3.

14. Ibid. para. 4.

15. UKNA FCO 31/2145: Lord Goronwy Roberts to Lord Bruce of Donington, 5 April 1977.

16. UKNA FCO 31/2145: 'Operation Utah: Incident involving Lieutenant Idi Amin', report dated 25 March 1977, para. 12.

17. Ibid. para. 13.

18. Ibid. para. 18.

19. UKNA FCO 31/2145: Minister of State (Lord Goronwy Roberts) to Lord Bruce of Donington, 5 April 1977.

20. UKNA FCO 31/2145: Briefing note: 'Operation Utah: Incident involving Lieutenant Idi Amin', dated 25 March 1977.

21. Ibid.

22. Ibid. para. 28.

23. Anderson (2005: 326).

24. UKNA FCO 31/2145: Briefing note: 'Operation Utah: Incident involving Lieutenant Idi Amin', dated 25 March 1977, para. 29.

25. Ibid. para. 30.

26. For example, the blame attributed by the report to senior KAR officers was omitted from the letter.

27. UKNA FCO 31/2145: Minister of State (Lord Goronwy Roberts) to Lord Bruce of Donington, 5 April 1977.

28. Ingham (1994: 90–91).

29. Ingham's biography of Obote was reviewed by the Ugandan legal scholar Joe Oloka-Onyango under the appropriate heading 'Biography as Apologia' (Oloka-Onyango, 1996). In fact, Ingham was wholly *un*apologetic about his deep admiration for the subject of his book.

30. Parsons (2003: 75).

31. Ingham (1994: 91).

32. Parsons (2003: 74).

33. The second battalion is covered in several documents in UKNA DO 213/53 (Uganda Army General Matters), and the air force in UKNA DO 213/149 (Formation of Uganda Air Wing). Both discuss the growing Israeli role.

34. Parsons (2003: 74).

35. UKNA DO 213/53 (Uganda Army General Matters): Despatch from Acting High Commissioner to Uganda to Secretary of State for Commonwealth Affairs.

36. Parsons (2003: 2).

37. Zanzibar and Tanganyika together became the new country of Tanzania in April 1964.

38. Parsons (2003: 101).

39. Ibid. 115.

40. Ibid. 116.

41. Ibid.
42. Ingham (1994: 92).
43. Parsons (2003: 125).
44. Ingham (1994: 92).
45. Amin and Akulia (2010: 124–125).
46. Parsons (2003: 214).
47. Ingham (1994: 92).
48. Parsons (2003: 150).
49. Ibid. 158.
50. Ibid. 195.
51. Ibid.
52. Ingham (1994: 92–93).
53. Otunnu (2016: 229).
54. Ibid.
55. Ibid. 228.
56. UKNA DO 213/50: Hunt to Garner, 21 January 1964.
57. UKNA DO 213/50: Telegram, Hunt to Commonwealth Relations Office (copied to Nairobi), 14 February 1964.
58. According to Hunt's 14 February telegram, Tillet also had asthma, and his father had recently died.
59. UKNA DO 213/50: Telegram, Hunt to Commonwealth Relations Office (copied to Nairobi), 15 February 1964.
60. Ibid.
61. Ibid.
62. This may have meant it was supplied by the British Secret Intelligence Service, generally known as MI6.
63. UKNA DO 213/50: Telegram, Walsh Atkins (Commonwealth Relations Office) to Hunt 28 February 1964. I have found no other trace of this Ghanaian link in the records.
64. UKNA DO 213/53: T.W. Aston, Acting High Commissioner, to Secretary of State, 10 September 1964, para. 7.
65. UKNA DO 213/50: Appendix to letter from Commander, British Land Forces: Army, 6 February 1964.
66. Ibid. para. 11.
67. Ibid. para 16.
68. Ibid.
69. Omara-Otunnu (1987: 61–62).
70. In UKNA DO 213/50. The implication that the British themselves did not use 'strong-arm techniques' is an interesting one.
71. UKNA DO 213/53: T.W. Aston, Acting High Commissioner, to Secretary of State, 30 September 1964, para. 25.
72. Ibid. paras 27–28.
73. Ibid. para. 31.
74. Ibid. para. 1.
75. However, as the British Military Attache remarked in a memo dated 16 March 1964: 'of course everyone knows that while still in Kenya they [i.e. British troops] are only four hours away'. UKNA DO 213/53: M. Reith to G.J. Price-Jones, EAD, Commonwealth Relations Office.
76. UKNA DO 213/53: T.W. Aston, Acting High Commissioner, to Secretary of State, 30 September 1964, para. 39.
77. Ibid. para. 41.
78. As well as being close to the Ganda aristocracy, Opolot had spent much of his military service in 5KAR, the Kenyan branch, which had not provided many useful contacts in the new Ugandan army.
79. Kyemba (1977: 24).

80. Karugire (1980: 196).
81. I have written elsewhere about this stereotype of 'the North', among both southern Ugandans and their British admirers. See particularly Leopold (1999).
82. Kanyeihamba (2010: 93).
83. Amin and Akulia (2010: 111).
84. Ibid. 113.
85. Idi Amin's oldest son, considered the head of the family since his father's death.
86. Amin and Akulia (2010: 117–119). 'Uhurus' were babies born around nine months after independence, supposedly conceived on the eve of self-determination.
87. Here, Decker cites 'Kamau and Cameron', the pseudonymous Rhodesian journalist and self-confessed fantasist.
88. Decker (2014: 16).
89. Grahame (1980: 82).
90. Ibid. 83.
91. Astles (2015: 48).
92. Omara-Otunnu (1987: 71).

4 AMIN AND OBOTE, 1965-69

1. Otunnu (2016: 158).
2. Ibid.
3. Karugire (1980: 189).
4. Kasozi (1994: 61).
5. Kanyeihamba (2010: 76–77).
6. Kasozi (1994: 71).
7. Ibid. 62.
8. Ibid. 63.
9. UKNA DO 213/35: Aston to N. Aspin, East and Central Africa Department, Commonwealth Relations Office, 22 June 1965.
10. UKNA DO 213/35: Aston to Ministry of Defence, 2 October 1964.
11. UKNA DO 213/35: Extract of a letter by Col. Senior, from W.F.S. No. 4/65, 27 February 1965.
12. UKNA DO 213/35: 'Uganda: The Politics of Defence', Confidential Print. British High Commissioner (Hunt) to Sec. of State for Commonwealth Relations, 20 August 1965.
13. Ibid.
14. UKNA DO 213/35: Col. V.J. Senior, Defence Advisor, Note for the Record, 22 October 1965.
15. UKNA DO 213/35: R.C.C. Hunt to G.W. St. J. Chadwick, CRO, 24 October 1965.
16. Karugire (1988: 55).
17. The Congo was a key Cold War ally of the West, not least because most of the world's known reserves of uranium, needed for nuclear bombs, were to be found in the country.
18. Jorgensen (1981: 228).
19. Kyemba (1977: 24).
20. Astles (2015: 101–102).
21. UKNA FCO 16/132: Newton Dunn to MOD [Ministry of Defence], etc., 28 August 1967.
22. Amin and Akulia (2010: 130–131).
23. Adoko (n.d. [1967]: 7).
24. Ibid. 9–10.
25. Ibid. 12.
26. Ibid. 16. Elgon and Ruwenzori are Ugandan mountains.
27. Ibid. 78–79.
28. Posnett was an interesting character, who knew Amin well, having been the district commissioner for West Nile for a number of years (he even spoke a little Kakwa, a very

rare accomplishment). For a couple of days during the 1962 transfer of power, he formally held the post of president of Uganda, before handing over to the Kabaka. He then returned to London to head the Commonwealth Office's EAD. I interviewed Sir Richard Posnett in 2008.

29. UKNA DO 213/62: R.N. Posnett, Commonwealth Relations Office, to P.M. Forster, British High Commissioner to Uganda, 22 April 1966.
30. UKNA DO 213/62: P.M. Forster, British High Commissioner to Uganda, to R.N. Posnett, Commonwealth Relations Office, 4 May 1966.
31. Ibingira (1973: 288).
32. Obote (1969: passim).
33. Kabaka of Buganda (1967: 186).
34. Quoted in Jorgensen (1981: 230).
35. Kyemba (1977: 26–27).
36. Amin and Akulia (2010: 139).
37. Kabaka of Buganda (1967: 13–22); the book was ghostwritten by a British Conservative journalist, Mark Amory.
38. Mutibwa (1992: 39).
39. UKNA DO 213/35: P.M. Forster to Michael Scott, EAD, Commonwealth Office, 8 November 1966.
40. Decker (2014: 17).
41. Ibid. 18.
42. Astles (2015: 145).
43. Ibid. 146–147.
44. Ibid. 147.
45. Amin and Akulia (2010: 152).
46. Kyemba (1977: 146).
47. Ibid. 147.
48. Decker (2014: 16–19).
49. Astles (2015: 150).
50. Jorgensen (1981: 231).
51. Kyemba (1977: 27).
52. Tabaire (2007).
53. Mujaju (1987: 502).
54. Karugire (1980: 196).
55. Kyemba (1977: 28).
56. Ibingira (1973: 288).
57. Reid (2017: 234).
58. Ibid. 234–235.
59. Ibid. 235.
60. Ibid.
61. UKNA FCO 31/182: Hunt, memo to Commonwealth Office, 23 February 1967.
62. At the time, Hunt had been severely and openly criticised by Obote in a press conference, and he may have been in an angry mood. See UKNA FCO 31/182: letter from the Private Secretary of the British Minister of State for the Commonwealth Office, to the Prime Minister's Office, dated 24 February 1967.
63. In a letter dated 10 February 1970, the high commissioner wrote to the EAD that Amin was 'chastened after his attempt in 1967 to get rid of Obote', in UKNA FCO 31/710.
64. UKNA FCO 16/132: M.C. Oatley (BHC, K'la [British High Commissioner, Kampala]) to M. Scott, esq, EAD, Commonwealth Office, 21 August 1967.
65. UKNA FCO 31/184: *The People*, 25 October 1967. Attachment to letter from High Commissioner Wenham-Smith to L. Reid of the FCO EAD dated 30 October 1967.
66. UKNA FCO 16/132: memo: Visit by Army Officers to Defence Advisor on Sunday 16 July 1967.

67. UKNA FCO 16/132: Newton Dunn to MOD, etc., 28 August 1967.
68. UKNA FCO 16/132: Col. T.N. Newton Dunn MC to Col. P.H. Noir, OBE, MC, Ministry of Defence, 16 August 1967.
69. UKNA FCO 16/132: Newton Dunn to Assistant High Commissioner, 5 January 1968. Record of conversation with Colonel Bar-Lev.
70. UKNA FCO 16/132: Newton Dunn to MOD, 24 January 1968.
71. UKNA FCO 16/132: enclosure dated 29 January 1968.
72. UKNA FCO 16/133: Crawford to High Commissioner, 21 June 1968.
73. UKNA FCO 16/133: Crawford to MOD, 1 October 1968.
74. UKNA FCO 31/184: Wenham-Smith to Tallboys, 2 October 1968.
75. UKNA FCO 31/184: Forster to Tallboys, 2 October 1968.
76. UKNA FCO 31/184: Scott to Tallboys, 4 October 1968.
77. UKNA FCO 31/468/1: R.J.R. Owen to Scott, 21 October 1968.
78. UKNA FCO 31/468/1: Tallboys to Scott, 25 October 1968.
79. UKNA FCO 31/493: Le Tocq to Tebbit, 14 January 1969.
80. UKNA FCO 31/493: Wenham-Smith to Tallboys, 2 January 1969.
81. Astles (2015: 153).

5 'MARTIAL MUSIC': THE BUILD-UP, THE COUP AND THE AFTERMATH, 1969-71

1. Bloch and Fitzgerald (1983: 167).
2. Obote (n.d. [1970]).
3. Ibid. 4.
4. Ibid. 9-10.
5. Ibid. 37-38.
6. Mazrui (1979: 262).
7. Lawoko (2005: 40).
8. See, for example, the article by Henry Lubega in the *Daily Monitor* newspaper of 17 June 2018.
9. UKNA FCO 31/472: Scott to FCO, 22 December 1969.
10. Ingham (1994: 125).
11. Lawoko (2005: 44).
12. Mutibwa (1992: 71).
13. Ibid. 72.
14. UKNA FCO 31/710: W.N. Wenham-Smith to R.N. Purcell, EAD, letter dated 10 February 1970.
15. UKNA FCO 31/710: N. Crawford, memo dated 4 February 1970 (enclosure to above letter to EAD).
16. UKNA FCO 31/710: Wenham-Smith to Purcell (EAD), 10 February 1970.
17. Ibid.
18. Martin (1974: 24).
19. Mamdani (1976: 292).
20. Ibid. 293.
21. Steiner (1978: 192).
22. Ibid. 212.
23. Ibid. 213.
24. Astles (2015: 15).
25. Kato (1989: xv).
26. Kasozi (1994: 102-103).
27. Mutibwa (1992: 74).
28. Kasozi (1994: 102).
29. Mamdani (1976: 292).
30. Mutibwa (1992: 76).

31. Kyemba (1977: 33).
32. Mutibwa (1992: 74–76).
33. Amin and Akulia (2010: 183).
34. Mutibwa (1992: 76).
35. See e.g. Kasozi (1994: 102–103), Mamdani (1976: 292–294), Mutibwa (1992: 74–76), Karugire (1988: 72), Otunnu (2016: 234), Kanyeihamba (2010: 109) and Kyemba (1977: 32–34).
36. Heath's comment is mentioned in Bloch and Fitzgerald (1983: 163) and in Hebditch and Connor (2009: 128), both citing the British satirical magazine *Private Eye* dated 27 April 1979 – rather a long time after the events. Various different wordings of this remark are quoted in the Amin literature, and the original source of the quote is unclear.
37. Lofchie (1972: 19). Mamdani, on the other hand, argued that the army was supported by the petty-bourgeoisie (especially in Buganda), while Obote's support he sees as being primarily among 'bureaucrats' and 'kulaks' (a Russian term for comparatively wealthy peasants, much used by Lenin).
38. Mamdani (1976: 287).
39. Omara-Otunnu (1987: 93).
40. Lofchie (1972: 35).
41. Ibid. 35.
42. Mamdani (1975: 54).
43. Mamdani (1984: 31).
44. UKNA FCO 31/1043: Slater to Harold Smedley (Foreign Office Permanent Secretary), 25 May 1971.
45. Otunnu (2016: 234).
46. Omara-Otunnu (1987: 97).
47. This is, for example, the view of Hebditch and Connor (2009).
48. UKNA FCO 31/1023: Slater to FCO, 25 January 1971.
49. Ibid.
50. From Government of Uganda (n.d. [1972a]), titled *Uganda, the First 366 Days of the Second Republic*. Slater's letter of 25 January (cited in note 51) contains a nearly identical contemporary account of Aswa's statement.
51. UKNA FCO 31/1023: Slater to FCO, 25 January 1971.
52. Ibid.
53. Kasozi (1994: 103).
54. Kanyeihamba (2010: 109).
55. UKNA FCO 31/1023: British High Commission Nairobi to BBC Monitoring Service, 25 January 1971.
56. Alibhai-Brown (1997: 172).
57. Alibhai-Brown (2008: 238).
58. Allen (2000: 310). As we have seen before, Allen's 'Diary' may be unreliable; no other source says that Wilfred Aswa was named in the broadcast; his name (sometimes spelt Waswa) became public later. His rank is also variously given; an official Amin government publication (Government of Uganda, 1972a) and Mutibwa (1992) both say he was a Warrant Officer.
59. Nabudere (1980: 280).
60. Measures and Walker (1998: 44).
61. Benson (1992: 73).
62. Wober (1973).
63. The Caversham House term 'Western-type' music sounds more like a description of pop tunes than military ones, but most listeners remember the latter.
64. A somewhat comparable case is that of Churchill's famous 'we shall fight on the beaches' speech, which very many contemporaries remembered clearly hearing on the radio at the time, though it was not broadcast then (see Stourton, 2017: 130–131).

65. Southall (1975: 100).
66. Quote from *Uganda Argus* newspaper, 27 January 1971.
67. Quote from (Kenyan) *Daily Nation* newspaper, 15 February 1971.
68. Mittelman (1975: 173–174).
69. Lawoko (2005: 53).
70. Ibid. 65.
71. Amin and Akulia (2010: 184–185).
72. Ibid. 189.
73. FCO 31/1024: W.E. Stober, Africa Section, Research Department (R707) to Purcell, EAD, 14 April 1971.
74. FCO 31/1024: 'The Uganda Coup: Amin Tells How It Happened', *The Daily Nation* (Nairobi), Monday 15 February 1971, attached to letter from R.A.C. Byatt to R.M. Purcell of the FCO, dated 5 March.
75. UKNA FCO 31/1023: Slater to FCO (and many more Whitehall addressees), 26 January 1971.
76. UKNA FCO 31/1023: EAD, FCO, to Sir Stuart Crawford (attachment: note on the security situation in Uganda for Chiefs of Staff meeting, 26 January 1971).
77. UKNA FCO 31/1023: Slater to FCO, telno 57 of 26 January 1971.
78. UKNA FCO 31/1023: telno 67 of 26 January 1971.
79. UKNA FCO 31/1023: telno 72 of 26 January 1971.
80. All quotes from UKNA FCO 31/1023: Slater to FCO, telno 77 of 27 January 1971.
81. UKNA FCO 31/1023: Slater to FCO, telno 78 of 27 January 1971.
82. From UKNA FCO 31/1023: telno 81 of 27 January 1971.
83. Campbell (1975: 51–56).
84. Ibid. 56.
85. Astles (2015: 141).
86. Ibid. 167.
87. Ibid.
88. Ibid. 140–141.
89. UKNA FCO 31/1043: Slater to Harold Smedley, 25 May 1971.
90. UKNA FCO 31/1023: Slater to FCO, telno 131 of 1 February 1971.
91. UKNA FCO 31/1023: Slater to FCO, telno 139 of 1 February 1971.
92. UKNA FCO 31/1024: Slater, letter to Sir Alec Douglas-Home, 15 February 1971.
93. Omara-Otunnu (1987: 101).
94. *Uganda Argus*, 25 February 1971, quoted in Otunnu (2016: 252).
95. Otunnu (2016: 254).
96. Ibid. 250.
97. Moghal (2010: 81).
98. Kiwanuka (1979: 55).
99. Otunnu (2016: 259).
100. Hebditch and Connor (2009).
101. Quoted in Otunnu (2016: 248).
102. Jorgensen (1981: 273).
103. Hansen (2013: 87).

6 A HONEYMOON AND FOUR DIVORCES: THE FIRST TWO YEARS OF UGANDA'S SECOND REPUBLIC, 1971-73

1. These include Mutibwa (1992) and Hansen (2013).
2. *Uganda Argus*, 27 January 1971.
3. Omara-Otunnu (1987: 102).
4. Ibid. 103.

5. UKNA FCO 31/1072: Booth, Assistant High Commissioner, Tg. [telegram] to EAD 2 July 1971.
6. The British high commissioner to Tanzania, to whom the telegram was copied as a matter of routine, described this as 'grossly exaggerated and it is difficult to believe he expects us to take it seriously', in UKNA FCO 31/1072: Tg, British High Commissioner Evans to FCO 5 July 1971.
7. Ibid.
8. UKNA FCO 31/1072: Booth Tg. to EAD 2 July 1971.
9. UKNA FCO 31/1072: Douglas-Home Tg. to British High Commissioner Kampala 5 July 1971.
10. UKNA FCO 31/1072: Booth to FCO Tg. 10 July 1971.
11. UKNA FCO 31/1072: Booth to FCO Tg. 12 July 1971.
12. UKNA FCO 31/1072: Booth to Le Tocq Tg. 12 July 1971.
13. UKNA FCO 31/1073: Account of press conference in memo from Mr Duggan, EAD, to Le Tocq, 14 July 1971.
14. UKNA FCO 31/1073: Foster, Tel Aviv to FCO 12 July 1971.
15. UKNA FCO 31/1072: FCO to High Commission Kampala, telno 726 of 9 July 1971.
16. UKNA FCO 31/1073: Briefing Note: General Amin's visit, call on Secretary of State, Annex D. 'Personality Notes'.
17. In UKNA FCO 31/1073.
18. Ibid.
19. *Daily Telegraph*, 12 July 1971.
20. In UKNA FCO 31/1073.
21. UKNA FCO 31/1073: Account of Press Conference in memo from Mr Duggan, EAD, to Le Tocq, 14 July 1971.
22. Wheen (2009).
23. UKNA FCO 31/1073: United Kingdom Passport Holders in Uganda: Note of a meeting at the Home Office on Tuesday, 13 July 1971.
24. UKNA FCO 31/1073: Duggan, EAD, memo: Ugandan Military Expenditure, 13 July 1971.
25. UKNA FCO 31/1073: Duggan, Brief for the Minister's Meeting with President Amin, 13 July 1971.
26. UKNA FCO 31/1073: Note of a Meeting Between the Minister for Overseas Development and Mr Wakhweya Minister of Finance Uganda ... on 15 July 1971.
27. That is, the aide-de-camp of his formal host, Lieutenant General Sir Henry Leask, General Officer Commanding, Scotland, and Governor of Edinburgh Castle.
28. UKNA FCO 31/1073: Seton Dearden, letter to William Patterson (FCO), 18 July 1971.
29. Quoted in UKNA FCO 31/1073: EAD to 'Savidge, Guidance Dept, FCO', 16 July 1971.
30. UKNA FCO 31/1073: 'Barnes', Tel Aviv, to FCO, 19 July 1971.
31. UKNA FCO 31/1073: Slater, letter to Le Tocq, EAD, 20 July.
32. This account is taken from the International Commission of Jurists' (ICJ) 1974 report into *Violations of Human Rights and the Rule of Law in Uganda*.
33. Kasfir (1976: 216).
34. Ibid. 219.
35. Ibid. 220.
36. Otunnu (2016: 261).
37. Omara-Otunnu (1987: 104).
38. Mutibwa (1992: 88).
39. UKNA FCO 31/1325: Acting British High Commissioner A.H. Brind, Uganda: annual review for 1971 (dated 11 January 1972).
40. Otunnu (2016: 262-263).
41. Omara-Otunnu (1987: 107-108).
42. Kasozi (1994: 112).
43. Omara-Otunnu (1987: 103).

44. UKNA FCO 31/1325: Acting British High Commissioner A.H. Brind, Uganda: annual review for 1971 (dated 11 January 1972).
45. Kasozi (1994: 116); see also Kanyeihamba (2010: 135).
46. UKNA FCO 31/1325: Acting British High Commissioner A.H. Brind, Uganda: annual review for 1971 (dated 11 January 1972).
47. Ibid.
48. Respectively, Government of Uganda (n.d. [1971], n.d. [1972b], n.d. [1972a], n.d. [1973]).
49. In these early publications, Amin gave himself no fancy medals or titles, apart from 'General', 'President' and 'His Excellency'.
50. See Omara-Otunnu (1987: 110).
51. Government of Uganda (n.d. [1972a]).
52. Ibid. i.
53. Ibid. 46–47.
54. Ibid. 49.
55. Ibid. 56–57.
56. Ibid. 59–60.
57. Ibid. 53–54.
58. Ibid. 55.
59. Kasozi (1994: 110).
60. Ibid. 107.
61. Otunnu (2016: 244).
62. Ibid.
63. Quoted in ibid. 245.
64. Government of Uganda (n.d. [1972a]: 59).
65. Otunnu (2016: 247).
66. Ibid. 247–248.
67. UKNA FCO 31/1325: Acting British High Commissioner A.H. Brind, Uganda: annual review for 1971 (dated 11 January 1972).
68. UKNA FCO 31/1587: Acting British High Commissioner A.H. Brind, Uganda: annual review for 1972 (dated 5 January 1973).
69. UKNA FCO 31/1338: Letter, Brind to Dawbarn, EAD, FCO 3 January 1972.
70. UKNA FCO 31/1338: Memo. P.M. Forster, EAD, 14 January 1972.
71. Ibid.
72. Mutibwa (1992: 89–90).
73. UKNA FCO 31/1325: Acting British High Commissioner A.H. Brind, Uganda: annual review for 1971 (dated 11 January 1972).
74. Mazrui (1975b: 221–222).
75. Amin and Akulia (2010: 180, 213, 220).
76. Ibid. 181.
77. Ibid. 211. Jaffar Amin gets the sequence wrong here (not for the only time). His father went to Libya first, *then* to Saudi Arabia, after first returning to Uganda to denounce Israel.
78. Ibid. Jaffar goes on to explain that: 'Dad was honoured with accolades and faithfully honoured those who revered him by pinning their numerous accolades on to his broad chest, to the amusement of the Western media. The Western media saw this action by Dad as self-aggrandizing behaviour and failed to note that the medals were to display the unwavering support he had for Arab people and Arab lands after severing ties with Israel' (ibid. 213–214).
79. Ibid. 220.
80. UKNA FCO 31/1338: Lt Col. B.H. Bradbrooke, British High Commission Kampala, to Maj. D.J. Cutfield, MOD London, 1 February 1972.
81. UKNA FCO 31/1027: Report appended to covering note from 'M.J. Macoum, Overseas Police Adviser' to Duggan and Le Tocq of the EAD, FCO dated 4 August 1971 (report is dated Friday 16 July).

82. Mazrui (1978: 19).
83. Mamdani (1976: 305).
84. Ibid. 305–306.
85. UKNA FCO 73/143: A.A. Ackland to Private Secretary, 13 December 1972.
86. UKNA FCO 31/1587: A.H. Brind, Acting British High Commissioner, Uganda: annual review for 1972 (dated 5 January 1973).
87. Ibid.
88. Mamdani (1976) gets this wrong.
89. UKNA FCO 31/1587: A.H. Brind, Acting British High Commissioner, Uganda: annual review for 1972 (dated 5 January 1973).
90. Leopold (2005: 26).
91. I am writing here only of the consequences for Uganda. The consequences for the expelled people themselves, and for Britain as a whole, were quite another matter. Initially they faced extreme racist hostility from many elements in British society; the British city of Leicester even took out adverts in Ugandan newspapers, telling Ugandan Asians not to go there, as there were too many immigrants in the area already (Moghal 2010: 98–99). Today, they are recognised as one of the most economically successful immigrant groups in British history.
92. UKNA FCO 31/1587: A.H. Brind, Acting British High Commissioner, Uganda: annual review for 1972 (dated 5 January 1973).
93. Swahili, literally 'too much fat', meaning, loosely, 'very wealthy'. It is not necessarily pejorative.
94. Mamdani (1984: 39).
95. Ibid.
96. Moghal (2010: 119).
97. Mutibwa (1992: 115–116).
98. Amin and Akulia (2010: 232).
99. UKNA FCO 31/1587: A.H. Brind, Acting British High Commissioner, Uganda: annual review for 1972 (dated 5 January 1973).
100. Ibid.
101. Ibid.
102. Ibid.
103. E.g. Kasozi (1994: 123).
104. Mutibwa (1992: 97).
105. Ibid. 98.
106. Ibid. 98.
107. Ibid. 101.
108. Government of Uganda (n.d. [1973]: i–ii).
109. Reid (2017: 236).

7 THE CENTRE CANNOT HOLD: PRESIDENT AMIN, 1973–76

1. Austin (1978: 69).
2. Nyeko (1997).
3. See UKNA FCO 31/1774: Uganda: annual review for 1973. Unsourced quotes in this section are from this document.
4. Mutibwa (1992: 108).
5. Ibid. 104.
6. Where not specified otherwise, the dates given in this chapter are from British High Commission annual reviews.
7. Coren (1974).
8. Ibid. 5.
9. Amin and Akulia (2010: 83).

10. UKNA FCO 31/1774: Hennessey (ACH) to FCO.
11. Ibid.
12. UKNA FCO 31/1951: Uganda: annual review for 1974.
13. Quotes in this paragraph are from UKNA FCO 31/1951: British High Commission's annual review on Uganda for 1974.
14. While this was going on, Britain was itself undergoing a political crisis. A general election in February led to a hung parliament, producing a second election in October, in which the Labour Party, led by Harold Wilson, was elected with a majority of just three MPs.
15. UKNA FCO 31/1951: Uganda: annual review for 1974.
16. It seems that in 1974 the FCO was prepared to lean on the BBC to go soft on Amin.
17. All quotes in this paragraph from UKNA FCO 31/1951: Uganda: annual review for 1974.
18. According to Decker (2014: 16).
19. Amin and Akulia (2010: 253).
20. Decker (2014: 101).
21. Amin and Akulia (2010: 289).
22. Cf. MacGaffey (1991).
23. UKNA FCO 31/1951: Uganda: annual review for 1974.
24. Ibid.
25. Iain Grahame interviewed in (US) PBS TV series *The Dictators' Playbook*, first broadcast 13 February 2019.
26. Kasozi (1994: 113).
27. Amnesty International (1983: 44).
28. Ibid. 44.
29. Ibid. 45.
30. Ibid. 45–46.
31. Ibid. 48. The word 'fairly' does a lot of work here.
32. Jorgensen (1981).
33. Ibid. 314–315.
34. Carver (1990: 399).
35. Ibid.
36. Ibid. 400.
37. Hayner (2002: 52). Unfortunately, international human rights organisations destroyed their hard copies of this document once it had been scanned and became (in theory) publicly available online. However, the scanning is very poor and what is now the only available copy of the report is in many places completely illegible. See also Decker (2014: 175–176).
38. Using the death rates given in the same report, this would imply that there were surprisingly few prisoners in Amin's jails.
39. Amnesty International (1983: 46).
40. Mutibwa (1992: 112). Here he is writing about the internationally reported 1977 killings of the Anglican Archbishop, Janani Luwum, and two government ministers.
41. Ibid. 120–121.
42. Published in 1977, and later editions.
43. Allen (2000: 635).
44. Makubuya (2018: 353–354).
45. Nayenga (1979: 133).
46. UKNA FCO 31/493: Le Tocq to Tebbit, 14 January 1969.
47. Decker (2014: 179).
48. Astles (2015: 166).
49. ICJ (1974).
50. Mutibwa (1992: 104).
51. Kibedi, 'Personal Letter' (attachment to ICJ, 1974).
52. Ibid.
53. Ibid.

54. Published in 1977.
55. Melady and Melady (1977: 175–176).
56. ICJ (1974: 1).
57. Peterson and Taylor (2013: 61).
58. Ibid. 76.
59. This is written in 'telegraphese'. To make it more readable I have inserted lower-case letters in place of capitals where appropriate, and have removed the usual spelt-out punctuation – e.g. 'COMMA' or 'STOP' every few words – replacing this with the relevant punctuation marks themselves. Apart from this, it is exactly as sent to the Queen, via the 'Crown Agents' in London.
60. UKNA PREM 16/1480: Telex, Amin to 'Her Majesty, Queen Elizabeth II', 22 January 1975.
61. UKNA PREM 16/1480: Hennessey to EAD, 23 January 1975.
62. UKNA PREM 16/1480: R.N. Dales to Patrick Wright Esq., 23 January 1975.
63. UKNA PREM 16/1480: Patrick Wright to Prime Minister Harold Wilson, 23 January 1975.
64. UKNA PREM 16/1480: PM's Office to Patrick Wright Esq., 24 January 1975.
65. UKNA PREM 16/1480: Hennessey to EAD, 24 January 1975.
66. UKNA PREM 16/1480: Hennessey to EAD, 27 January 1975.
67. UKNA PREM 16/1480: R.N. Dales to Patrick Wright, 27 January 1975.
68. Hills (1975: 331).
69. Makubuya (2018: 356).
70. In fact, all the photographs of this I have seen show the two men bowing down very low to get in the building – in full dress uniform; Blair with ostrich feathers on his hat – but not actually crawling on their knees. Most Ugandan commentators, however (e.g. Makubuya, 2018; Otunnu, 2016) suggest the latter.
71. Makubuya (2018: 356–358).
72. Peterson and Taylor (2013: 61).
73. UKNA FCO 31/1951: Uganda: Calendar of Events 1975.
74. Amin Dada (n.d. [1976]).
75. Dates and events from UKNA FCO 31/2147: British High Commission, Uganda: annual review for 1976.
76. Ibid.
77. Owen (2008: 353).
78. E.g. Ofer (1976), Stevenson (with Dan) (1976), Williamson (1976).
79. David's (2015) account is very readable, enlivened by long passages of invented 'reported speech', which makes it impossible to establish what he has evidence for and what is narrative creativity.
80. Ibid. 122.
81. This was the elder brother of the future president, 'Bibi' Netanyahu, who built much of his early political career on his brother's heroic status.
82. UKNA FCO 31/2147: Uganda: annual review for 1976.
83. Ibid.

8 DECLINE AND FALL: IDI AMIN AND UGANDA, 1977–79, AND AFTER

1. Omara-Otunnu (1987: 136).
2. Ibid.
3. See UKNA FCO 31/2386: Uganda: annual review for 1977. This was prepared by the EAD 'in the absence of diplomatic relations with Uganda' (ibid.).
4. Omara-Otunnu (1987: 138).
5. Mutibwa (1992: 112).
6. Ibid.

7. Cf. Omara-Otunnu (1987: 138).
8. Kasozi (1994: 124) and Omara-Otunnu (1987: 139).
9. Detailed in UKNA DEFE 70/439.
10. UKNA DEFE 11/860: Memo dated 26 May. This file, together with UKNA DEFE 70/439, holds the main documents concerning 'Operation Bottle', though there are others.
11. UKNA DEFE 11/860: Memo dated 26 May.
12. All quotes in this paragraph are from UKNA FCO 31/2386: Uganda: annual review for 1977.
13. Ibid.
14. Dates etc. from UKNA FCO 31/2674: Uganda: annual review for 1978.
15. Ibid.
16. Committee on Foreign Relations (1978: 10–11).
17. Ibid. 16
18. Ibid. 115.
19. UKNA FCO 31/2674: Uganda: annual review for 1978.
20. Owen (2008: 353).
21. UKNA FCO 31/2674: Uganda: annual review for 1978.
22. Amin and Akulia (2010: 386).
23. Ibid. 388.
24. Kasozi (1994: 126 127).
25. Kanyeihamba (2010: 146).
26. Interview, 6 February 1997, quoted in Leopold (2005: 65).
27. Kasozi (1994: 112).
28. Kasfir (1976: 219).
29. Omara-Otunnu (1987: 134, Table 10.1).
30. Mamdani (1984).
31. Ibid. 42.
32. Ibid. 43.
33. Mazrui (1973: 1).
34. Ibid.
35. Omara-Otunnu (1987: 124–125).
36. Ibid. 129–130.
37. Interview with Lugbara ex-soldier, 6 February 1997, quoted in Leopold (2005: 66).
38. Commonwealth Team of Experts (1979: 1–2).
39. Otunnu (2016: 328).
40. Reid (2017: 73–74).
41. Ibid. 74–75.
42. Amin and Akulia (2010: 425).
43. When I was in West Nile in the mid-1990s, the term 'Arua Boys' was applied to teams of smugglers who brought gold, fuel, cigarettes and many other commodities over the borders from Zaire and Sudan. *Magendo* has persisted in Uganda ever since Amin's day.
44. Amin and Akulia (2010: 427–428).
45. Ibid. 430.
46. Ibid. 458.
47. *The Mail on Sunday*, 15 August 2003.
48. Orizio (2004: 29–30).
49. Hansen (2013: 98).
50. Kyemba (1977: 240).
51. Ibid. 15.
52. Peterson and Taylor (2013: 64).
53. Ibid. 66.
54. Peterson and Taylor note that this was not unusual in the region at the time – Tanzania had previously introduced similar legislation (Peterson and Taylor, 2013: 66). Amin had banned miniskirts two years earlier.

55. Ibid.
56. Leopold (2009), Decker (2014).
57. Peterson and Taylor (2013: 75).
58. Kasozi (1994: 107).
59. Decker (2014: 237).
60. Listowel (1973: 7).
61. Ibid. 187.
62. Amin and Akulia (2010: 260).
63. Ibid.
64. Ibid.
65. In Machiavelli, *Discourses on Livy*, 3.2.
66. Otunnu (2016: 284).
67. UKNA FCO 31/1324: S.Y. Dawbarn (EAD) memo re Meeting with Mr Wendell Coote, State Department, 2 May 1972.
68. UKNA FCO 31/1324: File Note, 'Visit of Mr Clyde Ferguson, Recently US Ambassador to Uganda, 28 July 1972'.
69. A confusion of names; he was no relation to the imprisoned writer.
70. UKNA FCO 31/2145: Letter from Sir Denis Hill to Norman Aspin, 19 June 1975.
71. Wober (1973: 298).
72. Ibid.
73. Ibid.
74. Ibid. 298–299.
75. Ibid. 299.
76. Moghaddam (2013: 161).

AFTERWORD

1. UKNA FCO 31/2145: Memo, Ewans to Mansfield, 4 February 1977.
2. Achebe (1988: 252).
3. See Young (1995).
4. Quoted in Achebe (1988: 254).
5. Grahame (1980: 34, quoted in Chapter 2).

REFERENCES

ARCHIVAL SOURCES CITED

RHODES HOUSE LIBRARY, UNIVERSITY OF OXFORD

RHL A.E. Weatherhead: diary; RH Mss Afr.s.1638.
RHL KAR Files. Mss Afr.s.1715, Box 3.
RHL KAR Files. Mss Afr.s.1715, Box 10.
RHL KAR Files. Mss Afr.s.1715, Box 18.

UGANDA NATIONAL ARCHIVES

UNA A46/794: Northern Uganda Provincial Report for 1917.
UNA A46/811: Northern Province Annual Report for 1918–19.

UK NATIONAL ARCHIVES

UKNA DEFE 11/860: Uganda: Anglo/Ugandan relations; preparations for potential visit to UK by President Amin.
UKNA DEFE 70/439: Attendance of President Amin of Uganda at the Commonwealth Heads of Government Meeting London 8–15 June 1977.
UKNA DO 213/35: Commonwealth Relations Office Registered files (EA Series) Internal Security Situation, Uganda.
UKNA DO 213/50: Command Structure of the Uganda Army.
UKNA DO 213/53: Uganda Army General Matters.
UKNA DO 213/62: Judicial Committee of Enquiry: Uganda.
UKNA DO 213/149: Formation of Uganda Air Wing.
UKNA FCO 16/132: Defence Attache reports on Ugandan Army: Discussions with Brig. Amin and Bob Astles.
UKNA FCO 16/133: Defence Attache reports on Ugandan Army: Discussions with Brig. Amin and Bob Astles.
UKNA FCO 31/182: Personal Attack by President Obote on British High Commission and uncertain political situation.
UKNA FCO 31/184: Uganda: Internal Political Situation (1968–69).

REFERENCES

UKNA FCO 31/468: Situation report (1968–69).

UKNA FCO 31/472: Plots Against Government (1968–69).

UKNA FCO 31/493: Proceedings against Robert Astles.

UKNA FCO 31/710: Political Developments in Uganda (1970).

UKNA FCO 31/1023: Coup d'etat in Uganda, 25 January 1971, led by army commander, Major General Idi Amin.

UKNA FCO 31/1024: Coup d'etat in Uganda, 25 January 1971, led by army commander, Major General Idi Amin.

UKNA FCO 31/1026: Report on Leading Personalities in Uganda (1971).

UKNA FCO 31/1027: Inter-tribal violence within Uganda: plots against government.

UKNA FCO 31/1043: Political Relations between Uganda and Israel.

UKNA FCO 31/1055: Reports on armed forces in Uganda.

UKNA FCO 31/1072: Visit of President of Uganda, General Idi Amin, to UK.

UKNA FCO 31/1073: Visit of President of Uganda, General Idi Amin, to UK.

UKNA FCO 31/1324: Political Developments in Uganda.

UKNA FCO 31/1325: Uganda: annual review for 1971.

UKNA FCO 31/1338: Political relations between Uganda and Israel.

UKNA FCO 31/1587: Uganda: annual review for 1972.

UKNA FCO 31/1624: Diplomatic representation of the UK in Uganda: including valedictory despatch of Harry Brind.

UKNA FCO 31/1774: Uganda: annual review for 1973.

UKNA FCO 31/1781: Political relations between Uganda and UK.

UKNA FCO 31/1951: Uganda: annual review for 1974, Uganda: Calendar of Events 1975.

UKNA FCO 31/1961: Visit of James Callaghan, UK Secretary of State for Foreign and Commonwealth Affairs, to Uganda.

UKNA FCO 31/2145: President Amin of Uganda and Family.

UKNA FCO 31/2147: Uganda: annual review for 1976.

UKNA FCO 31/2386: Uganda: annual review for 1977.

UKNA FCO 31/2667: Leading Personalities in Uganda.

UKNA FCO 31/2674: Uganda: annual review for 1978.

UKNA FCO 73/143: Sir Alec Douglas-Home. Various correspondence and policy papers.

UKNA PREM 16/1480: Relations with Uganda, including correspondence from President Amin.

UKNA WO106/253: Papers relating to the Uganda Protectorate.

PUBLISHED WORKS CITED

Achebe, Chinua. 1988. 'An Image of Africa: Racism in Conrad's "Heart of Darkness"', in R. Kimbrough (ed.), *Joseph Conrad: Heart of Darkness*, 3rd Norton Critical Edition. New York, W.W. Norton.

Adoko, Akena. n.d. [1967]. *Uganda Crisis*. Kampala, African Publishers Ltd.

Alibhai-Brown, Yasmin. 1997. *No Place Like Home: An Autobiography*. London, Virago.

Alibhai-Brown, Yasmin. 2008. *The Settlers' Cookbook: A Memoir of Love, Migration and Food*. London, Portobello Books.

Allen, Sir Peter. 1987. *Days of Judgement: A Judge in Idi Amin's Uganda*. London, William Kimber.

Allen, Sir Peter. 2000. *Interesting Times: Uganda Diaries 1955–1986*. Lewes, Sussex, Book Guild Ltd.

Amin Dada, Al-Hajji Field Marshal Dr Idi. n.d. [1976]. *The Shaping of Modern Uganda*. Entebbe, Government Printer.

Amin, Jaffar and Margaret Akulia. 2010. *Idi Amin: Hero or Villain? His son Jaffar Amin and other people speak*. Kampala, Millennium Global Publishers.

338

REFERENCES

Amnesty International. 1983. *Political Killings by Governments*. London, Amnesty International Publications.

Anderson, David. 2005. *Histories of the Hanged: Britain's Dirty War in Kenya and the End of the Empire*. London, Weidenfeld and Nicolson.

Apter, David. 1961. *The Political Kingdom In Uganda: A Study in Bureaucratic Nationalism*. Princeton, NJ, Princeton University Press.

Arens, W. 1979. *The Man-Eating Myth: Anthropology and Anthropophagy*. New York, Oxford University Press.

Asiwaju, A.I. (ed.). 1985. *Partitioned Africans: Ethnic Relations across Africa's International Boundaries 1884–1984*. New York, St. Martin's Press.

Astles, Robert. 2015 [1988]. *Forty Tribes: A Life in Uganda*. Limited edition, privately published for the Robert Astles estate.

Atkinson, Ronald R. 1994. *The Roots of Ethnicity: The Origins of the Acholi of Uganda Before 1800*. Philadelphia, PA, Pennsylvania University Press.

Austin, Dennis. 1978. *Politics in Africa*. Manchester, Manchester University Press.

Beachey, R.W. 1967. 'The East African Ivory Trade in the Nineteenth Century', *Journal of African History* 8(2): 269–290.

Behrend, Heike. 2011. *Resurrecting Cannibals: The Catholic Church, Witch Hunts, and the Production of Pagans in Western Uganda*. Woodbridge, Suffolk and Rochester, New York, James Currey.

Benson, Heather. 1992. *A Dissolving Dream: A New Zealander in Amin's Uganda*. Wellington, Bridget Williams Books..

Blandford, Neil and Bruce Jones. 1994. *The World's Most Evil Men*. London, Octopus Books.

Bloch, Jonathan and Patrick Fitzgerald. 1983. *British Intelligence and Covert Action in the Third World*. London, Junction Books.

Brown, Douglas and Marcelle V. Brown (eds). 1996. *Looking Back at the Uganda Protectorate: Recollections of District Officers*. Dalkeith, Western Australia, Douglas Brown.

Campbell, Horace. 1975. *Four Essays on Neo-colonialism in Uganda: The Barbarity of Idi Amin*. Toronto, Afro-Carib Publications.

Carver, Richard. 1990. 'Called to Account: How African Governments Investigate Human Rights Violations', *African Affairs* 89(356): 391–415.

Castleden, Rodney. 2005. *The World's Most Evil People*. London, Time Warner Books.

Clark, Victoria and Melissa Scott. 2014. *Dictators' Dinners: A Bad Taste Guide to Entertaining Tyrants*. London: Gilgamesh Publishing.

Committee on Foreign Relations. 1978. *Uganda: The Human Rights Situation. Hearings before the Subcommittee on Foreign Economic Policy of the Committee on Foreign Relations, United States Senate, Ninety-Fifth Congress, Second Session on Uganda*, June 15, 21, 26. Washington, US Government Printing Office.

Commonwealth Team of Experts. 1979. *The Rehabilitation of the Economy of Uganda. Volume One. A Report . . ..* Commonwealth Secretariat.

Cooper, Frederick. 2005. *Colonialism in Question: Theory, Knowledge, History*. Berkeley, University of California Press.

Coren, Alan. 1974. *The Collected Bulletins of President Idi Amin*. London, Robson Books.

Coren, Alan. 1975. *The Further Bulletins of President Idi Amin*. London, Robson Books.

David, Saul. 2015. *Operation Thunderbolt*. London, Hodder and Stoughton.

Decker, Alicia C. 2014. *In Idi Amin's Shadow: Women, Gender and Militarism in Uganda*. Athens, OH, Ohio University Press.

'Donald, Trevor'. 1978. *Confessions of Idi Amin: The Horrifying, Explosive Exposé of Africa's Most Evil Man – in His Own Words*. London, W.H. Allen and Co.

Dougherty, Steve. 2010. *A Wicked History of the 20th Century: Idi Amin*. New York, Scholastic Inc.

Driberg, J.H. 1931. 'Yakan', *Journal of the Royal Anthropological Institute* 61: 413–420.

Edwards, Catharine. 1991. 'Review: The Truth about Caligula?', *The Classical Review*, NS 41(2): 406–408.

Elkins, Caroline. 2005. *Britain's Gulag: The Brutal End of Empire in Kenya*. London, Jonathan Cape.

Evans-Pritchard, E.E. 1963. *Essays in Social Anthropology*. Oxford, Oxford University Press.

Geria, S.A. 1973. 'A Traditional History of the Northwestern Lugbara of Uganda'. Undergraduate dissertation, Makerere University Kampala.

Gikandi, Simon. 1996. *Maps of Englishness: Writing Identity in the Culture of Colonialism*. New York, Columbia University Press.

Government of Uganda. n.d. [1971]. *Uganda, the Birth of the Second Republic*. Entebbe, published by the Government of the Republic of Uganda and printed by the Government Printer.

Government of Uganda. n.d. [1972a]. *Uganda, the First 366 Days of the Second Republic*. Entebbe, published by the Ministry of Information and Broadcasting and printed by the Government Printer.

Government of Uganda. n.d. [1972b]. *Achievements of the Government of Uganda during the First Year of the Second Republic*. Entebbe, published by the Government of the Republic of Uganda and printed by the Government Printer.

Government of Uganda. n.d. [1973]. *Uganda, the Second Year of the Second Republic*. Kampala, published by the Ministry of Information and Broadcasting and printed by the Government Printer.

Grahame, Iain. 1966. *Jambo Effendi*. London, J.A. Allen & Co.

Grahame, Iain. 1980. *Amin and Uganda: A Personal Memoir*. London, Granada Publishing.

Gutteridge, W.F. 1975. *Military Regimes in Africa*. London, Methuen.

'Gwyn, David'. 1977. *Idi Amin: Death-Light of Africa*. Boston, MA, Little, Brown.

Hale, Mary M. 2009. *On Uganda's Terms: A Journal of an American Nurse Midwife Working under Idi Amin's Regime*. British Columbia, CCB Publishing.

Hansen, Holger B. 1977. *Ethnicity and Military Rule in Uganda*, Research Report 43. Uppsala, Scandinavian Institute of African Studies.

Hansen, Holger B. 2013. 'Uganda in the 1970s: A Decade of Paradoxes and Ambiguities', *Journal of Eastern African Studies* 7(1): 83–102.

Hansen, Holger B. and Michael Twaddle (eds). 1988. *Uganda Now*. London, James Currey.

Hansen, Holger B. and Michael Twaddle (eds). 1991. *Changing Uganda*. London, James Currey.

Hansen, Holger B. and Michael Twaddle (eds). 1998. *Developing Uganda*. Oxford, James Currey.

Harrell-Bond, Barbara E. 1986. *Imposing Aid, Emergency Assistance to Refugees*. Oxford, Oxford University Press.

Hayner, Priscilla B. 2002. *Unspeakable Truths: Facing the Challenge of Truth Commissions*. New York and London, Routledge.

Hebditch, David and Ken Connor. 2009. *How to Stage a Military Coup: From Planning to Execution*. New York, Skyhorse Publishing.

Hespeler-Boultbee, J.J. 2012. *Mrs Queen's Chump: Idi Amin, the Mau Mau, Communists and Other Silly Follies of the British Empire: A Military Memoir*. British Columbia, CCB Publishing.

Hills, Denis. 1975. *The White Pumpkin*. London, George, Allen and Unwin.

Ibingira, G.S.K. 1973. *The Forging of an African Nation: The Political and Constitutional Evolution of Uganda from Colonial Rule to Independence, 1894–1962*. New York, Viking Press and Kampala, Uganda Publishing House.

Ingham, Kenneth. 1994. *Obote: A Political Biography*. London and New York, Routledge.

International Commission of Jurists. 1974. *Violations of Human Rights and the Rule of Law in Uganda*. https://www.icj.org/wp-content/uploads/2013/06/Uganda-violations-of-human-rights-thematic-report-1974-eng.pdf (accessed 11 June 2020).

Johnson, D.H. 1988. 'Sudanese Military Slavery from the Eighteenth to the Twentieth Century', in Leonie Archer (ed.), *Slavery and Other Forms of Unfree Labour*. London and New York, Routledge.

REFERENCES

Johnson, D.H. 1989. 'The Structure of a Legacy: Military Slavery in Northeast Africa', *Ethnohistory* 36(1): 72–88.

Johnson, D.H. 2009. 'Tribe or Nationality? The Sudanese Diaspora and the Kenyan Nubis', *Journal of Eastern African Studies* 3(1): 112–131.

Jorgensen, Jan Jelmert. 1981. *Uganda: A Modern History*. London, Croom Helm.

Kabaka of Buganda, The. 1967. *Desecration of My Kingdom*. London, Constable.

'Kamau, Joseph' and 'Andrew Cameron' [Angus Shaw]. 1979. *Lust to Kill: The Rise and Fall of Idi Amin*. London, Corgi Books.

Kanyeihamba, G.W. 2010. *Constitutional and Political History of Uganda from 1894 to Present*. Kampala, LawAfrica Publishing.

Karugire, Samwiri R. 1980. *A Political History of Uganda*. Nairobi, London, Heinemann Educational Books.

Karugire, Samwiri R. 1988. *Roots of Instability in Uganda*. Kampala, Fountain Publishers.

Kasfir, Nelson. 1976. *The Shrinking Political Arena: Participation and Ethnicity in African Politics, with a Case Study of Uganda*. Berkeley, University of California Press.

Kasozi, A.B.K. 1994. *The Social Origins of Violence in Uganda*. Kampala, Fountain Publishers.

Kato, Wycliffe. 1989. *Escape from Idi Amin's Slaughterhouse*. London and New York, Quartet Books.

King, A. 1970. 'The Yakan Cult and Lugbara Response to Colonial Rule', *Azania: Journal of the British Institute of History and Archaeology in East Africa*, 5: 1–25.

Kiwanuka, Semakula. 1979. *Amin and the Tragedy of Uganda*. Munich and London, Veltforum Verlag.

Kokole, Omari H. 1995. 'Idi Amin, the Nubi and Islam in Ugandan Politics', in H.B. Hansen and Michael Twaddle (eds), *Religion and Politics in East Africa*. London, James Currey.

Kyemba, Henry. 1977. *A State of Blood: the Inside Story of Idi Amin*. London, Paddington Press.

La Fontaine, Jean S. 1998. *Speak of the Devil: Tales of Satanic Abuse in Contemporary England*. Cambridge, Cambridge University Press.

Law, Diane. 2006. *The World's Most Evil Dictators*. Bath, Parragon Books.

Lawoko, WodOkello. 2005. *The Dungeons of Nakasero*. Stockholm, WodOkello Lawoko.

Leopold, Mark. 1999. ' "The War in the North": Ethnicity in Ugandan Press Explanations of Conflict, 1996–97', in T. Allen and J. Seaton (eds), *The Media of Conflict: War Reporting and Representations of Ethnic Conflict*. London and New York, Zed Books.

Leopold, Mark. 2001. 'The Roots of Violence and the Reconstruction of Society in North West Uganda'. D.Phil thesis, University of Oxford.

Leopold, Mark. 2003. 'Slavery in Sudan, Past and Present', *African Affairs* 102(409): 653–661.

Leopold, Mark. 2005. *Inside West Nile: Violence, History and Representation on an African Frontier*. Oxford, Santa Fe, Kampala, James Currey, School of American Research Press, Fountain Publishers.

Leopold, Mark. 2006. 'Legacies of Slavery in North-West Uganda: The Story of the "One-Elevens"', *Africa: Journal of the International African Institute* 76(2): 180–199.

Leopold, Mark. 2009. 'Sex, Violence and History in the Lives of Idi Amin: Postcolonial Masculinity as Masquerade', *Journal of Postcolonial Writing* 45(3): 321–330.

Leopold, Mark. 2013. ' "Print the Legend": Myth and Reality in *The Last King of Scotland*', in Nigel Eltringham (ed.), *Framing Africa: Portrayals of a Continent in Contemporary Mainstream Cinema*. New York, Oxford, Berghahn Books.

Listowel, Judith. 1973. *Amin*. Dublin and London, IUP Books.

Lofchie, Michael F. 1972. 'The Uganda Coup: Class Action by the Military', *Journal of Modern African Studies* 10(1): 19–35.

Low, D.A. 1971. *Buganda in Modern History*. London, Weidenfeld and Nicolson.

MacGaffey, J. 1991. *The Real Economy of Zaire*. Oxford, James Currey.

Makubuya, Apollo N. 2018. *Protection, Patronage or Plunder: British Machinations and (B)Uganda's struggle for Independence*. Newcastle upon Tyne, Cambridge Scholars Publishing.

Mamdani, Mahmoud. 1973. *From Citizen to Refugee*. London, Frances Pinter.

REFERENCES

Mamdani, Mahmoud. 1984. *Imperialism and Fascism in Uganda*. Trenton, NJ, Africa World Press.

Mamdani, Mahmoud. 1975. 'Class Struggles in Uganda', *Review of African Political Economy* 2(4): 26–61.

Mamdani, Mahmoud. 1976. *Politics and Class Formation in Uganda*. New York, Monthly Review Press.

Mamdani, Mahmoud (ed.). 1995. *And Fire Does Not Beget Ash: Critical Reflections on the NRM*. Kampala, The Monitor Newspaper.

Martin, David. 1974. *General Amin*. London, Faber and Faber.

Mazrui, Ali A. 1973. 'The Lumpen Proletariat and the Lumpen Militariat: African Soldiers as a New Political Class', *Political Studies* 21(1): 1–12.

Mazrui, Ali A. 1975a. 'The Resurrection of the Warrior Tradition in African Political Culture', *Journal of Modern African Studies* 13(1): 67–84.

Mazrui, Ali A. 1975b. *Soldiers and Kinsmen in Uganda: The Making of a Military Ethnocracy*. Beverly Hills, CA and London, Sage.

Mazrui, Ali A. 1977a. 'Religious Strangers in Uganda: From Emin Pasha to Amin Dada', *African Affairs* 76(302): 21–38.

Mazrui, Ali A. 1977b. 'The Warrior Tradition and the Masculinity of War', in Ali A. Mazrui (ed.), *The Warrior Tradition in Modern Africa*.

Mazrui, Ali A. (ed.). 1977c. *The Warrior Tradition in Modern Africa*. Leiden, Brill.

Mazrui, Ali A. 1978. *Political Values and the Educated Class in Africa*. Berkeley and Los Angeles, University of California Press.

Mazrui, Ali A. 1979. 'Casualties of an Underdeveloped Class Structure: The Expulsions of Luo Workers and Asian Bourgeoisie from Uganda', in W.A. Shack and E.P. Skinner (eds), *Strangers in African Society*. Berkeley and London, University of California Press.

McConnell, R.E. 1925. 'Notes on the Lugwari Tribe of Central Africa', *Journal of the Royal Anthropological Institute* 55: 439–467.

Measures, Bob and Tony Walker. 1998. *Amin's Uganda*. London, Minerva Press.

Melady, Thomas and Margaret Melady. 1977. *Idi Amin Dada: Hitler in Africa*. Kansas City, Sheed Andrews and McMeel.

Middleton, J.F.M. 1971. 'Some Effects of Colonial Rule Among the Lugbara', in Victor Turner (ed.), *Colonialism in Africa, 1870-1960*. Cambridge, Cambridge University Press.

Miller, Charles. 1971. *The Lunatic Express: An Entertainment in Imperialism*. London, Macmillan.

Mittelman, James H. 1975. *Ideology and Politics in Uganda: From Obote to Amin*. Ithaca, NY, and London, Cornell University Press.

Moghaddam, Fathali M. 2013. *The Psychology of Dictatorship*. Washington, DC, American Psychological Association.

Moghal, Manzoor. 2010. *Idi Amin: Lion of Africa*. Milton Keynes, AuthorHouse.

Montefiore, Simon Sebag. 2008. *Monsters: History's Most Evil Men and Women*. London, Quercus.

Moyse-Bartlett, Lieutenant Colonel H. 1956. *The King's African Rifles: A Study in the Military History of East and Central Africa, 1890-1945*. Aldershot, Gale and Polden Ltd.

Mujaju, Akiiki B. 1987. 'The Gold Allegations Motion and Political Development in Uganda', *African Affairs* 86(345): 479–504.

Mutibwa, P. 1992. *Uganda since Independence: A Story of Unfulfilled Hopes*. London, Hurst and Co.

Nabudere, D. Wadada. 1980. *Imperialism and Revolution in Uganda*. London, Onyx Press/Dar es-Salaam, Tanzania Publishing House.

Nader, Laura. 1969. 'Up the Anthropologist: Perspectives gained from Studying Up', in Dell H. Hymes (ed.), *Reinventing Anthropology*. New York, Pantheon Books.

Nayenga, Peter F.B. 1979. 'Myths and Realities of Idi Amin Dada's Uganda', *African Studies Review* 22(2): 127–138.

REFERENCES

Nyeko, Balam. 1997. 'Exile Politics and Resistance to Dictatorship: The Ugandan Anti-Amin Organisations in Zambia, 1972–79', *African Affairs* 96(382): 95–108.

Obote, A. Milton. 1969. *Uganda Revolution 1966*. Kampala, Uganda Publishing House.

Obote, A. Milton. n.d. [1970]. *The Common Man's Charter*. Entebbe, printed by the Government Printer.

Ofer, Yehuda. 1976. *Operation Thunder: The Entebbe Raid. The Israelis' Own Story*. Harmondsworth, Penguin Books.

Oloka-Onyango, Joe. 1996. 'Biography as Apologia' [review of Ingham, 1994, *op cit*], *Africa Today* 42(4): 118–121.

Omara-Otunnu, Amii. 1987. *Politics and the Military in Uganda 1890–1985*. New York, St. Martin's Press.

Orizio, Riccardo. 2004. *Talk of the Devil: Encounters with Seven Dictators*. London, Vintage.

Otunnu, Ogenga. 2016. *Crisis of Legitimacy and Political Violence in Uganda, 1890 to 1979*. Cham, Switzerland, Palgrave Macmillan.

Otunnu, Ogenga. 2017. *Crisis of Legitimacy and Political Violence in Uganda, 1979 to 2016*. Cham, Switzerland, Palgrave Macmillan.

Owen, David. 2008. *In Sickness and In Power: Illness in Heads of Government During the Last 100 Years*. London, Methuen.

Page, Malcolm. 2011. *King's African Rifles, a History* Barnsley, Pen and Sword Military.

Pain, D. 1975. 'The Nubians, Their Perceived Stratification System, and Its Relation to the Asian Issue', in Michael Twaddle (ed.), *Expulsions of a Minority*. London, University of London/Athlone Press.

Parkin, David (ed.). 1985. *The Anthropology of Evil*. Oxford, Basil Blackwell Ltd.

Parsons, Timothy H. 2003. *The 1964 Army Mutinies and the Making of Modern East Africa*. Westport, CT, Praeger.

Peterson, Derek and Edgar C. Taylor. 2013. 'Rethinking the State in Idi Amin's Uganda: The Politics of Extortion', *Journal of Eastern African Studies* 7(1): 58–82.

Pocock, David. 1985. 'Unruly Evil', in David Parkin (ed.), *The Anthropology of Evil*.

Reid, Richard J. 2017. *A History of Modern Uganda*. Cambridge, Cambridge University Press.

Schutt, Bill. 2017. *Eat Me: A Natural and Unnatural History of Cannibalism*. London, Profile Books.

Sembuya, Christopher C. 2009. *Amin Dada: The Other Side*. Kampala, Sest Holdings.

Shaw, Angus. 2013. *Mutoko Madness*. Harare, Zimbabwe, Boundary Books.

Smith, George Ivan. 1980. *Ghosts of Kampala: The Rise and Fall of Idi Amin*. London, Weidenfeld and Nicolson.

Soghayroun, Ibrahim El Zein. 1981. *The Sudanese Muslim Factor in Uganda*. Khartoum, Khartoum University Press.

Southall, Aidan. 1975. 'General Amin and the Coup: Great Man or Historical Inevitability?', *Journal of Modern African Studies* 18(4): 85–105.

Southall, Aidan. 1977. 'The Bankruptcy of the Warrior Tradition', in Ali A. Mazrui (ed.), *The Warrior Tradition in Modern Africa*.

Southall, Aidan. 1980. 'Social Disorganisation in Uganda: Before, During and After Amin', *Journal of Modern African Studies* 18(4): 627–656.

Southall, Aidan. 1988. 'The Recent Political Economy of Uganda', in H.B. Hansen and Michael Twaddle (eds), *Uganda Now*.

Southwold, Martin. 1985. 'Buddhism and Evil', in David Parkin (ed.), *The Anthropology of Evil*.

Steiner, Rolf. 1978. *The Last Adventurer: From Biafra to the Sudan*. London, Weidenfeld and Nicolson.

Stevenson, William (with Uri Dan). 1976. *90 Minutes at Entebbe*. London, New York, Bantam Books.

Stigand, C.H. 1923. *Equatoria, the Lado Enclave*. London, Constable (reprinted 1968, London, Routledge).

Stourton, Edward. 2017. *Auntie's War: The BBC During the Second World War*. London, Transworld.

REFERENCES

Tabaire, Bernard. 2007. 'The Press and Political Repression in Uganda: Back to the Future?' *Journal of Eastern African Studies* 1(2): 193–211.

Taylor, Donald. 1985. 'Theological Thoughts About Evil', in David Parkin (ed.), *The Anthropology of Evil*.

Twiss, Miranda. 2002. *The Most Evil Men and Women in History*. London, Michael O'Mara Books.

Vyner, Harriet. 1999. *Groovy Bob: The Life and Times of Robert Fraser*. London, Faber and Faber.

Wheen, Francis. 2009. *Strange Days Indeed: The Golden Age of Paranoia*. London, HarperCollins.

Williamson, Tony. 1976. *Counterstrike Entebbe*. London, Collins.

Wober, Mallory. 1973. 'An Attempt on the Mind of Idi Amin', *The Listener* 90 (6 September): 297–299.

Wooding, Dan and Ray Barnett. 1980. *Uganda Holocaust*. Glasgow, Pickering and Inglis.

York, Peter. 2005. *Dictators' Homes*. London, Atlantic Books.

Young, Robert. 1995. *Colonial Desire: Hybridity in Theory, Culture and Race*. London, Routledge.

INDEX

Aate/Atata, Aisha Chumaru (IA's mother): background, 25, 26, 27, 32–33; birth of IA, 29, 33–34; breakup with IA's father, 31, 35, 36; as 'camp-follower', 29, 50–51; death, 162; and Kabaka of Buganda, 33–34, 39, 52, 53, 142; as healer or witch, 36, 37, 39, 49, 51, 76; IA's paternity test and Aisha's curse, 33–35, 45, 52, 174, 187; marriage and children, 35, 52; pro-Israel, 227; as Yakan movement leader, 36–37, 39, 43

Achebe, Chinua, 5, 8, 11, 312

Acholi (district, language, people), 58–59, 64, 65, 69, 94, 119, 125, 126, 129, 199, 224, 236, 276; and 1971 coup, 185–189, 192, 215, 224, 236; 'disappearances' of and human rights violations against, 190, 192, 197, 202, 213, 214, 252; IA's attitude to, 3, 120, 124, 168, 169, 221–222, 240, 279, 287, 288, 298; see also Luo; Nilotic languages; 'northerners'

Adoko, Akena, 112, 134, 137–140, 168, 181, 185, 186, 258

Adroa, Kay, see Amin, Kay

Adume, Dudu Alias, 34–35

Africa, Africans, Western perceptions of, viii, xi–xii, 1, 3–6, 8, 11, 18, 21–23, 40–4, 46, 50, 59, 62, 65, 86, 97, 115, 123, 134, 192–193, 197, 209, 250, 310–313; see also 'mission boy' stereotype; 'warrior tribes' colonial stereotype

agriculture, 53, 92, 148, 165, 249, 280, 298; see also coffee; sugar

Allen, Peter Jermyn, 10, 72, 183, 256–257, 328

Alur (language, people), 5, 17, 52, 194, 216, 287, 288

Amin, Kay, 17, 18, 19, 52, 144–146, 152, 317

Amin, Idi (Idi Amin Dada): ancestry (as Kakwa and Nubi) x–xii, 2, 4, 5–8, 13–17, 26, 27–30, 31, 32, 35, 38, 41, 42, 46, 48, 177; birth and parentage; 2, 6, 24–30, 33–35, 37, 39, 45, 52, 54, 112, 162, 297; and Britain, see Britain; childhood, 6, 24, 49–54, 58, 61, 308; fascination exerted by, 8, 9, 23, 88, 242, 244, 249, 303–304; human rights violations, see human rights; image as icon of evil, 1, 3–5, 10–13, 17–19, 22, 23, 27, 38, 86, 135, 239, 242, 250, 309, 312–313; and Israel, see Israel; luck of, 64, 82, 102, 105, 121–122, 298, 305, 313; local policies, see under district/town names; marriages, 17, 18, 30, 120, 121, 144, 145, 155, 206, 221, 247, 248, 269, 296, 297, 300, see also individual wives' names; masculinity of, 1, 11, 19, 20, 72, 83; mental illness (supposed), xi, 16, 49, 294, 298, 305–309; military career in British army, see British Army; King's African Rifles; military career in Ugandan army, see army, Ugandan; and Milton Obote, see Obote, Milton; the name 'Dada', 30–31, 120, 315; overthrow of, 193, 210, 251, 276, 284–286, 288, 291–292; as parent, 17, 62, 82, 145, 150, 206, 295–297, 304; paternity test, see Aate, Aisha; representation as too African, 1, 4, 8–9, 11, 13, 18–23, 46, 250, 266, 295, 311–313; representation as buffoon, 4, 8, 55, 122, 196, 299, 309; representation as sadist, 1, 13, 16, 18, 37, 48, 49, 53, 64, 73, 75, 104, 305; representation as cannibal, 2, 9, 13, 14–19, 46, 48, 256, 314; responsibility for killings, 3, 96, 99, 104, 223, 250–256, 259–263, 294, 314; retirement, 8, 227, 294–296; sense of humour, 42, 55, 62, 81, 85, 89, 122, 157, 158, 265, 299, 300, 304, 310; violence of, 1, 7, 13, 14, 19, 20, 21, 48, 55, 72, 73, 87, 98–104, 172, 215, 238, 251–253, 283, 293, 312; as warrior, 2, 6,

345

14, 16, 20–22, 46, 65, 67, 70, 79, 85, 313;
Western image of, 1, 4, 16, 22, 84, 89, 120,
192, 195, 207, 209, 241, 246, 247, 249,
253, 266, 268, 301, 305, 209, 310; *see also*
British Army; King's African Rifles;
Obote, Milton; paranoia; sport;
Ugandan army; World War II

Amin, Jaffar, 23, 24, 30–35, 39, 44, 45, 51–54,
57, 58, 61, 62, 69, 71, 77, 80, 81, 82, 85, 110,
119–122, 135, 142, 144, 145, 162, 174, 186,
187, 227, 233, 242, 248, 259, 265, 285, 294,
295, 304, 331

Amin, Malyam, 120, 121, 144, 145, 146, 206

Amin, Nora, 145–146

Amin, Sarah, 17, 248, 269, 280

Amnesty International, 251–254, 263, 284

Anglican Church, 40, 125, 144, 222, 276,
279, 303; *see also* Christianity; Luwum,
Janani; Protestant Church

Ankole (district, language, people), 112, 125,
126, 128, 183, 203

anthropology, 4, 5, 11–13, 16, 18, 19, 27, 28,
43, 47, 54, 82, 136, 185

anti-colonialism, *see* colonialism

anti-semitism, 193–194, 261, 289

Anyanya 1 (Sudanese civil war), 170–172,
175, 216, 226, 228, 240, 287; *see also*
'Congo Gold Scandal'

Arabic, Arabs (language, people, states), 6,
28, 30, 45, 56, 57, 58, 108, 116, 170, 172,
176, 193, 212, 224, 226, 227, 228, 234, 238,
243, 244, 245, 248, 269, 270, 271, 280, 281,
294, 299, 309

archives, archival history, 49, 55, 79, 85, 92,
97, 164, 178, 179, 208, 215, 277, 337–338

aristocracy, Baganda, *see* Buganda

army, British, 2, 6, 7, 10, 23, 30, 42, 53, 55–90,
93, 94, 95, 96, 98, 103, 109–111, 117, 149,
208, 211, 244, 246, 277, 297, 304, 311, 312,
313; *see also* King's African Rifles

army, Ugandan, 7, 9, 28, 91, 102, 104–107,
122, 124, 125, 129–133, 136, 138, 151, 152,
153, 154, 155, 158, 159, 160, 166, 167, 168,
170–200, 202, 209, 212, 213–218, 221, 222,
233, 240, 241, 242, 243, 248, 251, 254, 271,
272, 279, 280, 285, 286, 288, 290, 291, 298,
299, 300, 304, 308; 1964 mutiny in,
107–116; used against Kabaka, 141–147;
see also 'Congo Gold Scandal'

Arua (town, district) 26, 27, 32, 33, 35, 52,
53, 57, 58, 118, 145, 162, 232, 285, 295, *see
also* Tangankiya Village

Asians in Uganda, 1, 2, 3, 7, 23, 40, 46, 47,
53, 92, 148, 149, 175, 199, 202, 204, 218,

237–238, 243; Obote's plan to expel,
165–166, 198, 302; Amin's expulsion of,
x, 205, 210, 228–235, 237, 241, 244, 245,
246, 263, 264, 270, 272, 274, 299, 308, 309,
314, 332

Astles, Robert (Bob), 16, 122, 123, 134,
135, 137, 144, 145, 146, 160, 161, 162,
163, 171, 186, 193, 194, 195, 257, 258,
259, 271, 300

Aswa/Waswa, Wilfred, 180, 182, 183, 184

Baganda, *see* Buganda

Bagaya, Elizabeth (Princess Elizabeth of
Tooro), 246, 248, 269

Bantu languages, cultures, 42, 66, 67, 106,
129, 132, 192, 288

Banyarwanda, *see* Rwanda

Banyoro, *see* Bunyoro

Bar-Lev, Baruch ('Burka'), 154–157, 163,
164, 168, 169, 176, 177, 178, 179, 190, 191,
192, 193, 225, 228, 273, 300

'Battle of Mengo', *see* Mengo

Belgian Congo, *see* Congo

Bloch, Dora, 273, 274, 311

boxing, *see* sport

Brind, Harry, 66, 217, 218, 226, 227, 229, 231,
232, 234, 235

Britain, British people, British Empire, xi, 4,
7, 9, 16, 22, 25, 29, 36, 39, 40, 42–45, 46,
48, 56, 63, 65, 66, 71, 73, 78, 82, 84, 86, 92,
94, 101, 105, 108, 115, 117, 118, 121, 123,
125, 127, 128, 135, 146, 151, 153, 157, 159,
160, 165, 167, 170, 175, 176, 178, 186, 190,
192–203, 210, 211, 212, 215, 218, 225, 226,
229, 233, 234, 235, 238, 241, 246, 261, 263,
266, 268, 272, 275, 277, 282, 288, 298, 300,
304, 305, 308, 309, 310, 313, 314, 319;
Amin's visit to, 204–212; *see also* army,
British; colonialism; Operation Bottle

British Broadcasting Corporation (BBC), 9,
183, 241, 246, 247, 268, 307

'British passport holders', British citizens of
Asian origin, *see* Asians in Uganda

Buganda (district, people, language,
culture), 2, 3, 7, 13, 24, 26, 30, 33, 35, 39,
40, 41, 42, 45, 46, 48, 52, 53, 58, 59, 67, 93,
94, 95, 105, 112, 125, 126, 126, 129, 133,
136, 140, 141, 143, 149, 164, 167, 173, 183,
190, 191, 195, 199, 200, 202, 236, 318, 324;
see also Kabaka

Bunyoro (district, people), 40, 52, 125, 128,
187, 203, 318

Burma, 6, 60, 61, 62, 69

Burundi, 142, 143, 243

Callaghan, James, 60, 268, 306
'Cameron, Andrew', see Shaw, Angus
Campbell, Horace, 193–194, 195
Canada, Canadians, 10, 29, 85, 86, 88, 190, 193, 231
cannibalism, 2, 9, 13–19, 46, 48, 79, 256, 314
Catholic church, 29, 30, 32, 40, 93, 95, 125, 126, 127, 137, 222, 224, 227, 276; see also Christianity
China, Chinese, 131, 132, 133, 154, 155, 156, 205, 208, 209, 210, 213, 253, 270
Christianity, 26, 29, 48, 170, 201, 224, 234, 241, 269, 276, 279; see also Anglican Church; Catholic Church; Protestant Church
Churchill, Winston S., 41–42, 328
Church of Uganda, see Anglican Church
coffee, 165, 181, 218, 249, 280, 281, 282, 298; see also agriculture
Cold War, 7, 108, 126, 129, 132, 137, 175, 210, 226, 258, 299
colonialism, colonial attitudes, colonial desire, xi, 2, 3, 4, 5, 6, 8, 12, 15, 20, 21, 25, 28, 36, 39–45, 46, 57, 58, 65, 67, 73, 75, 86, 87, 90, 92–96, 97, 102–103, 107, 111, 119, 125, 126, 127, 128, 131, 171, 175, 201, 203, 214, 224, 229, 233, 234
Commission of Enquiry into the Disappearances of People in Uganda since 25 January 1971, report of, see 'disappearances'
Common Man's Charter, see Obote, Milton
Commonwealth, British, 113, 114, 115, 132, 160, 173, 177, 185, 209, 264, 273, 277, 278, 281, 291, 293
communism, see Cold War; Marxism
Congo (incl. Belgian Congo, Zaire), 2, 5, 15, 37, 42, 18, 133, 142, 143; Amin as Congolese, 25, 26, 28; Mobuto, President, 243, 280, 282
'Congo Gold Scandal', 119, 133–140, 144, 160
Conrad, Joseph, 1, 2, 5, 312
Coren, Alan, 4, 88, 242, 310
Crawford, Col. H.N. (Nigel), 156, 157, 159, 168, 169
Czechoslovakia, 155, 156

Dada, Amin, see Tomuresu
Defence Council, 167, 168, 181, 194, 240, 245, 247, 269, 272
Democratic Party (DP), 95, 127, 128, 129, 166
Democratic Republic of Congo, see Congo

'disappearances', 213, 239, 248, 250–255, 259, 260, 269, 274, 276, 277, 298, 333; see also human rights
Douglas-Home, Sir Alec, 196, 205, 209

East Germany, see Germany
economy, economic policies, 2, 3, 6, 21, 40, 92, 108, 128, 129, 146, 148, 149, 163, 164, 165, 175, 180, 199, 204, 206, 212, 218, 229, 230, 231, 243, 248, 249, 264, 269, 270, 271, 280, 281, 291–293, 297, 298; 'Economic War', 233–234, 237, 238, 263, 264; see also Asians in Uganda
Elizabeth, Princess of Tooro, see Bagaya, Elizabeth
Elizabeth II, Queen, 38, 66, 73, 89, 205, 206, 207, 211, 212, 234, 245, 263, 266, 267, 268
Emin Pasha, 5, 6, 56, 59
Entebbe airport 110, 116, 117, 180, 189, 206, 236, 280, 280, 298
Entebbe raid, 1, 270–273
Ethiopia, 60, 97, 203, 223, 243, 269
ethnicity, 2, 3, 4, 13, 14, 19, 24, 26, 28, 29, 33, 41, 48, 54, 56, 59, 64, 65, 93, 94, 111, 112, 125, 127, 129, 132, 136, 171, 175, 185, 198, 201, 212, 213–217, 224, 251, 287, 288, 290; see also Amin, Idi, ancestry
evil, concept of, and IA as icon of, 1, 4, 9, 10–13, 17–19, 22, 86, 135, 239, 242, 250, 309, 312–313
Evans, Martin, 66, 271, 274, 275, 280, 281, 310–312
exiles, see opposition groups

fascism (incl. Nazism), 11, 163, 232, 233, 261, 288–289
father (IA's), see Tomuresu, Amin Dada Nyabira
Fraser, Robert, 82–83
Freud, Sigmund, 8, 20, 33, 304, 312
Foreign Office, British (incl. Colonial Office, Foreign and Commonwealth Office, Foreign Secretary), 42, 60, 66, 78, 96, 97, 167, 196, 205, 208, 228, 247, 258, 265, 266, 268, 269, 271, 272, 274, 277, 284–285, 288, 303, 306, 309, 310, 312, 313; see also 'Turkana incident', Operation Bottle
foreign policy, see individual countries
Forster, Peter N., 140, 159, 225
France, French government, 61, 274, 280, 282

Ganda, see Buganda
General Idi Amin Dada: A Self Portrait (film), see Schroeder, Barbet

General Service Unit, 112, 137, 168, 252, 258

Germany (incl. East Germany, West Germany), 5, 57, 61, 171, 242, 243, 245, 272, 318

Ghaddafi, Muamar, 226, 244, 280, 294

Ghana, 14, 203, 223, 277, 324

General Service Unit (GSU), 112, 137, 168, 181, 252, 258

Grahame, Iain, 7, 10, 14, 15, 17, 29, 31, 46, 48, 68, 69, 70, 71, 73, 77–81, 83, 84, 86, 91, 104, 122, 251, 268, 302, 313, 315

Greece, alleged role in coup, 194–195, 200

Gulu (town, district) 156, 168, 169, 186, 196, 285, 303; see also Acholi

Hartley, Lt. Col., see 'Turkana incident'

Heath, Edward, 175, 177, 207, 245, 265, 328

Hennessey, J.P.I (Jim), 241, 243, 244, 245, 246, 247, 249, 265, 266, 267, 270, 273

Hills, Denis, 3, 10, 267–269, 303, 306

Hitler, Adolf, see fascism

human rights, 119, 175, 239, 241, 250–263, 271, 277, 281, 282, 284, 294; see also 'disappearances'; torture

Hunt, R.C.C. (Roland), 131, 132, 149, 326

Ibingira, Grace, 128, 129–133, 140, 146, 147

Imperial British East Africa Company (IBEAC), 6, 40, 56

India, 57, 65, 79, 84, 122, 230, 271, 320

Ingham, Kenneth, 105, 106, 109, 110, 112, 126, 167

International Commission of Jurists (ICJ), 250, 253, 259–263, 353

International Monetary fund (IMF), 211, 218, 281

Ireland, Northern, 245, 264, 265

Islam (incl. Muslims), 2, 5, 6, 15, 26, 27, 30, 32, 35, 52, 53, 56, 57, 76, 120, 125, 145, 170, 173, 199, 201, 206, 208, 222, 224, 226, 227, 228, 233, 248, 269, 276, 286

Israel, Israelis, 7, 31, 106, 107, 113, 114, 115, 116, 117, 118, 131, 146, 155, 156, 157, 162, 163, 164, 167, 169, 172, 175, 176, 177, 178, 179, 186, 187, 190, 193, 194, 196, 200, 202, 203, 207, 212, 218, 223, 224, 225, 238, 261, 271, 275; Amin's visit to, 204–207, 212, 213, 215, 280, 299, 300, 309, 314; expulsion from Uganda, 224–228, 234, 237, 244; see also Anyanya 1; Bar-Lev; Entebbe raid

Jinja (town), 39, 50, 51, 72, 85, 101, 109, 110, 112, 113, 116, 120, 121, 150, 151, 154, 167, 174, 185, 209, 213, 215, 285

jokes, see Amin, Idi, sense of humour

Kabaka (King) of Buganda, 53, 93, 94, 95, 119, 128, 136, 137, 140, 141, 142, 143, 151, 153, 192, 199, 200, 203, 258; as suspected father of IA, 2, 33, 34, 39; see also Buganda; Kampala

Kabaka Yekka Party, see Kabaka

Kagera salient, see Tanzania

Kakwa (culture, language, people), 2, 4, 21, 26, 27, 28, 29, 30, 31, 22, 34, 35, 36, 37, 45, 50, 51, 58, 69, 82, 89, 105, 120, 122, 194, 216, 286, 316–317, 318; as cannibals, 15, 16, 17, 48; as 'primitive', 13, 14, 38, 41–42; split between countries, 15, 25, 48, 177; as 'warrior tribe' and as KAR soldiers, 6, 16, 19, 48, 58, 59, 64–70, 76, 125, 185, 287; see also Amin, Idi, ancestry; Yakan movement

'Kamau, Joseph', see Shaw, Angus

Kampala, 6, 18, 29, 32, 33, 68, 69, 10, 111, 115, 140, 141, 161, 192, 196, 198, 199, 203, 230, 236, 237, 239, 248, 269, 271, 274, 285, 286, 292, 300, 311; birth of IA in, 2, 28, 30, 34; coup in 176–179, 182–186, 188, 189, 190, 191; see also Kabaka; Makerere University

Karamoja, Karamojong, xiv, 73, 74, 77

Kaunda, Kenneth, see Zambia

Kenya, Kenyans, 3, 6, 7, 19, 28, 37, 40, 60, 69, 70, 71, 73, 74, 76, 89, 91, 92, 94, 102, 107, 108, 109, 111, 114, 122, 126, 133, 139, 166, 178, 179, 181, 198, 210, 239, 241, 243, 271, 272, 276, 277, 279, 280, 281, 282; see also Kenyatta, Jomo; Luo; Mau Mau uprising; Mazrui, Ali

Kenyatta, Jomo, 82, 111, 123, 164, 206, 210, 223, 282; see also Kenya

Khartoum, see Sudan

Kibede, Sarah Mutesi, see Amin, Malyam

Kibede, Wanume, 240–241, 261

Kikuyu (people), see Kenya; Kenyatta, Jomo; Mau Mau uprising

King's African Rifles (KAR), 6, 7, 29, 35, 43, 45, 125, 153, 157, 208, 247, 251, 268, 288, 297, 302, 304, 312, 313, 320; see also army, British; Nubi

Koboko (town), 2, 25, 26, 27, 28, 30, 34, 47, 58, 68, 69

kondoism, 180, 241, 252

Kyaloba, Sarah, see Amin, Sarah

Kyemba, Henry, 2, 10, 14, 16, 17, 18, 46, 118, 133, 141, 145, 146, 147, 174, 198, 256, 260, 279, 280, 299, 300, 305, 316

Lagu, Joseph, *see* Anyanya 1
Lango, Langi (district, people), 65, 94, 126, 137, 168, 181, 185, 189, 196, 221, 288; *see also* Obote, Milton; Luo; Nilotic languages; 'northerners'
Last King of Scotland, The (book, film), 1, 15, 135, 206
Legislative Council (LEGCO), 93, 94, 97, 126
Le Tocq, E.G., 160, 206, 258
Libya, *see* Ghadaffi, Muamar
Listowel, Judith (Lady Listowel), 9, 13, 25, 30, 31, 36, 37, 38, 41, 46, 50, 69, 70, 73, 80, 242, 303, 304
Lugard, Frederick (Lord Lugard), 6, 56, 59
Lugbara, (language, people), 2, 5, 17, 25, 26, 27, 29, 31, 33, 36, 37, 39, 46, 58, 144, 217, 286, 287, 288, 316–317; *see also* Aate, Aisha
Luo, or Lwo (language, people), 166, 215, 216, 229, 240, 288, 315; *see also* Acholi; Langi
Luwum, Archbishop Janani, 276–277, 279, 303; *see also* Anglican Church

Madi (language, people), 5, 17, 58, 194, 217, 282, 286, 287
mafuta mingi, *magendo* system, 232, 237, 249, 269, 280, 292, 297, 335
Makerere University, 20, 126, 144, 152, 183, 184, 185, 193, 213, 214, 233, 255, 256, 267, 271, 302, 306, 307
Mamdani, Mahmoud, 170, 173, 175, 176, 229, 230, 232, 288, 289
Mao Zedong, 150, 154, 236, 253, 270
Martin, David, 10, 13, 26, 36, 48, 50, 51, 66, 74, 75, 76, 170, 261, 262, 306
Marxism, Marxist analyses of Amin, 3, 163, 175, 232, 289, 290, 316, 328; *see also* Mamdani, Mahmoud; Mazrui, Ali; Nabudere, Dan Wadada
Masaka (town), 236, 248, 279
masculinity, 1, 4, 11, 19, 20, 21, 72, 83
Mau Mau uprising, 7, 15, 60, 73, 78–79, 82, 86, 89, 91, 92, 96, 97, 102, 104, 126, 297; *see also* Kenya; Kikuyu
Mazrui, Ali, 4, 20, 21, 46, 47, 67, 68, 166, 176, 227, 229, 232, 290
Mbarara (town), 154, 183, 213, 215
media, 5, 107, 162, 223, 260, 279, 288, 307; Amin's use of, 16, 153, 185, 188, 191, 207, 209, 271, 285, 299–303, 307; Ugandan media, 22, 110, 123, 135, 161, 166, 179, 179, 180, 183–184, 191, 223, 254, 257, 265, 270, 274, 280, 301; *see also*, Amin, Idi, Western image of
Melady, Thomas, 10, 16, 27, 261, 282
'mission boy' stereotype, 21, 65, 313; *see also* Obote, Milton; 'warrior tribes'
Mobuto Sese Seko, *see* Congo
Moroto (barracks, town), 209, 213, 215
mother (IA's), *see* Aate, Aisha
Museveni, President Yoweri Kaguta, 8, 236, 256, 277, 294
Muslims, *see* Islam
Mutesa, Edward, *see* Kabaka

Nabudere, Dan Wadada, 3, 173, 175, 184
Nakan (sacred snake), *see* Amin, Idi, birth and parentage; Yakan movement
National Association for the Advancement of Muslims (NAAM), *see* Islam
Nazis, Nazism, *see* fascism
Nekyon, Adoko, 132, 136, 149, 160
Newton Dunn, T.N. ('Tommy'), 135, 149, 152, 153, 154, 155, 156
Ngwatella people, *see* 'Turkana incident'
Nilotic languages, 25, 27, 29, 50, 66, 67, 129, 133, 168, 288; *see also* Acholi; Langi; Luo
'northerners', 'northern tribes', northern Ugandans, 45, 48, 58, 65, 66, 67, 68, 69, 73, 79, 93, 107, 110, 112, 119, 125, 126, 129, 131, 132, 136, 170, 171, 192, 214, 226, 276; *see also* Acholi; Langi; Luo; Nilotic languages; Nubi; 'warrior tribes'
Northern Ireland, 245, 264, 265
Nubi, Nubians, (people, language), 5, 6, 7, 15, 20, 25, 28, 33, 36, 38, 39, 40, 42, 44, 48, 49, 56, 57, 58, 59, 67, 111, 119, 120, 171, 216, 233, 286, 287; reputation as killers and cannibals, 13, 15, 17, 42, 48, 79; IA as: 13, 14, 19–21, 27, 29, 46, 49, 51, 52, 53, 58, 72
Numeiri, Jaafar, 175, 226, 284; *see also* Sudan
Nyerere, Julius, *see* Tanzania

Obote, Apolo Milton, 3, 4, 7, 8, 9, 13, 14, 31, 94, 95, 96, 101, 105, 106, 107, 123, 124, 126–130, 134, 146, 147, 148, 159, 160, 161, 164, 167, 174, 177, 183, 184, 209, 220, 222, 257, 258, 287, 293, 298, 312, 313, 314; and 1964 army mutiny, 108–112; and 1966 'revolution', 140–144; and Amin, 7, 31, 118–120, 125, 130, 134–136, 141–143,

144, 145, 147, 150, 154, 156, 159, 160, 162, 168–173, 181, 185–191, 196, 198, 209, 215, 220, 221, 229, 235, 236, 237, 238, 240, 261, 262, 263, 268, 293, 294, 299, 300, 302, 309, 316; and Asian expulsion, 165–166, 175–176, 210, 214, 215, 228, 229, 237–238; and British, 21, 110, 113–115, 117, 131, 175, 178, 179, 192, 193, 197, 226; and Congo gold crisis, 136–140; economic policies 148–149, 199, 218, 237, in exile: 198, 200, 202, 223, 235, 241, 260, 261, 262, 277, 285, 288

Observer (newspaper), 241, 247, 261, 268; *see also* Martin, David

Ocheng, Daudi, 129, 136, 138, 139, 140

Okoya, Pierino Yere, 167, 168, 169, 174, 175

Onama, Felix, 106, 109, 110, 113, 115, 116, 117, 118, 131, 133, 136, 149, 155, 159, 160, 169, 176, 186, 190

Operation Bottle, 277–279

Operation Utah, 97–104

Opolot, Shaban (or 'Opoloto'), 84, 85, 96, 105, 110, 111, 113, 115, 116, 118, 119, 130, 131, 132, 133, 138, 140, 143, 150, 198

opposition groups, 7, 22, 210, 213, 216, 223, 236, 239, 241, 254, 255, 256, 259, 260, 261, 272, 277, 284, 285

Organisation of African Unity (OAU), 110, 203, 209, 212, 223, 226, 242, 269, 271, 280, 284

Orizio, Riccardo, 296–297

Oryema, Erinayo, 179, 182, 186, 191, 276

Palestine, Palestinians, 78, 223, 224, 269, 272

paranoia, 209–210, 214

Pasha, *see* Emin Pasha

Posner, Michael, 261, 282–283

postcolonialism, *see* colonialism

Protestant Church, 40, 93, 95, 125, 126, 127, 222, 224, 241, 269, 276, 279; *see also* Anglican Church

public relations (PR) techniques, *see* media

Punch magazine, 4, 88, 242

Queen Elizabeth II, *see* Elizabeth II, Queen

radio, *see* media

refugees, viii, 7, 27, 214, 223, 224, 231, 235, 253, 284; *see also* opposition groups

Roman Catholics, *see* Catholic Church

Royal Marine Commandos, *see* army, British

rugby, *see* sport

Russia, *see* Soviet Union

Rwanda, Rwandans, 3, 208, 243, 281

Sandhurst, military academy, 89, 96, 105, 187, 208

Sandys, Duncan, 97, 102, 114

Saudi Arabia, see Arabic, Arabs

Schroeder, Barbet, 268–269, 303

Scotland, 69, 70, 159, 167, 208, 211–212, 277, 297

Scots Guards regiment, *see* army, British

Shaw, Angus (alias 'Joseph Kamau and Andrew Cameron'), 10, 28, 29, 36, 37, 38, 49, 50, 51, 63, 75, 76, 79

Slater, R. ('Dick'), 178–179, 182, 190, 191, 195, 196, 204, 212, 235

slavery, slaves, 'slave soldiers', *see* Nubi

Smith, George Ivan, 15, 26, 31, 36, 37, 38, 48, 49, 51, 67, 71, 73, 74, 76, 84

Somalia, 60, 76, 81, 82, 175, 243, 269

South Africa, 173, 174, 175, 177, 193, 198, 200, 203, 223, 224, 234

Southall, Aidan, 19–21, 28, 185

Southern Rhodesia, *see* Zimbabwe

Soviet Union, 133, 155, 156, 164, 205, 242, 270, 280, 282, 299

sport, importance to Amin, 62, 63, 70, 71, 72, 73, 75, 77, 80, 87, 150, 302, 313

Staffordshire regiment, *see* army, British

State Department, *see* United States of America

State Research Bureau, 194, 252, 254, 255, 257, 272

Steiner, Rolf, 171–172

Sudan, Sudanese people, viii, 2, 5, 7, 9, 15, 17, 25, 28, 29, 37, 39, 42, 47, 48, 53, 56, 57, 61, 72, 111, 116, 135, 154, 170, 171, 172, 175, 176, 177, 178, 190, 195, 198, 202, 203, 209, 215, 223, 224, 226, 227, 228, 240, 243, 271, 282, 285, 288, 289, 320; *see also* Anyanya 1; Nubi; Numeiri, Jaafar

Sudanic languages, 26, 27, 48, 67, 288

Swahili, Kiswahili (language, people), 6, 28, 30, 50, 57, 65, 68, 70, 73, 98, 150, 158, 189, 201, 320

Tallboys, R.G., 158, 159, 160, 161

Tanganyika, *see* Tanzania

Tanganyika Village (Arua town), 32, 35, 52, 57, 58

'Tank Hill incident', 122–123, 157

Tanzania, Tanzanian people, 7, 8, 22, 32, 57, 86, 107, 108, 109, 111, 113, 116, 133, 139, 178, 193, 197, 202, 203, 205, 208, 209, 210,

213, 214, 223, 235, 236, 239, 242, 243, 271, 272, 277, 280, 285, 288, 294, 318; invades Uganda, 245, 280, 284–287, 293; Nyerere, Julius, 133, 164, 181, 198, 200

Teso district, 65, 84, 105

Tillet, J.M.A., 106, 108, 110, 111, 113, 114

Tomuresu, Amin Dada Nyabira (IA's father), 2, 6, 26, 27, 29, 30, 31, 33, 34, 35, 45, 50, 52, 57

Tooro/Toro district, 128, 203, 246

torture, viii, 18, 37, 75, 76, 186, 194, 251, 252, 254, 255, 283, 293; see also 'Turkana incident'

'Turkana incident', 97–104

Uganda National Congress (UNC), 94, 106, 282

Uganda People's Congress (UPC), 94, 95, 112, 126–130, 134, 136, 140, 148, 147, 164, 166, 173, 175, 192, 223

Uganda Rifles, see army, British; army, Ugandan; King's African Rifles

Ugandan Asians, see Asians in Uganda

United States of America, 8, 10, 11, 62, 186, 126, 129, 159, 160, 175, 184, 186, 213, 28, 231, 244, 277, 279, 280, 281, 282, 299, 306

'warrior tribes' colonial stereotype, 2, 6, 14, 16, 20–22, 46, 65, 67, 70, 79, 85, 313, 316; see also 'mission boy'

Waswa, Wilfred, see Aswa

Wenham Smith, W.N. (Nigel), 158, 159, 161, 168, 169

West Germany, see Germany

West Nile, West Nilers, viii, x, xii, xiii, 48, 49, 50, 52, 57, 58, 59, 64, 65, 69, 94, 118, 119, 124, 125, 133, 144, 145, 68, 171, 172, 183, 185, 186, 90, 194, 196, 202, 214, 215, 216, 268, 281, 282; Amin's origins in, 2–7, 15, 19, 21, 25, 26, 27, 30, 33, 34, 36, 37, 39, 40, 41–45; post-Amin repression in, 285–288; see also Alur; Kakwa; Lugbara; Madi; Nubi

Wilson, Harold, 265, 266, 270

'wind of change' speech, 91, 93, 96

witchcraft, witches, 12, 13, 15, 16, 29, 36, 37, 47, 49, 51, 52, 76; see also Aate, Aisha

World War 1, 32, 40, 42, 57, 58

World War 2, 6, 59, 244, 257; IA's claimed role in, 60–64

Wright, Patrick, 265, 266, 267

Yakan movement, 36–39, 40, 43–45, 48, 54, 77, 227

Yoma, SS, see World War 2, IA's claimed role in

Zaire, see Congo

Zambia, 150, 164, 174, 239, 245, 277

Zanzibar, see Tanzania

Zimbabwe, 10, 28, 49, 174, 177, 223, 224, 234, 281